Behavior Management

A Practical Approach for Educators

Behavior Management

A Practical Approach for Educators

FIFTH EDITION

James E. Walker
University of Northern Colorado

Thomas M. Shea
Southern Illinois University—Edwardsville

Merrill, an imprint of
Macmillan Publishing Company
New York

Collier Macmillan Canada, Inc.
Toronto

Maxwell Macmillan International Publishing Group
New York   Oxford   Singapore   Sydney

Cover art: © Karen Guzak, 1987
Editor: Ann Castel
Production Editor: Constantina Geldis
Photo Editor: Gail Meese
Cover Designer: Russ Maselli

This book was set in Korinna.

Photo credits: pp. 1 and 289 by Lloyd Lemmerman/Merrill Publishing; p. 35 by Mark Freado/Merrill Publishing; p. 56 by Jean Greenwald/Merrill Publishing; pp. 100 and 137 by Kevin Fitzsimmons/Merrill Publishing; p. 165 by David Napravnik/Merrill Publishing; p. 199 by Bruce Johnson/Merrill Publishing; p. 243 by Gale Zucker.

Macmillan Publishing Company
866 Third Avenue, New York, New York 10022

Collier Macmillan Canada, Inc.

Library of Congress Cataloguing-in-Publication Data

Walker, James Edwin, 1941-
    Behavior management : a practical approach for educators / James
E. Walker, Thomas M. Shea.—5th ed.
        p.   cm.
    Includes bibliographical references and index.
    ISBN 0-675-21385-1
    1. Teaching.   2. Behavior modification.   3. Individualized
instruction.   4. Problem children—Education—United States.
I. Shea, Thomas M., 1934-   .   II. Title.
LB1027.W29   1991
371.1′024—dc20   90-41173
                                                                    CIP

Printing: 1 2 3 4 5 6 7 8 9   Year: 1 2 3 4

To
Gwenn, Jamell, and Jabrina
and
Dolores, Kevin, and Keith

PREFACE

This fifth edition of *Behavior Management: A Practical Approach for Educators* has been extensively revised to improve its readability and usability. Revisions are based on developments in the field of behavior management reported in the literature since the original manuscript was prepared and on feedback from many professionals and students.

During the last 2½ decades, the proliferation of behavior management philosophies, techniques, and instructional methodologies has increased the complexity of the educator's responsibilities and functions. New information is being published almost daily on the various perspectives of human behavior, including the psychodynamic, biophysical, environmental, and behavioral points of view. Of these perspectives, the behavioral point of view appears to have had the most significant impact on classroom and school management procedures and practices. However, because of their overall importance in the broad field of behavior management, the theories and techniques associated with the psychodynamic, biophysical, and environmental perspectives are also reviewed in detail in this edition.

Revisions in the text are, in large part, a result of direct and indirect feedback from many undergraduate and graduate students of education, from teachers participating in in-service programs, and from our professional colleagues who have studied the fourth edition.

The text is written to provide a practical guide to experienced teachers, teachers-in-training, parents, and paraprofessionals for applying behavior management techniques both in general and special educational settings and in the home. It is designed to aid teachers working in self-contained classes and resource centers; teachers engaged in itinerant and consultative service; and elementary and secondary regular classroom teachers having responsibility for normal and exceptional children. It may be used as a basic text for preservice and in-service courses and as a self-study guide. It is designed for use by parents of normal and exceptional children.

Behavior management is introduced in Chapter 1. This chapter includes presentations on guidelines for behavior management and on the application of behavior management techniques to individualized education programs (IEPs), mandated for all handicapped children by Public Law 94-142. The chapter includes an extensive discussion of teacher effectiveness and introduces an integrative framework for viewing behavior management. Chapter 1 concludes with an overview of the psychodynamic, biophysical, environmental, and behavior modification perspectives of human behavior and educational practice.

The basic principles of behavior modification are presented in Chapter 2. The exposition of each principle is supplemented by practical examples from classroom teaching experiences. In addition, the schedules of reinforcement have been completely rewritten.

In Chapter 3 the reader is given step-by-step instructions for modifying behavior in the classroom. Each step is discussed and exemplified. Chapter 3 includes an extensive list of reinforcers for use in the classroom and school setting. The chapter also includes a discussion of prompting and the reinforcement area.

Several specific methods changing behavior are reviewed in Chapters 4 and 5, including a new discussion on "time-out."

Chapters 6 and 7 provide an overview of behavior management techniques associated with the psychodynamic, biophysical, and environmental theoretical perspectives presented in Chapter 1.

Chapter 8 is an overview of behavior management procedures and practices for implementation by educators wishing to involve parents in coordinated home-school management programs. The chapter includes a parent-teacher interview technique for assessment purposes. This material is also applicable to the training of paraprofessionals. In the final chapter, the ethics of behavior management are discussed.

As an aid to students, chapter objectives are presented at the beginning of each chapter. Skill-building projects are presented at the end of each chapter. A copy of each work sheet and form presented earlier is provided at the end of the text.

The text is written in nontechnical language for maximum readability by a broad audience of professionals, paraprofessionals, college students, and parents. This style was chosen in order to avoid the unnecessary technical jargon that causes so much of the professional literature to lose its significance and impact. Although based on the results of current research, the text does not provide an extensive review of the literature. However, the reader will find, in the reference sections, lists of journals and texts to serve as a beginning point in a review of the literature.

The primary goal of this work is the *ethical, effective,* and *efficient* management of the behavior and learning problems of children and youth as they learn to explore, manipulate, and ultimately control their world for their personal satisfaction and benefit and for the benefit of society.

Acknowledgments

We thank the reviewers of this and previous editions—Dr. Andrew Brulle of Eastern Illinois University, Dr. Tom Kampwirth of California State University—Long Beach,

Dr. Robert N. Freeman of Georgia Southern College, and Dr. Frances T. Harrington of Radford University—for their time and their constructive suggestions that strengthened the fifth edition. We would like to acknowledge the assistance and support of our many colleagues, friends, and long-suffering students who have been exposed to and have responded to the materials in this text. We have profited greatly by their comments.

CONTENTS

CHAPTER ONE

An Introduction to Behavior Management

Ms. Justine watches as Tami, wiping her eyes with a tissue from the decorative dispenser on the corner of the teacher's desk, slowly leaves the fourth-grade classroom. It has been a long, trying day for both of them.

As the little Swiss clock on the desk chimes 4 o'clock, Ms. Justine leans back in her chair to ponder her dilemma. Right now, she hates teaching. She hates reprimanding and scolding children, especially Tami, who tries so very, very hard to sit still and pay attention during her lessons. It seems as if this little drama has happened with Tami and some of the other children a dozen or more times since the school year began last month.

The children are too active to settle down to their lessons. Ms. Justine yells and hollers, scolds and reprimands, but it doesn't appear to help. They never change. Perhaps they never will.

Something must be done. The children have to learn their lessons. Tami in particular needs help. She is 2 years behind in reading and a full year behind in spelling; she has practically no measurable skills in subtraction and division. Tami must learn these skills before the end of the school year or confront another failure in the fifth grade.

Ms. Justine knows her present methods of behavior management are not only ineffective but also are taking too much out of her personally. She is exhausted when she gets home after school. Her stomach is always upset. She is grouchy and short-tempered with her husband and children.

Perhaps there are more effective methods Ms. Justine could apply in an effort to help Tami and the others attend to their lessons.

Larry sits in the gym bleachers, anxiously waiting for Mr. Veritas to finish organizing the volleyball game. The whole class, except Larry, is choosing sides and preparing to begin the game.

Larry wishes he could be part of the activity, but he can't. He's afraid to let the others know that he's a poor player. He doesn't know exactly why he's a poor player, but every time a group game is organized, he must refuse to participate. He says, "No, I won't," "I can't," "I don't feel good," or "That's a dumb game."

Larry knows Mr. Veritas is unhappy with him but also very concerned about him. But Larry just can't play those games. He thinks it's really too bad that Mr. Veritas doesn't like him, because Mr. Veritas is a nice guy and would be an interesting friend.

Mr. Veritas quickly organizes the teams, and the volleyball game begins. He believes that he must hurry and talk to Larry.

"Poor kid," Mr. Veritas thinks, "he's really OK, but he just won't play team games. Perhaps he refuses because of his weight problem. No, others in the class are as rotund as Larry, and they play team sports. Perhaps Larry is afraid he's not a good enough player. I'll talk to him again and see what I can do to help."

Perhaps there are effective methods for helping Larry increase his participation in team activities.

Ms. Komfort hums a little tune to herself as she cruises along Interstate 55 out of Memphis. What a marvelous day! What a great year it has been at John F. Kennedy Elementary School with her 25 first graders!

For the first time in her teaching career Ms. Komfort has interested, responsive and enthusiastic children in her class. If the last 4 months of the school year are as good as the first 5 months, she will remain in teaching forever.

"Sure hope it continues," she thinks.

Perhaps there are techniques to help Ms. Komfort maintain her children's enthusiasm for learning throughout the year.

Teachers wish to teach; it is what they are trained to do, their function, and the purpose for which they are employed and assigned to a school, a classroom, and a group of children for approximately 180 days each school year. Frequently teachers are frustrated in efforts to attain their goals because of the behavioral and remedial problems of the individual children in their classrooms.

As a result of the theoretical, experimental, and pragmatic efforts of many scholars and practitioners, teachers have been made increasingly aware of a number of variables that must be considered if effective and efficient classroom transactions are to be established between teachers and children. Teachers have become keenly aware of the following:

1. Every child is a unique individual, *similar* to all other children in many respects, yet *different* from all other children.
2. No single set of therapeutic or remedial procedures is effective under *all conditions* with *all children*. We must remain open-minded and give thoughtful consideration to many theoretical and methodological points of view if we are to effectively aid children.
3. No matter how well designed and executed classroom-centered intervention processes may be, their effectiveness will be limited unless they relate to the individual child's needs and desires (Morse, 1985).

Educators have also become aware that the child's cognitive, affective, and psychomotor learning domains are inextricably interwoven. We understand that the child acts and reacts as a whole being. We recognize that a remedial intervention in the cognitive domain may influence the child's affective behavior, that intervention in the psychomotor domain will in all probability affect the child's cognitive and affective learning, and so on.

EXAMPLES
■ Todd, a 6-year-old first grader, was diagnosed by a neurologist as "a hyperactive child with suspected minimal brain damage." According to his teacher, Todd was disruptive in the classroom, constantly running about, hitting children, tearing paper, and so on.

Todd's neurologist prescribed medication to slow the boy down in school. The medication has been effective in modifying Todd's behavior. He has begun to identify his letters and numbers; he has learned to use scissors for cutting-and-pasting activities; and his behavior has improved in the classroom, especially during group activities. Todd has been heard to say, "See how good I am," and "I'm a big boy now."

It is evident that changes in Todd's hyperactive psychomotor behavior have influenced his cognitive skills (learning his letters and numbers) and his affective behavior (in group activities). In addition, his self-concept appears to have improved. ■

■ Scott, an 11-year-old fifth grader with a visual-perceptual handicap, had experienced difficulty in throwing and catching a ball and in running bases.

Scott is now enrolled in a program that includes physical therapy and adaptive physical education. As a result of these interventions, he has developed skills in throwing, catching, and running.

Scott's teacher has noted that as Scott is increasing his competency in the psychomotor area, he is also improving cognitively (in such activities as reading and writing) and socially (his group behavior and peer relationships have improved).

Again, it is evident that changes in one learning domain influence the individual's competency in the other areas of learning. ■

■ Maryellen, a 13-year-old ninth grader, was diagnosed by a school psychologist as a "slow learner."

Maryellen had experienced difficulty in academic subjects throughout her school years. Although she could learn and did learn the basic skills, she required more time and instruction than her classmates. As a consequence of her academic difficulties, Maryellen usually received Ds and Es on report cards. Over the years she developed an "I don't care" attitude toward school work and school. This attitude caused her to be frequently reprimanded and punished by her teachers.

On entering high school, Maryellen was placed in a remedial program. In this special program, academic work was designed to be responsive to Maryellen's rate and level of learning. Evaluations were based on individual performance.

Presently Maryellen's teacher reports she is a happy, highly motivated slow learner.

It is evident that changes in Maryellen's academic program influenced her affective behavior. ■

This text is written primarily from the point of view of learning theory and behavior modification. However, behavior modification is but one of the conceptual frameworks available to the practitioner for use in efforts to change behavior. *Behavior modification is not a panacea that can effectively solve all problems of all children.*

Other conceptual frameworks (biophysical, psychodynamic, and environmental) have made and continue to make significant contributions to our knowledge of the behavior of children. The reader is encouraged *not* to cast aside these other points of view—not to become an exclusivist.

Behavior management interventions based on social learning and behavior modification theory are presented in Chapters 2 to 5. Interventions based on psychodynamic theory are presented in Chapter 6; those derived from environmental and biophysical theory are presented in Chapter 7.

The remainder of this chapter is devoted to an operational definition of behavior management and several teacher effectiveness guidelines. Four frequently applied models of the etiology of human behavior are discussed and related to an integrative framework for the analysis of behavior and the selection of interventions. Also included are brief discussions of Public Law 94-142, related legislation, and the individualized education program (IEP).

CHAPTER OBJECTIVES

After completing this chapter, you will be able to do the following:

1. Define behavior management and explain its purposes.
2. Identify several personal traits and knowledge and skill competencies of effective teachers.
3. Understand the relationship between ideas, actions, and outcomes (theories, interventions, and results).
4. Explain the four historical determiners of human behavior.
5. Characterize the basic principles and components of the four traditional models of the etiology of human behavior (psychodynamic, biophysical, environmental, and behavioral).
6. Describe the integrative framework and discuss its implications for analyzing behavior management problems and selecting, implementing, and evaluating interventions.
7. Define the Public Law 94-142 mandate and the components of the individualized education program (IEP).

Definition of Behavior Management

The majority of school staff meeting and discussion time is often devoted to considerations of behavior management. The same few, but important, questions are asked repeatedly:

☐ How can this child's behavior be changed?
☐ How can this classroom's group behavior be changed?
☐ Should I punish this behavior?

☐ Should I discuss this behavior with the individual?
☐ Should I ignore this behavior?
☐ Will this intervention work?
☐ Is it ethical to use this intervention technique?
☐ Will it harm or hurt the child?

Hour after hour of teacher and parent time is devoted to discussions of these and similar questions and concerns about the management of children's behavior in the classroom, school, and home.

In this text *behavior management interventions* are defined as all those actions (and conscious inactions) teachers and parents engage in to enhance the probability that children, individually and in groups, will develop effective behaviors that are personally fulfilling, productive, and socially acceptable (Shea & Bauer, 1987).

Behavior management is a complex problem that cannot be approached from a simplistic point of view. It is a teacher function that must be studied, planned, and objectively used and evaluated, with equal emphasis given to all relevant variables: the individual or group whose behavior is being studied; the behavior under consideration; the setting in which the behavior occurs; the individual applying the intervention; and the purpose of the intervention. A specific technique that is an effective intervention for one specific behavior of one specific child in a particular setting may be ineffective under another set of circumstances when applied by a different individual to change a different behavior. More specifically, behavior management must be individualized.

Self-discipline is the goal of all behavior management. It is the process of attaining control over one's personal behavior in a variety of circumstances in association with many individuals and groups. Self-discipline is discussed in greater detail in the next section.

Teacher Effectiveness Guidelines

Kampwirth (1988) conducted an observational study of the behavior management techniques in 15 regular and special education classrooms from kindergarten through senior high school. Four of the classes were special education programs. The classes were selected on the basis of principals' evaluation of teachers who were within the top 10% in the management of behavior. Kampwirth found several preventive and class-in-session factors essential to effective management. The preventive factors included: an attractive and functional classroom; behavior management rules and consequences; preparation for instruction; preplanned continuum of interventions for inappropriate behavior; and preplanned responses to appropriate behavior. The class-in-session factors included: expectations for good behavior; properly paced instruction; review of rules and consequences; control of group attention; emphasis on success rather than on errors and failure; modeling of appropriate behavior; teacher communication that is positive, sensitive, and assertive; and a sense of humor.

In a discussion of teacher-child-peer relationships using an ecological perspective, Kauffman, Pullen, and Akers (1986) and Kauffman (1985) noted several factors that teachers may contribute to the misbehavior of students. These factors included: inconsistency in the use of management techniques; reinforcement of incorrect or inappropriate behavior; inappropriate expectations for children; presentation of subject matter that is inappropriate, nonfunctional, or irrelevant; a lack of responsiveness to children's individuality; modeling or encouraging others to model inappropriate behavior; irritability with children and reliance on punishment to manage children; and an unwillingness to seek help and implement different interventions.

The following teacher effectiveness guidelines and discussion were derived from these works and the work of Tisdale (1985) and Shea and Bauer (1987). They are presented here primarily to stimulate thought and discussion.

Model and Leader

Outside of the family, the teacher is in all probability the most important element in the child's environment. No other variable in the school appears to have a greater potential impact on a student than the interpersonal relationship developed between teacher and child.

Educational programs can be operated successfully under extremely adverse conditions (without adequate facilities, materials, equipment, funds, personnel, transportation, and so on). However, no program has ever been successfully operated without teachers who can and do relate positively and productively with children.

Personal Traits

Authentic teachers must be authentic people—real people. It is difficult to select for employment an authentic teacher by the traditional means of application and personal interview. However, there are several personal traits that effective teachers appear to have in common:

- *Self-insight:* They know why they wish to work with children. They have an understanding of why they engage in the activities that make up their life style.
- *Self-acceptance, self-appraisal and realistic self-confidence:* They accept themselves as they are but seek to improve themselves. They are realistically confident in themselves and their capability to be effective but are not so overconfident of their abilities as to be considered naive; they do not have an "I can do anything" attitude. They can make honest and forthright statements concerning their strengths and weaknesses without excuses.
- *Love and acceptance of children:* They love and are able to demonstrate their love for children. They understand that love and compliance are not identical. Sometimes love is demonstrated through discipline. They accept children as worthwhile human beings even though they must at times reject a child's behavior.

They are capable of accepting, without reservation, individuals who are different from themselves—whether these individuals are short or tall, male or female, black, white, brown, red, or yellow, rotund or slim, deformed or normal, intelligent or retarded, or conforming, deviant, or radical.

☐ *An understanding of the behavior of children:* They not only understand human behavior at a cognitive level but are also able to empathize with children who manifest deviancy. They continually seek insight and understanding into such a child's behavior.

☐ *Curiosity and willingness to learn:* They have a bit of the child in their adult person. Like children, they are curious about their environment and enthusiastically explore it. They enjoy learning.

☐ *Patience with self and others:* They realize that they are imperfect and that they make mistakes. They also recognize this quality in others. They realize that learning is a slow, complex, process for many individuals. However, they continually strive to attain learning goals for themselves and their students.

☐ *Flexibility:* They are flexible. They know when to change a lesson, intervention, or activity for the benefit of the students and when to change in order to attain a broader objective.

☐ *Humor:* They have a well-developed sense of humor. (Mistakes, accidents, and humorous happenings occur in the classroom daily. Teachers who cannot laugh will certainly cry.) They are capable of laughing at themselves and with their students. They never laugh at their students.

Teachers become models for the children they instruct. For better or worse, children will probably model at least some of their behavior after a teacher. It is of questionable value for children to have teachers who are highly skilled and knowledgeable in specific subject areas and activities but who lack the capacity to understand and accept themselves and their students.

Knowledge and Skills

In addition to the personal traits just presented, effective teachers need specific knowledge and skills to successfully work with children. Following are work characteristics of such individuals:

1. They establish routines in the daily lives of those in the classroom group.
2. They establish and enforce behavioral limits. They accomplish this difficult task without personal emotional involvement.
3. They do not permit emotionally charged situations to get out of control. They intrude themselves into conflicts and cause them to end with fairness to all involved.
4. They are consistent. All children are confused by teachers who condone a specific deviant behavior one day but do not condone the same deviation the next day.

5. They personally investigate an incident before acting rather than taking action on the basis of second- or third-person information and rumors. They confer with all children and adults involved in the incident before acting.

6. They ignore certain behaviors. Many unacceptable behaviors manifested by children are normal, age-appropriate behaviors. Others are simply not of sufficient potential impact to require a response by the teacher. Effective teachers are selective in responding to and ignoring behaviors.

7. They communicate verbally and nonverbally with their students. They talk *with* students, not *to* them. They learn that many of the concepts they considered to be universal knowledge are mysteries to many students. They are tuned-in to the language and action of children and youth.

8. They learn to avoid personal confrontations with students when it is therapeutically appropriate. However, they confront an individual or group when necessary for the benefit of that person or group.

9. They learn to change activities and lessons for therapeutic purposes. They are not so personally committed to their lesson or subject that they fail to recognize student disinterest, dislike, and resistance.

10. They work both independently and as team members by communicating with colleagues and supervisors. They hold themselves accountable for their actions or lack of action. They know they cannot succeed in isolation.

11. They make a direct appeal to students when the students' actions are confusing and discomforting to them personally. Frequently a direct appeal to a child's basic humanness and common sense will solve behavior problems as quickly and as effectively as sophisticated behavior management interventions.

12. They provide each child under their supervision with security. Effective teachers communicate to students that they will be provided needed security from physical and psychological harm while under teacher supervision.

The new teacher seldom arrives in the classroom with fully developed behavior management skills in addition to instructional competence in all the needed subject matter areas. These skills are developed through experience and with the assistance of colleagues and supervisors.

Self-Discipline

Self-discipline is the desired result of all behavior management interventions presented in this text. Self-discipline, or the process of attaining self-control over one's personal behavior in a variety of circumstances in association with a variety of individuals and groups, is not an instantaneous process. Self-control is developed by nearly all human beings over many years and includes a number of developmental phases. During the process of attaining self-control, children naturally progress and regress as they and their environment change. A child may appear perfectly self-controlled one day and not the following day. Progress—maturing and growing—is often measured in slowly increasing lengths of time between occurrences of unacceptable behavior exhibited by the child.

The word *discipline* is derived from *disciple*, or follower of a master's teaching. This concept contains the idea of something learned from a teacher whose example the learner personally desires to model or imitate. The best discipline is derived from the respect and understanding of one human being for another. Discipline should be cooperative and voluntary, not simply imposed from above by an authority figure. Harsh, punitive, and negative disciplinary techniques are avoided in education. The majority of children, especially those with behavior problems, have a poor or distorted self-image as a result of repeated failure and negative discipline. Many of these children have psychologically isolated themselves from the effects of negative discipline. Benign and positive interventions leading ultimately to self-discipline are suggested to teachers of both regular and special classes.

Time

All children at one time or another during their school years exhibit some behavior problems. This simple fact is all too frequently overlooked by teachers.

It is not unusual to have a teacher become extremely frustrated with a child because the child's deviant behavior does not respond to intervention immediately. This same frustration among teachers is also exhibited relative to academic training. Perhaps we are too impatient and too easily frustrated as a result of living most of our adult lives in a society conditioned to instant change, instant solutions to problems, and minimal frustration. The teacher must be patient and adjust to slow, time-consuming progress. Miracles and instant "cures" are few in number and difficult to observe when they do occur.

Children learn certain habitual ways of acting and reacting in their environment. These coping skills are developed over a span of years. Although unacceptable to others, they have been and continue to be more or less successful for the child. The child cannot and should not be forced to relinquish these coping mechanisms or survival behaviors immediately and begin using new more acceptable and productive ways of coping.

To change deviant behavior requires time and energy. Teachers must be patient and focus on the child's progress rather than on the desired end product.

Objectives and Goals

Although teachers develop long-term goals for the children with whom they work, such goals are generally not a daily concern. Long-term goals are divided into a series of properly sequenced short-term objectives. These objectives provide structure for the group's (teacher and students) daily, weekly, and/or monthly program of lessons and activities. The long-term goals provide the needed direction for the overall program for the individual child.

An important objective for each child enrolled in school should be to have a pleasant and positive experience. The program must be enjoyable and rewarding for the child, or it will not meet the normal childhood needs of seeking out and exploring the new, the different, the unknown, and the exciting.

Although the teacher has many academic remedial objectives for a particular child, these remedial tasks cannot be so demanding of the child's time and energy that school becomes drudgery. School must be a positive experience, offering the child a variety of opportunities to learn new skills and to participate in new activities of a nonacademic as well as of an academic nature.

Empathy

Behavior problem children do not need their teacher's sympathy. Ill-founded sympathy distorts the problems the teacher is attempting to help the child overcome. It places the teacher in an emotional situation that prohibits objective analysis of the child's behavior. A teacher who becomes too emotionally involved in a child's problem frequently functions in a biased, nonhelpful way. Such a teacher reacts to the child and others concerned with the child's welfare on a subjective rather than an objective level.

Although relationships based on sympathy are to be avoided in the educational setting, those based on empathy are necessary and should be encouraged. The teacher must be able to understand how the child feels and must be able to perceive the child's world from the child's point of view. This capacity is frequently referred to as "taking the position of the other" or "being in the other person's shoes."

The capacity to empathize permits the teacher to provide the child or group with direction, guidance, and support when such assistance is needed.

Expectations

Many years ago we might have been told by our grandparents or parents, "As the twig is bent, so grows the tree." Some teachers ignore this simple truth. However, researchers have confirmed what our grandparents took for granted: Our expectations for children have a significant effect on their performance (Beez, 1972; Rosenthal & Jacobsen, 1966; Rubin & Balow, 1971, among others).

This self-fulfilling prophecy means that, to a significant extent, if we believe a child is and will continue to be an incompetent, the probability is increased that the child will function as an incompetent. If we believe and communicate to a child that he or she will not learn to read, behave, compute, socialize, speak, and so on, the probability is significantly increased that the child will not accomplish these tasks. Conversely, if we believe and communicate to a child that he or she will learn to behave, read, play, socialize, and speak, the probability is increased that the child will respond to our expectations and learn these tasks.

As educators, we must maintain high but realistic expectations for students. Classrooms should be environments developed around a "can do" attitude. Children must be told repeatedly throughout each day: "You can do it." "You know and I know you can do it." "You did it!" "Great!" "Super!" "Beautiful!"

Obviously such a "can do" attitude is meaningless and perhaps harmful unless the program is designed to ensure that the child receives the needed social-emotional support and skill training required to complete a task and fulfill our expectations.

Freedom and Independence

As a general policy students should be encouraged to grow and learn as much as possible without teacher assistance. Within realistic limits, anything that children can do for themselves, they should do. The instructor's function is to facilitate, not to dominate, the child's activity program. The teacher is available to instruct, demonstrate, assist, counsel, and offer encouragement. All young people need freedom to explore, investigate, and implement new behaviors without adult interference if they are to grow. Often they will succeed in their efforts; occasionally they will fail and require assistance.

Although constant failure is not recommended, occasional failure is a part of every person's life. The teacher cannot and should not shelter children from all failure; at times they should be allowed to confront the logical consequences— success and failure—of their actions. (Dreikurs & Grey, 1968). It is the teacher's function to help the child learn to cope appropriately with both success and failure.

Complete freedom for many children becomes counterproductive. A child attends school to learn productive skills and behaviors. The teacher is responsible for planning the curriculum for or, preferably, in cooperation with the child. To do otherwise would be irresponsible and a disservice to the child. Behavior management and curriculum are partners; one is of little value without the other.

Democracy without structure, discipline, or predictability becomes anarchy. Children are learners; they are not adults skilled in the principles and practices of democracy. They must be encouraged to learn and apply democratic principles in the classroom and school under teacher supervision if they are to live by these principles as adults.

Models of Human Behavior

What makes us behave as we do toward self, others, and the environment? How can we change our behavior and the behavior of others from inappropriate to appropriate? From unacceptable to acceptable? From destructive to constructive? From "bad" to "good"?

These questions are the age-old queries that have gnawed at our intellect and emotions since the beginning of time.

What makes us behave as we do? How can behavior be changed?

Four of the responses theoreticians have made and continue to make to these questions are the psychodynamic, biophysical, environmental, and behavior modification explanations of human behavior. Argyris and Schon (1974) call the perspective from which we analyze and attempt to understand behavior our "theory-of-action," philosophy, or "espoused beliefs." They are those beliefs that guide our actions in our work with children. In this section these theoretical models are related to the behavior of children.

Ideas, Actions, and Outcomes

"What we believe about the behavior of students affects how we respond and act toward them" (Wood, 1978). In an intervention, ideas, actions, and outcomes are tied together and greatly affect each other. Ideas, in and of themselves, are inert unless active energy is added to their influence. Active energy, by itself, is meaningless and chaotic unless it is directed. In an intervention, the conceptual framework or theory directs and channels action by providing an analysis of the nature of the problem that dictates the intervention and by suggesting the outcome or result toward which the intervention is directed. According to Fink (1988), it is often presumed that teachers' "espoused beliefs" govern their actual behavior. However, we frequently find that considerable variance exists between behavior and philosophy. Training and experience can decrease this discrepancy.

"One form of intervention, carried out within two different conceptual frameworks, can have radically different meanings and lead to radically different experiences and outcomes for the participants" (Rhodes & Tracy, 1972b, pp. 23 and 24).

Educators' perceptions of children, if Rhodes and Tracy are correct, are in large part determiners of the behavior management interventions selected and imposed. For example, the teacher who perceives the child as primarily determined by the environment approaches the problems of behavior management from a radically different point of view from the teacher who perceives a child as controlled primarily by intrapsychic or biophysical factors.

Historical Perspective*

According to Hewett and Forness (1984), there are four historical determiners of our behavior toward ourselves and others:

1. The need and desire to *survive* in a harsh and hostile environment
2. *Superstition*, or the need to respond in some manner to the unknown

---

*The reader is especially referred to Hewett and Forness (1984), and Rhodes and Tracy (1972a, 1972b) for excellent overviews and discussions of our attitude toward and treatment of the handicapped during the various historical periods.

3. *Science*, or the need to investigate, analyze, and explain the unknown
4. *Service*, or the need to assist, guide, protect, and make whole fellow human beings of lesser fortune

Humans have moved among these determiners throughout recorded history, first emphasizing one explanation then another. Movement among these forces is determined by natural forces, irrational and rational beliefs, social and economic conditions, religion, law, and knowledge. We have striven for a rational explanation of behavior but we have frequently regressed to irrational explanations during trying times. However, during each historical period we have developed some explanation of our behavior, frequently a combination of two or more of the historical determiners.

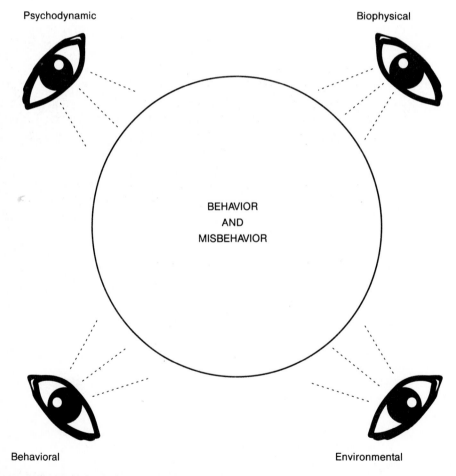

FIGURE 1.1
Conceptual frameworks of children's behavior and misbehavior.

As we approached the twentieth century, our explanations of human behavior focused more on science and service and less on survival and superstition. However, with all of our contemporary knowledge of human beings and our environment, the elements of survival and superstition still exist in our explanations of human behavior.

Each of the models of human behavior presented in the following section is an explanation of behavior; each has led to the development of an educational strategy or methodology for application with children having behavior problems.* Figure 1.1 depicts the relationship of the various theories or conceptual frameworks to the behavior and misbehavior of children. More specifically, conceptual frameworks are ways of looking at behavior and misbehavior.

Psychodynamic Model

As used in this text, the psychodynamic model refers to a group of theoretical constructs that have evolved during the past several decades from the original theoretical formulations of Freud (1949). These formulations have in common a belief in the existence of a dynamic intrapsychic life. Proponents of this model vary in their views on the following: the impact of the environment on the individual's intrapsychic life, the basic instinctive forces energizing psychic life, and the functions of the components of the personality (Roberts, 1975). The effects of nonintrapsychic variables, such as the environment and heredity, have been discussed by Adler and Jung (Munroe, 1955), Erikson (1963), and many others.

Psychodynamic theorists see the causes of human behavior as being within the individual. Behavior is determined by a dynamic intrapsychic life. The relationship between the individual and behavior problems from the psychodynamic perspective is depicted in Figure 1.2.

FIGURE 1.2
Etiology of behavior from the psychodynamic perspective.

---

*The material on the psychodynamic, biophysical, environmental, and behavior modification models of behavior is adapted from Shea, T. M., and Bauer, A. M. (1987). *Teaching children and youth with behavior disorders* (2nd ed.). Englewood Cliffs, N. J.: Prentice-Hall.

Freud perceived the personality as being composed of three interrelating components: the id, the superego, and the ego.

> The id is the lusty infant who wants immediate gratification. Physical pleasure is what the id is after, and it will use the libido (sexual energy) to get what it wants. The id's typical remark in the personality dialogue is, "Gimmie. I want it. Now!" Because of its animalistic antisocial nature, the rest of the personality and society have kept the id mostly unconscious. It still influences us, but unconsciously. . . .
>
> The superego is the conscience. Should and shame are the staples of its vocabulary, and its favorite line is, "You should be ashamed of yourself!" While the id is predominantly unconscious, the superego is partly conscious and partly unconscious. The unconscious part contains the remonstrations and rules we were taught. "Don't do that. Don't play with . . . Nasty! Nice people don't . . ." The superego is judgmental.
>
> Between the id and the superego lives the hero and executive of the Freudian personality structure, the ego. Not only is he caught between the id and the superego and forced to moderate their conflicting pressures, he also is the one who is mostly aware of outside, social reality. Thus, his line to the others is, "Now, let's be realistic about this. . . ." The ego generally straddles the conscious and the unconscious. In a healthy personality he is the manager and can call the shots without being overpowered by the id or the superego. Each of the three parts has a genius all of its own. The ego's armamentarium includes his "ego defenses." Sublimation, for example, is the redirection of socially unacceptable impulses into acceptable channels: Don't play in the toilet, dear. Why don't you go out and play in the sandbox? A large part of our work as teachers is to provide socially acceptable outlets for otherwise destructive desires.*

From the psychodynamic perspective, personality development occurs as the child moves through a series of psychosexual steps that must be completed in order for the individual to avoid later problems (Erikson, 1963). The first stage is the *oral* stage, in which the individual's first contact with the environment occurs, relationships are initiated, and a basic attitude of trust or mistrust is developed. The *anal* stage follows, centering on elimination and conformity to demands for control. At the end of this stage, the individual either accomplishes autonomy or experiences shame and doubt. The third stage is *phallic*, in which the child becomes increasingly interested in the feelings of pleasure associated with the genitals. At this time the individual must develop his or her personality and self-identification. The next stage of psychosexual development, *latency*, usually occurs during the elementary school years. During this period the individual channels energy into learning. Finally, during adolescence, the *genital* stage occurs, in which the individual's previous identities are consolidated.

Efforts to apply psychodynamic theories to educational processes have led teachers to develop the psychodynamic-interpersonal educational, or psychoeducational, strategy. This strategy is

---

*From Roberts, T. B. (1975). *Four psychologies applied to education: Freudian-behavioral-humanistic-transpersonal.* Cambridge, MA: Schenkman Publishing Co.

. . . concerned with the psychic origin and meaning of maladaptive behavior, as well as the child's interpersonal relationships with others, particularly the teacher. This orientation, shared by most psychotherapists, is consistent with the high priority given by them to understanding psychological causal factors and the development of a positive, trusting relationship between adult and child in formal education training. (Hewett, 1968, p. 9)

Significant contributions to this educational strategy have been made by Berkowitz and Rothman (1960), Bower (1961), Morse (1985), Long, Morse, and Newman (1980), Nichols (1984), and others. Although diversification exists among these theorists and practitioners, the primary objectives and methodologies to be applied in the educational setting remain relatively constant.

A primary goal is to understand why the child is behaving as he is in school. This goal may be achieved by some through interpretation of behavior in a psychodynamic context, using psychoanalytic concepts. Others may view the child more in relationship to his total environment and be concerned with understanding why he lacks adaptive capacities for dealing with the stresses and demands associated with learning and adjustment in school. For the teacher, a major goal is the communication of acceptance to the child and the establishment of a secure and meaningful relationship. Formal educational goals are of secondary importance. (Hewett, 1968, pp. 17 and 18)

In the classroom emphasis is placed on (1) developing a mentally healthy atmosphere, (2) accepting the child and the pathological conditions without reservation, and (3) encouraging and assisting the child in learning, beginning at a level and under circumstances in which the child can perform successfully. Assuming the role of educational therapist, the teacher accepts the child, tolerating and interpreting the child's behavior.

Psychodynamic theories no longer dominate educational programs as they did in the 1950s and 1960s. However, this theoretical perspective remains a dominant force in contemporary society in the United States in such forms as popular literature, child care books, movies, novels, television shows, and casual conversations.

In Chapter 6 several intervention strategies associated with the psychodynamic model are reviewed in detail.

Biophysical Model

The biophysical theory of the etiology of learning and behavior problems of children places emphasis on organic origins of human behavior. The proponents of this conceptual model postulate a relationship between physical defects, malfunctions, and illnesses and the individual's behavior. This relationship is depicted in Figure 1.3.

Schroeder and Schroeder (1982) discussed the two primary subgroups of biophysical theories: (1) deficit and (2) developmental. The deficit subgroup includes theories related to genetics, temperament, neuropsychopharmacology, nutrition, and

FIGURE 1.3
Etiology of behavior from the biophysical perspective.

neurologic dysfunction. Development theories include neurological organization, perceptual motor learning, physiological readiness, sensory integration, and development. Several interventions evolving from these subgroups of biophysical theory are discussed in Chapter 7.

Although not the dominant theory of causation in the education of children, the biophysical model does have proponents among professionals and parents concerned with severely emotionally disturbed, autistic, learning-disabled, perceptually handicapped, and developmentally disabled children.

The practitioner who is influenced by the biophysical model is concerned primarily with changing or compensating for the individual's malfunctioning organic mechanisms or processes that are causing the inappropriate behavior. Organic defects may be a consequence of either heredity or environment (trauma). Environmental effects may occur before, during, or after birth. Biophysical handicaps can be classified into four groups (National Foundation-March of Dimes, 1975):

1. *Structural defects:* One or more parts of the body are defective in size or shape (spina bifida, clubfoot, cleft lip).
2. *Functional defects:* One or more parts of the body are malfunctioning (blindness, deafness).
3. *Inborn errors of metabolism:* The body is unable to convert certain chemicals to other chemicals needed for normal body functioning (phenylketonuria [PKU], Tay-Sachs disease).
4. *Blood diseases:* The blood is unable to conduct its normal functions (sickle-cell anemia, hemophilia).

Several curative and preventive medical interventions have been developed to mitigate or modify the effects of biophysical defects. Among these interventions are prenatal and postnatal health care, proper nutrition and diet, megavitamin and similar therapies, general and specific physical examinations, symptom control medications, and genetic counseling. These interventions are presented in detail in Chapter 7.

Among the proponents of biophysical theories as they apply to the education of children and youth are Cruickshank and others (1961), Fernald (1943), and Kephart (1971).

An excellent summary of this theoretical perspective as it applies in the educational setting is provided by Hewett (1968):

> The primary goal of the sensory-neurological strategy is to discover the child's sensory and neurologically based deficit, often through extensive observation and diagnostic testing. Once these deficits are uncovered, the child is viewed as a learner who must be trained to accurately perceive and comprehend stimuli and to demonstrate motor efficiency before he is given complex learning tasks. (p. 24)

In the educational setting, the teacher who is influenced by the biophysical model will emphasize order and routine in the classroom and daily schedule, frequent repetition of learning tasks, the sequential presentation and learning of tasks, and a reduction of extraneous environmental stimuli.

Environmental Model

The impact of the environment on human behavior is a dominant theme in contemporary society. Many decisions made by governments, corporate groups, and individuals are made with a conscious awareness of the relationship between people and the environment. Environmental impact studies are standard, accepted components of all proposals to construct highways, airports, dams, lakes, industrial complexes, high-rise buildings, and so on. Both professionals and lay persons are increasingly concerned with any environmental changes that may affect human behavior, such as those concerning recreation areas, water pollution, waste disposal, strip mining, or nuclear power. Many are concerned with the effects of environmental changes on issues such as employment, human services, and neighborhood composition.

Sociology traditionally is the study of the development, structure, interaction, and behavior of organized groups of humans. Sociology is composed of a number of subgroups focusing on specific areas of this social science, such as social psychology, small-group study, or educational sociology.

In an educational setting, sociology focuses on the formal and informal composition of and interactions among groups. It is concerned with groups that affect an organization both within the organization and outside it. Applied to the education of children, sociology is the study of social forces that in some manner affect individuals and groups.

Ecology is the study of the interrelationships between an organism and its environment. As it applies to education, ecology is the study of the reciprocal relationship between the child or group and others (individuals, groups, and objects) in the environment.

Sociology and ecology as etiological models of human behavior are depicted in Figure 1.4.

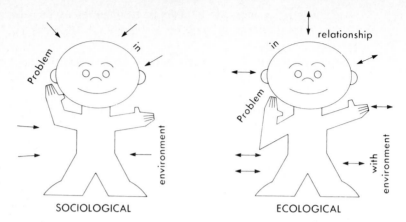

FIGURE 1.4
Etiology of behavior from the sociological and ecological perspectives.

The environmental theorists maintain that isolating a child's behavior from the environment in which it occurs denies the phenomenal nature of that behavior (Rhodes & Paul, 1978). Environmental theorists assume instead that "the child is an inseparable part of a small social system, an ecological unit, made up of the child, his family, his school, his neighborhood, and community" (Hobbs, 1966, p. 1108). Reactions of others in the child's ecosystem influence the way the child acts (Algozzine, 1980). The environmental perspective emphasizes the individual's behavior problem as a product of a "particular collective in a particular environment or place at a particular time in history" (Rhodes & Paul, 1978).

An environmental theory of importance to educators is the *deviance perspective.*

> The deviance perspective focuses on mental illness as the breaking of social rules. In particular, mental illness is related to implicit rules governing ordinary social interaction. From a deviance perspective, two important questions arise. (1) What are the social forces promoting conformity or rule-breaking? (2) What relationships exist between those enforcing the rules and those breaking the rules? (Des Jarlais, 1972, p. 263)

In an effort to respond to these two central questions, theorists have generated several models to account for deviant behavior. Reviewed by Des Jarlais (1972), these frameworks include:

☐ *Anomie:* The theory of anomie as a cause of mental illness was first proposed by Durkheim (1951). Anomie is defined as a lack of social rules or inhibitors within the structure of a society that effectively limit or regulate individual and group behaviors. This phenomenon occurs in rapidly developing or changing societies, such as contemporary society, in which socially sanctioned norms have not evolved or been institutionalized rapidly enough to monitor the efforts of individuals and groups to attain their needs and desires.

☐ *Social disorganization:* The theory of social disorganization was developed from the findings of a series of urban studies. Among the researchers associated with this school of thought were Hawley (1950) and Park and Burgess (1925). This perspective attempts to measure and characterize the differences between communities considered organized or "natural" and communities considered disorganized. Characteristics of the organized community, in opposition to those of the disorganized community, include low crime and delinquency rates, stable family units, a low rate of mental illness and so on. The sources of such characteristics of the community (both organized and disorganized) are assumed to be related to such variables as the availability of employment, education, religious services, recreational facilities, and the like. The disorganized community lacks appropriate services.

☐ *Labeling theory:* The labeling of children who deviate from the norms and rules of the school and community has long been a concern of educators. Many fear the effects of the label and its implications for the child's behavior and educators' expectations of the child (Algozzine, Mercer, & Countermine, 1977).

The theory of labeling emphasizes that one does not become a deviant by breaking rules. One must be labeled a deviant before the social expectations defining the particular form of deviance are activated. Once an individual is officially labeled a deviant, this person assumes the role expectations of that particular form of deviance in order to conform to the expectations of society.

This theoretical perspective is closely related to Parsons's (1951) concept of the sick role. He proposed four societal expectations that encourage individuals labeled "sick" to assume this role:

1. Sick persons are relieved of their normal role obligations.
2. Because they are sick, they are not morally responsible for their condition.
3. Sick persons must express their desire to return to normal functioning.
4. Sick persons must seek technically competent help from appropriate caretakers (psychiatrists, psychologists, social workers, teachers).

Reviewed by Wagner (1972), a variety of interventions have evolved out of environmental theories. Many of these interventions are reviewed in detail in Chapter 7.

The application of the environmental model in educational programs for children is characterized by (1) an awareness of the impact of the environment on the group and/or individual and the monitoring and manipulation of the environment for the benefit of the individual and/or group, and (2) an awareness of the dynamic reciprocal interrelationship that exists between the group and/or individual and the environment and the monitoring and manipulation of this relationship for the benefit of the individual and/or group.

In summary, the environmental framework is based on several assumptions about behavior, the environment, and the interactions between an individual and environment (Swap, Prieto, & Harth, 1982). These assumptions are as follows:

1. The child is not disturbed. Disturbance is a consequence of either the environment's effect on the child or the interactions between the child and the environment.
2. Environmental interventions, to be effective, must in some manner alter the ecological system in which the child functions. The implementation of environmental interventions is based on an assessment of the child, the specific environment in which the child is functioning, and the interactions between these two elements. Although the interventions may focus on one or more of these factors, it impacts on all of them.
3. Environmental interventions are eclectic. It will be apparent in the discussion in Chapter 7 that environmental interventions are chosen from many theoretical perspectives. Interventions are selected and applied as needed within the environmental framework.
4. Interventions in an ecological system may have unanticipated consequences. Because of the complexity of the child, the environment, and the relationship between the two elements, it is difficult to predict with certitude the specific effects an intervention may have on the relationship's many variables. Thus, frequent and careful evaluation of the impact of interventions is essential.
5. Each interaction between child and setting is unique. This assumption recognizes the uniqueness of each child, the environment in which he or she is functioning, and the reciprocal relationship between child and environment.

Behavioral Model

Behavioral psychology is the predominant educational psychology taught in colleges and universities in the United States today (Kavale & Hirshoren, 1980).

The statement "what you do is influenced by what follows what you do" (Sarason et al., 1972, p. 10) is an excellent summary of the essence of the behavioral theory, specifically in reference to behavior modification. Behavior modification is the primary focus of Chapters 2 to 5 of this text. A brief overview of this model is presented here to facilitate the reader's efforts to compare and contrast it with the three previously presented models of human behavior.

The behavior modifier is concerned primarily with what behavior an individual exhibits and what intervention can be designed and imposed to change this observable behavior.

For the behavior modification practitioner *behavior* is defined as all human acts that are observable and measurable, excluding biochemical and physiological processes (Roberts, 1975).

The behavioral theorists and practitioners see the causes of human behavior as existing outside the individual in the immediate environment. Thus the individual's behavior is primarily determined by external forces. The relationship between the individual and his or her behavior as perceived by the behaviorist is depicted in Figure 1.5.

FIGURE 1.5
Etiology of behavior from the behavior modification perspective.

Those adhering to the behavior modification model assume that all human behavior (adaptive and maladaptive) is the consequence of the lawful application of the principles of reinforcement.

According to Roberts, the principles of reinforcement are as follows:

1. Reinforcement always follows the exhibition of the behavior. According to "Grandma's law," you eat your vegetables first, then you may have dessert.
2. The behavior should be reinforced as soon as possible after it occurs. Teachers who do not return papers or who delay their return a long time are guilty of professional misconduct in the perception of the behaviorist.
3. The reinforcement must be appropriate for the individual or group being reinforced. A reinforcer is only effective if the individual or group being reinforced perceives the reinforcer as rewarding or punishing.
4. Many small rewards, presented frequently, are more effective than a few big ones.

The principles of reinforcement are presented in depth in Chapter 2. These rules are an indication of the behavior modifier's belief that human behavior is controlled by the individual's impinging environmental stimuli. The individual's behavior is changed by manipulation of environmental stimuli.

Behavioral theory, including behavior modification techniques and their applications to individual and group behavior problems, has its roots in the writings and research of Bandura (1969), Skinner (1971), Thorndike (1932), and Wolpe (1961), among others. Although there have been and continue to be debates among theorists relative to various constructs and interventions within this theoretical model, practitioners have successfully applied its principles to a variety of human problems. Among the problem behaviors that have been modified as a consequence of the application of behavior modification interventions are the symptoms of psychoses, autism, neuroses, marital conflicts, specific learning problems, motivational handicaps, and speech problems. Researchers and practitioners have successfully modified tantrums, verbal and physical aggression, interpersonal interaction patterns, eating habits, mutism, and so on.

Various behavior modification interventions in the school have been successfully implemented with children with exceptionalities by Haring and Phillips (1962), Hewett and Taylor (1980), Orme and Purnell (1970), and others.

The goal of behavior modification interventions in the classroom with children with behavioral disorders (and, indeed, with all individuals) is best summarized by Hewett (1968).

> The basic goal for the behavior modifier is the identification of maladaptive behaviors which interfere with learning and assisting the child in developing more adaptive behavior. Every child is considered a candidate for learning something regardless of his degree of psychopathology and other problems. This "something" may only represent a starting point (e.g., chair sitting) and be but a small part of the eventual "something" the teacher hopes to accomplish (e.g., reading), but care will be taken to insure its mastery before more complex goals are introduced. The child's behavior is viewed in the broadest possible context without rigid adherence to a priority ranking of behavioral goals on the basis of inferences regarding emotional conflicts or brain dysfunctions.

There are a variety of behavior modification interventions that may be applied in the effort to change behavior. These interventions are presented in detail with practical examples in Chapters 4 and 5.

The procedures for applying behavior modification in the educational setting require the teacher to (1) observe and clarify the behavior to be changed, (2) select and present potent reinforcers at the appropriate time, (3) design and impose, with consistency, an intervention technique based on the principles of reinforcement, and (4) monitor and evaluate the effectiveness of the intervention. These steps in the behavior change process are presented in detail in Chapter 3.

Integrative Framework

As is evident from the discussion in the previous section, the behavior of children is a complex, dynamic phenomenon that may be perceived from a psychodynamic, biophysical, behavioral, or environmental point of view. The very complexity and diversity of the theoretical perspectives and children's behavior preclude simple assessment and intervention. However, through the application of an integrated, ecological framework, it may be possible to coordinate the extant perspectives into a manageable assessment-intervention model (Shea & Bauer, 1987).

From an ecological perspective, rather than being seen as rooted within the child or in the environment exclusively, behavior is seen as a result of the interaction between the child, the child's idiosyncratic behaviors, and the unique environments in which the child functions (Forness, 1981). Ecological practitioners would suggest that traditional practitioners are missing educationally and socially relevant variables due to their limiting single-theory perspective.

Before discussing the integrative framework, it is necessary to become familiar with a few specialized terms.

Ecology is the interrelationship of humans with the environment, and involves reciprocal association (Thomas & Marshall, 1977). According to Scott (1980), ecology is all the surroundings of behavior. From this point of view, it is assumed that the child is an inseparable part of an ecological unit, which is composed of the child, the classroom, the school, the neighborhood, and the community. *Development* is defined as the continual adaptation of the child and the environment to each other. It is seen as progressive accommodation that takes place throughout the life span between growing individuals and their changing environments. It is based on "the person's evolving conception of the ecological environment and his relationship to it, as well as the person's growing capacity to discover, sustain, and alter its properties" (Bronfenbrenner, 1979, p. 9).

Behavior is the expression of the dynamic relationships between the individual and the environment (Marmor & Pumpian-Mindlin, 1950). Behavior occurs in a setting that includes specific time, place, and object props as well as the individual's previously established pattern of behavior (Scott, 1980). To understand behavior, it is necessary to examine the systems of interaction surrounding the behavior; assessment is not restricted to a single setting. In addition, according to Bronfenbrenner (1977), examination must take into account those aspects of the environment beyond the immediate situation in which the individual is functioning and that impact on the behavior. *Congruence* is the match or goodness-of-fit between the individual and the environment. Thurman (1977) suggests that the individual whom we judge to be normal is functioning in an ecology that is congruent: the individual's behavior is in harmony with the norms of the environment. When there is a lack of congruence, the individual is viewed as either deviant or incompetent.

The integrated, ecological framework, presented here, includes several interrelated ecological contexts in which individuals may function. These contexts, which affect the individual's development and behavior, are the *ontogenic system*, the *microsystem*, the *mesosystem*, the *ecosystem*, and the *macrosystem* (Bronfenbrenner, 1979; Belsky, 1980). The relationship of the five systems is depicted in Figure 1.6.

The ontogenic system includes the child's personality, skills, abilities, and competencies. Each student exhibits intraindividual factors for working the environment. Among the many factors included in this system are the child's intelligence, coping skills, and academic skills.

The microsystem includes the interrelationships within the immediate setting in which the individual is functioning, such as the teacher-child and child-child relationships in the classroom. It must be remembered that both teacher and child are actors and reactors in the classroom environment (Carroll, 1974).

The mesosystem is the interrelationships between the settings in which the child is actually functioning at a particular point in time. It is a system of microsystems.

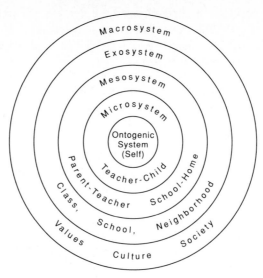

FIGURE 1.6
The five systems of the integrative framework.
From Shea & Bauer, 1987.

The mesosystem may include relationships among school, home, church, and community.

The exosystem is the larger social system in which the microsystem and mesosystem are imbedded. It includes both formal and informal social structures, such as law enforcement, recreational, political, and transportation systems. Though a child may not actively participate in these systems or be directly influenced by them, they do influence the child's microsystem and mesosystem and, thus, indirectly influence the child.

The final system—the macrosystem—includes the overriding cultural belief and values, as well as the general perceptions, of the social institutions common to a particular culture in which the child is functioning. The beliefs, values, and attitudes of the macrosystem directly and indirectly influence the child's behavior. Areas of the macrosystem that may impact on the child include society's perceptions of education, teachers, special education, children, children with exceptionalities, and so on.

As can be seen, the ontogenic system is related most closely with psychodynamic and biophysical conceptual frameworks. Interventions of an ontogenic nature are discussed in Chapters 6 and 7. The microsystem is closely related to the behavioral perspective and is discussed in Chapters 2 through 5 of the text. The interventions related directly and indirectly to the mesosystem, ecosystem, and macrosystem are discussed in Chapters 7, 8, and 9.

Public Law

On November 29, 1975, President Ford signed Public Law (PL) 94-142, which in a bipartisan effort was passed by both the House of Representatives and the Senate. This legislation, the *Education of All Handicapped Children Act of 1975* mandates throughout the United States a *free, appropriate public education for all handicapped children.*

Congress emphasized the key elements of the act in its use of the words *free, appropriate, public,* and *all.* It is the intention of Congress that *all* handicapped children receive an education regardless of race, religion, sex, or the characteristics of their particular handicaps. They are to receive an education that is *appropriate* to their individual needs. This education is to be *free* (without cost) to the child and the parents or guardian. Finally, the handicapped child's *free, appropriate* education is to be provided by the *public* school system rather than in private school or institutional settings (Shea and Bauer, 1987).

Among the provisions of PL 94-142, of greatest significance to the topics presented in this text are (Abeson & Weintraub, 1977):

1. Each handicapped individual needing special education and related services is to have an individualized education program (IEP) written in response to his or her individual educational needs.
2. Parents are to be involved in the child's IEP. As partners with professionals in the child's education, parents have several important functions. They participate in the child's assessment, the IEP development process, the approval of the IEP and educational placement, and the evaluation of the IEP. Parents may participate directly in the child's educational program.
3. The regular and special classroom teachers are to be fully participating members of the IEP decision-making team. As the professionals primarily responsible for the delivery of services to the handicapped individual, the teacher—general or special—has full and active involvement in the IEP development, implementation, and evaluation.
4. Handicapped children are to be placed in the least restrictive environment necessary to meet their unique educational needs. This concept is frequently referred to as *mainstreaming*, an often misunderstood term.

Mainstreaming is defined as

. . . a belief which involves an educational procedure and process for exceptional children, based on the conviction that each such child should be educated in the least restrictive environment in which his educational and related needs can be satisfactorily provided. This concept recognizes that exceptional children have a wide range of special educational needs, varying greatly in intensity and duration; that there is a recognized continuum of educational settings which may, at a given time, be appropriate for an individual child's needs; that to the maximum extent appropriate, exceptional children should be educated with non-exceptional children; and that special classes, separate schooling, or other removal of an exceptional child from education with non-exceptional children should occur only when the intensity of the child's special education and related need is such that they cannot be satisfied in an environment including non-exceptional children, even with provisions of supplementary aides and services. (Council for Exceptional Children, Delegate Assembly, 1976, p. 3)

Public Law 99-457, enacted in 1986, reauthorized Public Law 94-142 and provided a national directive for further services for young children with exceptionalities and their families. All the rights and protections of Public Law 94-142 were extended to children 3 to 5 years old in the 1990-91 school year. Parents are to be involved in their child's programs through a written Individualized Family Service Plan developed by a multidisciplinary team and the parents.

Individualized Education Programs

A key provision of PL 94-142 is the individualized education program (IEP) to be written for each child who is declared eligible for special education services, whether service is provided in the general or special educational setting. The IEP is developed in response to each child's educational needs.

The IEP is

> . . . a written statement for each handicapped child developed in any meeting by a representative of the local educational agency or an intermediate educational unit who shall be qualified to provide, or supervise the provision of, specially designed instruction to meet the unique needs of handicapped children, the teacher, the parents or guardian of such child, and, whenever appropriate, such child, which statement shall include (A) a statement of the present levels of educational performance of such child, (B) a statement of annual goals, including short-term instructional objectives, (C) a statement of the specific educational services to be provided to such child, and the extent to which such child will be able to participate in regular educational programs, (D) the projected date for initiation and anticipated duration of such services, and (E) appropriate objective criteria and evaluation procedures and schedules for determining, on at least an annual basis, whether instructional objectives are being achieved. (Public Law 94-142, Section 4)

As noted previously, the law specifically requires the direct participation of parents, teachers, and, when appropriate, the child in the IEP development process. In addition, PL 9-142 mandates that the child be integrated into the regular school programs for educational activities unless such integration is detrimental to child's overall educational progress.

A correlation can be made between the IEP process and the steps in the behavior change process, described in detail in Chapter 3. Briefly, the behavior change process requires the following steps:

☐ Collection of baseline data (IEP assessment)
☐ Selection of objectives for the behavior change program (IEP short-term instructional objectives)
☐ Design and implementation of a specific behavior change intervention or strategy (IEP instructional or educational program)
☐ Collection of intervention data to evaluate the effectiveness of the behavior change intervention (IEP evaluation)

These similarities are demonstrated on the sample IEP in Figures 1.7 and 1.8 (pp. 30-31).

SUMMARY

In this introductory chapter, an effort is made to prepare the reader for the discussion of behavior management strategies presented in Chapters 2 through 7.

First, a definition of behavior management and several teacher effectiveness guidelines are presented and discussed.

Next, the relationship between models of human behavior (conceptual frameworks) and behavior management interventions evolving from these models are discussed. Four models of behavior are discussed in detail. These are psychodynamic, biophysical, environmental, and behavioral. It is suggested that each of the models contributes to our understanding of human behavior. To increase understanding of the relationships between behavior and the conceptual models, an integrative framework is discussed.

Several important components of PL 94-142 (Education for All Handicapped Children Act of 1975) and PL 99-457 having bearing on the role and function of general and special educators and parents are presented. The major components of the IEP are reviewed and exemplified. The similarities between the IEP and the behavior change process are discussed.

In Chapters 2 through 5, the reader's attention is turned to processes and techniques associated with the behavioral model. Chapters 2 and 3 present the principles of reinforcement and the steps in the behavior change process, respectively. Chapters 4 and 5 present several behavior modification techniques applied to change behavior.

Individualized Education Program

Student's name: *E.J. Jolpe*   Planning conference date: *May 12, 1990*
IEP manager's name: *T.J. Waller*   Date for review/revision: *May, 1991*

PRESENT LEVELS OF PERFORMANCE

Academics: *One year below grade level in reading and spelling, as noted on PIAT, Botel, and a teacher informal assessment*

Speech/Language: *Age appropriate as noted on Utah and district speech and language therapist*

Motor: *Below age level in visual perception on DTVP. Below age level in auditory discrimination on Wepman. Visual and hearing tests negative*

Social Behavior: *Inattentive and hyperactive as observed by teacher, district psychologist, and speech and language therapist*

Prevocational/Vocational: *Not applicable*

Self-Help: *Not applicable*

Extent of Participation in Regular Education: *All activities except 1 hour daily in resource room*

Type of Physical Education Program: *Regular physical education*

Services to be provided for current year

Type	Initiation date	No. minutes per week	No. weeks
Resource room	*Aug. 23, 1990*	*300*	*36*
Second grade teacher consultation	*Aug. 23, 1990*	*150*	*36*

Placement: *Special Education Resource Room, 2nd grade with consultation on behavior problem*

Justification for Placement: *Needs assistance in visual perception and auditory discrimination which cannot be provided in regular 2nd grade classroom*

FIGURE 1.7
Sample IEP statement.

(Modified from *Illinois primer on individualized education programs.* Springfield, Ill.: State Board of Education, Department of Specialized Educational Services and Regional Resource Center, 1981.)

Student's name: E.J. Jolpe
Implementer's names:
    T.J. Waller, resource room
    J.J. Topel, second grade

Instruction areas:
1. Visual perception
2. Auditory discrimination
3. a. Inattentiveness
   b. Hyperactivity

SHORT-TERM INSTRUCTIONAL OBJECTIVES

Condition	Behavior	Criteria	Special media and materials	Evaluation/Schedule	Date objective mastered
1. Visual perception	Cannot discriminate between b/d, d/p, etc.	100% accuracy	Kephart (1960)	Teacher on-going evaluation with formal evaluation every 9 weeks	
2. Auditory discrimination	Cannot discriminate between "was/saw," etc.	100% accuracy	Valett (1974)	As above	
3. a. Inattentive	a. Attends to teacher directions and on-going group activities less than 20% of time	Increase attend behavior to 60%	Token economy	Count and chart daily; summary weekly; reevaluate at 9 weeks	
b. Hyperactive	b. On an average, during seat work, is in seat less than 30% of time	Increase in-seat behavior to 70%	Token economy and time-out by exclusion Communication via token economy card carried by child to all special and regular school activities	As above	

FIGURE 1.8
Sample IEP short-term objectives.
(Modified from *Illinois primer on individualized education programs.* Springfield, Ill.: State Board of Education, Department of Specialized Educational Services and Regional Resource Center, 1981.)

PROJECTS

1. Conduct a class discussion of the definition of behavior management presented in the text.
2. Using the professional literature, locate three definitions of behavior management. Compare these definitions with that presented in the text.
3. Using the professional literature, write a five- or six-page paper on one of the models of human behavior discussed in this chapter.
4. Discuss the impact of the four historical determiners (survival, superstition, science, and service) on contemporary human behavior.
5. Invite to class for a presentation or conduct an interview with a special education administrator or teacher to discuss the impact of PL 94-142 on general and special education.
6. Discuss the sample IEP presented in the text. Write an IEP using a child who is familiar to you or your instructor.

REFERENCES

Abeson, A., & Weinstraub, F. (1977). Understanding the individualized education program. In S. Torres (Ed.), *A primer on individualized education programs for handicapped children* (pp. 3-8). Reston, VA: The Foundation for Exceptional Children.

Algozzine, B. (1980). The disturbing child: A matter of opinion. *Behavioral Disorders, 5*(2), 112-115.

Algozzine, B., Mercer, D. C., & Countermine, T. (1977). The effects of labels and behavior on teacher expectations. *Exceptional Children, 44*(2), 131-132.

Argyris, C., & Schon, D. A. (1974). *Theory in practice: Increasing professional effectiveness.* San Francisco, CA: Jossey-Bass.

Bandura, A. (1969). *Principles of behavior modification.* New York: Holt, Rinehart & Winston.

Beez, W. V. (1972). Influence of biased psychological reports on teacher behavior and pupil performance. In A. Morrison & D. McIntyre (Eds.), *The social psychology of teaching* (pp. 324-332). Baltimore: Penguin Books.

Belsky, J. (1980). Child maltreatment: An ecological integration. *American Psychologist, 53*, 320-335.

Berkowitz, P., & Rothman, E. (1960). *The disturbed child.* New York: New York University Press.

Bower, E. M. (1961). *The education of emotionally handicapped children: A report to the California Legislature.* Sacramento: California State Department of Education.

Bronfenbrenner, U. (1977). Toward an experimental ecology of human development. *American Psychologist, 32*, 513-531.

Bronfenbrenner, U. (1979). *The ecology of human development.* Cambridge, MA: Harvard University Press.

Carroll, A. W. (1974). The classroom as an ecosystem. *Focus on Exceptional Children, 6* (4), 1-11.

Council for Exceptional Children, Delegate Assembly. (1976). Mainstreaming. *CEC Update, 7*(4) 3.

Cruickshank, W., Bentzen, F., Ratzenburg, F., & Tannhauser, M. (1961). *A teaching methodology for brain-injured and hyperactive children.* New York: Syracuse University Press.

Des Jarlais, D. C. (1972). Mental illness of social deviance. In W. C. Rhodes and M. L. Tracy (Eds.), *A study of child variance: Vol. 1. Conceptual project in emotional disturbance* (pp. 259-322). Ann Arbor: The University of Michigan Press.

Dreikurs, R., & Grey, L. (1968). *Logical consequences: A new approach to discipline.* New York: Hawthorn Books.

Durkheim, E. (1951). *Suicide.* New York: Free Press.

Erikson, E. H. (1963). *Childhood and society.* New York: W. W. Norton & Co.

Fernald, G. (1943). *Remedial techniques in basic school subjects.* New York: McGraw-Hill Book Co.

Fink, A. H. (1988). The psychoeducational philosophy: Programming implications for students with behavioral disorders. *Behavior in Our Schools, 2* (2), 8-13.

Forness, S. R. (1981). Concepts of learning and behavior disorders: Implications for research and practice. *Exceptional Children, 48,* 56-64.

Freud, S. (1949). *An outline of psychoanalysis.* New York: W. W. Norton & Co.

Haring, N. G., & Phillips, E. L. (1962). *Educating emotionally disturbed children.* New York: McGraw-Hill Book Co.

Hawley, A. (1950). *Human ecology: A theory of community structure.* New York: Ronald Press Co.

Hewett, F. M. (1968). *The emotionally disturbed child in the classroom: A developmental strategy for educating children with maladaptive behavior.* Boston: Allyn & Bacon.

Hewett, F. M., & Forness, S. R. (1984). *Education of exceptional learners* (3rd ed.). Boston: Allyn & Bacon.

Hewett, F. M., & Taylor, F. D. (1980). *The emotionally disturbed child in the classroom.* Boston: Allyn & Bacon.

Hobbs, N. (1966). Helping disturbed children: Psychological and ecological strategies. *American Psychologist, 21*(12), 1105-1115.

Illinois primer on individualized education programs. (1981). Springfield, IL: State Board of Education, Department of Specialized Educational Services and Regional Resource Center.

Kampwirth, T. J. (1988). Behavior management in the classroom: A self-assessment guide for teachers. *Education and Treatment of Children, 11*(3), 286-293.

Kauffman, J. M. (1985). *Characteristics of children's behavior disorders* (3rd ed.). Columbus, OH: Merrill.

Kauffman, J. M., Pullen, P. L., & Akers, E. (1986). Classroom management: Teacher-child-peer relationships. *Focus on Exceptional Children, 19*(1), 1-10.

Kavale, K., & Hirshoren, A. (1980). Public school and university teacher training programs for behaviorally disordered children: Are they compatible? *Behavior Disorder, 5*(3), 151-155.

Kephart, N. (1971). *The slow learner in the classroom.* Columbus, OH: Merrill.

Long, N. J., Morse, W. C., & Newman, R. G. (1980). *Conflict in the Classroom* (4th ed.). Belmont, CA: Wadsworth.

Marmor, J., & Pumpian-Mindlin, E. (1950). Toward an integrative conception of mental disorders. *Journal of Nervous and Mental Disease, 3,* 19-29.

Morse, W. C. (1985). *The education and treatment of socioemotionally impaired children and youth.* Syracuse, NY: Syracuse University Press.

Munroe, R. L. (1955). *Schools of psychoanalytic thought: An exposition, critique, and attempt at integration.* New York: Holt, Rinehart & Winston.

National Foundation-March of Dimes. (1975). *Birth defects: The tragedy and the hope.* White Plains, NY: The Foundation.

Nichols, P. (1984). Down the up staircase: The teacher as therapist. In J. Grosenick, S. Huntze, E. McGinnis, & C. Smith (Eds.). *Social/affective intervention in behavioral disorders* (pp. 43-66). Des Moines: State of Iowa Department of Public Instruction.

Orme, M. E. J., & Purnell, R. F. (1970). Behavior modification and transfer in an out-of-control classroom. In G. Fargo, C. Behms, & P. Nolen (Eds.). *Behavior modification in the classroom* (pp. 166-138). Belmont, CA: Wadsworth Publishing Co.

Park, R. E., & Burgess, E. W. (1925). *The city.* Chicago: University of Chicago Press.

Parsons, T. (1951). *The social system.* New York: Free Press.

Rhodes, W. C., & Paul, J. L. (1978). *Emotionally disturbed and deviant children: New views and approaches.* Englewood Cliffs, NJ: Prentice-Hall.

Rhodes, W. C., & Tracy, M. L. (Eds.). (1972a). *A study of child variance: Vol. 1. Conceptual project in emotional disturbance.* Ann Arbor: The University of Michigan Press.

Rhodes, W. C., & Tracy, M. L. (Eds.). (1972b). *A*

study of child variance: Vol. 2. Interventions. Ann Arbor: The University of Michigan Press.

Roberts, T. B. (1975). *Four psychologies applied to education: Freudian-behavioral-humanistic-transpersonal.* Cambridge, MA: Schenkman Publishing Co.

Rosenthal, R., & Jacobson, L. (1966). Teacher's expectancies: Determinants of pupils' IQ gains. *Psychological reports, 19,* 115-118.

Rubin, R., & Balow, B. (1971). Learning and behavior disorders: A longitudinal study. *Exceptional children, 38,* 293-298.

Sarason, I. G., Glaser, E. M., & Fargo, G. A. (1972). *Reinforcing productive classroom behavior.* New York: Behavioral Publications.

Schroeder, S. R., & Schroeder, C. (1982). Organic factors. In J. L. Paul and B. Epanchin (Eds.), *Emotional disturbance in children.* Columbus, OH: Merrill.

Shea, T. M., & Bauer, A. M. (1987). *Teaching children and youth with behavior disorders* (2nd ed.). Englewood Cliffs, NJ: Prentice-Hall.

Skinner, B. F. (1971). *Beyond freedom and dignity.* New York: Alfred A. Knopf.

Scott, M. (1980). Ecological theory and methods for research in special education. *Journal of Special Education, 4,* 279-294.

Swap, S. M., Prieto, A. G., & Harth, R. (1982). Ecological perspective of the emotionally disturbed child. In R. L. McDowell, G. W. Adamson, & F. H. Wood (Eds.), *Teaching*

emotionally disturbed children. Boston: Little, Brown & Co.

Thomas, E. D., & Marshall, M. J. (1977). Clinical evaluation and coordination of services: An ecological model. *Exceptional Children, 44,* 16-22.

Thorndike, E. L. (1932). *The fundamentals of learning.* New York: Teacher's College Press.

Thurman, S. K. (1977). Congruence of behavioral ecologies: A model for special education programming. *Journal of Special Education, 11,* 329-333.

Tisdale, P. C. (1985). The teacher's ten commandments. *The Directive Teacher, 7*(1), 6-8.

Wagner, M. (1972). Environmental interventions in emotional disturbance. In W. C. Rhodes & M. L. Tracy (Eds.), *A study of child variance: Vol. 2. Intervention.* Ann Arbor: The University of Michigan Press.

Wolpe, J. (1961). The systematic desensitization treatment of neuroses. *Journal of nervous and mental disease, 132,* 189-203.

Wood, F. H. (1978). Punishment and special educators: Some concluding comments. In F. H. Wood & K. C. Lakin (Eds.), *Punishment and aversive stimulation in special education: Legal, theoretical and practical issues in their use with emotionally disturbed children and youth* (pp. 119-122). Minneapolis: University of Minnesota.

CHAPTER TWO

Basic Principles of Behavior Modification

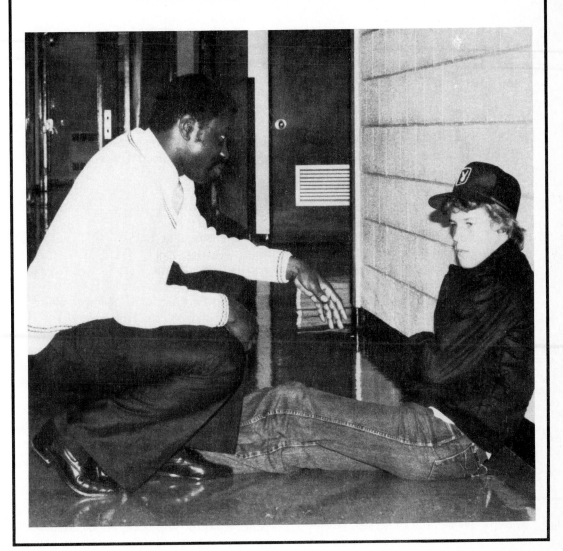

Mr. Rodrigues has completed his first semester as principal of San Jose Mission High School. It has been a challenging semester for the new principal, but something is not going right among the faculty and staff. The morale of the office staff is low; teachers are not motivated; students are going through the motion of learning; and the community acts as if it doesn't know the school exists. Mr. Rodrigues wonders how he might create a more positive, exciting educational atmosphere. Conversations among staff and teachers suggest that Mr. Rodrigues is an administrator who believes that if a person is being paid for a job, that should be ample reward. The teachers and staff think their efforts are not appreciated. The students appear to reflect the attitudes of the staff and teachers.

Maybe if Mr. Rodrigues were taught something about the basic principles of reinforcement, his relations with his staff, teachers, students, and the community would improve.

Linda has about had it with her husband, Bob, and football. Saturday football, Sunday football, Monday night football, Tuesday night football from Canada, Wednesday night college football highlights, Thursday night pro football highlights, and Friday night football forecasts are more than she can take. In the prime of her life, she has lost Bob to oversized giants who wear funny uniforms with team names like Lions, Falcons, Raiders, Bears, Fighting Irish, Trojans, and Pioneers, some of which stand in front of television cameras and wave, "Hi, Mom."

Linda has attended workshops for football widows. She has gone so far as to have the name and number of Bob's favorite player printed on a very "naughty" nightgown and dance seductively in front of the television, only to be told, "Linda, would you please move; I can't see the game."

Is it possible that Linda could change Bob's behavior? Perhaps if Linda knew something about the basic principles of reinforcement, she could become the football player in Bob's life.

Most persons go through life unaware of the many factors in their lives and the influences these factors have on the way they behave. They appear unaware of the fact that as "normal" *Homo sapiens* they tend to be attracted to those experiences that are pleasurable and avoid those that are not pleasurable. Most persons receive pleasure from smiles, positive comments, a pat on the back, an excellent grade in a course, and a bonus in their paychecks. They avoid situations where physical or mental pain is inflicted, and they avoid associating with persons they don't like to be around.

"What you do is influenced by what follows what you do" (Sarason et al., 1972). The consequences and probable consequences of behavior, more than any other factor, determine the behavior that an individual exhibits (Shea & Bauer, 1987). In the field of behavior modification, the consequences of behavior are called *reinforcers*. These reinforcers may increase or decrease behavior (Axelrod, 1983; Morris, 1985).

Reinforcers can be classified in a number of ways. Basically, they are classified as tangible or primary reinforcers (food, drinks, and tokens) and social or secondary reinforcers (praise, smiles, and other signs of approval).

For example, why does a child attend school? What reinforces school-attending behavior? A child may go to school because:

1. It is warmer in the school than in the home.
2. The people at school give the child more attention than the people at home or in the neighborhood.
3. The child plans after-school activities with friends during the morning recess.
4. The child eats the hot meal provided each noon by the school.

It can be understood, then, that a child attends school for both tangible (heat and food) and social (attention and friends) reinforcers.

Reinforcers may be positive (rewarding, pleasure giving) or negative (aversive, punishing). Tangible and social reinforcers may be positive reinforcers, that is, desirable consequences for which behavior is exhibited. Or they may be negative, that is, undesirable consequences for which behavior is not exhibited.

A child who considers school aversive might exhibit inappropriate behavior in an attempt to avoid school. If the child were successful in this attempt, the inappropriate behavior would increase; thus school-attending behavior would decrease. For example, two situations that would result in an increase in school-avoiding behavior are the following:

1. The child is allowed to remain at home during the school day because he or she complains of being ill.
2. The child is allowed to remain at home because a homework assignment is not completed.

If the child were not allowed to avoid school by exhibiting these behaviors, they would probably decrease.

Punishment would also be effective in getting a child to attend school. Among the punishments that could be employed are (1) a spanking from the child's parent, (2) a reprimand from the child's parent, (3) loss of allowance or the use of a bike, (4) loss of privileges, such as watching television or attending the movies, and (5) the threat of being sent to juvenile court or a detention center.

The consequences of behavior, then, are the determiners of behavior. Human beings tend to repeat behaviors that are, in their perception, rewarded or praised. They tend not to repeat behaviors that are, in their perception, punished.

In the remainder of this chapter the basic principles of reinforcement are presented and exemplified. These principles can be systematically applied by the teacher in the classroom and by the parents in the home.

The effective and efficient application of behavior modification techniques involves more than the simple memorization and application of the principles of reinforcement. For effective implementation it is necessary that the teacher or parent be intuitive, creative, and empathetic.

CHAPTER OBJECTIVES

After completing this chapter, you will be able to do the following:

1. Discuss and exemplify the principles of reinforcement.
2. Identify and illustrate the consequences of behavior.
3. Understand and characterize the concepts of generalization and discrimination.
4. Describe and give examples of the five most common schedules of reinforcement.

Principles of Reinforcement

The principles of reinforcement are a set of rules to be applied in the behavior change process. The successful behavior modifier relies heavily on these principles when planning and implementing a behavior change program.

Principle 1: Reinforcement Is Dependent on the Exhibition of the Target Behavior

If we are attempting, via a planned intervention, to change a specific behavior in an individual, we must reinforce *only* the behavior we are planning to change and only after that behavior is exhibited. In planning and implementing an intervention, we must *take caution to ensure that nontarget behaviors are not reinforced unwittingly.*

EXAMPLES ■ Ms. Jones was attempting to decrease Bill's out-of-seat behavior in her classroom. It had been ascertained through systematic observation that Bill received attention from her for out-of-seat behavior. When Bill was out of his seat, Ms. Jones proceeded to yell or otherwise reprimand him. Although Bill was receiving negative attention (in Ms. Jones' perception), his attempts to receive attention—positive or negative—were apparently being met in this situation. Bill's inappropriate behavior (being out of his seat) kept increasing as Ms. Jones's behavior (yelling or scolding) kept increasing. ■

■ Ms. Long was faced with a problem similar to Ms. Jones'—Jerry's out-of-seat behavior. She was reported to have said that she had to dust Jerry's chair every morning because he never used it.

At first she applied Ms. Jones' technique, that is, yelling. Then she planned a behavior modification intervention. She would totally ignore Jerry's out-of-seat behavior. She would in *no* way reinforce this particular inappropriate behavior. However, whenever Jerry's overactive bottom hit his assigned seat, she would immediately reward him. She would praise him in front of the whole class, if necessary, and pat his shoulder.

As a result of this intervention, Jerry not only learned to sit in his seat, but Ms. Long discovered she liked him. ■

In the second example the approach was effective in bringing about the desired behavior. In the first example, however, Ms. Jones is still yelling and Bill is still high on all the attention he is receiving.

In conclusion, Principle 1 suggests that if we desire to modify a specific behavior, we must reinforce *only* that behavior and *only* after it is exhibited.

Principle 2: The Target Behavior Is To Be Reinforced Immediately after It Is Exhibited

The importance of presenting the reinforcer immediately after the target behavior is exhibited cannot be overstressed. This principle is especially true during the initial stages of the behavior change process, when we are attempting to establish a new behavior. Inappropriate and nonfunctional behaviors occur from time to time in every individual's behavioral repertoire. If reinforcers are delayed in a planned intervention program, nontarget behaviors (rather than the target behavior) may be accidentally or unwittingly reinforced, thus increasing the probability that a nontarget behavior will be exhibited in the future.

EXAMPLE ■ Mr. Flamer was attempting to increase the number of math problems Pat completed during the period. He planned to reward Pat immediately after he completed each assigned group of problems. The number of problems in each group would be increased on a weekly basis if Pat responded to the intervention as predicted.

Mr. Flamer was very inconsistent in the presentation of the reinforcer (tokens). As a result, Pat spent considerable time waiting at his desk and waving his hand frantically to gain Mr. Flamer's attention.

After a few weeks it was found that the intervention program was ineffective in increasing the number of completed problems. However, Pat now sat at his desk for much longer periods of time with a bored expression.

Mr. Flamer became aware of Pat's behavior and of his personal inconsistency. He began to reinforce Pat immediately after Pat had completed each group of problems. Within a short time, Pat was completing his problems and had doubled his production. ■

When attempting to establish a new behavior or increase the frequency of an existing behavior, we must reinforce that behavior as soon as it occurs.

Principle 3: During the Initial Stages of the Behavior Change Process, the Target Behavior Is Reinforced Each Time It Is Exhibited

If newly acquired behavior is to be sustained at the appropriate frequency rate, the reinforcer must be administered each time the behavior is exhibited. Frequently beginning behavior modifiers reinforce new, but not yet habituated, behaviors with such inconsistency and so infrequently that the child becomes confused and the target behavior does not become an established part of the child's behavioral repertoire.

EXAMPLES   ■ Ms. Traber worked several months with Matt, rewarding approximations of a desired behavior (in this case, a complete sentence). Finally, after 6 months Matt said a complete sentence: "I want a candy." Matt was immediately rewarded with a candy, and for the next several weeks he consumed many candies; he was given many opportunities to receive the reward. In addition, during this phase of the behavior change process Matt increased his variety of complete sentences to include "I want a glass of milk," " I want some juice," "I want some soda," "I want a puzzle," and the like.   ■

■ Russell never requested any materials or assistance in the junior high school classroom without whining, screaming, or both. he would yell, "I want my paper," or "Give me some help." Mr. Hicks had taken about as much of this behavior as he could tolerate. He decided to ignore all whining and screaming from Russell. Russell's initial reaction to being ignored dramatically increased his inappropriate behavior, but Mr. Hicks stuck to the plan.

After 2 weeks of mutual frustration Russell raised his hand one day during social studies. He politely requested Mr. Hicks' assistance. He immediately received the assistance, verbal praise, and a pat on the back. Mr. Hicks was very pleased with Russell (and himself). A mutual admiration society developed and continued very consistently for a few days.

Mr. Hicks then focused his attention on the problem of another boy in the class. As a result, Mr. Hicks became an inconsistent reinforcer and Russell began whining and screaming anew.

Mr. Hicks forgot that Russell's inappropriate behavior had been learned over 12 or 13 years and could not be changed overnight and after only a few successes.   ■

A newly acquired, unconditioned, or not fully habituated behavior cannot be sustained if it is not reinforced each time it occurs. Consistent reinforcement during the initial stages of the behavior change process is essential.

Principle 4: When the Target Behavior Reaches a Satisfactory Frequency Level, It Is Reinforced Intermittently

Although this principle may appear to be a contradiction of Principle 3, it is not. The behavior modifier must be consistent in the application of inconsistent (intermittent) reinforcement *after* the target behavior is established. This practice appears to be the only way in which a newly acquired behavior can be firmly established and become self-sustaining.

Once a target behavior has been established at a satisfactory level, the presentation of the reinforcer is changed from continuous to intermittent. This change in the reinforcer presentation increases the probability that the behavior will be maintained at a satisfactory level. It appears that if the child whose behavior is being changed does not know exactly when the reinforcer will be given *but does know reinforcement will occur,* the target behavior will continue to be exhibited at a satisfactory level.

EXAMPLES
■ Ms. Williams wished to increase Phil's frequency of voluntary responses during current events discussions. In this situation poker chips were used as a reinforcer. The chips could be saved and cashed in at the end of the discussion period for a tangible reward from the class store.

Initially Ms. Williams reinforced Phil each time he volunteered a response during the discussion. After several weeks Phil's frequency of responses was at a satisfactory level; that is, it was equal, or nearly equal, to the average frequency of responses of the other members of the discussion groups. At this point in the behavior modification process Ms. Williams changed from giving continuous to intermittent reinforcement.

With intermittent reinforcement Phil's behavior remained at a high level. Phil became aware that he would be rewarded when he responded, but not every time. It also became evident to Ms. Williams that Phil was enjoying his participation in the class discussions. ■

■ Mr. Jones and Ms. Walker had similar problems in their classroom groups. In Mr. Jones' room Jared would not participate in class discussions. In Ms. Walker's room Herman presented the same problem.

Mr. Jones wished to increase the frequency of Jared's responses during group discussions. He introduced an intervention similar to the one used by Ms. Williams in the previous example. However, once Jared had attained an acceptable level of performance, Mr. Jones discontinued all reinforcement. Because of the lack of reinforcement, Jared's newly acquired behavior decreased.

Ms. Walker also initiated an intervention program to increase Herman's level of participation. Ms. Walker kept Herman on the continuous reinforcement schedule until he became bored with the tokens and the tangible rewards he could purchase with them. Like Mr. Jones' program, Ms. Walker's was ineffective. Herman's participation decreased to its original level. He remained an infrequent participant in group discussions. ■

The reinforcement schedules most commonly applied in behavior modification intervention are discussed later in this chapter.

Principle 5: Social Reinforcers Are *Always* Applied with Tangible Reinforcers

All reinforcement, even during the initial phases of the behavior change process, must include the presentation of social and tangible reinforcers simultaneously, if a tangible reinforcer is used. The purpose of the behavior change process is to help the child perform the target behavior, not for a tangible reward but for the satisfaction of personal achievement. As discussed in the previous chapter, the goal of all behavior management is self-control or self-discipline.

If tangible reinforcers, such as tokens, chips, candy, stars, smiling faces, or checks, are presented, they must always be accompanied by a social reward, such as a smile, a pat on the back, praise, or a wink. In this way the child associates the social reinforcer with the tangible reinforcer. As the behavior change process progresses, the tangible reinforcer is extinguished (phased out) and the target behavior is maintained by social reinforcers alone. If the change process is effective, behavior is maintained by self-satisfaction, occasional unplanned social reinforcers, and delayed tangible rewards.

EXAMPLES ■ When Ms. Williams was initially attempting to increase Phil's discussion group participation (see example in previous section), she provided Phil with verbal praise and a token each time he exhibited the desired behavior. However, when Phil was placed on an intermittent schedule, Ms. Williams continued to provide consistent social reinforcement but only occasional token reinforcement. During the final phase of the behavior change process Phil was provided only intermittent social reinforcement to maintain the desired behavior. ■

■ Mr. Whiteface wanted to modify George's hand-raising behavior. A grape was given to George every time he raised his hand. The reward was delivered by a dispenser affixed to George's desk. When George raised his hand, Mr. Whiteface would push a button to activate the dispenser and release a grape.

In this way, Mr. Whiteface rewarded George consistently. In addition, he gave George social reinforcers for the new behavior. He would say, "That was very good, George"; "I like the way you are raising your hand, George"; or "Fine," "Great," "Good."

After 6 months on the program George functioned with intermittent social reinforcement only. The dispensing of grapes had been terminated, and George's hand-raising behavior remained at a high rate. ■

Beginning behavior modifiers are cautioned to apply this important principle when using reinforcers: *Always apply tangible and social reinforcers simultaneously, if tangible reinforcers are used.*

Potentially effective reinforcers, both tangible and social, are discussed in Chapter 3.

Consequences of Behavior

Behavioral consequences (results) have a direct influence on the behavior a child exhibits. Behavior can be modified, that is, increased, decreased, initiated, or extinguished by systematic manipulation of its consequences. The possible consequences of human behavior are classified as positive reinforcement, extinction, negative reinforcement, and punishment.

In Table 2.1 are several examples of (1) classification of the consequence, (2) appropriate and inappropriate behavior, (3) the consequence of that behavior *(not necessarily a planned intervention),* and (4) the probable effect of the consequence on the behavior in the future. The reader is encouraged to study Table 2.1 carefully.

TABLE 2.1
Behavior: consequence, probable effect, and classification

Classification	Original Behavior Exhibited	Consequence	Probable Effect on the Original Behavior in the Future
Positive reinforcement	Jane cleans her room	Jane's parents praise her	Jane will continue to clean her room
Positive reinforcement	Shirley brushes her teeth after meals	Shirley receives a nickel each time	Shirley will continue to brush her teeth after meals
Extinction	Jim washes his father's car	Jim's car-washing behavior is ignored	Jim will stop washing his father's car
Positive reinforcement	Alton works quietly at his seat	The teacher praises and rewards Alton	Alton will continue to work quietly at his seat
Punishment	Gwenn sits on the arm of the chair	Gwenn is spanked each time she sits on the arm of the chair	Gwen will not sit on the arm of the chair
Negative reinforcement	Bob complains that older boys consistently beat him up, and he refuses to attend school	Bob's parents allow him to remain at home because of his complaints	Bob will continue to miss school
Punishment	Elmer puts Elsie's pigtails in the paint pot	The teacher administers the paddle to Elmer's posterior	Elmer will not put Elsie's pigtails in the paint pot
Extinction	Shirley puts glue on Joe's seat	Shirley is ignored	Shirley will stop putting glue on Joe's seat
Negative reinforcement	Jason complains of headaches when it is time to do homework	Jason is allowed to go to bed without doing his homework	Jason will have headaches whenever there is homework to do

Positive Reinforcement

Positive reinforcement is the presentation of a reinforcer after a behavior has been exhibited. These reinforcers, or consequences of behavior, tend to increase or sustain the frequency with which the behavior is exhibited in the future (Alberto & Troutman, 1986). Everyone receives positive reinforcement throughout each day. The process of positive reinforcement involves increasing the probability of a behavior recurring by reinforcing it with a reinforcer that is appropriate and meaningful to the individual.

Remember, a reinforcer is reinforcing only if it is perceived as reinforcing by the individual.

EXAMPLES   ■   Kevin has received a superior report card and is praised by his parents and siblings. As a result of the positive reinforcer (praise), the probability of Kevin's continuing to study hard and receive superior report cards in the future is increased. If Kevin's report card were ignored or severely criticized because of a single poor grade, the probability of his continuing his efforts and receiving superior report cards in the future would be decreased.   ■

■   Ms. Pompey has identified stars as positive reinforcers with her classroom group. She puts a star on Cynthia's paper because Cynthia has successfully completed her homework assignment. Cynthia enjoys receiving stars. By placing a star on Cynthia's paper, Ms. Pompey knows she is increasing the probability of Cynthia's completing her homework assignments in the future.   ■

Extinction

Extinction is the removal of a reinforcer that is sustaining or increasing a behavior (Alberto & Troutman, 1986). Extinction is an effective method for decreasing undesirable behaviors exhibited by individuals. Unplanned and unsystematically applied extinction techniques have been naturally applied throughout history. For example, parents tend to *ignore* many unacceptable behaviors exhibited by children, such as roughhousing, arguing, and showing reluctance to go to bed, in the hope that these behaviors will decrease in frequency. The ineffectiveness of ignoring as an unplanned intervention is frequently a result of the inconsistency of its application rather than its inadequacy as a behavior change technique. We insist that there be no roughhousing or arguing and that the children be in bed at the designated time one day but do not insist on these rules the next day. The inconsistency on our part, as a teacher or parent, tends to confuse children and reinforce the unacceptable behavior.

Extinction involves the removal or withdrawal of the reinforcer responsible for maintaining behavior. In the classroom setting the target behavior will be extinguished once the reinforcer has been withdrawn for a sufficient period of time.

EXAMPLES   ■   John, a ninth grader, was always making funny sounds with his mouth in Mrs. Rawlin's class. These activities not only got him a lot of attention from his peers but from Mrs. Rawlin. She usually stopped the class and told John how immature he was behaving for his age and that he was making a fool of himself. The class responded with laughter. John laughed the loudest. After several meetings with the school counselor about John's classroom behavior, Mrs. Rawlin agreed to implement another approach.

The next time John made a funny sound, Mrs. Rawlin told the class to ignore him and those students that did would be rewarded with free time. John continued to make sounds for a few days, but because of the lack of attention from peers and teacher, the behavior began to change. Over the course of 7 school days John's behavior was extinguished. Mrs. Rawlin was able to conduct her class without disruptions. John is now receiving attention from his peers and Mrs. Rawlin for appropriate behavior. ■

■ Eight-year-old Robin was constantly tattling on every child who committed the slightest transgression within his purview. Robin's teacher, Ms. Fye, was reinforcing Robin's behavior by responding and attending to him when he tattled on others. Finally, she planned an intervention program employing extinction to decrease Robin's behavior. She would ignore all of his tattling.

Each time Robin approached her to tattle on a classmate, Ms. Fye did one of the following:

Intervened before Robin had an opportunity to tattle and focused his attention on another topic, picture, book and so on;

Turned her back on him and attended to another child who was performing appropriately;

Turned her back on him and walked away without any sign of recognition.

During the initial phase of the behavior change process, Robin's tattling increased for a brief period. As the program continued, the behavior decreased and was extinguished (Figure 2.1). ■

During the extinction process, there are two behavior response phases. During the initial phase, immediately after the reinforcer sustaining the behavior has been removed, the target behavior usually increases or decreases dramatically. During the second phase, the target behavior changes systematically.

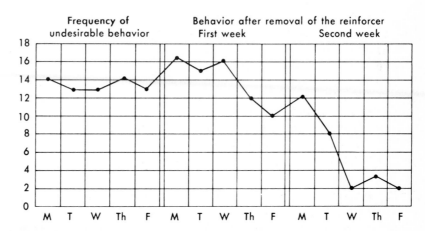

FIGURE 2.1
Frequency of Robin's tattling behavior a week before the removal of the reinforcer and 2 weeks afterward.

The response during the initial phase is a natural, human one that occurs when an individual is suddenly confronted with a situation wherein established methods of gaining goals become nonfunctional. It is natural to become confused under such conditions and continue to try the previously effective method of attaining a goal.

It is during this initial phase that beginning behavior modifiers frequently throw up their hands in frustration and abandon a project. However, if they will persist, the behavior will in all probability extinguish.

Robin's rate of tattling before and during the extinction process is presented in Figure 2.1. The reader should note that Robin's tattling behavior increased on the first 3 days of extinction, then decreased dramatically during the next 7 days.

The teacher or parent should be patient and consistent; the behavior will change.

Negative Reinforcement

Negative reinforcement is one of the most difficult concepts in behavior modification to explain and exemplify. Consequently, several examples of this process are presented. The reader is urged to study this section and Tables 2.1 and 2.2 carefully.

Negative reinforcement is the removal of an already-operating aversive stimulus (negative reinforcer). As a consequence of the removal of the aversive stimulus, the target behavior is strengthened.

Axelrod (1983) has described the technique of negative reinforcement in the classroom setting as "an operation in which a student performs a behavior and the teacher removes something the student dislikes" (p. 8).

As stated earlier, negative reinforcement is the removal of an aversive stimulus in an effort to change the frequency of a behavior. In contrast, punishment is the addition of an aversive stimulus or the subtraction (taking away) of a pleasurable item or activity in an effort to change the frequency of a behavior.

Axelrod provides two excellent examples.

EXAMPLE ■ A group of students are working very diligently at their desks *after* the teacher has stated that they will not be required to do homework assignments that evening if their classroom assignments are completed during the allotted time during the school day. ■

In this example the homework assignment, which was already given by the teacher, is the aversive stimulus (most students perceive homework as aversive). It is removed, and as a result the students' in-classroom work is increased.

EXAMPLE ■ Jimmy is in the process of twisting Tommy's arm. This situation is causing Tommy considerable pain. Jimmy says, "Say Uncle Dudley-Do-Good, and I'll let you go." Tommy, in agony, screams, "Uncle Dudley-Do-Good." Jimmy with a smile on his innocent face releases Tommy's arm, and the pain ends. ■

TABLE 2.2
Effects of consequences

	Positive Reinforcer	Aversive Stimulus
Add	Positive reinforcement (behavior increases)	Punishment (behavior decreases)
Remove	Extinction (behavior decreases)	Negative reinforcement (behavior increases or decreases)

In this example the arm twisting, which was already giving Tommy pain (and Jimmy pleasure), is the aversive stimulus. It is removed, and as a result Tommy's comfort level is increased.

The following examples are provided to offer additional clarification of negative reinforcement.

EXAMPLES   ■   The Reynoldses have a 2-year-old daughter, Alice, who wakes up crying (aversive stimulus) in the middle of the night. She wants to sleep with Mommy and Daddy. In an effort to get their sleep and stop Alice from crying, the parents permit her to sleep with them (thus removing the aversive stimulus of crying). By allowing Alice to sleep in their bed, the parents are increasing both their and Alice's sleeping behavior.

However, the parents' method of stopping Alice's crying (allowing Alice to sleep with them) actually reinforces the frequency of the crying.   ■

■   Bobby was absent 141 of 180 days during the school year. He gave no reason for his nonattendance except that he simply did not want to come to school. After several hours of discussion, it was discovered that Bobby remained away from school so his mother would not die, disappear, or become ill. Bobby's mother unconsciously reinforced his staying-at-home behavior. Many times each day she would say, "Bobby, I always feel safe when you're with me," or "I hope I will be here when you get home," or "I am not well, you know."

Bobby, a very sensitive and concerned son of 11 years, applied the following logic to this predicament: "I love my mother and want her to remain with me. If I leave her to go to school, she may die, become ill, or have an accident. Thus I will not attend school; I will remain with her, and she will be OK."

During the discussion that followed this discovery of why Bobby stayed home, his mother was made aware of her statements and their probable effect. She was asked to cease making these and similar comments (aversive stimulus). After a reasonable time Bobby returned to part-time and eventually full-time attendance at junior high school.   ■

In this example Bobby's mother used her concerns of becoming ill, dying, or having an accident to keep him home. Each time his mother complained of being afraid to be at home alone, Bobby would stay with her, thereby reinforcing the mother's inappropriate behavior as well as Bobby's inappropriate behavior.

Punishment

Punishment appears to be the most familiar and frequently used behavior change technique. Although it is frequently used on children by some parents and teachers, punishment is perhaps the least effective of the behavior modification interventions discussed in this text. Those using punishment have been reinforced by its immediate result; however, it has been determined that the long-term effects of punishment are limited. McDaniel (1980) points out that punishment tends to *suppress* the undesirable behavior rather than extinguish it. This suppression is of short duration, and frequently the behavior recurs in the absence of the punisher.

Punishment is viewed by the behavior modification practitioner as two distinct operations. Punishment is accomplished by the *addition* of an aversive stimulus to the environment. Examples of this operation are paddling, electric shock, additional homework, and the like. Punishment may also be seen as the *subtraction* (taking away) of a pleasurable item or activity. Examples of this operation include loss of extracurricular activities, recess, and the like. Punishment is not to be confused with extinction (see earlier section).

EXAMPLES ■ Anita, one of Mr. Cooper's fifth-grade pupils, constantly talks in class. She disturbs her classmates when she should be completing her assignments. To stop Anita's inappropriate behavior, Mr. Cooper scolds her, and has her stand in the corner of the classroom with a dunce cap on her head.

These techniques are very effective while Mr. Cooper is in the room. However, when Mr. Cooper leaves the classroom for whatever reason, the long-term ineffectiveness of punishment becomes apparent. On these occasions Anita goes around the room yelling and screaming, to the glee of her classmates ■

■ Joe is in Mr. Dee's junior high school class for the socially maladjusted. Joe enjoys using four-letter words. In addition, he takes great pleasure in the expression on Mr. Dee's face when he tosses a few well-chosen words at him. Mr. Dee believed he could eliminate this behavior via the 3-P method, that is a punishing paddle on the posterior. He designed the following intervention, which he explained to Joe:

"Each time you swear in my presence, you will assume the hands-on-ankle position and receive four swats."

Mr. Dee's intervention has had the following results:

1. Joe's language has improved in Mr. Dee's presence but not in his absence (according to a burnt-eared substitute).
2. Mr. Dee has a very tired arm.
3. Joe continues to use his vocabulary on Mr. Dee to gain attention, especially when there are visitors in the classroom.
4. Others in the class encourage Joe to curse so that they can enjoy the circus. ■

It can be seen that *some punishments will remove some unacceptable behaviors* (Wood & Lakin, 1978; Shea, Bauer, & Lynch, 1989). It has been found, however, that when a punished behavior recurs, it usually does so at a rate higher than before the punishment was originally imposed. Another concern associated with punishment is its potential and actual effect on the physical and emotional health of the child. In some cases punishment may cause emotional problems. The fact that the punished child identifies the punishment with the punisher rather than with the inappropriate behavior should be of great concern to teachers and parents who, as previously discussed, are models for children. Children who are punished or abused often punish or abuse their children. The results of punishment do not appear sufficient to justify its use as a behavior change agent.

Effects of Consequences

A thorough understanding of the relationships among the four basic consequences of behavior is a primary requisite for the effective application of behavior modification principles and techniques.

In general, positive reinforcement *increases* the target behavior; punishment and extinction *decrease* the target behavior. Negative reinforcement may increase or decrease behavior depending on the particular target behavior (see Table 2.2).

Generalization

Generalization, or the transfer of learning, is the process by which a behavior reinforced in the presence of one stimulus will be exhibited in the presence of another stimulus (Morris, 1985). The generalization process is an important element of learning. If the process of generalization did not occur, each response would have to be learned in every specific situation. "Transfer of behavior does not occur automatically, but needs to be planned and programmed as part of the training process" (Vaughn, Bos, & Lund, 1986).

EXAMPLES ■ A young child learns the name of an animal (dog). He calls a specific dog "dog" and will soon generalize the name "dog" to all four-legged animals within the classification. He will at times label other four-legged animals, such as cats, cows, and crawling brothers and sisters, with the name "dog." ■

■ A toddler is reinforced for calling her father "Daddy." She will generalize and call all male figures "Daddy" at an early stage of her development. She may call the mailman, milkman, and others "Daddy." This may result in considerable stress between husband and wife. ■

If we wish to function successfully in the environment, we must apply the concepts learned in one situation to many and varied situations. For example, as young children we learn honesty, respect for authority, and the basic principles of computation. It is hoped that each year we can generalize this learning to the completion of our income tax returns.

Stokes and Baer (1977) and Baer (1981) make several suggestions for teaching students to generalize. They suggest that natural contingencies facilitate the learning of generalization. Natural contingencies are those which commonly occur in the environment as a consequence of a behavior. In addition, training more exemplars may help students to generalize. Reinforcing generalization and self-reports of the target behavior assists in generalization. It is important to remember that just because a student behaves in a desired way in one situation does not mean that generalization of that behavior to other settings has occurred. At least initially, generalization should be programmed.

Vaughn, Bos, and Lund (1986) recommend several practical strategies for teachers wishing to help their students develop generalization skills. The recommended strategies include:

1. Varying the amount, power, and type of reinforcers applied to students, such as fading reinforcers, changing from tangible to social reinforcers, or using the same reinforcers in different settings.
2. Varying the instructions given to students, such as using alternative and parallel directions, rewording directions, and using photographs and pictures.
3. Varying the medium and the media of the instructional materials used by students to complete tasks. In the written medium, this could mean varying things such as paper size and color, writing instruments, and inks. The teacher may use other instructional media, such as films or computers.
4. Varying the response modes students use to complete tasks, for instance, changing from written to oral responses, or using a variety of test question formats.
5. Varying the stimulus provided to students, such as changing the size, color, and shape of illustrations, or using concrete objects.
6. Varying the instructional setting, such as changing the work location, or changing from individual to small group study.
7. Varying instructors, such as using aides, peers, or parents.

Vaughn, Bos, and Lund recommend that teachers carefully plan, monitor, and evaluate the effects of generalization instruction on students.

Discrimination

Discrimination is another important learned behavior. Through discrimination we learn that we act one way in one situation and another way in a different situation (Axelrod, 1983). If it were not for the process of discrimination, we would generalize behaviors to a variety of situations in which they would be inappropriate.

EXAMPLE   ■ We behave differently in church than we do at a cocktail party (most of us) and differently in class than we do at a football game (although some classes are stimulating and some football games are boring). Our behaviors in these situations are reinforced by the rewards we receive. ■

Discrimination is the result of differential reinforcement. Reinforcing a behavior in the presence of one stimulus and not reinforcing it in the presence of another stimulus is differential reinforcement.

EXAMPLE ■ Teaching a young child to discriminate between the words *cat* and *rat* may be accomplished by listening and reacting to the child's responses. The child is reinforced for the appropriate response only. In this way the child discriminates between the words *rat* and *cat* when they are presented in the future. ■

Schedules of Reinforcement

A schedule of reinforcement is the pattern with which the reinforcer is presented in response to the exhibition of the target behavior (Rusch, Rose, & Greenwood, 1988). The schedule of reinforcement that is applied has a significant effect on the behavior change process. The most common types of reinforcement schedules are continuous (C), fixed ratio (FR), variable ratio (VR), fixed interval (FI), and variable interval (VI).

Continuous Schedules

The continuous schedule of reinforcement requires the presentation of the reinforcer immediately after each occurrence of the target behavior (Cooper, Heron, & Heward, 1987). The continuous schedule is most often applied during the initial stage of a behavior change program. Frequently, its use will change the behavior rapidly in the desired direction. It is not recommended for long-term use, however, because individuals tend to satiate on this schedule and initial behavior change gains may be lost. In addition, it presents a very unrealistic and artificial procedure for classroom application.

EXAMPLES ■ Ms. Bantle wished to increase Deanna's hand-raising behavior during history. To do this she decided, at least initially, to reinforce Deanna each time she raised her hand. Application of this continuous schedule rapidly increased the target behavior to an acceptable level. ■

■ Mr. McCloud was disturbed by Bobby's out-of-seat behavior. He planned an intervention to increase Bobby's in-seat behavior. During the initial intervention, he reinforced Bobby's in-seat behavior each time it occurred. This continuous schedule quickly increased Bobby's in-seat behavior. ■

Fixed and Variable Schedules

The primary distinctions among fixed and variable ratio and interval schedules are related to the timing and frequency with which the reinforcer is presented. The ratio schedules, fixed and variable, focus on the *completion of specific tasks* before the reinforcer is presented to the child. Reinforcer presentation on the interval schedules, fixed and variable, depends on the exhibition of specific behaviors for *definite periods of time.*

Table 2.3 summarizes the schedules discussed in the following sections.

Fixed Ratio Schedules

When a fixed ratio schedule is applied, the reinforcer is presented after a specific number of appropriate responses are emitted by the child.

EXAMPLES
- Every time John answers 15 social studies questions correctly, he is given 10 minutes to read a comic book. John's reward (comic book reading) is based on his successful completion of a fixed number (15) of social studies questions. ■

- Every time Sheila reads five brief passages in her reading workbook with 80% accuracy, she is allowed to listen to her favorite record album for 5 minutes. In this case Sheila is on a fixed ratio schedule. ■

The fixed ratio schedule usually results in a high rate of response. Consequently it is most effectively and appropriately applied during the beginning phase of the behavior change process.

Variable Ratio Schedules

The variable ratio schedule is designed to sustain the level of response to reinforcement once the acceptable level of behavior has been attained by means of a continuous or fixed ratio schedule. When the variable ratio schedule is applied, the ratio of the reinforcer presentation varies around a response mean or average. This variability is instrumental in sustaining the appropriate level of response.

TABLE 2.3
Relationships among the common reinforcement schedules

	Ratio	Interval
Fixed	Child completes 20 problems to receive 10 minutes of free time	Child is rewarded for remaining in seat for 5 minutes
Variable	Teacher rewards child, on an average, every third time child raises hand	Teacher gives child individual attention, on an average, every 15 minutes in response to acceptable behavior during the time period

EXAMPLES ■ Mr. Davis has Kerry raising his hand and participating in class discussions. He accomplished this via a fixed ratio schedule. He now wishes to change to a variable ratio schedule. Kerry is placed on a variable ratio schedule of 5 (the reinforcer is presented around a response mean of 5). Kerry may be reinforced the seventh time he raises his hand, the sixth time, the third, the fourth, or the fifth. If this schedule (7, 6, 3, 4, and 5) is averaged, the response mean or variable ratio is 5. The fact that Kerry does not know when Mr. Davis will call on him to respond (but does know that he will be called on) maintains his hand-raising behavior at a high level. ■

■ Las Vegas slot machines (in our experience) operate on a variable ratio schedule. The gambler puts quarters in the slot and is occasionally reinforced with small rewards. This occasional reinforcement keeps the person playing until he or she is broke, but the loser always has the hope that the next pull of the arm will result in the super jackpot. ■

Inexperienced behavior modifiers are cautioned not to change from a continuous or fixed ratio to a variable ratio schedule too early in the behavior change process. The desired behavior must be adequately established on a fixed ratio schedule before it can be changed to a variable ratio schedule. Many behavior change programs have failed as a result of the practitioner's impatience in making this transition.

Fixed Interval Schedules

On the fixed interval schedule a specified period of time must elapse before the reinforcer is presented. The reinforcer is presented immediately *after the first response after* the specified time has elapsed. The following examples should clarify this seeming confusion.

EXAMPLES ■ Debbie does not remain in her seat during language lessons. Mr. Quick has decided to reinforce Debbie on a fixed interval schedule of 10. Thus every time Debbie remains in her seat for 10 minutes during language lessons, she is rewarded. ■

■ Most people work on a fixed interval (1 week, 2 weeks, or 1 month) pay schedule. They receive their paychecks after the pay period has elapsed. ■

With fixed interval schedules, the longer the time interval between reinforcements, the lower will be the level of performance. This would suggest that initially during an intervention reinforcers should be presented at frequent intervals.

Variable Interval Schedules

The variable interval schedule is similar to the variable ratio schedule. However, the presentation of the reinforcer is based on a behavioral response mean or average. The individual whose behavior is being modified is not aware of when reinforcement will occur. However, the individual does know that he or she will be reinforced for exhibiting a certain behavior.

EXAMPLE   ■ Mr. Quick has decided to place Debbie on a variable interval schedule of 10. On this schedule Debbie will continue to be reinforced for in-seat behavior. She may be reinforced the first time after only 9 minutes of appropriate behavior, the second time after 4 minutes; the third time after 9 minutes, the fourth time after 15 minutes, and the fifth time after 13 minutes. This is a reinforcement schedule of 9, 4, 9, 15 and 13. It is based on a variable interval with a mean or average of 10 minutes. ■

Again, the behavior modifier should be cautious when changing from fixed ratio or fixed interval to variable ratio or variable interval schedules. If this is done too early or too late in the behavior change process, the newly acquired behavior may be extinguished.

The specific schedule to be applied varies with the behavior being changed. For example, if the concern is to keep an individual in his or her seat for a period of time, an interval schedule would be the most appropriate. However, if the behavior is related to the completion of specific numbers or kinds of tasks, a ratio schedule should be applied. The selection and application of the appropriate schedule is part of the art of behavior modification. Knowing when and how to apply a specific schedule of reinforcement becomes less confusing with experience.

SUMMARY

The basic principles of reinforcement are presented in this chapter, followed by a discussion of the concepts of positive and negative reinforcement, extinction, and punishment. An understanding of these operations and their effects on behavior is essential. To use the aforementioned operations, the reader must understand how they are different as well as how they are interrelated.

The concepts of generalization and discrimination are discussed. Generalization increases the probability that a behavior reinforced in the presence of one stimulus will be exhibited in the presence of another stimulus. Discrimination is the process by which we learn to behave differently in different situations.

A discussion of the schedules of reinforcement is also presented. A schedule of reinforcement is the pattern with which the reinforcers are presented in response to the exhibition of a behavior. The most common types of schedules are continuous, fixed ratio, fixed interval, variable ratio, and variable interval. It is essential that the new practitioner of behavior modification have a thorough knowledge of these schedules.

PROJECTS

1. Explain the five basic principles of reinforcement.
2. Give examples of how positive reinforcement, extinction, negative reinforcement, and punishment can be used to change the behavior of children.
3. List several factors involved in the use of punishment as a behavior change technique.
4. Describe two examples for each of the following: continuous, fixed ratio, fixed interval, variable ratio, and variable interval schedules of reinforcement as applied in the classroom or home setting.
5. Compare the concepts of generalization and discrimination.

REFERENCES

Alberto, P. A., & Troutman, A. C. (1986). *Applied behavior analysis for teachers* (2nd ed.). Columbus, OH: Merrill.

Axelrod, S. (1983). *Behavior modification for the classroom teacher.* New York: McGraw-Hill Book Co.

Baer, D. M. (1981). *How to plan for generalization.* Austin, TX: Pro-Ed.

Cooper, J. O., Heron, T. E., & Heward, W. L. (1987). *Applied behavior analysis.* Columbus, OH: Merrill.

Gardner, W. I. (1977). *Learning and behavior characteristics of exceptional children and youth.* Boston: Allyn & Bacon.

Geller, C. H. (1986). Clarification of negative reinforcement: Once and for all. *The Directive Teacher, 8*(1), 16.

McDaniel, T. (1980). Corporal punishment and teacher liability: Questions teachers ask. *The Clearing House, 54*(1) 10-13.

Morris, R. J. (1985). *Behavior modification with exceptional children: Principles and practices.* Glenview, IL: Scott, Foresman & Co.

Rusch, F. R., Rose, T., & Greenwood, C. R. (1988). *Introduction to behavior analysis in special education.* Englewood Cliffs, NJ: Prentice-Hall.

Sarason, I. G., Glaser, E. M., & Fargo, G. A. (1972). *Reinforcing productive classroom behavior: A teacher's guide to behavior modification.* New York: Behavioral Publications.

Shea, T. M., & Bauer, A. M. (1987). *Teaching children and youth with behavior disorders.* Englewood Cliffs, NJ: Prentice-Hall.

Shea, T. M., Bauer, A. M., & Lynch, E. M. (1989, September). *Changing behavior: Ethical issues regarding behavior management and the control of students with behavioral disorders.* Paper presented at the CEC/CCBD conference, "Find the answer for a decade ahead." Charlotte, NC.

Stokes, T. F., & Baer, D. M. (1977). An implicit technology of generalization. *Journal of Applied Behavior Analysis,10*(2), 349-67.

Vaughn, S., Bos, C. S., & Lund, K. A. (1986) . . . . But they can do it in my room: Strategies for promoting generalization. *Teaching Exceptional Children, 18*(3), 176-180.

Wood, F. H., & Lakin, K. C. (1978). *Punishment and aversive stimulation in special education: Legal, theoretical and practical issues in their use with emotionally disturbed children and youth.* Minneapolis: University of Minnesota, Advanced Training Institute.

CHAPTER THREE

Steps in the Behavior Change Process

George, a junior high student at the John T. Belfast School, appears to be having problems in school. Mrs. Chung, a social studies teacher, notices that George does not participate in class discussions, associate with other students, or take part in cocurricular activities. Mrs. Chung wishes there were some way she could help George become involved with his peers. She feels guilty about George's isolation and believes that she has in some manner let him down. The one thing Mrs. Chung has noticed about George is that he likes to draw.

One day, out of frustration, Mrs. Chung refers George for placement in a special class. However, the school psychologist's report reveals that George has an IQ of 144 with no signs of learning disabilities. Next she decides to show some of George's drawings to the school art teacher, Mr. Bonetti, who is impressed by the creative quality of George's efforts. He shows the drawings to an art professor at the university. He agrees that the drawings are the work of a genius.

Perhaps if Mrs. Chung could learn the steps in the behavior change process, George, her young genius, may become more involved with other students.

Mrs. Anderson teaches algebra and geometry at the Thomas Edison High School. She enjoys teaching and is a conscientious instructor. Her students respect her; she is admired by her colleagues; and the principal refers to her as "my perfect teacher." Mrs. Anderson has been presented the "Outstanding Teacher of the Year" award twice by the school board. She was voted "Teacher of the Year" by the state education association. However, Mrs. Anderson has a serious problem. It is not at school, but at home.

Mrs. Anderson is a single parent. She is head of a household that includes three teenagers, ages 13, 15, and 17. Her children take little responsibility for caring for themselves or the house. After Mrs. Anderson has taught school, attended faculty meetings, corrected papers, called parents, changed her bulletin board, prepared monthly reports, and planned for the next day, she goes home to her other job. At home she must prepare meals, wash and iron, clean the house, do the yardwork, take out the garbage, wash and fuel the car, shop for food and clothing, care for the dog, and finally care for three teenagers.

Perhaps if Mrs. Anderson could learn the steps in the behavior change process, she could change her home situation.

57

In this chapter the specific steps and procedures applied during the behavior change process are discussed and exemplified in detail. Teachers and parents should follow these steps closely: (1) selecting a target behavior, (2) collecting and recording baseline data, (3) identifying reinforcers, (4) implementing the intervention and collecting and recording intervention data, and (5) evaluating the effects of intervention. The chapter also includes a discussion of observer reliability, prompting, and design of the classroom reinforcement area.

CHAPTER OBJECTIVES

After completing this chapter, you will be able to do the following:

1. Characterize the steps in the behavior change process including:
   a. selecting target behaviors;
   b. collecting and recording baseline data;
   c. identifying reinforcers;
   d. implementing interventions and collecting and recording intervention data;
   e. evaluating the effects of intervention.
2. Describe and exemplify the observer reliability process.
3. Define the various forms of prompting.
4. Design a classroom reinforcement area.

Selecting a Target Behavior

The initial step in the behavior change process is the identification of the target behavior. The target behavior is the behavior to be changed or modified. A target behavior may be an existing behavior that the teacher or parent desires to increase or decrease or a nonoccurring behavior; that is, a behavior that is not observable in the individual's behavioral repertoire but one to be developed.

In most classroom situations it is not difficult for the teacher to identify a variety of behaviors needing change (target behaviors). The teacher may recognize the following:

1. Percy does not communicate verbally.
2. Jake should increase his reading skills.
3. Mary should stop yelling in the classroom.
4. Joseph needs to learn to listen to instructions before he begins an assignment.
5. Ellis should improve his table manners in the lunchroom.

All of the aforementioned are potential target behaviors that the teacher could identify in the classroom.

It should be remembered that whenever an individual or a group is singled out for observation and study for the purpose of initiating a behavior change program, it is inevitable that several individual and group target behaviors will be identified. All children and adults manifest behaviors that are unacceptable to some other individuals or groups of individuals under certain conditions.

Decisions leading to the selection of a behavior for modification should be governed by the following considerations, among others:

☐ Type of behavior.
☐ Frequency of the behavior.
☐ Duration of the behavior.
☐ Intensity of the behavior.
☐ Overall number of behaviors needing modification.

It is generally recommended that the beginning behavior modifier not attempt to change more than one individual or group behavior at a time. Implementing several behavior change programs simultaneously frequently results in inefficiency, and otherwise useful interventions prove ineffective. Individual and group behaviors needing modification should be ranked in priority (Morris, 1985). The teacher then systematically works down the priority list from the most important to the least important of the potential target behaviors. The importance of a specific behavior should be determined on the basis of its effect on the child's functioning. Schopler, Reichler, and Lansing (1980) suggest the following order of priorities be applied to changing the behaviors of severely developmentally disabled children:

1. Problems that risk the child's life.
2. Problems that risk the child's continuing to live with the family.
3. Problems that limit the child's participation in special education.
4. Problems that limit the child's adaptation to the community outside home and school.

EXAMPLE   ■ Peter, an autistic-like child, manifests a variety of unacceptable behaviors. Among the behaviors of greatest concern to his teacher, Mr. Wise, are (1) withdrawal from group activities, (2) unacceptable eating habits, (3) inability to communicate with his classmates and Mr. Wise via speech, and (4) unsatisfactory gross motor skills.

Mr. Wise recognizes that a program cannot be initiated to modify all of Peter's potential target behaviors at a single time. Because of the nature of the behaviors, the proposed interventions could be in conflict with one another. Mr. Wise must respond to the following question: "Is it more important for Peter, at this time, to participate in the luncheon discussion [behaviors 1 and 3 would be targets], or is it more important to improve his gross motor skills and eating habits [behaviors 2 and 4 would be targets]?"

In response to this question, Mr. Wise develops the following priority list for Peter's program:

☐ First priority: Increase participation in group activities.
☐ Second priority: Increase verbalization with others.

☐   Third priority: Increase gross motor skills.
☐   Fourth priority: Increase acceptance of a variety of foods.   ∎

Priorities vary with individual student needs and the setting in which the behavior change intervention is applied. However, the objective of all behavior change is to benefit the student (Alberto & Troutman, 1986).

Cooper, Heron, and Heward (1987) suggest these nine factors that should be considered when establishing target behavior priorities:

1. Determine if the behavior is of danger to the individual or others.
2. Determine if the frequency of the behavior or, in the case of a new behavior, the opportunities to use the behavior warrant intervention.
3. Determine the duration of the problem or, in the case of a new behavior, how long the individual's need for the new behavior has existed.
4. Determine if the behavior will produce a higher level of reinforcement for the individual than other behaviors under consideration. Generally, behaviors that produce a high level of reinforcement take priority over behaviors that produce a low level of reinforcement.
5. Determine the impact of the behavior on the individual's skill development and independence.
6. Determine if learning the behavior will reduce the negative attention that the individual receives.
7. Determine if learning the behavior will increase reinforcement for others in the individual's environment.
8. Determine the difficulty (time and energy) to be expended to change the behavior.
9. Determine the cost involved in changing the behavior.

With an increase in experience and skill in the behavior change process, the teacher or parent may wish to program more than one individual or group target behavior simultaneously. However, the beginning practitioner should refrain from multiple programming.

When selecting a target behavior, the practitioner must consider the frequency of the behavior. Some behaviors occur so infrequently that they do not necessitate or respond to a formal behavior modification intervention. Of course, the reverse is also true; some behaviors occur so frequently that they obviously require a behavior change program.

EXAMPLE   ∎   Ms. Lochman was very concerned about Martin, a member of her class, and on many occasions she became very angry with him. Six-year-old Martin appeared to be constantly out of his assigned seat. When out of his chair, he would grab other children's work, work tools, and lunches. Using a time-sampling technique (see p. 68), Ms. Lochman collected baseline data on Martin's out-of-seat behavior for 1 hour a day for 5 days. She found that during these observation periods Martin was out of his seat 17 times an hour on an average.

This behavior was so frequent and so obtrusive that it usually brought all productive classroom activity to a halt until Ms. Lochman could corral Martin and return him to his seat. ■

Teachers and parents are confronted daily with behaviors that are responsive to behavior change intervention. Such behaviors include lack of attention to tasks, incomplete assignments, fighting, not cleaning their room, tardiness to and from school, weight loss, excessive television watching, neglecting music or dance practice, and independent reading, to name a few.

left off here

EXAMPLE ■ Ms. Derry, like many of her peers, does not approve of chewing gum in school. Johnny, a member of her classroom group, was seen chewing gum on the second day of school this year. Ms. Derry grabbed him, removed the gum from his mouth, and stuck it on his nose, where it stayed for the remainder of the day. Ms. Derry then proceeded to make plans for a formal behavior change program. After several hours of planning, she was satisfied with her elaborate scheme for gathering baseline data and applying the chosen intervention. Unfortunately (or fortunately), Johnny never chewed gum in school again (that she observed). ■

There are many behaviors like Johnny's that appear so infrequently that they do not require a formal behavior change program. Examples of such behaviors are

- George's annual 2-minute tantrum
- Barbara's occasional reading reversal
- Don's infrequent falling out of his seat
- Judy's monthly bus-missing behavior

If a proposed target behavior is both obtrusive and occurs frequently, the teacher should next consider the duration of the behavior.

EXAMPLES ■ For several weeks Gerald was very nervous in school. His teacher, Ms. Farley, noted that he was frequently out of his seat, irritable, and ready to burst into tears. She had never seen Gerald in this condition. She attempted to discuss the situation with him but was rebuffed.

Ms. Farley decided to establish a formal behavior modification program to decrease the behaviors. However, before initiating the program, she discussed the situation with Gerald's mother. During the conversation the mother indicated that she had observed similar behavior at home and was attempting to help Gerald regain his old composure. She thought the behavior was the result of the recent death of Gerald's grandfather. Gerald and his grandfather had been pals; they had always been together in the evenings. The death left a great void in Gerald's daily life. Gerald's mother said that her husband was rescheduling his evening activities so that he and Gerald could spend more time together.

Ms. Farley decided to hold the intervention program in abeyance for another few weeks. Within a short time Gerald was his normal self. The program was never implemented. ■

■ Mr. Parker is Maryann's kindergarten teacher. He thoroughly enjoys his work with Maryann and her 16 classmates. The kindergarten is an interesting and exciting learning place for the children.

During the first few weeks of the school year Mr. Parker observed that Maryann, although involved in the classroom activities, seldom if ever spoke to him, the paraprofessional, or her classmates. He decided to collect some baseline data on the frequency of Maryann's verbal behavior. In cooperation with the kindergarten paraprofessional, an observation schedule was set up to obtain some objective data. Using a time-sampling technique, they observed Maryann's behavior on an average of 1 hour a day for 10 days. Data indicated that Maryann spoke only 4 times a day, on an average, while in school. She directed all her verbalizations to one classmate.

Although Mr. Parker was very concerned about the behavior, he did not implement a behavior change program at this time. He had worked with kindergarten children in the past who were shy and quiet and did not begin to interact verbally in the classroom until just before Christmas vacation.

The paraprofessional continued to collect data 1 day each week until mid-December. No change was noted in Maryann's behavior.

Mr. Parker concluded that the behavior had endured too long and that a behavior change program was needed to help Maryann. He conferred with the school's language therapist, who evaluated Maryann. He also discussed the problem with Maryann's mother, who agreed to participate in a home-school behavior change program. The intervention was implemented immediately after the Christmas holidays. ■

The teacher or parent must also consider the intensity of the behavior. Some behaviors, although unacceptable, are relatively mild and unobtrusive. They do not generally interfere with the classroom process or the individual child's overall functioning. Of course, other behaviors, although infrequent, are so intense that they are extremely obtrusive. Not only do they adversely affect the individual's overall functioning, but they also interfere with the classroom program and group process. Such behaviors must be modified.

EXAMPLES   ■ Ricky is 7 years old and in a special class for children with behavioral disorders. Ricky has temper tantrums that are totally unpredictable, frequent, and analogous to all of the Fourth of July fireworks in all the towns of the United States igniting simultaneously. These tantrums involve lying on the floor with feet and arms flying and verbalizations that are interesting but disturbing combinations of four-letter words. The tantrums last up to 45 minutes, averaging about 25 minutes.

These tantrums destroy the classroom program, frighten the other children, and interfere with Ricky's overall functioning. This behavior must be changed. ■

■ Keith is 13 years old and in the seventh grade. Occasionally he manifests some behaviors, normal for his age-group, that are bothersome, such as know-it-all behavior, big-shotism, and negativism. These behaviors are of minimal intensity. They are manifested by a wise remark at the termination of a conversation, his saying "No, I won't" before beginning a task, and the like. The behaviors are generally ignored by others and have little effect on either the classroom process or Keith's overall functioning. ■

The final characteristic to be considered in the selection of a target behavior is the type of behavior. Some behavior that is disturbing to some adults and children is really quite normal from a child development point of view. In fact, a child who did not manifest such behavior might be considered abnormal.

EXAMPLES ■ Paul is a sixth grader and a straight-A student. When he is asked if he likes school, his teacher, or the like, he says "No, I hate it." In addition, he insists on having long hair, wearing jeans and sneakers to school, and other equally "obnoxious" things.

As most teachers realize, these behaviors are quite normal for sixth-grade boys. The behavior manifested by Paul is within normal limits and of a kind that does not necessitate a formal intervention program. ■

■ Russell is 12 years old and in a junior high school special class. He has an uncontrolled temper and frequently tells his teacher to "go to hades" or "drop dead" (among other things). Russell gets into occasional fights with his classmates. These fights are extremely vicious. On two occasions he has inflicted severe injury on his opponent.

Russell's behavior is of a type that cannot simply be ignored. An intervention must be implemented for both his benefit and the safety of his peers. ■

After all of these variables have been considered and a target behavior selected, the teacher must decide the direction of the behavior change process. A behavior may increase or decrease as a consequence of an intervention. Table 3.1 presents these behavior change directions and examples of each.

Behavior change programs, then, are implemented to increase acceptable behaviors or decrease unacceptable behaviors. Teachers can easily select behaviors they wish to increase or decrease. In most instances the practitioner takes the child's manifestation of acceptable behaviors for granted and does not systematically reward such behaviors. More effort should be made to prevent unacceptable behaviors from developing, via the systematic rewarding and maintenance of existing acceptable behaviors.

TABLE 3.1
Behavior change directions

Direction	Example
Increase	Group participation
	In-seat behavior
	Interaction with peers
	Typing skills
	Reading rate
	Number skills
	Visual-perceptual skills
Decrease	Verbal outbursts
	Inattentiveness
	Use of four-letter words
	Food intake
	Smoking
	Talking in study period
	Spelling errors

Two other important characteristics of the target behavior are observability and measurability (Rusch, Rose, & Greenwood, 1988). The behavior must be readily observable in the environment in which it occurs. In addition, the behavior must be quantifiable.

EXAMPLES ■ Ernest, in Ms. Moral's words, is "an unhappy child." Ms. Moral would like to decrease his unhappiness (and increase his happiness). However, when she attempted to observe and quantify Ernest's unhappiness, she abandoned the behavior change program before the baseline data were collected. ■

■ Brian seldom participated in organized group activities on the playground. Mr. Spencer wished to increase his level of activity. He recorded Brian's group participation rate on the playground during morning recess. Mr. Spencer easily established Brian's baseline of activity; he could thus directly observe and quantify the frequency and duration of Brian's participation in group activities. ■

■ Roy is in Mr. Watson's fourth-grade class. He has perfect school attendance during the first 7 months of the school year. Mr. Watson would like to have Roy maintain his present level of attendance for the remaining 2 months of the school year. Roy is the only student in his class with a perfect attendance record. Mr. Watson and the class praise Roy for his attendance. If Mr. Watson and Roy's classmates have anything to do with it, Roy's perfect attendance will be maintained. ■

Statements describing the target behavior, the precise intervention, and the criteria for success or acceptability of performance should be written or otherwise communicated in objective and specific terminology. The following objectives are written so that the target behavior and the result of the intervention can be observed, quantified, and evaluated:

☐ Decrease the number of times Jack interrupts during social studies class.
☐ Increase the number of pages Susan reads during each 15-minute study period.
☐ Decrease the number of times Marion yells during the first hour of the morning.
☐ Increase the number of times Ken uses the reference books on the science table.
☐ Decrease the amount of time Sharon sucks her thumb during the school day.
☐ Increase Benji's skill in recognizing and naming the letters of the alphabet during language development class.

Program objectives should be written as instructional objectives, whether the target behavior is in the cognitive, affective, or psychomotor learning domain. The instructional objective in its written form should respond to the following guidelines:

1. What is the child or group of children whose behavior is being modified expected to do or not to do?
   a. Use action verbs to denote the behavior change process.

   b. List the specific resources and materials to be used by the child during the behavior change process.

   c. Indicate specifically the desired interaction between the child and the environment, including persons and objects.

2. What is the level of performance (in terms of accuracy, duration, and skill) expected of the child?

3. What percentage of time or what percentage of occurrences of the desired behavior is the child expected to perform at the criterion level?

4. How will the anticipated changes in behavior be measured for evaluative purposes? What instrumentation is needed for the evaluation?

5. How long will the proposed intervention program be in force before its effectiveness is evaluated?

Further information on the writing of specific objectives may be found in Mager (1984) and Cooper, Heron, and Heward (1987).

The following guidelines summarize the process of selecting a target behavior:

1. Select only one individual or group target behavior to change at a time. This requires the establishment of priorities.

2. Analyze the potential target behavior for its frequency, duration, intensity, and type. The importance and pertinence of these variables vary with the characteristics of the specific target behavior under consideration.

3. Consider the direction or course the behavior is to take during the change process. Is the behavior to be decreased or increased?

4. Determine whether the behavior is observable.

5. Determine whether the behavior is measurable in numeric terms.

6. Describe the target behavior in precise, descriptive terminology in all verbal and written communication.

The beginning behavior modifier is advised to use the checklist in Figure 3.1 to assist in the target behavior selection process. An additional copy of this checklist is provided in the back of the text.

Collecting and Recording Baseline Data

Information collected before the behavior change intervention has been implemented is referred to as *baseline data*. Baseline data provide the foundation on which the behavior change process is established. These data are also used to determine the effectiveness of the intervention during the evaluation step of the behavior change process.

Target Behavior Selection Checklist

1. What is the target behavior to be modified? _____

   _____

   _____

   _____

   _____

2. Each characteristic of the behavior that should be considered in the target behavior selective process is listed below. An X should be marked by each characteristic as it is considered. The pertinency of these characteristics varies with the specific target behavior under consideration.

(X)	Characteristic	Comment
( )	1. Frequency	
( )	2. Duration	
( )	3. Intensity	
( )	4. Type	
( )	5. Direction	
( )	6. Observability	
( )	7. Measurability	

3. Restate the target behavior in precise and specific terminology. _____

   _____

   _____

   _____

   _____

FIGURE 3.1
Sample checklist to assist in the selection of a target behavior.

EXAMPLE ■ The behavior change program Mr. Dixon selected for Jean concerned increasing the amount of time Jean remained in her seat during history class. Mr. Dixon collected baseline data for 1 week. The data demonstrated that Jean usually remained in her seat an average of 10 minutes at a time before she was up and about the classroom. This information provided Mr. Dixon with the data he needed to determine the kind and characteristics of the reinforcement schedule to be implemented. In order to be sure Jean received immediate reinforcement for staying in her seat, a fixed interval schedule of 7 minutes was used.

The selection of the fixed interval 7 schedule was not a haphazard choice. It was based on the fact that Jean had demonstrated that she could, on the average, remain in her seat for 10 minutes without interference. Therefore it was reasonable to select a 7-minute interval because that was a level of performance that Jean could easily attain. Consequently she could be frequently reinforced for appropriate behavior.

If Mr. Dixon had not collected baseline data but had proceeded on a hunch, he might have selected a fixed interval schedule of 11 minutes. With this interval there would be a strong possibility that Jean would be infrequently rewarded and that her behavior would not change significantly. ■

Reinforcement is initiated at a level of performance either above or below the baseline depending on whether the behavior is to be increased or decreased. For instance, you want to work with a student on increasing the number of words he can read per minute. You know that the student can read 75 words per minute. To start at baseline or above baseline will usually mean waiting too long to get the appropriate behavior, and your behavior change program may not be effective. If, however, you start your reinforcement at a level below baseline, in this case, for example, at 65 words per minute, you have then established a level at which you can provide immediate success for the student and can begin the program on a positive note.

EXAMPLE ■ Ms. Waters has a little terror in her class who responds occasionally to the name of Emmet. Emmet is constantly yelling in the classroom, to the annoyance of Ms. Waters and the other members of the group. Ms. Waters initiated a behavior change program but did not collect baseline data, since Emmet appeared to yell constantly. She withdrew attention from Emmet each time he yelled and praised him when he was not yelling.

After 2 weeks, Ms. Waters was convinced that no change had occurred in the frequency of the behavior. Emmet seemed to yell in class more frequently. Ms. Waters concluded that "this behavior modification stuff" only works in textbooks, and she abandoned the project. Emmet is still yelling in class. ■

It should be stressed here that behavior modification *always* works. The failure of an intervention does not lie in the principles of reinforcement but in the application of those principles by the practitioner. In the preceding example Ms. Waters would have been wise to collect baseline data. She would have been able to evaluate the effectiveness of the behavior change process. Baseline data would have revealed that Emmet yelled in class on an average of 21 times a day. When the intervention was abandoned, the behavior was occurring only 18 times a day (Figure 3.2). The behavior was, in fact, changing in the desired direction. However, without appropriate data, 18 yells a day sound very much like 21 when you are immersed in a situation, as in the case of Ms. Waters.

There are a variety of methods for observing and recording baseline data behavior. The efficiency of a particular technique varies with the expertise of the practitioner, the characteristics of the behavior, and the setting in which the behavior occurs.

To obtain meaningful baseline data, the behavior modifier must engage in two activities: counting the behavior and charting or graphing the behavior. Counting

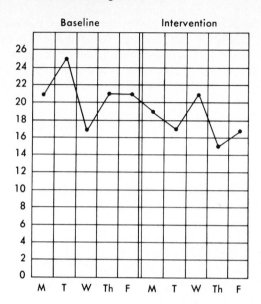

FIGURE 3.2
Frequency of Emmet's yelling behavior before and during the intervention.

the behavior means enumerating the number of times the behavior occurs in a given period of time. Charting or graphing the behavior means preparing a visual display of the enumerated behavior in graphic form.

These two processes are of paramount importance in the behavior change process. When the number of occurrences or the average duration of the occurrences of a behavior in a temporal framework are known, the behavior modifier can select an efficient reinforcement schedule before implementing an intervention. Equally important is the application of the baseline data to the intervention evaluation process. By comparing baseline data with intervention data, the teacher can determine the effectiveness of the reinforcer and the reinforcement schedule. Judgments can be made regarding the responsiveness of the target behavior to the intervention; that is, is the behavior increasing, decreasing, or remaining unchanged?

The recommended method of collecting baseline data is direct observation of the child in the environment in which the behavior occurs. The beginning behavior modifier is well advised to obtain observation data by means of a time-sampling technique.

A trained observer realizes that it is impossible to observe *all* of the behavior occurring within the environment; neither is it possible to efficiently observe all of the occurrences of a single behavior over an extended period. This is particularly true in a busy classroom with many students and a variety of activities occurring simultaneously.

With the time-sampling technique, the teacher first selects the behavior to be observed and then selects the periods of time that can be devoted to observing that behavior each day during the baseline phase. Each occurrence of the target behavior during the observation period is tallied or recorded.

EXAMPLE   ■   Joshua's teacher, Mr. Cates, wished to modify Joshua's hitting behavior during the 2-hour language arts period. With all his other teaching duties, he could not observe Joshua the full 2 hours for the 5 days required to collect reliable baseline data. Thus Mr. Cates used a time-sampling technique; he observed Joshua's behavior during two 10-minute periods for each hour of the language arts period for 5 days. He designed a behavior-tallying sheet to record his observations (Table 3.2).

Mr. Cates noted several things as a result of his data-collecting efforts:

1. Joshua hit other children a total of 32 times during the observation periods.
2. Mr. Cates only observed one third of the total language arts period, that is, 20 minutes out of each 60 minutes. Thus, in all probability, Joshua hit others approximately 96 times during language arts that week.
3. Joshua hit others, on an average, approximately 6 times a day. However, he hit others less on Friday than on any other day of the week.
4. Joshua hit others more frequently with the passing of each observation period of the day.

During the intervention phase of the behavior change program, Mr. Cates would isolate Joshua for 2 minutes each time he hit another child.

Before initiating the intervention, Mr. Cates transferred the baseline data to a graph to improve his visual image of the behavior (Figure 3.3).

Mr. Cates first made a chart for a 2-week period. His baseline data was entered in the section of the chart reserved for the first week. The remainder of the chart would be used for intervention data; he would enter the number of occurrences of hitting behavior during his observations each day of the intervention phase.

Mr. Cates used the horizontal axis of the chart for the days of the week and the vertical axis for the frequency of the behavior. He plotted the behavior and drew lines between the daily occurrences.   ■

Although the same basic methods of counting and charting behavior are applied in all cases, certain modifications may be necessary, depending on the behavior under consideration.

TABLE 3.2
Baseline data: Joshua's hitting behavior

Time	Day					Time Total
	Mon.	Tue.	Wed.	Thur.	Fri.	
9:00-9:10	/	/		/	/	4
9:30-9:40	/	/	//	/	/	6
10:00-10:10	//	///	/	//	/	9
10:30-10:40	///	/	////	///	//	13
DAY TOTAL	7	6	7	7	5	32

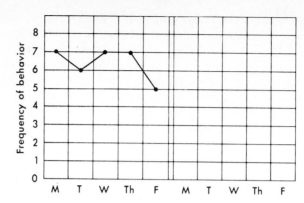

FIGURE 3.3
Joshua's hitting behavior (frequency).

In the example of Joshua's hitting behavior, the frequency of the behavior was the primary concern. The behavior itself was instantaneous; thus the duration of the occurrences was not germane to the objective of the behavior change program.

However, if we were concerned with the duration of Bucky's tantrums, for example, we would focus our observation on both the frequency of occurrence and the duration of each occurrence. In this case we would collect raw observation data in the manner shown in Table 3.3.

Table 3.3 is a tally log for Monday only, but the tally logs for the remaining 4 days of the baseline period are similar. The teacher, Mr. Wagner, is interested in decreasing both the frequency of the behavior and the duration of the behavior when it does occur.

Mr. Wagner has noted in the comments column that the tantrums occur when changes in group activities are taking place, such as at the end of reading period, at the beginning of science, at the beginning of lunchtime, and when it's time to go home.

TABLE 3.3
Bucky's tantrums (duration and frequency)

Time			
Begin	*End*	*Total Minutes*	*Comments*
9:31	9:38	7	End of reading
11:03	11:12	9	Beginning of science
12:07	12:17	10	Lunchtime
2:30	2:39	9	Time to go home

Total occurrence for day: *4*
Average duration: *9* minutes
Day: *Monday*

The planned intervention is as follows:

1. Intervene before the transition period and assist Bucky through the potential tantrum period.
2. If a tantrum does occur, isolate Bucky immediately until 2 minutes after the tantrum ceases.

As a result of this data-collecting procedure, Mr. Wagner designed two graphs to visually display the behavior. Figure 3.4 is concerned with the number of tantrums a day. Figure 3.5 represents the average duration of the tantrums.

Regardless of the specific target behavior being charted, the practitioner should remember that the ordinate points are generally located on the vertical axis of the chart and the abscissa points on the horizontal axis. Ordinate points represent the behavior's frequency, duration, and percent of occurrence. Abscissa points represent the hours, days, and sessions of observation (Axelrod, 1983).

To facilitate the data collection and graphing processes, Shea and Bauer (1987) and Fabry and Cone (1980) suggest that practitioners apply self-graphing procedures. Examples of these procedures are presented in Figures 3.6 and 3.7. By using these or similar procedures, the teacher can reduce the time and energy devoted to graphing.

If the practitioner wishes to record only the number of responses or behaviors, the system presented in Figure 3.6 is recommended. In this system, the total number of responses or behaviors exhibited by the student is circled for each day or time period. The circles are connected to form a graph.

In the example in Figure 3.6, Mr. Baden was interested in collecting and graphing data on the number of times Christina speaks without permission during Industrial Arts class. To begin, Mr. Baden completed the identifying information at the top and bottom of the form. During class, each time Christina spoke without permission, the appropriate number in the day's column was slashed. Next, Mr. Baden circled the highest slashed number for the day. He connected the circled numbers as the days passed and formed the graph in Figure 3.6.

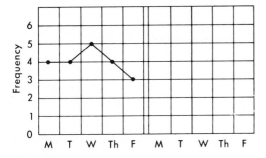

FIGURE 3.4
Bucky's tantrums (frequency).

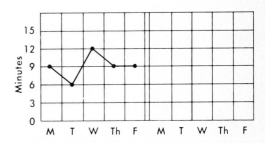

FIGURE 3.5
Average duration of Bucky's tantrums.

Student _Christina_   Date Initiated _9/12/90_

Objective _Frequency of speaking in IA class without permission_

FREQUENCY OF BEHAVIOR

15	15	15	15	15	15	15	15	15	15	15	15	15	15	15	15
14	14	14	14	14	14	14	14	14	14	14	14	14	14	14	14
13	13	13	13	13	13	13	13	13	13	13	13	13	13	13	13
12	12	12	12	12	12	12	12	12	12	12	12	12	12	12	12
11	11	11	11	11	11	11	11	11	11	11	11	11	11	11	11
10	10	10	10	10	10	10	10	10	10	10	10	10	10	10	10
9	9	9	9	9	9	9	9	9	9	9	9	9	9	9	9
8	8	8	8	8	8	8	8	8	8	8	8	8	8	8	8
7	7	7	7	7	7	7	7	7	7	7	7	7	7	7	7
6	6	6	6	6	6	6	6	6	6	6	6	6	6	6	6
5	5	5	5	5	5	5	5	5	5	5	5	5	5	5	5
4	4	4	4	4	4	4	4	4	4	4	4	4	4	4	4
3	3	3	3	3	3	3	3	3	3	3	3	3	3	3	3
2	2	2	2	2	2	2	2	2	2	2	2	2	2	2	2
1	1	1	1	1	1	1	1	1	1	1	1	1	1	1	1
0	0	0	0	0	0	0	0	0	0	0	0	0	0	0	0

criteria

9/12   9/13   9/14   9/15   9/16   9/19   9/20

DATES

Directions:
- Indicate behavior counted.
- Enter criteria line.
- Cross out one number each time the behavior occurs.
- Circle number of times the behavior occurs each date.
- Connect the circles to form graph.

FIGURE 3.6
Frequency data collection and graphing form.

Student *Herm*   Date Initiated *1/15/91*

Objective *Recognize safety words and phrases*

TRIAL RESPONSES   DATES

		1/15	1/16	1/19	1/20	1/21	1/22	1/25	1/26	1/27	1/28
A	Stop	15	15	15	15	15	15	15	15	15	15
B	Go	14	14	14	14	14	14	14	14	14	14
C	Caution	13	13	13	13	13	13	13	13	13	13
D	Yield	12	12	12	12	12	12	12	12	12	12
E	Don't walk	11	11	11	11	11	11	11	11	11	11
F	Walk	10	10	10	10	10	10	10	10	10	10
G	Keep to right	9	9	9	9	9	9	9	9	9	9
H	Do not enter	8	8	8	8	8	8	8	8	8	8
I	Merge	7	7	7	7	7	7	7	7	7	7
J	No right on red	6	6	6	6	6	6	6	6	6	6
K	Right on red	5	5	5	5	5	5	5	5	5	5
L	4-way stop	4	4	4	4	4	4	4	4	4	4
M		3	3	3	3	3	3	3	3	3	3
N		2	2	2	2	2	2	2	2	2	2
O		1	1	1	1	1	1	1	1	1	1
P		0	0	0	0	0	0	0	0	0	0

Directions:
- Enter objective.
- Place a slash (/) over the number in the dated column for a correct response.
- At the end of the lesson, circle the number in the column which corresponds to the total correct responses (slashes) for the lesson.
- Connect the daily circles to make a graph.

FIGURE 3.7
Self-graphing event recording form.

A self-graphing event recording procedure is presented in Figure 3.7. To use this format, list the trial responses in the first column; note the dates in the other columns moving from left to right. As the student responds to each trial, make a slash over the corresponding number for the correct response. At the end of the session, the number corresponding to the total number of correct responses is circled. As sessions progress, the circles are connected to form a graph.

In the example in Figure 3.7, Mrs. Angie is teaching safety words and phrases to Herm using a predetermined sequence. If Herm responds correctly, the corresponding number in the day or session column is slashed. At the end of the session, the number of slashes are counted, and Mrs. Angie circles the appropriate number under the day's column. As the days or sessions progress, the circled numbers are connected to form a graph.

The methods of counting and charting behavior presented in this section are the ones used most frequently in the field, probably because of the ease with which the practitioner can visually perceive and evaluate the data and thus determine the status of the behavior at a given point in time.

Observer Reliability

Successful application of the behavior change process is dependent on the reliability with which target behaviors are observed or measured. If unreliable measurement procedures are used, then (1) behaviors that change may be recorded as stable, and (2) behaviors that are stable may be recorded as changed (Hall & Houten, 1983).

To increase confidence in their skills as observers, it is recommended that teachers conduct interobserver reliability checks. To do this, a second observer should be invited to observe and record the target behavior. This should be done occasionally during both the baseline and intervention phases of the behavior change process. It is important that the second person observe the target behavior at the same time, under the same circumstances, and use the same definition of the behavior as the first observer.

By comparing the results of the two observations, using the following formula, an interobserver reliability percent or quotient can be calculated. The closer to 100% the quotient is, the greater the confidence the practitioner has in the observation data. Hall and Houten (1983) suggest calculating interobserver reliability for interval data by dividing the number of intervals during which two observers agree by the total number of intervals they observed and multiplying the result by 100.

For example, Mrs. Sims and Mr. Horner observed Darlene's behavior together for a total of 20 five-minute intervals. Mrs. Sims observed the target behavior 20 times; Mr. Horner observed it 18 times. Using the preceding formula, their interobserver reliability quotient is

$$\frac{18}{18+2} \times 100 = 90\%$$

To obtain an interobserver reliability quotient for frequency data, divide the frequency reported by the observer with the "lower" frequency by the frequency reported by the observer with the "higher" frequency and multiply the results by 100. For example, Mr. Luther and Ms. Shanks were both observing Angel's frequency of cursing. They observed during the same time period. Mr. Luther recorded 12 curses; Ms. Shanks recorded 11. Using the formula, their interobserver reliability quotient is

$$\frac{11}{12} \times 100 = 91.66\%$$

Identifying Reinforcers

A behavior modification intervention is only as effective as its reinforcer. Regardless of the intervention applied in any behavior change program, if the exhibition of the behavior is not reinforced, the behavior will probably not change. In a behavior change program, all factors may be carefully planned and the intervention precisely implemented, but if the child is not reinforced by the result of his or her behavior, little probability exists for a permanent behavior change.

Remember, a reinforcer is not necessarily a desirable or undesirable consequence for a child merely because the child's teacher or parent believes it should be (Hall & Hall, 1980; Shea & Bauer, 1987). Likewise, a reinforcer is not necessarily desirable to John simply because it is desirable to Mary, Herm, or Lucinda. The *only* true test of the effectiveness of a specific reinforcer with a specific child is implementation— that is, to try it.

How can the teacher or parent identify potential reinforcers for the child whose behavior is to be modified? There are several procedures recommended for identifying reinforcers having a high probability of changing behavior in the desired direction. Among the available procedures are (1) preference scales, (2) lists, (3) interview with the child, (4) interview with the parent or teacher about the child, and (5) direct observation.

Preference Scales

Commercially available reinforcement preference scales are designed to assist the practitioner in eliciting and ranking the child's preferences. By means of pictures and questions, the teacher or parent presents the child with a variety of objects and activities, both tangible and social. The child selects from these reinforcers. The teacher or parent systematically guides the child through the process of selecting, comparing, and ranking the reinforcers. With these materials, however, the possibility exists that the child will not respond to the selected reinforcers during the behavior change process.

The Children's Reinforcement Survey Schedule (CRSS) (Cautela & Meisels, 1977) is a reinforcement preference scale. The CRSS includes three parts or forms. Forms A and B are parallel short forms for application with children in kindergarten through third grade. Form C is applied with children in grades four through six. Form A consists of 25 items; the individual is asked to indicate how much he or she likes a certain material object, organism (animal, person), or activity. The choice categories are "dislike," "like," and "like very much." Form B consists of 25 similar items scored in the same manner. Form C consists of 75 items scored as in Forms A and B and 5 open-ended questions concerning other possible reinforcers. The three forms of the CRSS are presented in Supplement One at the end of this chapter.

The child's interpersonal skills may prohibit communication of his or her real desires to the teacher. It is also possible that the reinforcers suggested in the scale are not desirable to the child or are not appropriate for the child's age. Of course, the possibility always exists that the child does not know or simply cannot articulate what is desirable to him or her.

Another problem with commercially prepared materials is that they are frequently both costly and time consuming to administer.

Preference Lists

Reinforcement lists, such as the one presented in Supplement Two (also at the end of this chapter), are frequently helpful to the teacher or parent who is having difficulty thinking of potential reinforcers. The list may be used in a manner similar to the reinforcement preference scale discussed previously. The disadvantages of the reward list are similar to those of the preference scale.

The reinforcement list's greatest practical value to the practitioner is that it stimulates consideration of a broad spectrum of potential reinforcers; new reinforcers can be added to the list as the teacher or parent becomes aware of them.

The reinforcers listed in Supplement Two are suggestions for classroom use. Each child has unique personal likes and dislikes. The reinforcers must be selected and decided on in consultation with and by observation of the child whose behavior is to be changed. A list for home use is presented in Chapter 8.

Interview with Child

Interviewing a child to determine what he or she finds reinforcing is frequently productive. The interview should be structured, and the reinforcement list or scale may be used to stimulate discussion. The child is encouraged to express and discuss desires; he or she is asked questions such as "What kinds of things do you like to do?" "What are your favorite toys?" "What do you like to do more than anything else?" The child's responses will be of great help in attempting to pinpoint those items and activities to be used as reinforcers. Also, the interviewer has an opportunity to thoroughly explain the behavior change program and answer the child's questions.

There is evidence to indicate that when a child is involved in decision making concerning important ingredients of his or her program, the overall quality and rate of the program are enhanced (Raschke, 1979). Thus involving the child in the selection of reinforcers enhances the probability that the intervention will be successful.

The use of the interview technique provides the child with an opportunity to learn to select reasonable and positive reinforcers. Many children initially have difficulty making reasonable selections because of a lack of experience in decision making. In this situation the interview is in itself a learning experience for the child.

The interview technique can be used with small groups as well as individuals. The disadvantage of the technique is that it is time consuming, and its success is dependent on (1) the child's or group's ability to communicate with the interviewing adult, and (2) the adult's skill as an interviewer.

In the interview situation the following steps should be used as guidelines (Shea et al., 1974a, 1974b):

1. Establish rapport with the child or group.
2. Explain the purpose of the meeting.
3. Define and explain the meaning of individual and/or group reinforcers.
4. Elicit suggestions for individual and/or group rewards.
   a. Ask the child or group which rewards could be used as individual reinforcers. Record these suggestions. If working with a group, ask the individuals which suggested rewards could be used as group rewards.
   b. Give the child or group an opportunity to add to the list of rewards.
   c. Request that the child or each member of the group choose three rewards and rank them according to their desirability. If working with a group, determine the group's ranking of the rewards. Have the members vote to decide on the reward.
   d. Make arrangements for another meeting at which the child or group may choose to add to or change the reinforcers. It is useful to record the reinforcers suggested by the child or group on the chalkboard.

Raschke (1981) published a procedure for designing reinforcement surveys that permit a child to choose personal reinforcers. The procedure is responsive to the needs and interests of the child and teacher in a specific instructional setting. To develop a survey, the teacher follows four steps: select content items, design a survey inventory, administer the inventory, and summarize the results.

The content of the inventory reflects not only the child's likes and dislikes but what is practical and possible in the specific instructional setting. To assist in the selection of the survey's content, the teacher is encouraged to consult the list of potential reinforcers presented in Supplement Two.

The survey itself may take one of several forms, an open-ended format, multiple choice format, or a rank-order format. Examples of the open-ended format and multiple choice format are presented on the following pages.

The administration of the survey includes very specific instructions that emphasize the confidentiality of responses and the fact that there are no right or wrong answers. From the information obtained, the teacher develops individual and group preference lists.

REINFORCEMENT ASSESSMENT: OPEN-ENDED FORMAT

1. If I had 10 minutes free time during this class, I would most like to . . .
2. The favorite type of activity that I wish we would do more often in this class is . . .
3. My favorite seating arrangement in this class is . . .
4. My favorite place to sit in this class is . . .
5. My favorite way to learn new information in this class is . . .
6. My favorite instructional equipment to use in this class is . . .
7. The special jobs I like to help the teacher with the most in this class are . . .
8. If I could change one class rule for 1 hour in this class, the rule I would change would be . . .
9. If I were to choose two students in this classroom to do a fun activity with, I would select . . .
10. If I went to the store and had 50 cents to spend on whatever I wanted, I would buy . . .
11. The person in this school I like most to praise me when I do good work is . . .
12. In this class, I feel proudest of myself when . . .
13. The thing that motivates me the most to do well in this classroom is . . .
14. The nicest thing that has ever happened to me in this class for doing good work is . . .
15. The very best reward in this class that the teacher could give me for good work is . . .*

REINFORCEMENT ASSESSMENT: MULTIPLE CHOICE FORMAT

1. The way I best like to learn about something new in this class is
   a. Lecture
   b. Books
   c. Pamphlets
   d. Films
   e. Tapes
   f. Language master
   g. Small-group work
   h. Guest speakers
2. My favorite writing tool to use in this class is
   a. Magic Markers™
   b. Felt pens
   c. Colored pencils
   d. Colored chalk

---

*From "Designing Reinforcement Surveys—Let the Students Choose the Reward" by D. Raschke, 1981, *Teaching Exceptional Children, 14,* p. 93. Copyright 1981 by The Council for Exceptional Children. Reprinted by permission.

3. My favorite seating arrangement in this class is
   a. Desks in rows
   b. Chairs at tables
   c. Desks randomly scattered
   d. Study carrels randomly scattered
4. The special job I like to help the teacher with the most in this class is
   a. Handing out papers
   b. Putting away supplies
   c. Decorating a bulletin board
   d. Running the filmstrip projector
   e. Writing the assignment on the chalkboard
   f. Straightening up cupboards and bookcases
5. The best privilege I could earn in this class for good work would be to
   a. Sit anywhere I want in the class
   b. Help the teacher grade papers
   c. Put an assignment on the chalkboard
   d. Give the class announcements
   e. Pick a partner to work with
6. When I do well in this class, I like it most when the teacher
   a. Smiles at me
   b. Informs the class of my good work
   c. Writes a note on my paper
   d. Tells me privately in words
   e. Draws a big happy face on my paper
   f. Puts my good work on the bulletin board
7. When I do good work in this class, I would most like to earn
   a. Free time
   b. Praise from the teacher
   c. A favorite activity with a friend
   d. A favorite activity with a teacher
   e. Good work displayed on a bulletin board
8. My favorite free-time activity in this class is
   a. Playing checkers or a card game
   b. Listening to radio or playing records
   c. Working a puzzle or doing a craft
   d. Visiting with a friend
   e. Reading a favorite book
   f. Playing a computer game
9. The nicest thing that could happen to me for doing good work in this class would be
   a. Receiving an award in front of the class
   b. Receiving an A+ on a project
   c. A phone call to my parents describing my good work
   d. Having my work displayed in the hallway
   e. Earning free time for the whole class
10. The best tangible reward I could earn in this class would be a
    a. Gold star
    b. Happy gram
    c. Good work badge

    d. Certificate of achievement
    e. Scratch-n-sniff sticker
    f. Spacemen stamp
11. If I had 50 cents to buy anything I wanted, I would buy
    a. A yo-yo
    b. A Frisbee™
    c. A poster
    d. Some Silly Putty™
    e. A comic book
12. Something really different I would work hard for in this class would be
    a. A warm fuzzy
    b. A monster tattoo
    c. Some space dust
    d. A creepy spider
    e. Some monster teeth
    f. A vampire fingernail
    g. A squirt ring*

Interview with Parent or Teacher

An interview with a parent or teacher can also be used in an effort to obtain and rank the child's reinforcers. Although less desirable than a direct interview with the child, the parent or teacher interview can be helpful in determining which reinforcers have been applied successfully and unsuccessfully by others. It may also be used to determine the range of successful reinforcers within the child's response repertoire.

The parent or teacher interview is especially valuable to the consultant who is trying to determine the level of understanding and acceptance of behavior change techniques by the individual who works directly with the child.

The obvious disadvantage in applying this technique is that the parent's or teacher's level of sophistication as an objective observer is unknown. It should be recognized that the parent or teacher may not be of real assistance in the selection of potent rewards because of a distorted perception of the child's likes and dislikes. However, the use of the technique can be an excellent learning experience for parents and teachers; frequently it can sensitize them to the importance of meaningful reinforcers for children.

This topic is discussed in detail in Chapter 8.

Direct Observation

The most productive strategy for identifying effective reinforcers is direct observation. According to an old saying, "If you want to see a person do something well, observe him doing something he enjoys."

---

*From "Designing Reinforcement Surveys—Let the Students Choose the Reward" by D. Raschke, 1981, *Teaching Exceptional Children, 14,* p. 93. Copyright 1981 by The Council for Exceptional Children. Reprinted by permission.

Direct observation requires the teacher to observe the child's self-selected activities in a variety of situations, such as on the playground, in the classroom, during structured time, and during free time, and to list those activities the child chooses. These self-selected activities and items can be used during the intervention as reinforcers.

EXAMPLES ■ Ms. Maron observed that Marvin liked to congregate with his friends during recess to trade baseball cards. She decided to allow the boys to have an additional trading time after they finished their arithmetic lesson. The total arithmetic period was 40 minutes. After 30 minutes the boys who had finished the assignment could go to a special area of the room and quietly trade cards. The longer Marvin took to complete the lesson, the less time he had to trade cards. ■

■ Mr. Dee knew that most 8-year-old boys like to play baseball. Mr. Dee wished to improve Jamie's performance in spelling. He told Jamie that each day that he got 80% of his spelling words correct, he could play baseball for 20 minutes on the playground. Mr. Dee was astonished when Jamie did not respond to this reward.

There were several reasons why Jamie did not respond, and Mr. Dee had failed to take them into consideration. Jamie had not only a visual-perceptual handicap but also a gross motor handicap, and these problems interfered with his skill in large muscle activities. It was far more difficult to play baseball than to flunk spelling. Mr. Dee's fundamental error was that he did not include Jamie in the reinforcer selection process. ■

Different children value different consequences. It is nearly impossible to identify any event or item that will serve as a positive reinforcer for all children.

In the end, the potency of a reinforcer selected as a result of using any technique can only be determined by implementation. Many reinforcers, thought to be highly potent, fail to be effective with some children; whereas some reinforcers, discovered only on a teacher's hunch, prove to be most powerful in changing behavior.

A few additional suggestions for the selection and use of reinforcers may be useful.

1. Except for a few basic items such as food and water, no item or activity can be identified with certitude as an effective reinforcer before it has been demonstrated to be effective for a specific child. What is highly reinforcing for one child may not be for another.
2. When satiation occurs, even the most powerful reinforcer will lose strength and must be replaced. The teacher should provide a variety of reinforcers, not only to prevent satiation but also to satisfy the individual and his ever-changing preferences. Many teachers provide a "menu of reinforcers" for their children. On any given day a variety of items or activities are available to satisfy the diverse needs and interests of the children. They are permitted to select from this menu.
3. The task of observing the effects of existing reinforcers and searching for new reinforcers is a continuous process. A good reinforcement system is an ever-changing blend of established and potential reinforcers.
4. Reinforcers should not be thought of only in terms of tangible items. There are many activities and privileges that are potent reinforcers. Frequently teachers

use a tangible reinforcer (with a social reinforcer) initially during the behavior change program. Later they change the reward from the tangible reinforcer to a special activity or privilege (always keeping the social reinforcer). In the final stages of the behavior change process, the social reinforcer used alone should be adequate.

Although several methods for identifying reinforcers are discussed in this section, the two procedures most recommended are direct observation and a direct interview with the child. Both have proved effective for identifying reinforcers (Karraker, 1977).

The fact that a child is motivated by a specific reinforcer today does not necessarily mean the child will respond to that particular reinforcer next week. A change in performance may be the signal to initiate a new reward. The fact that Lisa correctly completed 25 addition problems on Monday to play with a puzzle, 27 problems on Tuesday to play with a puzzle, and 28 problems on Wednesday for the same privilege does not mean she will respond in a similar fashion on Thursday. To avoid this situation, a reward menu, as discussed in Chapter 4, is recommended. The menu allows the practitioner to systematically vary the rewards a child can work for on different days. With proficiency gained through practice in the techniques for changing behavior, the practitioner can predict when it is time to change reinforcers.

Schedules of reinforcement are discussed in Chapter 2; however, it should be reemphasized that the schedule on which the reinforcement is delivered has considerable influence on the behavior change process.

Phasing Out Reinforcers

As stated previously, a goal of the behavior change process is to train an individual to respond to appropriate and occasional social reinforcers *only*. Consequently it is necessary that the behavior modification practitioner focus particular attention to phasing out the reinforcers over a period of time. This difficult task is accomplished primarily by changing from a fixed interval or ratio reinforcement schedule to a variable interval or ratio reinforcement schedule and by the systematic attenuating of the average frequency of reinforcer presentation. It must be remembered that a social reinforcer is always presented concurrently with a tangible reinforcer, if tangible rewards are used.

Procedures applied to phasing out reinforcers are as follows:

Step 1: Social and tangible reinforcers are presented simultaneously to the individual on a fixed reinforcement schedule. This statement assumes that tangible reinforcers are needed initially in the particular situation.

Step 2: Social reinforcers are continued on a fixed schedule, and tangible reinforcers are presented on a variable schedule. Tangible reinforcers are attenuated over time and are finally extinguished. Social reinforcers are presented simultaneously with tangible reinforcers during this step.

Step 3: Social reinforcers are presented on a variable schedule. They are attenuated over time and are finally extinguished as the formal behavior change program is terminated.

Reinforcement Area

A special area may be set aside in the classroom to serve as a reinforcement area. This area should be selected before a behavior change program is implemented and should contain those items needed to provide reinforcers. Among the items may be the following:

A table and chairs

A rug

Reading material (books, comics, magazines)

Art materials (clay, paint, paper, crayons)

Games (bingo, checkers, chess, cards)

Listening equipment (record player, tape deck)

Viewing equipment (television, slide or filmstrip projector)

For additional examples see the section on reinforcers in Supplement Two.

Obviously, the furnishings, materials, and equipment in a reinforcement area must be selected in response to the age, physical size, developmental levels, and interests of the students using the area. Figure 3.8 is an illustration of a classroom with a reinforcement area.

Implementing the Intervention and Collecting and Recording Intervention Data

The next step in the behavior change process is selecting and implementing the intervention and collecting and recording intervention data. Chapters 4 and 5 are devoted to a detailed description of interventions applied to increase and decrease target behaviors.

Intervention data involve information collected on the effects of the intervention during the implementation phase. Equally as important as baseline data, intervention data provide a yardstick for comparing baseline behavior with new behavior. By comparing baseline data with intervention data, the teacher can determine the changes that have occurred as a result of the intervention. Figure 3.9 presents a comparison of Joshua's hitting behavior before and during the intervention.

In this graph the target behavior shows an increase during the initial 2 days of intervention. The behavior then decreases to zero over the remaining days of the program.

The initial increase in the behavior (days 6 and 7) was probably a result of Joshua's testing of the teacher's response to his original behavior. In all probability Joshua was confused by the fact that his previously effective response was no longer effective. Of course, this increase might also have been a result of the initial inefficiency

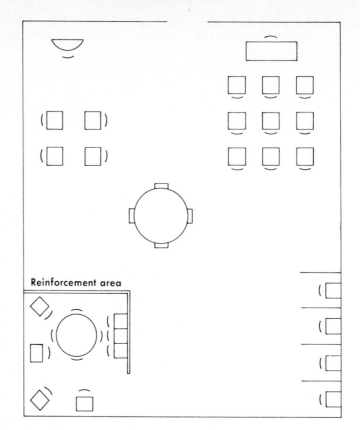

FIGURE 3.8
Classroom with reinforcement area.

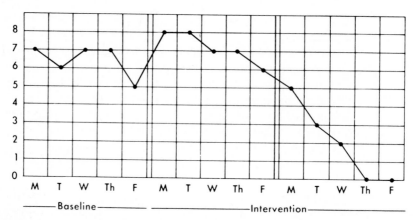

FIGURE 3.9
Frequency of Joshua's hitting behavior before and during the intervention.

of either the reinforcer or the practitioner. However, the initial increase in behavior, as discussed in Chapter 2, is normal and should be anticipated during the beginning days of the intervention.

The importance of continuing to count and chart the target behavior during the intervention can be readily seen on Joshua's graph. This procedure provides the practitioner with a visual image to be used in comparing the baseline and intervention behaviors. The data alerts the teacher to the child's response to the intervention and thus to the overall effectiveness of the program at a particular point in time.

Prompting

Children often need special assistance during the behavior change process. This special assistance may be manual or verbal and is called *prompting*. Prompts may include such activities as guiding a child's hand or foot in the completion of a task, moving the child's head to gain his or her attention, talking a child through a task by repeated precise verbal instruction, providing a verbal model for imitation, and providing printed or three-dimensional material that structures a task (Schloss, 1986). Prompts are used to increase the probabilities of success in a task. Prompting is applicable with several behavior change interventions discussed in Chapters 4 and 5.

Although prompts of various kinds may be a necessary component of the behavior change intervention initially, they must eventually be eliminated; the child must learn to complete the task independently. The gradual elimination of prompts is called *fading* (Panyan, 1980). Fading includes the reduction of the amount and quality of manual guidance, verbal assistance, and printed or three-dimensional material used to structure an activity. It is important that the practitioner consider the procedures to be used to fade the prompt before it is implemented.

EXAMPLE ■ Marie, a 6-year-old child, was enrolled in a motor therapy program in an effort to remediate her physical coordination problems. One of the objectives of her program was walking a 10-foot balance beam without assistance.

During the therapy program's assessment phase, Marie fell off the balance beam seven times in her effort to walk its length unaided. It was decided that during the initial stages of her motor therapy Marie would be manually guided by a therapist. He would hold her right hand as she walked the beam.

With manual guidance Marie learned to walk the 10-foot beam with efficiency within a few days. The therapist decided to fade the prompt (manual guidance) and applied the following schedule during the fading process:

1. The therapist reduced the firmness of his grasp on Marie's right hand.
2. The therapist grasped only one finger of Marie's hand.
3. The therapist positioned his hand in progressive steps approximately 6, 9, and 12 inches from Marie's right hand.

4. The therapist walked beside Marie with his hands at his side.
5. The therapist withdrew to the position he normally assumed to observe a person's efficiency on the balance beam. ■

An example of the use and elimination of a prompt can also be seen in the example of Jeff (p. 104).

Evaluating the Effects of Intervention

Once the new behavior has been established at the acceptable level, the practitioner may question whether the observed changes were a result of the intervention or of an unknown intervening variable. This query cannot be responded to with exactitude. However, there is a procedure to test the effectiveness of the intervention. This is the process of extinction, or of reestablishing the baseline (Baseline 2). The process of reestablishing the baseline in this situation is as follows: If a behavior is thought to be maintained at a specific level by a reinforcer, the practitioner can evaluate the effectiveness of the reinforcer by withdrawing it.

EXAMPLE   ■   Mr. Curtain had established Shirley's hand-raising behavior at an acceptable level. He then wondered if the reinforcer applied in the intervention phase was the *factor* that had resulted in her change in behavior. The reinforcer was a smile and verbal praise each time Shirley raised her hand in class.

To check the potency of the reinforcer, Mr. Curtain withdrew it; that is, he ceased smiling at Shirley and praising her when she raised her hand in class. Within a few days, as demonstrated in Figure 3.10, Shirley's hand-raising response began to be extinguished. Because of the decrease in Shirley's hand-raising behavior, Mr. Curtain could assume that the reinforcer (smiles and verbal praise) was instrumental in increasing the hand-raising behavior. He had evaluated the effect of reinforcement on the behavior. ■

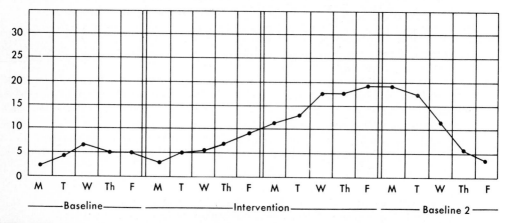

FIGURE 3.10
Frequency of Shirley's hand-raising behavior before and during the intervention and as a result of reestablishing the baseline (Baseline 2).

Reestablishing the baseline is not always an effective means of evaluating the potency of a reinforcer. If a behavior has been firmly habituated into the child's behavioral repertoire, it will not respond to extinction.

Establishing and then extinguishing a behavior is *not* a standard procedure applied in the behavior change process. However, this technique may assure new students of behavior modification that their efforts are effective in changing behaviors.

The use of Baseline 2 in an intervention is at the discretion of the practitioner. However, once a teacher or parent has determined that the reinforcer was instrumental in the behavior change program, it would be a disservice to the child not to reinstate it or not to return to the intervention state.

SUMMARY

In this chapter the steps for changing behavior are discussed. They are (1) *selecting a target behavior,* (2) *collecting and recording baseline data,* (3) *identifying reinforcers,* (4) *implementing the intervention and collecting and recording intervention data,* and (5) *evaluating the effects of the intervention.*

When selecting a target behavior, the practitioner should choose only *one* individual or group behavior to change at a time. The practitioner should analyze the potential target behavior in relation to its frequency, duration, intensity, and type; determine the direction the behavior is to take (whether it is to increase or decrease); determine whether the behavior is observable and quantifiable; and finally, describe the behavior in precise, descriptive terminology. Collecting and recording baseline data allow an analysis of the changes in behavior that occur during the intervention.

Three forms of the Children's Reinforcement Survey Schedule (CRSS) are presented in Chapter Supplement One. A list of tangible and social reinforcers for application in the classroom and school are presented in Supplement Two of this chapter. Consideration is given to consumable rewards, tangible and token rewards, games, activities, social rewards, and jobs. The two most effective methods of identifying reinforcers are direct observation and an interview with the child.

Comparison of baseline and intervention data provides the practitioner with an evaluation technique for determining changes occurring in the target behavior as a result of intervention.

It is highly recommended that the new practitioner of behavior modification carefully follow each step in the behavior change process presented in this chapter.

PROJECTS

1. Select five potential target behaviors and observe them. After observing the behaviors, discuss their characteristics in terms of frequency, duration, intensity, and type.
2. Collect and record accurate baseline data on two of the behaviors observed.
3. List 25 reinforcers that may be useful in modifying the behavior of children in your present teaching situation. Classify these as tangible or social reinforcers. At least 12 of the 25 reinforcers should be classifiable as social rewards.

4. Observe a child and develop a list of potential reinforcers for this child. Observe the child in a variety of situations.
5. a. As outlined in the text, interview the same child and develop another list of reinforcers.
   b. Interview the child's parent or teacher and develop a third list of reinforcers.
6. Conceptualize and write a detailed description of an intervention to be applied to one of the behaviors observed in Project 1.

REFERENCES

Alberto, P. A., & Troutman, A. C. (1986). *Applied behavior analysis for teachers* (2nd Ed.). Columbus, OH: Merrill.

Axelrod, S. (1983). *Behavior modification for the classroom teacher.* New York: McGraw-Hill Book Co.

Cautela, J. R., & Meisels, L. B. (1977). Children's reinforcement survey schedule. In J. R. Cautela (Ed.), *Behavior analysis forms for clinical intervention* (pp. 53-62). Champaign, IL: Research Press Co.

Cooper, J. O., Heron, T. E., & Heward, W. L. (1987). *Applied behavior analysis.* Columbus, OH: Merrill.

Fabry, B. D., & Cone, J. D. (1980). Autographing: A one-step approach to collecting and graphing data. *Education and Treatment of Children, 3,* 361-368.

Hall, R. V., & Hall, M. C. (1980). *How to select reinforcers.* Austin, TX: Pro-Ed.

Hall, R. V., & Houten, R. V. (1983). *The measurement of behavior.* Austin, TX: Pro-Ed.

Karraker, R. J. (1977). Self versus teacher selected reinforcers in a token economy. *Exceptional Children, 43*(7), 454-455.

Mager, R. F. (1984). *Preparing instructional objectives* (2nd rev. ed.). Belmont, CA: Pitman Learning Press.

Morris, R. J. (1985). *Behavior modification with exceptional children: Principles and practices.* Glenview, IL: Scott, Foresman & Company.

Raschke, D. (1979). The relationship of internal-external control and operant reinforcement procedures with learning and behavior disordered children. *Dissertation Abstracts International, 40,* 4533. (Unpublished doctoral dissertation, University of Wisconsin, Madison.)

Raschke, D. (1981). Designing reinforcement surveys—let the students choose the reward. *Teaching Exceptional Children, 14,* 92-96.

Rusch, F. R., Rose, T., & Greenwood, C. R. (1988): *Introduction to behavior analysis in special education.* Englewood Cliffs, NJ: Prentice-Hall.

Schopler, E., Reichler, R. J., & Lansing, M. (1980). *Individualized assessment and treatment for autistic and developmentally disabled children; Vol. II. Teaching strategies for parents and professionals.* Austin, TX: Pro-Ed.

Shea, T. M., & Bauer, A. M. (1987). *Teaching children and youth with behavior disorders* (2nd ed.). Englewood Cliffs, NJ: Prentice-Hall.

Shea, T. M., Whiteside, W. R., Beetner, E. G., & Lindsey, D. L. (1974a). *Psychosituational interview.* Edwardsville: Southern Illinois University.

Shea, T. M., Whiteside, W. R., Beetner, E. G., & Lindsey, D. L. (1974b). *Selecting reinforcers.* Edwardsville: Southern Illinois University.

Children's Reinforcement Survey Schedule
Part A

Directions:

This is a list of many different things or activities. Explain how much you like each choice by making an "X" in the appropriate box.

If you dislike the choice, make an "X" in the box under *Dislike:*

Dislike	Like	Like Very Much
X		

If you like the choice, make an "X" in the box under *Like:*

Dislike	Like	Like Very Much
	X	

If the choice is something which you like very, very much, make an "X" in the box under *Like Very Much:*

Dislike	Like	Like Very Much
		X

	Dislike	Like	Like Very Much
1. Do you like candy?			
2. Do you like raisins?			
3. Do you like milk?			
4. Do you like stuffed toy animals?			
5. Do you like coloring?			
6. Do you like making things out of clay?			
7. Do you like listening to music?			
8. Do you like animal stories?			
9. Do you like playing on swings?			
10. Do you like kickball?			
11. Do you like going on field trips at school?			
12. Do you like being the teacher's helper?			
13. Do you like going to the library?			
14. Do you like people to tell you that you did a good job?			

CRSS—Part A, cont'd

	Dislike	Like	Like Very Much
15. Do you like your teacher to buy materials that you especially like?			
16. Do you like teaching things to other people?			
17. Do you like watching trucks, bulldozers, and tractors?			
18. Do you like to go shopping?			
19. Do you like to eat out in a restaurant?			
20. Do you like going to a circus or a fair?			
21. Do you like playing with dogs?			
22. Do you like to play with some children younger than you?			
23. Do you like to play with some special grown-ups?			
24. Do you like people to take care of you when you are sick?			
25. Do you like taking care of pet animals?			

(Reprinted with permission of authors and publisher from: Cautela, J. R., and Brion-Meisels, L.A., Children's reinforcement survey schedule. *Psychological Reports*, 1979, 44, 327-338.)

CRSS—Part B

Directions:

This is a list of many different things or activities. Explain how much you like each choice by making an "X" in the appropriate box.

If you dislike the choice, make an "X" in the box under *Dislike:*

Dislike	Like	Like Very Much
X		

If you like the choice, make an "X" in the box under *Like:*

Dislike	Like	Like Very Much
	X	

If the choice is something which you like very, very much, make an "X" in the box under *Like Very Much:*

Dislike	Like	Like Very Much
		X

	Dislike	Like	Like Very Much
1. Do you like apples?			
2. Do you like breakfast cereals?			
3. Do you like fruit juice?			
4. Do you like to play with toy cars?			
5. Do you like painting?			
6. Do you like making things out of wood?			
7. Do you like to sing?			
8. Do you like cartoons and comic books?			
9. Do you like swimming?			
10. Do you like riding a bike?			
11. Do you like outdoor recess?			
12. Do you like to be the winner of a contest?			
13. Do you like arithmetic and working with numbers?			
14. Do you like being better than everyone else at something?			

CRSS—Part B, cont'd

	Dislike	Like	Like Very Much
15. Do you like saving your school papers to show to other people?			
16. Do you like your parents to ask you what you did in school today?			
17. Do you like to watch television?			
18. Do you like traveling to different, far-away places on vacation?			
19. Do you like to go to the movies?			
20. Do you like playing with cats?			
21. Do you like to go to the zoo?			
22. Do you like playing with some children older than you?			
23. Do you like being alone rather than being with other people?			
24. If your friend is sick, do you like to take some things to your friend's house to make your friend feel happier?			
25. Do you like someone to take care of you when you are scared?			

(From: Cautela, J. R., *Behavior analysis forms for clinical interventions.* Champaign, Ill.: Research Press Co., 1977.)

CRSS—Part C

Directions:

This is a list of many different things or activities. Explain how much you like each choice by making an "X" in the appropriate box.

If you dislike the choice, make an "X" in the box under *Dislike:*

Dislike	Like	Like Very Much
X		

If you like the choice, make an "X" in the box under *Like:*

Dislike	Like	Like Very Much
	X	

If the choice is something which you like very, very much, make an "X" in the box under *Like Very Much:*

Dislike	Like	Like Very Much
		X

	Dislike	Like	Like Very Much
1. Do you like candy?			
2. Do you like fruit?			
3. Do you like cooking?			
4. Do you like to drink soda?			
5. Do you like to make models?			
6. Do you like to play with model cars and trains?			
7. Do you like to draw and paint?			
8. Do you like to do crafts?			
9. Do you like carpentry and woodworking?			
10. Do you like making things out of clay?			
11. Do you like working with motors?			
12. Would you like to have sports equipment of your own?			
13. Do you like to play on playground equipment?			
14. Do you like to go bike riding?			

CRSS—Part C, cont'd

	Dislike	Like	Like Very Much
15. Do you like to go swimming?			
16. Do you like to go skiing?			
17. Do you like hockey?			
18. Do you like baseball?			
19. Do you like football?			
20. Do you like basketball?			
21. Do you like kickball?			
22. Do you like camping?			
23. Do you like listening to music?			
24. Do you like singing?			
25. Do you like learning how to play musical instruments?			
26. Do you like cartoons and comic books?			
27. Do you like fairytales?			
28. Do you like science fiction?			
29. Do you like mysteries?			
30. Do you like biographies (stories about peoples' lives)?			
31. Do you like having field trips at school?			
32. Do you like outdoor recess?			
33. Do you like puzzles?			
34. Do you like being a leader in your class, such as being a class officer?			
35. Do you like giving reports in front of the class?			
36. Do you like creative writing (making up stories or poems)?			
37. Do you like science?			
38. Do you like math?			
39. Do you like spelling?			

CRSS—Part C, cont'd

	Dislike	Like	Like Very Much
40. Do you like go-carts?			
41. Do you like mini-bikes?			
42. Do you like to sell things?			
43. Do you like to go shopping?			
44. Do you like to watch television?			
45. Do you like to go to different, far-away places on vacation?			
46. Do you like to eat out in a restaurant?			
47. Do you like to go to the movies?			
48. Would you like to go to a circus or a fair?			
49. Do you like playing with dogs?			
50. Do you like playing with cats?			
51. Do you like to go to the zoo?			
52. Do you like to play with some children younger than you?			
53. Do you like to play with some children older than you?			
54. Do you like to play with some special grown-ups?			
55. Do you like being alone rather than being with other people?			
56. Would you like to talk to a sports' star you know about?			
57. Would you like to talk to a TV or movie star you have seen?			
58. Do you like going to parties?			
59. Do you like to stay overnight at a friend's house?			
60. Do you like earning money?			
61. Do you like it when your teacher buys materials that you especially like?			

CRSS—Part C, cont'd

	Dislike	Like	Like Very Much
62. Do you like to be praised for your good work?			
63. Do you like your parents to ask you what you did in school today?			
64. Do you like to be the winner of a contest?			
65. Do you like to have your teacher ask you to help?			
66. Do you like getting the right answer?			
67. Do you like to show your good work to other people?			
68. Do you feel good when you have just finished a project or job you had to do?			
69. Do you like it when all the other kids think you are terrific?			
70. Do you like taking care of pet animals?			
71. Do you like fixing broken things?			
72. Do you like having a birthday party and getting presents?			
73. If your friend is sick, do you like to take some things to your friend's house to make your friend feel happier?			
74. Do you like someone to take care of you when you are scared?			
75. If you are sick, do you like people to take care of you?			

76. What do you think is the best thing about you?

_____

_____

_____

CRSS—Part C, cont'd

77. What do you daydream about?

_____

_____

78. What do you do for fun?

_____

_____

79. What would you like for your birthday?

_____

_____

80. Do you have any collections? _____ If so, what do you collect?

_____

_____

(From: Cautela, J. R., *Behavior analysis forms for clinical interventions.* Champaign, Ill.: Research Press Co., 1977.)

CHAPTER 3, SUPPLEMENT TWO

Preference List
Consumable Food Reinforcers

Apples

Grapes

Oranges

Raisins

Crackers

Cookies

Popcorn

Potato Chips

Peanuts

Gumdrops

Jelly beans

Small candies

Mints

Juice

Fruit-flavored drink

Milk

Soda

Ice cream

Lollipops

Sugarless gum

Reinforcing Activities in Relation to the
Consumable Foods

Distributing reinforcers

Cleaning the area after reinforcers have been distributed

Popping popcorn

Scooping ice cream

Baking cookies

Preparing snacks

Tangible Reinforcers Other Than Food

Tickets to games, movies

Personal grooming supplies

Toys, games, and so on, from the class store

Special materials such as colored chalk, pencils, or felt-tipped pens

Token Reinforcers

Check marks and points

Happy faces and stars

Behavior and achievement charts

Individual behavior and achievement cards and bankbooks

Rubber stamp marks of various designs

Gold stars next to child's name on the class chart

Trading stamps

Conservation stamps

Good citizen tags and certificates

Social Reinforcers

Receiving verbal praise
Having photograph displayed
Getting personal time with the teacher, aide, counselor, or principal
Participating in small-group discussions
Having work and projects displayed
Participating in show and tell
Demonstrating a skill
Clapping and cheering by others when successful
Being leader or organizer of an event
Getting a hug, handshake, or pat on the back
Sitting next to the teacher at lunch
Playing with a classmate of choice
Sitting and talking with a friend (child or adult)

Job Reinforcers

Conducting an auction in class
Passing out paper, pencils, and so on
Taking a note to the office
Erasing the chalkboard
Helping the teacher with a project
Conducting a class raffle
Being teacher for a lesson
Managing the class store
Shopping for the class store
Being messenger for the day
Helping in the cafeteria
Assisting the custodian
Cleaning the erasers
Watering the plants
Running the ditto machine
Stapling papers together
Feeding the fish or other animals
Giving a message over the intercom
Picking up litter on the school grounds
Cleaning the teacher's desk

Taking the class roll
Carrying messages to other teachers
Serving as secretary for class meetings
Raising or lowering the flag
Emptying the wastebasket
Carrying the wastebasket while other children clean out their desks
Distributing and collecting materials
Operating a slide, filmstrip, or movie projector
Using the overhead projector
Recording own behavior on a graph
Teaching another child
Helping the librarian
Telling the teacher when it is time to go to lunch
Sharpening the teacher's pencils
Opening the teacher's mail
Sweeping the floor of the classroom
Adjusting the window shades

CHAPTER FOUR

Methods of Increasing Behavior

Judy, a second grader, is more socially mature than her peers. This social maturity is a result of her close association with her sister Joanne, who is a fifth grader. The girls spend most of their time playing together and with Joanne's friends. Judy thinks that second graders are babies and therefore does not associate with them at recess; she associates with them only when necessary in the classroom. Judy is not only socially mature for her age but intellectually mature as well.

Behavior problems are developing for Judy among her peers, as well as among Joanne's friends. Joanne's friends often invite her to their homes for parties or to the movies. They do not invite Judy because they think she is too young. As Joanne gets older, Judy is finding herself alone more and more frequently. Not having anyone to play with upsets her greatly.

Maybe if Judy's parents knew more about behavior management, they might increase Judy's socialization with her peers.

Mr. Peterson is a basketball coach at William Tolbert Community College. Over the past 2 years he has developed a winning basketball team and an excellent reputation as a coach. Mr. Peterson is employed by the college part-time to coach and recruit basketball players. He is a full-time employee of a local high school where he teaches physical education. Because of over-staffing and declining budgets, the college is unable to offer Coach Peterson a full-time position.

Mr. Peterson is worried that additional budget cuts will eliminate his position at the college. He fears he will be replaced by the former basketball coach, who is teaching full-time in the physical education department. If so, he believes he is developing a winning basketball team for another coach. He is so paranoid about the former basketball coach taking his team away from him that it is affecting his coaching and his relationship with the college faculty. Mr. Peterson dwells on one topic in all conversations: "I'm working day and night to build a team for someone else."

Maybe if the physical education department chairperson knew more about increasing behaviors, he would be able to help Coach Peterson be more positive toward his part-time position.

The five most common techniques applied in behavior modification interventions for increasing a target behavior are (1) positive reinforcement, (2) shaping, (3) modeling, (4) contingency contracting, and (5) the token economy. These basic methods should be of assistance to the beginning practitioner attempting to establish acceptable behaviors in children. The techniques are applicable with both individual and group behaviors.

CHAPTER OBJECTIVES

After completing this chapter, you will be able to do the following:

1. Characterize positive reinforcement.
2. Describe shaping.
3. Understand and exemplify modeling.
4. Define and explain contingency contracting.
5. Identify and illustrate token economy.

Positive Reinforcement

Positive reinforcement, which is discussed in some detail in Chapter 2, is reviewed in this section. Positive reinforcement is known by various other labels, such as positive attention, approval, social reinforcement, and rewarding. Here it is defined as the process of reinforcing an appropriate target behavior in order to increase the probability that the behavior will recur. The advantages of positive reinforcement are (1) it is responsive to the child's natural need for attention and approval, and (2) it decreases the probability that the child will exhibit inappropriate behavior in an effort to obtain needed attention.

Two rules are essential for the effective application of positive reinforcement. First, when a child is initially exhibiting a new appropriate behavior, it must be positively reinforced each time it occurs. Second, once the target behavior is established at a satisfactory rate, the child should be reinforced intermittently.

To apply positive reinforcement, the teacher should follow these steps (Shea & Bauer, 1987):

Step 1: Carefully select a target behavior (do not attempt to reinforce every positive behavior a child exhibits).

Step 2: Observe the child's behavior to ascertain when he or she engages in the behavior.

Step 3: During the initial stage, reinforce the behavior immediately after it is exhibited.

Step 4: Specify for the child the behavior that is being reinforced ("I like the _____," or a similar comment).

Step 5: When reinforcing, speak with enthusiasm and show interest in the child's behavior.

Step 6: When appropriate, the practitioner may become involved in the child's behavior, that is, give the child help.

Step 7: Vary the reinforcer.

A note of caution: Public reinforcement is unwelcome to some children under some circumstances. They may be embarrassed by positive reinforcement in the presence of peers, teachers, parents, and others.

Gross and Ekstrand (1983) studied increasing and maintaining rates of teacher praise and their effects on student behavior. They found that teacher positive reinforcement decreased student scolding, increased productivity, and increased teacher enthusiasm in the classroom.

EXAMPLES ■ Michael has extremely poor table manners. He not only eats with his hands and fingers, but also he eats very rapidly. His teacher, Ms. Vandan, is attempting to improve the boy's table manners by positively reinforcing Michael's use of a fork and placement of the fork on the plate between each bite of food.

Michael is pleased with the extra attention, and over a period of several weeks his table manners have dramatically improved. Ms. Vandan used first a continuous reinforcement schedule, and then a variable schedule to help Michael. ■

■ Fourteen-year-old George, a member of the "Wild and Crazy Bunch," likes his math teacher, Ms. Chinn, very much. He enjoys receiving her attention, but sometimes it is a little annoying. This is especially true when Ms. Chinn makes a big show in front of the whole class of his successfully completing a difficult problem. It seems the other members of the "Bunch" hassle him after class when this occurs. ■

Shaping

To initiate an intervention for the purpose of increasing a behavior, the teacher or parents need only wait until the target behavior is emitted by the child. When the behavior occurs, it must be immediately rewarded with a potent reinforcer.

However, suppose a situation arises in which the level of performance of the behavior is at zero or near zero. What can the teacher or parent do to establish the behavior? There are two alternatives:

1. Wait an undetermined length of time (in some cases, forever) for the behavior to naturally occur.
2. Use a behavior-shaping technique.

Shaping is the systematic, immediate reinforcement of successive approximations of the target behavior until the behavior is established (Panyan, 1980; Shea & Bauer, 1987). It is primarily used to establish behaviors that have not been previously manifested in the individual's behavioral repertoire (Cooper, Heron, & Heward, 1987).

Just as the sculptor shapes and molds an object of art from clay, the behavior modifier shapes and molds a new behavior from an undifferentiated behavioral response (Neisworth and others, 1969). Shaping may also be used to increase infrequently exhibited behaviors. This technique is applicable to both behavioral and academic problems.

The behavior-shaping process includes the following steps:

Step 1: Selecting a target behavior.
Step 2: Obtaining reliable baseline data.
Step 3: Selecting potent reinforcers.
Step 4: Reinforcing successive approximations of the target behavior each time they occur.
Step 5: Reinforcing the newly established behavior each time it occurs.
Step 6: Reinforcing the behavior on a variable reinforcement schedule.

Many of these steps are explained in Chapters 2 and 3. However, some of them require additional comments here for clarification.

The behavior selected for shaping must be carefully specified. The teacher or parent must be positive that the selected behavior is meaningful to the child in terms of the child's present life context and developmental level.

If the performance level of the target behavior is at zero, the teacher or parent must initiate the shaping process from the child's undifferentiated behavioral manifestations.

EXAMPLES ■ Tommy's teacher, Ms. Allen, wishes to establish intelligible verbal responses in Tommy's behavioral repertoire. However, the child enunciates no understandable words. His entire verbal behavior consists of vocal noises such as screeches, howls, and gutteral sounds. The teacher must begin the shaping process with the manifested behavior, that is, vocal noise. She must reinforce successive approximations of intelligible verbal responses. ■

■ Jeff, a severely handicapped child, was having great difficulty interacting appropriately on the playground during circle or ball games requiring running from one specific location to another. When he was required to engage in a game of this type, he ran about at random, dashing here and there, jumping up and down, and in general confusing himself and his playmates.

Mr. Speer, the physical education teacher, wished to modify this behavior. He realized he had to start the change process with the behavior presently being manifested by Jeff. He determined that Jeff did attend to the action of the game and attempted to play by the rules. In his effort to help Jeff, Mr. Speer modified the rules of the game; he established a "new rule" in which all team members ran hand-in-hand in pairs from one location to another. Jeff was Mr. Speer's partner until he was conditioned to the new running pattern. The game was played by the traditional rules after Jeff developed acceptable skills. ■

During the behavior-shaping process, the teacher or parent reinforces only those behavioral manifestations that most approximate the desired behavior.

EXAMPLE   ■ Mr. Jackson designed a shaping intervention to increase the number of assigned math problems that Robert would successfully complete in his workbook during independent study. Robert never completed the 20 problems given for practice. However, baseline data revealed that Robert consistently solved the first 9 problems successfully in each practice section. He simply did not attempt the remaining 11 problems.

During the shaping process, Mr. Jackson reinforced Robert for *improvements* over his baseline of 9. Robert was rewarded for successfully completing 10 problems, 11 problems, 12 problems, and so on. Robert was *never* rewarded for completing a quantity of problems below his highest level of accomplishment. Within a short time Mr. Jackson's intervention data confirmed the fact that Robert was consistently completing the 20 problems successfully. The reinforcer was phased out. ■

Reinforcing less than the existing baseline results in rewarding behavior in a direction of change that is the reverse of the proposed direction. Remember, *only* the *highest* approximations of the target behavior should be reinforced.

Another important consideration in the shaping process is the teacher's or parent's knowledge of how long to provide reinforcement at one level of performance before moving to the next level. Such a movement increases the demands on the child. Determining when to move on is the teacher's or parent's greatest dilemma. If reinforcement continues too long at a given performance level, the child's behavior may become so rigidly established that further progress will be difficult. However, if the practitioner insists that the child progress too rapidly from one level to the next, there is a great possibility that the new behavior will be extinguished.

Knowing when to progress from one level of performance to the next is of utmost importance. Unfortunately, this knowledge is part of the skill needed for behavior modification, and developing it is not easy. The teacher or parent develops this needed sensitivity and skill only with practice and experience in behavior shaping and through knowing the individual child.

The following two examples are presented to clarify the steps in the behavior-shaping process.

EXAMPLES   ■ Ms. Simpkins wished to increase Jim's letter identification skills. Jim could identify 7 of the 26 letters of the alphabet consistently. Before implementing a shaping intervention, Ms. Simpkins determined that gumdrops were an effective reinforcer for Jim.

During the intervention phase of the behavior change program, Jim was exposed to one new letter of the alphabet at a time. He was to learn each new letter before another letter was presented. Jim was only reinforced with a gumdrop if he identified the new letter and all previously identified letters. The new letter was always presented last in the daily sequence of letters. After he had learned a letter, it was presented randomly with all the other previously learned letters in the daily session.

This procedure was continued until Jim successfully identified all the letters in the alphabet. ■

■ Mr. Behe wished to increase Barry's in-seat behavior. Baseline data revealed that on an average, Barry remained in his seat approximately 6 minutes. Mr. Behe had determined through observation that Barry enjoyed listening to story records. This activity was selected as a reinforcer for acceptable in-seat behavior.

During the intervention a timer was placed on Barry's desk. He was told that each time he remained in his seat until the timer bell sounded, he would be allowed to go to the reinforcement area of the classroom and listen to his favorite story record for a specified number of minutes. The reinforcement schedule Mr. Behe used to shape the in-seat behavior is presented in Table 4.1.

Barry's behavior was shaped with little difficulty. However, during the 20-minute interval between reinforcement Barry became bored. As a consequence, he remained at the 20-minute interval longer than the teacher had anticipated. At Barry's suggestion, Mr. Behe changed the reinforcer from story records to jigsaw puzzles. ■

According to Panyan (1980), there are two distinct types of behavior-shaping interventions: progressive and chain.

In backward shaping or chaining, the last component or link of a complex task or chain is taught to the individual first, the second to last component of the task is taught second, and so on. In other words, the components or links in the chain are taught in reverse order. In forward shaping or chaining, the first component or link in the chain or series of links is taught first, the second link is taught second and so on. Both forms of chaining are useful; their application depends on the particular task being taught, the individual being instructed, and other variables such as time and personnel availability.

EXAMPLE   ■   Both Mr. McGinnis and Mr. Solomon were responsible for teaching their daughters, Angie and Beth, to make their beds before they left for school in the morning. Both Mr. McGinnis and Mr. Solomon were very busy in the morning and had little time to teach the task. Mr. McGinnis had a little more time in the morning because he was a professor of behavior management at the local university and left for work later than Mr. Solomon. Both men decided to use shaping.

TABLE 4.1
Reinforcement schedule for in-seat behavior

Minutes of In-seat Behavior	Minutes in Reinforcement Area
5	2
5	2
7	2½
8	2½
10	2½
15	3
20	3
25	3
30	3½
45	4
60	4
90	5
120	7½
150	10

Mr. McGinnis and Mr. Solomon analyzed the complex task of bed making into the following discrete steps:

STEP	TASK
1.	Remove the pillows.
2.	Pull back the blanket and top sheet.
3.	Smooth the bottom sheet.
4.	Pull up the top sheet and smooth.
5.	Pull up the blanket and smooth.
6.	Fold the top of the top sheet over the top of the blanket.
7.	Put the bedspread on the bed.
8.	Fold the top one-fourth of the bedspread back.
9.	Put the pillow on the top of the bed, above the fold in the bedspread.
10.	Place the top one-fourth of the bedspread over the pillow.
11.	Smooth and check.

Mr. McGinnis used forward chaining to teach Angie to make her bed. During the teaching process, he and Angie proceeded from Step 1 to Step 11 in order. In the first session, Angie was required to complete Step 1 and was reinforced when the step was completed. After Angie completed Step 1, Mr. McGinnis completed making the bed (Steps 2 through 11). During the second session Angie completed Steps 1 and 2, was reinforced, and Mr. McGinnis completed making the bed.

Mr. Solomon used backward chaining to teach Beth to make her bed. He did this because he could reinforce "completed bedmaking" more frequently and, in addition, the teaching task would be quicker and the bed would look better. During the teaching process, Mr. Solomon and Beth proceeded from Step 11 to Step 1. In the first session, Mr. Solomon completed Steps 1 through 10, and Beth was required to complete Step 11 and reinforced for making her bed. During the second session, Mr. Solomon completed Steps 1 through 9, and Beth completed Steps 10 and 11 and was reinforced. (By the way, both Angie and Beth learned to make their beds each morning before departing for school. However, Beth enjoyed the learning task more than Angie.) ■

In the progressive shaping intervention, the child is required to engage in a series of steps, each of which is a continuation and progression of the previously learned step or steps. Examples of this intervention are bathing, hand-washing, putting on a sweater or socks, and so on.

A chain intervention is composed of two or more separate and distinct steps or skills that are learned and combined sequentially to complete a specific task (Alberto & Troutman, 1986). Examples of this intervention are tying shoes, polishing shoes, eating, buttoning clothing, and so on.

The following example and conceptual model summarize this discussion of the behavior-shaping process.

EXAMPLE ■ Five-year-old Stephen was nonverbal. His speech teacher selected the initiation of verbal exchanges with his preschool teacher as the target behavior. Baseline data revealed that Stephen's only verbal behavior consisted of babbling, yelling, and screaming. This behavior was frequent when he was in the company of adults he knew. However, he did not consistently emit this behavior in response to queries from others.

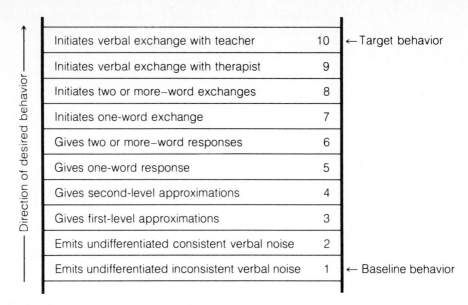

Initiates verbal exchange with teacher	10	← Target behavior
Initiates verbal exchange with therapist	9	
Initiates two or more–word exchanges	8	
Initiates one-word exchange	7	
Gives two or more–word responses	6	
Gives one-word response	5	
Gives second-level approximations	4	
Gives first-level approximations	3	
Emits undifferentiated consistent verbal noise	2	
Emits undifferentiated inconsistent verbal noise	1	← Baseline behavior

Direction of desired behavior →

FIGURE 4.1
Behavior-shaping model (Stephen's verbal behavior).

Stephen was observed by the speech teacher, who determined that he consistently responded to four tangible reinforcers: pickles, potato chips, prunes, and Popsicles.

The behavior-shaping intervention was initiated on a daily basis for 30 minutes during the preschool sessions that Stephen attended at a local school. The effectiveness of the intervention was to be evaluated by means of direct observation of the behavior-shaping sessions and the boy's activities in the preschool classroom with his teacher and playmates.

Shaping began with undifferentiated, inconsistent verbal responses. Within a single school year Stephen had progressed to initiating some verbal exchanges with others in both the shaping sessions and the preschool class. By the end of the year he would ask his teacher for milk, juice, cookies, toys, and the like. Although he seldom played with his classmates, he did verbally object to their attempts to confiscate his toys and snacks.

Stephen's ascent up the behavior-shaping ladder is presented in Figure 4.1. The steps of the ladder are self-explanatory with the possible exception of steps 3 and 4. During these steps, Stephen consistently used specific verbal noises in place of words. For example, "ah" was used for the word "milk," "eh" was used for the word "no," and the like. Emphasis here was put on converting these emissions into meaningful words. ■

Contingency Contracting

When one considers contemporary emphasis in the media on deferred payment purchasing and organized crime, one believes that every child should have some idea of the meaning of a contract. A *contract* is an agreement, written or verbal, between two or more parties, individuals, or groups, that stipulates the responsibilities of the parties concerning a specific item or activity. Contingency contracting in behavior modification parlance was well defined by Becker (1979) when he stated, "Arrange the conditions so that the child gets to do something he wants to do following something you want him to do."

We are all parties of contracts in daily living. Some of us are fortunate enough to have a written contract stating the terms of employment. This contract explains what duties we are to perform, for what period of time, and for what compensation. If we perform as specified in the contract, we cannot be fired under normal circumstances. A verbal contract exists between spouses. The terms of the contract state that they will love, honor, and respect one another until death (or divorce) does them part.

There are many lesser contracts in American society, such as home loans, loans on new automobiles, boats, and the like. Contracts such as these are indispensable to the efficient operation of the business system.

There are some contracts, seldom written, that are often taken for granted but nevertheless are indispensable in a complex urban society. Among these unwritten contracts are trust arrangements with utility services that the rubbish will be collected on certain mornings, the lights will go on when we turn a switch, or the water will flow when we open a faucet.

The use of contingency contracting as a behavior modification technique is based on a principle developed by Premack (1965). Premack's principle states: "A behavior that has a high rate of occurrence can be used to increase a behavior with a low rate of occurrence." What Premack stated was a very ancient and frequently used principle. For centuries people have applied this principle to raising their children, teaching their students, and supervising their employees. *If you do X, then you can do or get Y.* This principle has often been referred to as "Grandma's law." Most persons remember the power of this law from childhood:

- "Eat your spinach; then you can have some ice cream."
- "Clean your room; then you can go to the movies."
- "Cut the lawn; then you can use the car."

This same principle carries over to adult life:

- "Write 27 articles and 10 books; then you will be promoted to professor."
- "Don't join the union; then you will retain your job."
- "Don't make waves on the bureaucratic sea of calm; then you will be granted tenure."

Table 4.2 presents a series of *X* and *Y* statements found in the classroom.

Within the last two decades, teachers and parents have recognized the significance of individual differences caused by such factors as maturation, general knowledge, locus of control, and experience. Various instructional programs have been developed in response to these differences. Contingency contracting is one method that can

TABLE 4.2
X, then Y, statements

X	Then	Y
Sit in your seat 2 hours		Get a 10-minute recess
Complete your term paper		Get an A
Be a "good" student		Receive a good report card
Volunteer for the football team		Receive recognition from the cheerleaders
Learn a letter of the alphabet		Immediately receive a gumdrop

be used to individualize instruction and behavior control to respond to the child's interests, needs, and abilities; it can be applied to the cognitive, affective, and psychomotor domains of learning.

According to Kelly and Stokes (1982), there are few published empirical studies on the use of contingency contracting in the schools. In his review of the research, however, Murphy (1988) cited school-based studies on contingency contracting and academic productivity, performance accuracy, study skills, school attendance, and social behavior. He suggests that contracting is an excellent method for facilitating self-management, academic, and social development.

The advantages of contingency contracting are many. The method is positive; that is, the child takes an active role in deciding the type and amount of work required. Consequently personal responsibilities are understood by the child. At regular intervals the contract is reviewed for the child's reaffirmation. Accountability factors are built into this intervention. The teacher collects empirical data that indicate where the child was, where the child has progressed, and the child's current needs. The teacher can use this information to develop the program, instructional objectives, and developmental objectives with the child.

Salend (1987) suggests that student involvement will increase the effectiveness of the contingency contracting system. He notes several areas of this management system in which students may be involved:

□ Selecting the target behavior.
□ Gaining an understanding of the specific behavior to be changed through discussion with the teacher, by giving examples and explanations, and defining the behavior.
□ Selecting reinforcers.
□ Writing and reviewing the contract.
□ Evaluating the system from a student's perspective.

The teacher serves as contract manager, providing facts and explaining the principles. The teacher encourages the child to choose realistic limits. The teacher ensures that both the task and the reinforcer are fair to both parties of the contract (child and teacher).

When contingency contracting is first used with a child, small tasks and small reinforcers are most effective because they allow frequent reinforcement. Lengthy or complex tasks and small reinforcers are unfair and defeat the motivational factors inherent in this intervention. If the task is more demanding than the reinforcer is desirable, the learner is not sufficiently motivated to perform. Likewise, the reinforcer should not be greater than the task warrants; otherwise the instructional objective established for the child is difficult to obtain.

Initially contracts may encourage and reward approximations of desired behavior. Short work periods are desirable because they permit frequent reinforcement. Low-achieving children usually require immediate reinforcers; consequently short-term contracts (daily) are appropriate. Higher-achieving children can usually delay reinforcements; therefore long-term contracts (1 or 2 weeks) are feasible.

Some practitioners believe it is beneficial to separate the locations for task performance and reinforcer delivery. In this way the learner equates the task performance as a means to a desirable end, that is, going to the reinforcement area. This also broadens the type and variety of reinforcers that can be made available to the students. Teachers are encouraged to establish a reinforcement area in their classroom. The establishment of reinforcement areas is discussed in Chapter 3.

The teacher must encourage the child to adhere to the contract for the designated period of time. The child should be cautioned that if the agreed-on task is not performed, the child will not receive the reinforcer. However, if the original contract is too difficult, a new contract must be written for the learner to perform successfully. However, every effort should be made to ensure the success of the original contract.

The underlying principle of contingency contracting is constant: the learner, by making decisions concerning personal productivity, develops critical thinking skills, self-control, and the independence that increases productivity (Hall & Hall, 1982).

There are two types of contracts applicable in the classroom setting: verbal and written. Educators have generally found verbal contracts more useful than written contracts. The following are examples of verbal contracts that can be used in the classroom:

- □ "John, when you have completed 8 addition problems correctly, you may play with the puzzles."
- □ "Mary, if you remain in your seat for 5 minutes, you may work in your coloring book."
- □ "James, if you come to school on time tomorrow, you may be first in line for lunch."
- □ "Tom, if you don't hit anyone this morning, you may have an extra milk at lunch."
- □ "Mike, if you complete your seat work, you may watch 'Sesame Street' on television."

Verbal contracts such as these are made daily in the classroom. They work effectively for both the teacher and the child.

Written contracts are more elaborate than verbal contracts. The elaborateness of the written contract depends on the child for whom it is designed. Contracts frequently lose their effectiveness when they include pseudolegal jargon such as "the parties of the first part," "the party of the second part," or "henceforth and forevermore." It is recommended that the teacher or parent use the contract format in Figure 4.2 or a similar one. An additional copy of the contract is provided in the back of the text.

Date _____

Contract

This is an agreement between _____
Child's name

and _____. The contract begins on
Teacher's name

_____ and ends on _____. It will be re-
Date   Date

viewed on _____ .
Date

The terms of the agreement are:

Child will _____

_____

_____

_____

Teacher will _____

_____

_____

_____

If the child fulfills his or her part of the contract, the child will receive the agreed-on reward from the teacher. However, if the child fails to fulfill his or her part of the contract, the rewards will be withheld.

Child's signature _____

Teacher's signature _____

FIGURE 4.2
Contingency contract.

Homme and others (1979) have suggested ten basic rules for writing a contract for classroom use. These rules are as follows:

1. The contract payoff (reinforcer) should be immediate.
2. Initially contracts should call for and reinforce approximations of target behavior.
3. The contract should provide for frequent reinforcers in small amounts.
4. The contract should call for and reinforce accomplishments rather than just obedience.
5. The performance should be reinforced after it occurs.
6. The contract must be fair to both parties.
7. The terms of the contract must be clear.
8. The contract must be honest.
9. The contract must be positive.
10. Contracting must be used systematically as an integral part of the on-going classroom program.

In addition to the preceding rules, the practitioner should consider the following factors when developing and implementing a contract:

1. The contract must be negotiated and freely agreed on by both child and teacher.
2. The contract must include the target achievement or production level.
3. The reinforcer must be consistently delivered in accordance with the terms of the contract.
4. The contract must include the date for review and renegotiation.

One of the major functions of contingency contracting is to get children to the level of development at which they will initiate a contract instead of waiting for suggestions from the teacher.

The key to successful contracting is a negotiation session during which (1) the system of contracting is explained and discussed, (2) the contract is written, and (3) the contract is signed by the child and the teacher.

Negotiation should be systematic and precise. The teacher, as manager, has an obligation to ensure that the session is productive. It is recommended that the new practitioner use the following negotiation procedure (Shea et al., 1974):

1. Teacher establishes and maintains rapport with the child.
2. Teacher explains the purpose of the meeting by saying something such as, "I know you've been working hard on your schoolwork [reading, writing, spelling, arithmetic], and I'd like to help you."
3. Teacher gives a simple definition of a contract, explaining that a contract is an agreement between two people.
   a. Teacher gives an example of a contract such as: "When your mother takes your TV to the repair shop, the clerk gives her a ticket. The ticket is a contract between your mother and the repairman. He will repair and return the TV, and your mother will pay him."

    b. Teacher asks the child to give an example of a contract.

    c. If child cannot respond, the teacher gives another example and repeats 3b.

4. Teacher explains to the child that they are going to write a contract.

5. Teacher and child discuss tasks.

    a. Child suggests tasks for the contract.

    b. Teacher suggests tasks for the contract.

    c. Child and teacher discuss and agree on the specific task.

6. Teacher and child discuss reinforcers.

    a. Teacher asks the child which activities the child enjoys doing and which things he or she likes (see Chapter 3). The teacher may also suggest reinforcers.

    b. Teacher writes a reinforcer menu of child-suggested reinforcers.

    c. Child selects reinforcers for which he or she would like to work.

    d. Teacher and child rank the reinforcers in the child's order of preference.

7. Teacher and child negotiate the ratio of task to reinforcer.

8. Teacher and child agree on the time to be allotted for the child to perform the task; for example, the child works 10 addition problems in 15 minutes to receive the reinforcer, or the child completes a unit of science and does the laboratory experiments in 2 weeks to receive an A.

9. Teacher and child identify the criteria for achievement; that is, the child will work the 10 addition problem in 15 minutes with at least 80% accuracy.

10. Teacher and child discuss evaluation procedures.

    a. Teacher discusses various types of evaluations with the child.

    b. Teacher and child agree on a method of evaluation.

    c. Teacher asks the child to explain the method of evaluation. If the child appears confused, the teacher clarifies the evaluation procedure.

11. Teacher and child negotiate delivery of the reinforcer.

12. Teacher and child agree on a date for renegotiation of the contract.

13. Teacher or child writes the contract. If feasible, the child should be encouraged to write it. Teacher gives a copy of the contract to the child.

14. Teacher reads the contract to the child as the child follows on his or her own copy.

15. Teacher elicits the child's verbal affirmation to the contract terms and gives affirmation.

16. Child and teacher sign the contract.

17. Teacher congratulates the child for making the contract and wishes the child success.

A properly conducted negotiating session is complex and time consuming, particularly if the teacher has not previously introduced the concept of contracting in the classroom. Both the complexity and time consumed by the negotiation process decrease as the student and teacher gain experience in contracting. As an aid to reducing confusion on the part of the teacher or the child and in an effort to facilitate the negotiation process, a contract work sheet is provided (see Figure 4.3). An additional copy of the work sheet can be found in the back of the text.

Contract Work Sheet

Child _____

Teacher _____ Date _____

(X)	Tasks	Comments
( )	1. Establish and maintain rapport.	
( )	2. Explain the purpose of the meeting.	
( )	3. Explain a contract.	
( )	4. Give an example of a contract.	
( )	5. Ask the child to give an example of a contract; if there is no response, give another example.	
( )	6. Discuss possible tasks.	
( )	7. Child-suggested tasks: _____ _____ _____ _____	
( )	8. Teacher-suggested tasks: _____ _____ _____ _____	
( )	9. Agree on the task.	
( )	10. Ask the child what activities he or she enjoys and what items he or she wishes to possess.	
( )	11. Record child-suggested reinforcers.	
( )	12. Negotiate the ratio of the task to the reinforcer.	

FIGURE 4.3
Sample work sheet for contract negotiation.

Contract Work Sheet—cont'd

(X)	Tasks	Comments
( )	13. Identify the time allotted for the task.	
( )	14. Identify the criterion or achievement level.	
( )	15. Discuss methods of evaluation.	
( )	16. Agree on the method of evaluation.	
( )	17. Restate and clarify the method of evaluation.	
( )	18. Negotiate the delivery of the reinforcer.	
( )	19. Set the date for renegotiation.	
( )	20. Write two copies of the contract.	
( )	21. Read the contract to the child.	
( )	22. Elicit the child's verbal affirmation and give your own affirmation.	
( )	23. Sign the contract and have the child sign it.	
( )	24. Congratulate the child (and yourself).	

FIGURE 4.3
Continued.

The left-hand column of the work sheet should be checked as the practitioner and child complete each of the specified tasks. The tasks to be accomplished are specified in the middle column. The tasks are presented in logical order. It is strongly recommended that the order of presentation be followed during the session. The right-hand column of the work sheet is reserved for comments and notations.

Three examples of contracts drawn from classroom experience are found in Figures 4.4-4.6.

Contract forms need not be as formal as suggested by these procedures. Many home and school situations are responsive to less formal contracts. Examples of

Date _____ February 3, 1991 _____

Contract

This is an agreement between _____ Bob Wellrock _____ and _____ Mr. Bare _____. The contract
                                    Child's name   Teacher's name

begins on _____ 2/8/91 _____ and ends on _____ 2/10/91 _____. It will be reviewed on _____ 2/9/91 _____.
              Date   Date   Date

The terms of the agreement are:

Child will _____ spell with 90% accuracy the 20 assigned spelling words for Friday. _____

Teacher will _____ provide a ticket good for admission to the school movie on February 10, 1991 _____

If the child fulfills his or her part of the contract, the child will receive the agreed-on reward from the teacher. However, if the child fails to fulfill his part of the contract, the rewards will be withheld.

Child's signature _____

Teacher's signature _____

FIGURE 4.4
Sample contract.

Date _____ April 5, 1991 _____

Contract

This is an agreement between _____ Russell Palmer _____ and _____ Mr. Davis _____. The contract
                                    Child's name   Teacher's name

begins on _____ 4/8/91 _____ and ends on _____ 4/13/91 _____. It will be reviewed on _____ 4/11/91 _____.
              Date   Date   Date

The terms of the agreement are:

Child will _____ not engage in any fights during the school day for the period of the contract. _____

Teacher will _____ take the child to a Golden Gloves boxing match at the local arena. _____

If the child fulfills his or her part of the contract, the child will receive the agreed-on reward from the teacher. However, if the child fails to fulfill his part of the contract, the rewards will be withheld.

Child's signature _____

Teacher's signature _____

FIGURE 4.5
Sample contract.

Date _____ *March 7, 1991* _____

Contract

This is an agreement between _____ *Tom Hawk* _____ and _____ *Mr. George* _____ . The contract
_____Child's name_____Teacher's name

begins on ____ *3/10/91* ____ and ends on ____ *3/30/91* ____ . It will be reviewed on ____ *3/28/91* ____ .
_____Date_____Date_____Date

The terms of the agreement are:

Child will ____ *participate in a teacher-prescribed physical education program for 30 minutes*

a day during the period of the contract. _____

Teacher will ____ *provide one out-of-town basketball trip and admission to the game.* _____

If the child fulfills his or her part of the contract, the child will receive the agreed-on
reward from the teacher. However, if the child fails to fulfill his part of the contract, the rewards will be withheld.

Child's signature _____

Teacher's signature _____

FIGURE 4.6
Sample contract.

less formal contracts, developed by Kaplan and Hoffman (1981), are shown in Figures
4.7-4.11 (pp. 120-124).

Token Economy

When most of us think of learning, we recall our participation in formal educational
systems, which involved acquiring knowledge by listening to teachers, having
discussions, taking tests, and the like. This symbolic or verbal learning is essential
to our development, but it is not the only kind of learning in which we participate.
Human nature permits us to learn directly from experiences in our environment.
It is through learning that we develop habitual ways of working our environment
for our reinforcers, that is, to obtain and sustain pleasure and to avoid discomfort
and pain.

Although they differ in some ways, all learning environments are similar in that
they are worked by individuals for reinforcers. Reinforcers may be defined as stimuli

that induce changes in the person. These are positive reinforcers if they induce a pleasant state and negative reinforcers if they induce an aversive or painful state. Generally we work the environment to acquire positive reinforcers and to avoid or escape negative reinforcers. Learning occurs by discovering behaviors that produce rewards and then repetitively working the environment to continue to obtain the reward. In general, the strength of a reinforcer is judged by the magnitude of the change it produces in the individual. The stronger or more desirable the reinforcers, the more quickly and easily the individual learns.

Learning environments generally provide feedback process cues that predict the presentation of delayed reinforcers. The immediacy of feedback, whether it is reinforcement per se or a process cue predictive of later reinforcement, is an important determinant of the rate of learning. In general, learning occurs more easily and more rapidly when feedback is immediate.

Learning environments vary in the consistency of feedback that they provide for the learner; the more consistent the feedback, the more quickly and easily the individual learns. Learning environments also vary in the degree to which individuals are allowed to set their own work rate. In other words, some environments allow individuals more freedom to work at a self-selected rate than others. Individuals learn more easily and quickly when they are free to set their own pace in working the environment for the desired reinforcer (Ayllon & McKittrick, 1982).

Many children are not able to function appropriately if they must wait an extended time for their reinforcer. In addition, there are some children who have not developed to the level at which social rewards alone are satisfactory reinforcers. In these cases the use of a token economy has proved to be an effective behavior change intervention.

The tokens are usually valueless to the children when originally introduced to them. Their value becomes apparent as the children learn that tokens can be exchanged for a variety of reinforcers, such as being first in the lunch line, getting 10 minutes of free time, listening to phonograph records, watching television, purchasing a favored toy, and so on. This versatility makes the token system superior to many interventions.

It is an accepted fact that the child who is first in line for lunch today may not wish to be first in line next week. A properly administered token economy adjusts to this human tendency by providing a variety of rewards, that is, a reward menu.

When the teacher "sells" admission to a movie, use of Play-doh, or the like, the tokens rapidly take on value for the children. When the teacher states the price and asks a child to count out the needed quantity of tokens, they are engaged in a token economy.

In this manner the tokens become potent reinforcers. They can be awarded over a period of time for acceptable academic and nonacademic work. The system allows the teacher to structure the learning environment for positive reinforcement and to provide immediate feedback to the children via tokens. Hence, a moderately well run token exchange can promote direct learning regardless of the content of the activity.

Contract Your Way
Out of a

If I can squeeze through

_____

_____

_____

by _____
   (date)

then I will have a clean start to_____

_____

_____

_____	_____	_____
Squeezer	Squeezee	Date

FIGURE 4.7
Informal contract between student and teacher.

(From Kaplan, P., and Hoffman, A. *It's absolutely groovy.* Denver: Love Publishing Co., 1981.)

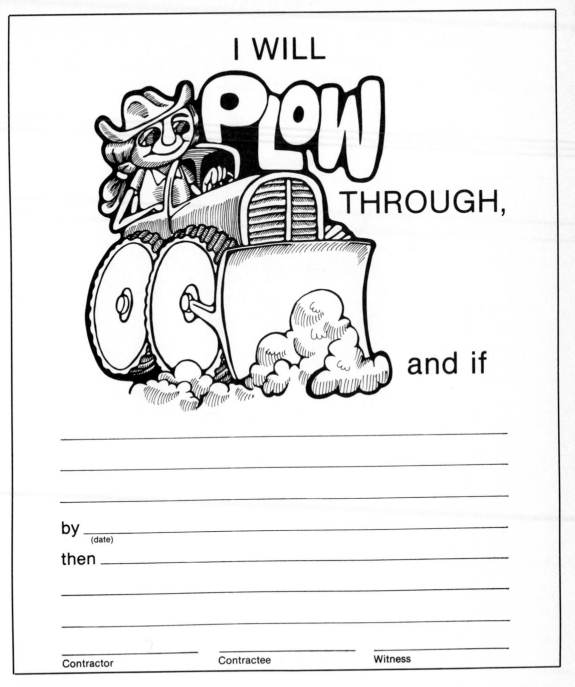

FIGURE 4.8
Informal contract between student and teacher.

(From Kaplan, P., and Hoffman, A. *It's absolutely groovy.* Denver: Love Publishing Co., 1981.)

_____ and _____
will

PITCH IN

and help each other to

_____ by _____
(date)

When we are done, we will be able to _____

_____

_____

_____   _____
Friend #1   Friend #2

_____ _____ _____
Witness   Contractor   Date

FIGURE 4.9
Informal contract between students.

(From Kaplan, P., and Hoffman, A. *It's absolutely groovy.* Denver: Love Publishing Co., 1981.)

I hereby agree to help

_____

OUT OF A PICKLE

by

_____

_____

on or before _____

When this pickle of a problem is
solved, we will be able to

_____

_____

_____

Pickle #1 _____ Pickle #2 _____

Pickler _____ Date _____

I hereby

AGREE

to

_____

_____

_____

To do this, I will need _____

_____

When I deliver the finished
product, I will receive _____

_____

_____

Builder _____ Supplier _____

FIGURE 4.10
Informal contracts.

(From Kaplan, P., and Hoffman, A. *It's absolutely groovy.* Denver: Love Publishing Co., 1981.)

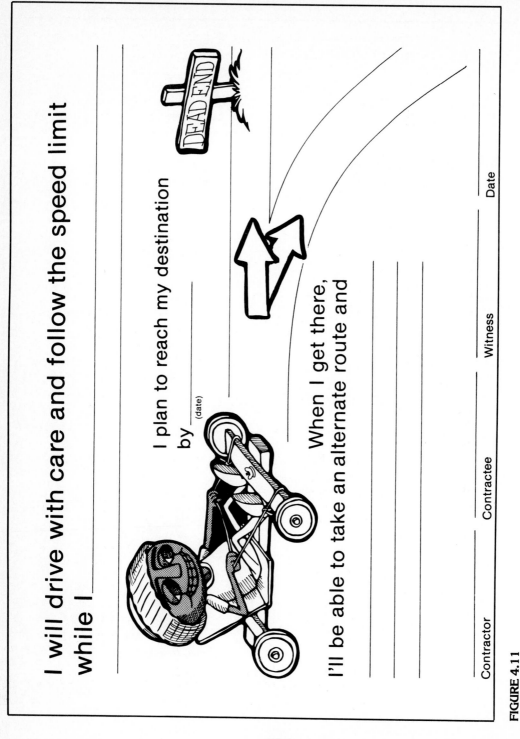

I will drive with care and follow the speed limit while I _____

I plan to reach my destination by _____
(date)

When I get there, I'll be able to take an alternate route and

| Contractor | Contractee | Witness | Date |

FIGURE 4.11
Informal contract.

(From Kaplan, P., and Hoffman, A. *It's absolutely groovy.* Denver: Love Publishing Co., 1981.)

We are all exposed to and use tokens daily. The most common form of token exchange is the use of currency to purchase various items and services. It is generally agreed (especially in today's economy) that money itself has no value; only the objects for which it is exchanged have real value. In the classroom the token takes on the same meaning as currency has in the marketplace.

The classroom token economy suffers the same problems as the marketplace economy, that is, loss, theft, and counterfeiting. Some of these problems can be prevented by not using poker chips and other readily available objects for tokens.

For instance, what would you do if Joel came to your classroom every morning with his pockets filled with poker chips? Not only is Joel selling the chips to his classmates, but they are constantly dropping them on the floor—a very distracting practice.

Items that could be used include:

Check marks	Conservation stamps
Points	Trading stamps
Stars	Animal stickers
Smiling faces	Fairy tale character stickers
Point cards	Teacher-made tokens
Point tally forms	Play money

These tokens have several advantages over tokens made of rigid, hard materials such as metal, plastic, and wood. They are made of soft, flexible materials, that is, paper, vinyl, or simple pen and pencil markings. They are less distracting to have in the classroom atmosphere because they neither rattle nor make noise if dropped on a hard surface. These characteristics eliminate much potential and actual distraction and confusion in the classroom. The tokens are easily glued to a paper, desk top, record card, or chart. They can be permanently affixed to various surfaces to minimize the incidence of misplacement, loss, or theft. However, they must be sufficiently distinctive to prohibit unauthorized duplication.

The following are the basic rules when establishing a token economy system for the classroom:

1. Select a target behavior. This topic is thoroughly discussed in Chapter 2 and does not warrant further elaboration here.
2. Conceptualize and present the target behavior to the child or group. It is a well-known fact that an emphasis on "what you can do" is more palatable to children than an emphasis on "what you cannot do." Many unsuccessful behavior modification practitioners have determined their own failure by introducing a program by saying. "Now you boys and girls are going to stop that noise and fooling around in here. I have this new . . . [and so on]." The children are immediately challenged; they prepare to defeat the teacher and defend their personal integrity.
3. Post the rules and review them frequently.

4. Select an appropriate token.
5. Establish reinforcers for which tokens can be exchanged.
6. Develop a reward menu and post it in the classroom. The children should be permitted to thoroughly discuss and consider the items on the menu. They should be encouraged to make their selections from among the items available. The children should not be permitted to debate the cost (number of tokens) of the various rewards after prices have been established.
7. Implement the token economy. Introduce the token economy on a limited basis initially. A complex sophisticated system as an initial exposure confuses and frustrates the children. *Start small and build on firm understanding.* Explain the system to the children with great clarity and precision. Be patient and answer all the children's questions. It is better to delay implementation than create confusion and frustration.
8. Provide immediate reinforcement for acceptable behavior. The children will lose interest in the program if the process for obtaining the tokens is more effort than the reward is desirable. Many systems fail because the teacher neglects to dispense tokens at the appropriate time. Rewarding the children immediately reduces frustration and overconcern with the system. When the children are sure they will receive the tokens at the proper time, they can ignore the delivery system and concentrate on their work or behavior.
9. Gradually change from a continuous to a variable schedule of reinforcement. As discussed in Chapter 2, quick, unpredictable, or premature changes in a reinforcement schedule can destroy the program.
10. Provide time for the children to exchange tokens for rewards. If the token economy is a legitimate class program, time during the school day should be made available for the exchange. Time should not be taken from the children's recess, lunch, or free time.
11. Revise the reward menu frequently. Children, like adults, become bored with the same old fare day after day.

Rosenberg (1986) studied the effects of daily rule-review and rehearsal procedures on the effectiveness of a token economy with five disruptive and distractible elementary school-age students in a resource room program. He found that daily review of classroom rules resulted in an overall time-on-task improvement of 12% and a 50% reduction in disruptive talkouts.

The token economy has worked very effectively in the classroom. Two reasons for its success are its lack of emphasis on competition with others and the fact that the reward menu provides sufficient variety to prevent boredom.

Table 4.3 is an example of a reward menu for classroom use.

The menu need not be lengthy or elaborate but should contain at least 10 items and activities. The children should exchange their tokens daily; they should not be allowed to take them home. If they are deferring their reinforcers and saving tokens for long-range ones, their tokens should be collected and recorded each day.

TABLE 4.3
Reward menu

Reward	Time	Cost (Points)
Getting free time	10 minutes	20
Watching television	30 minutes	45
Reading comic books	5 minutes	15
Listening to records	10 minutes	20
Cutting and pasting	5 minutes	10
Purchasing modeling clay	—	55
Purchasing crayons	—	45
Purchasing coloring books	—	50
Finger painting	12 minutes	25
Playing with toys	10 minutes	25
Borrowing a book	48 hours	35
Borrowing a game	48 hours	50

The number of tokens earned may be recorded on a point card or tally form. The teacher can affix the card or form to each child's desk and then either record or circle the points earned by the child. The points are totaled at the end of each day. The child may either delay the reward or accept it immediately.

In a discussion of token economy reinforcers, Raschke, Dedrick, and Thompson (1987) recommended the use of contingency packages to motivate reluctant learners. The packages are tangible reminders of potential reinforcers. They consist of three-dimensional displays designed specifically to advertise rewards. The packages should be novel, exciting, and age-appropriate. Two packages described in detail by Raschke et al. (1987) included the "Flip-The-Lid-Robot," a multi-drawered container in which each drawer holds various rewards, and "Touchdown Triumph," a football game board designed for adolescents. Raschke (1986) suggested a similar package using available classroom materials (construction paper, sponges, pipe cleaners) to make "delicious" incentives (hamburgers, french fries, ice cream cones) for display in the classroom.

Clark (1988) recommended the use of "Behavior Tickets" to extend the token economy outside the classroom. The tickets may be used by approved adults in any class or area of the school in which the student works or plays. When the student leaves the classroom to go to the restroom, lunchroom, playground or elsewhere, he or she is given a ticket. To earn points, the students must return to class with the ticket in one piece. If the student is caught misbehaving by another teacher, that teacher stops the student, requests the ticket, and tears it into two pieces. Missing tickets are considered to be torn tickets. This technique, according to Clark, has two advantages: The student can be reinforced for appropriate out-of-classroom behavior, and misbehavior can be addressed as soon as the student returns to the classroom. All tickets must be returned to the teacher at the end of the class period or day.

Of course, the system assumes that all adults in the school are trained in the technique and willing to participate.

Examples of the point card and tally form to be used for specific behaviors are presented in Figures 4.12 and 4.13. Maher (1989) suggested a "punch out" card for use as a behavior recording technique. The teacher punches a hole in the card when the student exhibits the appropriate behavior. Punching the card is paired with social and tangible reinforcement if tangible reinforcement is used.

The teacher, with little difficulty, may plan and implement a multipurpose token economy in the classroom. In this situation the children earn tokens for a variety of appropriate behaviors as well as academic effort and academic success.

Tokens or points can be presented to the child for any or all of the following behaviors:

☐ Being present at the work station on time.
☐ Having appropriate work tools available for use.
☐ Attending to the instructor's directions.
☐ Exhibiting appropriate social behavior during the work period (raising hand for attention, remaining at the work station, not talking without permission).
☐ Engaging in the assigned work task during the work period; that is, showing effort.
☐ Correctly or satisfactorily completing the assigned work task.
☐ Returning work tools to their appropriate place.

Tokens are presented for various appropriate behaviors and withheld for inappropriate behaviors.

A point card for a multipurpose token economy is presented in Figure 4.14. Copies of each of the forms for recording points in a token economy are provided in the back of the text.

Point Card*

Child's name _____ Date _____

1	2	3	4	5	6	7	8	9	10
11	12	13	14	15	16	17	18	19	20
21	22	23	24	25	26	27	28	29	30
31	32	33	34	35	36	37	38	39	40
41	42	43	44	45	46	47	48	49	50
51	52	53	54	55	56	57	58	59	60
61	62	63	64	65	66	67	68	69	70
71	72	73	74	75	76	77	78	79	80
81	82	83	84	85	86	87	88	89	90
91	92	93	94	95	96	97	98	99	100

*Teacher circles the cumulative total.

FIGURE 4.12
Point card for specific behavior.

Point Tally Form

Child _____ Date _____

Monday												
Tuesday												
Wednesday												
Thursday												
Friday												

TOTAL

Monday	
Tuesday	
Wednesday	
Thursday	
Friday	
Week	

FIGURE 4.13
Tally form for specific behavior.

129

Point Card for Multipurpose Token Economy

Child _____ Day _____ Date _____

Work period	Readiness	Social behavior	Work effort	Work success	Teacher comments
9:00-9:15			*	*	
9:15-10:00					
10:00-10:30					
10:30-10:45			*	*	
10:45-11:30					
11:30-12:00					
12:00-1:00			*	*	
1:00-1:30					
1:30-2:45					
2:45-3:00			*	*	

*Points for work effort and work success are not available during these periods due to the nature of the activity: opening exercises, recess, lunch, and closing exercises.

FIGURE 4.14
Point card with spaces for behavior notation and comments.

EXAMPLES ■ Mr. Newman, a junior high school math teacher, was having difficulty with Charlie, who had developed the habit of counting and computing aloud while doing math assignments. At first this behavior was not a serious problem, but then it began to distract many of the other students.

Mr. Newman decided to implement a token economy system to modify Charlie's behavior. He discussed the system with the class, established a set of rules, and developed a reward menu before implementing this intervention.

The reward menu is presented in Table 4.4.

The token economy was used with the entire class and effectively modified the behaviors of Charlie and his peers.

Tokens were initially presented on a fixed interval schedule; as the group progressed, however, a variable interval schedule was introduced. Throughout the program Mr. Newman conscientiously paired social rewards with the tokens. ■

■ Two physical education teachers were having problems with the student participation in PE class. They were being bombarded with complaints such as headaches, back pains, sore toes, and sore ears. After discussing the token economy system between themselves and with their students, they decided to initiate a program to increase participation. A student delegation aided the teachers in developing the reward menu shown in Table 4.5. ■

■ Mrs. Thomas has been attempting to get Mary, her 16-year-old daughter, to share in the housekeeping. Mrs. Thomas has had very little success.

One day Mary asked if she and three of her friends could go into the city for dinner and the theater. The big evening was to be in 4 weeks. Mrs. Thomas said "yes" if Mary would pay for the trip by helping with the housekeeping. Mrs. Thomas made a list of tasks Mary was responsible for around the house. It included cleaning her room, washing and drying clothes, helping with the cooking, ironing, washing windows, cleaning the bathroom, and so on. Each task was assigned a specific point value. The points could be exchanged for money.

When the time for the trip arrived, Mary had sufficient money for the evening. In addition, she had an improved attitude about helping to take care of the house. ■

TABLE 4.4
Mr. Newman's reward menu

Reward	Time (Minutes)	Cost (Points)
Checkers	10	15
Cards	10	15
Puzzles	15	20
Magazines	18	25
Chess	12	30
Model car kits	10	20
Comic books	5	10
Bingo	15	25
Quiet conversation	10	30

TABLE 4.5
Physical education class reward menu

Reward	Time (Minutes)	Cost (Points)
Getting free time	15	50
Using trampoline	10	40
Shooting baskets	5	30
Acting as activity leader	—	25
Talking with friend	10	40
Playing badminton	10	30
Using trapeze	15	50
Sitting out an activity	—	100

In these three examples the token economy system proved to be effective in increasing participation. In two of the cases, the teachers changed the reward menu frequently in cooperation with their students throughout the duration of the program.

Modeling

One of the most common forms of human learning is accomplished through the processes of observation and imitation. All parents and teachers can relate a variety of acceptable and unacceptable behaviors exhibited by their children and students that are imitations of their own (the adults') personal acceptable and unacceptable behaviors. This form of learning at various times and by various theorists and practitioners has been called modeling, observational learning, identification, copying, vicarious learning, social facilitation, contagion, role playing, and so on (Bandura, 1969; Striefel, 1981). In this text the term *modeling* is used to describe learning by observation and imitation.

As a behavior change method, modeling is the provision of an individual or group behavior to be imitated or not imitated by a child. This is one of the oldest and most frequently applied methods of changing behavior.

Mothers and fathers, husbands and wives, and teachers and principals have been suggesting models to their sons, daughters, spouses, and students for generations.

- □ "Be a good boy like your brother John."
- □ "Why can't you be like George, an excellent father, a great lover, and a good provider?"
- □ "Mary, can't you be a good student like Eileen?"
- □ "Why can't you behave like the other boys and girls?"

Several state and national organizations exist for the purpose of providing children with an acceptable social model. These organizations provide children with either the direct services of a live model or an abstract model inherent in their program and printed materials. Among these organizations are Big Brother and Big Sister, Boy Scouts and Girl Scouts, 4-H, and Little League.

According to Bandura (1969), and Clarizio and Yelon (1967), exposure to a model has three effects:

1. *Modeling effect or observational learning.* Children may acquire behavior from a model that was not previously a part of their behavioral repertoire. In this situation the model performs a behavior that is imitated by the child in substantially identical form. Examples of the modeling effect are teaching a nonverbal child to verbalize in imitation of a model and teaching a child signing skills as a method of communication.

2. *Inhibitory and disinhibitory effects.* Modeling is not confined exclusively to the learning of new behaviors as in the preceding modeling effect. Modeling includes

imitating a model for the purpose of disinhibiting or inhibiting a behavior. For example, a child may observe and imitate a peer who is positively reinforced for exhibiting a behavior. Or the child may observe and *not* imitate a peer who is punished or ignored for exhibiting a behavior. In these situations the child may be said to be experiencing the other child's behavior and its consequences vicariously.

3. *Eliciting or response facilitation effect.* In this situation the model's behavior is employed to facilitate the occurrence of a previously learned but dormant behavior from the child. For example, a child may know that it is appropriate to say "Thank you" when given a cookie at snack time. However, this child may not say "Thank you" as a matter of common practice. Appropriate social responsiveness may be facilitated if all the children who receive cookies previous to this child during snack time say "Thank you."

Before implementing a modeling intervention, the teacher or parent should consider the following factors:

1. Is the child able developmentally and cognitively to imitate the model? Practitioners must be cognizant of the fact that some children are simply not ready to use modeling.
2. Will the child be rewarded for imitating the model? Some children are simply not intrinsically rewarded by performing behaviors that others consider acceptable.
3. Is the model "good"? Caution must be taken when a model is being selected for a child. Remember, what the model does in science class may be quite different from what this individual does in English, shop, on the playground, at home, or behind the barn.
4. Is the model acceptable to the child? A model who is too good, too bright, too fast, or just plain obnoxious will be rejected by the child.

Modeling techniques can be effectively applied by teachers in an effort to change behavior only when consideration is given to these factors.

EXAMPLES ■ Ms. Simpson is a resource teacher of educable mentally handicapped children. Dave and Carl work with Ms. Simpson in the resource room for 1 hour each day. Until recently Dave would usually attempt his assigned tasks, whereas Carl would seldom attempt his assigned work.

It was determined by Ms. Simpson that both boys were reinforced by her attention. Therefore she decided to use her attention as a reward they received for completing their work. Dave was reinforced by Ms. Simpson's attention. She praised him each time he did his class work, attended to the appropriate stimulus, or completed an assigned task; she ignored Carl's inappropriate behavior.

After several sessions during which Dave's behavior was rewarded, Carl began to imitate Dave to receive Ms. Simpson's attention. She immediately reinforced Carl whenever he exhibited the appropriate behavior.

The result of this intervention was a dramatic change in Carl's behavior. He is now completing his work to gain approval from Ms. Simpson. ■

■ Mr. Cohen is an instructor of three boys and one girl in a class for behaviorally disordered children. The students' names are John, James, Charles, and Shirley. Of the four students, Charles is the most troublesome. Charles constantly moves about the room, exhibiting feelings of indignation at assignments and disrupting the activities of Mr. Cohen and his classmates. This behavior occurs throughout the school day. Originally when the behavior occurred, the other children remained busy at their seats. On these occasions, Mr. Cohen would chase after Charles or provide him with attention for the unacceptable behavior he was exhibiting. The acceptable behaviors manifested by Shirley, John, and James were ignored. Lately Shirley, John, and James have begun to move about the room and exhibit behaviors that disturb Mr. Cohen. They are imitating the behavior of Charles.

One can conclude that Shirley, John, and James are modeling Charles' behavior for the purpose of receiving attention from their teacher. ■

In both of these examples the procedure of modeling is effective; in fact, it is effective in developing both appropriate and inappropriate behaviors. The consequence of behavior is again the key factor.

In too many classrooms appropriate behavior is taken for granted. Modeling is a potentially effective preventive technique.

SUMMARY

In this chapter the practitioner of behavior modification is provided with an overview of the five common techniques used to increase appropriate behavior: (1) positive reinforcement, (2) shaping, (3) contingency contracting, (4) the token economy, and (5) modeling.

Positive reinforcement is defined as the process of reinforcing an appropriate target behavior to increase the probability that the behavior will be repeated. Also known as positive attention, approval, social reinforcement, and rewarding, this technique requires two things: (1) during the initial stage, the target behavior must be reinforced each time it occurs, and (2) when the target behavior is established at a satisfactory rate, it should be reinforced intermittently.

Shaping is the reinforcement of successive approximations of the target behaviors that have not been previously manifested in the individual's behavioral repertoire. The steps in behavior shaping are (1) selecting a target behavior, (2) collecting baseline data, (3) selecting a reinforcer, (4) reinforcing successive approximations of the target behavior, (5) reinforcing the approximations immediately and continuously, and (6) changing to a variable reinforcement schedule.

Contingency contracting involves the completion of behavior X before reinforcement Y is given or allowed. This process is actively used in day-to-day living. Contracts may be verbal or written. Verbal contracts are commonly used in schools, but written contracts are appealing to the reluctant learner. When developing a contract, the practitioner should know the developmental level of the child or children with whom the contract is being negotiated. Contracting is more effective when the child is allowed to share in its development.

A token economy is a system of exchange. Children earn tokens that are exchanged for specific reinforcers. The tokens themselves are valueless; their value lies in the reinforcers for which they can be exchanged. There are a number of objects that can be used as tokens, such as check marks, points, smiling faces, stars, and other similar items. An important component of a token economy is the reward menu, which should be developed with the child or group.

Modeling, one of the oldest and most frequently applied methods of behavior change, has been effective in developing appropriate behaviors in children. Modeling is the provision of an individual or group behavior to be imitated or not imitated by the child.

PROJECTS

1. Select a target behavior to change and describe how you would implement each step of shaping the behavior.
2. Write two examples of modeling as a technique for increasing behaviors.
3. Develop and implement a contract for (a) an individual child in a class and (b) an entire class.
4. Develop a reward menu for your class.
5. Develop a token economy system.

REFERENCES

Alberto, P. A., & Troutman, A. C. (1986). *Applied behavior analysis for teachers.* Columbus, OH: Merrill.

Ayllon, T., & McKittrick, S. M. (1982). *How to set up a token economy.* Austin, TX: Pro-Ed.

Bandura, A. (1969). *Principles of behavior modification.* New York: Holt, Rinehart & Winston.

Becker, W. C. (1979). Introduction. In L. Homme, Csanyi, A. P., Gonzales, A. M., & Rechs, J. R. (Eds.), *How to use contingency contracting in the classroom.* Champaign, IL: Research Press.

Clarizio, H. F., & Yelon, S. L. (1967). Learning theory approaches to classroom management: Rationale and intervention techniques. *Journal of Special Education, 1,* 267-274.

Clark, J. (1988). Behavior tickets quell misconduct. *Behavior In Our Schools, 1*(3), 19-20.

Cooper, J. O., Heron, T. E., & Heward, W. L. (1987). *Applied behavior analysis.* Columbus, OH: Merrill.

Gross, A. M., & Ekstrand, M. (1983). Increasing and maintaining rates of teacher praise. *Behavior Modification, 7*(1), 126-135.

Hall, R. V., & Hall, M. C. (1982). *How to negotiate behavioral contracts.* Austin, TX: Pro-Ed.

Homme, L., Csanyi, A. P., Gonzales, M. A., & Rechs, J. R. (1979). *How to use contingency contracting in the classroom.* Champaign, IL: Research Press.

Kaplan, P. G., & Hoffman, A. G. (1981). *It's absolutely groovy.* Denver: Love Publishing Co.

Kelly, M. L., & Stokes, T. F. (1982). Contingency contracting with disadvantaged youths: Improving classroom performance. *Journal of Applied Behavior Analysis, 15,* 447-454.

Maher, G. B. (1989). "Punch out": A behavior management technique. *Teaching Exceptional Children, 21*(2), 74.

Murphy, J. J. (1988). Contingency contracting in the schools: A review. *Education and Treatment of Children, 11*(3), 257-269.

Neisworth, J. T., Deno, S. L., & Jenkins, J. R. (1969). *Student motivation and classroom management: A behavioristic approach.* Newark, DE: Behavior Technics.

Panyan, M. C. (1980). *How to use shaping.* Austin, TX: Pro-Ed.

Premack, D. (1965). Reinforcement theory. In D. LeVine (Ed.), *Nebraska symposium on motivation.* Lincoln: University of Nebraska Press.

Raschke, D. (1986). "Delicious" incentives: A technique to motivate reluctant learners. *Teaching Exceptional Children, 19* (1), 66-67.

Raschke, D., Dedrick, C., & Thompson, M. (1987). Motivating reluctant learners: Innovative contingency packages. *Teaching Exceptional Children, 19*(2), 18-21.

Rosenberg, M. S. (1986). Maximizing the effectiveness of structured classroom management programs: Implementing rule-review procedures with disruptive and distractible students. *Behavioral Disorders, 11*(4), 239-248.

Salend, S. J. (1987). Contingency management systems. *Academic Therapy, 22*(3), 245-253.

Schloss, P. J. (1986). Sequential prompt instruction for mildly handicapped learners. *Teaching Exceptional Children, 18*(3), 181-184.

Shea, T. M., & Bauer, A. M. (1987). *Teaching children and youth with behavior disorders* (2nd ed.). Englewood Cliffs, NJ: Prentice-Hall.

Shea, T. M., Whiteside, W. R., Beetner, E. G., & Lindsey, D. L. (1974). *Contingency contracting in the classroom.* Edwardsville: Southern Illinois University.

Striefel, S. (1981). *How to teach through modeling and imitation.* Austin, TX: Pro-Ed.

CHAPTER FIVE

Methods of Decreasing Behavior

Mrs. Hamilton dreaded coming to school today. It is raining, and her fourth-grade students will have to remain inside during recess. When the students do not get to go outside for recess, they seem to go crazy. As the recess period approaches, they become increasingly disruptive.

On this day, when the recess period arrives, Mrs. Hamilton tells the students that they are to engage in silent reading. They can choose any book from the classroom library. With little enthusiasm each student selects a book. Within 5 minutes the disruptive behavior begins. Charlie pinches George; Mary reports that Mike is pulling her hair; Fred and Martin are using their desks as drums; Gloria is blowing kisses at Larry; Sharon, Pat, and Carol are giggling; Walter is asleep; Mrs. Hamilton is angry.

Maybe if Mrs. Hamilton knew something about methods of decreasing disruptive behavior, her rainy day recesses could be filled with sunshine.

Mr. Bell hates teaching, schools, students, other teachers, and most of all, his principal, whom he refers to as "the superintendent's flunky." Mr. Bell never wanted to be a teacher. But after failing premed, prelaw, and biology, his college advisor counseled him into education. After completing college, Mr. Bell planned to teach a year or two and begin another career. That was 15 years ago.

At Washington High School where he teaches physical science, Mr. Bell is viewed as the most negative person on the faculty. His colleagues tend to avoid him, especially in the faculty lounge, because of his constant complaining. He complains about the following: the school not being clean; teachers trying to act as young as their students; how dumb the students are; the limited exposure the faculty has to the world; a lack of materials with which to work; crime on the streets; drugs; sex; athletic program expenses; overpaid administrators; the do-nothing union; school board members being afraid of the superintendent; and so on.

Maybe if the faculty and principal knew something about methods of decreasing unacceptable behavior, the teacher's lounge would provide a positive and relaxing environment.

During the course of a single school day, a teacher may observe a number of behaviors that should be either decreased in frequency or eliminated. These examples include:

- ☐ Rusty's incessant talking
- ☐ Richard's constant bullying
- ☐ Mary's endless complaining
- ☐ Barbara's inability to keep her hands off things and people
- ☐ Martin's thumb sucking

In this chapter several methods of decreasing and eliminating behavior are discussed and exemplified. These are (1) extinction, (2) time-out, (3) satiation, (4) punishment, (5) reinforcement of incompatible behaviors, and (6) desensitization.

CHAPTER OBJECTIVES

After completing this chapter, you will be able to do the following:

1. Define extinction.
2. Describe and exemplify the major forms of time-out.
3. Characterize satiation.
4. Describe the various forms of punishment and discuss their ethical application.
5. Explain reinforcement of incompatible behaviors techniques.
6. Characterize desensitization techniques for classroom application.

Extinction

The discontinuation or withholding of the reinforcer of a behavior that has previously been reinforcing it is called *extinction*. This process is also known as systematic ignoring (Hall & Hall, 1980a). (This process is also discussed in Chapter 2.)

EXAMPLE ■ Timmy was constantly attempting to obtain Mr. Calm's attention in class by jumping up and down in his seat, frantically waving his hand, and whispering in a loud voice, "Mr. Calm, Mr. Calm, me, me, I know."

Mr. Calm knew he would have to change his name to Mr. Storm if this behavior did not stop or at least decrease in frequency. In an effort to retain his composure and aid Timmy, he commenced to study the situation.

Baseline observation data indicated that Timmy exhibited the target behavior an average of 8 times per day, or 40 times during the 1-week baseline data-collecting phase. During this phase Mr. Calm also collected data on his personal overt reactions to the unacceptable behavior. He discovered that 90% of the time he responded to the behavior by either permitting Timmy to answer the question, telling the child to be quiet and sit still, or signaling his disapproval nonverbally. Regardless of his specific reaction, Mr. Calm realized that he was *attending* to Timmy's attention-getting behavior.

Mr. Calm devised an intervention whereby he *would not* reinforce the behavior with his attention and would thus extinguish it. He would only respond to Timmy when he was exhibiting acceptable behavior in response to questions directed to the class.

As indicated in Figure 5.1, the behavior was extinguished within 2 weeks, although there were brief periods of regression thereafter.

Timmy's behavior (attempts to obtain attention) increased during the days immediately following the implementation of the intervention. This increase in the target behavior appeared to be an attempt by the child to defend his method for obtaining attention against the loss of effectiveness. This phenomenon known as an "extinction burst" is discussed in detail in Chapter 2, and the reader is referred to that section for further clarification. ■

As demonstrated in the case of Timmy, extinction techniques, when properly applied, result in a gradual decrease in the target behavior and its eventual elimination.

Extinction is only as effective as the teacher or parent is consistent and persistent in implementation of the intervention. The most effective approach to extinguishing behavior that has been previously reinforced is ignoring that behavior. This is easier said than done. Most of us are conditioned to the point that we find it difficult to ignore inappropriate behavior. But to ignore a behavior means exactly that— to totally and consistently ignore the target behavior. We are aware that there are some behaviors so serious that they cannot be ignored. However, if the individual is not inflicting pain to himself or others or disrupting the ongoing classroom program, then extinction may be the intervention of choice.

The following are some guidelines for those wishing to apply extinction:

1. When the target behavior is exhibited, remain impassive; give no indication that you are aware of the behavior.
2. Continue whatever activity you are presently doing.
3. If the behavior persists, turn your back and walk away.

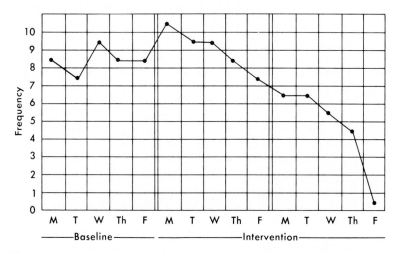

FIGURE 5.1
Frequency of Timmy's attention-getting behavior before and during the intervention.

Time-Out

In general, time-out is the removal of a child from an apparently reinforcing setting to a presumably nonreinforcing setting for a specified and limited period of time. Time-out is "time away from positive reinforcement" (Powell & Powell, 1982). According to Cuenin and Harris (1986), the definition of time-out includes two important factors: (1) time-out is contingent upon the exhibition of the target behavior, and (2) a discrepancy that is meaningful to the student exists between the time-in and time-out environments. Such removal can effectively decrease a target behavior (Hall & Hall, 1980b). Time-out is a frequently used behavior management intervention. In a questionnaire survey of preschool teachers and teachers of students with behavioral disorders in Kansas and Nebraska, Zabel (1986) found that 70% of her sample applied some form of time-out in the classroom. Teachers of young children used time-out more frequently than teachers of older children.

Harris (1985) noted five types of time-out: (1) isolation, (2) exclusion, (3) contingent observation, (4) removal of reinforcing stimulus conditions, and (5) ignoring. Systematic ignoring or extinction is discussed in the previous section. According to Lewellen (1980), there are three types of time-out: (1) observational, (2) exclusion, and (3) seclusion.

Observational time-out is a procedure in which the student is withdrawn from a reinforcing situation by doing one of the following: (1) placing him or her on the outer perimeter of the activity, where the child can see and hear the activity, but not participate in it, (2) requesting the child to place his or her head on the desk (called "head-down"), (3) removing activity materials, or (4) eliminating or reducing response maintenance stimuli, for example, room illumination.

Exclusion is a procedure in which the student leaves a reinforcing situation to a presumed nonreinforcing situation while remaining in the classroom. The student is not allowed to observe the group. An example is placing a screen between the student and the group.

Seclusion is a procedure that makes use of a "time-out room." In this situation the student leaves the classroom and goes to an isolated room.

EXAMPLE   ■   Benji is a hyperactive child in first grade. The boy was having difficulty remaining in his seat and refraining from impulsive grabbing of persons and objects near him. He was also appropriating and ingesting his classmates' lunches. Benji's teacher realized that these behaviors were interfering with his classroom progress and that of his classmates. She attempted several procedures to help Benji control his behavior. Among these were verbal reprimands, ignoring the inappropriate behavior and reinforcing appropriate behavior, and peer pressure. Observation data revealed that none of these interventions was effective, although her efforts were sufficient.

A behavior management consultant observed Benji and recommended time-out as a potentially effective intervention. Together, the teacher and the consultant decided that *each time Benji left his seat, he was to be sent to time-out for 2 minutes.*

This intervention necessitated defining and specifying several factors:

1. Out-of-seat behavior was defined as any time Benji's posterior was not in contact with his chair.
2. When the unacceptable behavior did occur, the teacher's aide was to escort Benji to the time-out area. Benji was to remain in time-out for 2 minutes; during this time he had to be quiet and seated.
3. After the time-out period Benji would return to the group. There would be no discussion or reprimand.
4. Benji's desk and chair were relocated in the classroom to ensure that he would not participate in unacceptable behavior such as grabbing people and lunches without leaving his seat.
5. A time-out area with a chair was arranged in the corner of the classroom. The time-out area was constructed by rearranging two 5-drawer filing cabinets. A chair was provided outside the area for the aide, who was to monitor Benji whenever he was in time-out.

The intervention was imposed, and although the behavior did not decrease immediately, significant progress was observed during the first months, as indicated in Figures 5.2 and 5.3.

Benji's out-of-seat behavior was brought under control within a period of several months. However, it remains an occasional problem; therefore time-out procedures remain in effect. ■

Ribbon time-out is a nonexclusionary procedure (Foxx & Shapiro, 1978). It may be applied as an individual or group contingency. While the individual or group is behaving appropriately, a ribbon or other symbol is visible (a ribbon may be worn by a child or the group may see a ribbon on the bulletin board). While the ribbon is visible, positive reinforcement is available to the student or group. If the student or group act inappropriately, the ribbon is removed and reinforcement is not available for a specific predetermined period of time. The ribbon is returned and reinforcement is again available after the nonreinforcement time expires.

Salend and Gordon (1987) researched the effects of an interdependent group contingency ribbon time-out procedure to decrease the inappropriate verbalizations of two groups of students who attended a resource room. They found that the ribbon time-out procedure effectively decreased inappropriate verbalizations. In an earlier study, Foxx and Shapiro (1978) conducted an experiment using ribbon time-out with severely retarded children. They found that on average, the children misbehaved 42% during baseline, 32% during a reinforcement-only intervention, and only 6% during the ribbon time-out condition.

The time-out intervention includes the reinforcement of acceptable behavior. A child who is performing or approximating the desired behavior in the classroom should be reinforced for these efforts.

The effectiveness of time-out as an intervention is contingent on several factors (Cuenin & Harris, 1986):

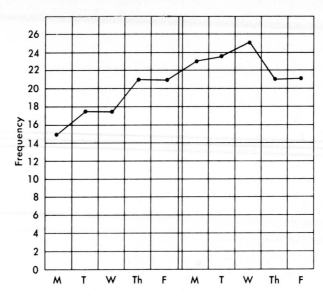

FIGURE 5.2
Frequency of Benji's out-of-seat behavior before and during the first week of intervention.

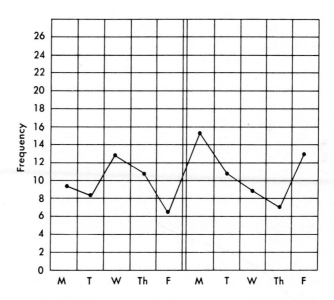

FIGURE 5.3
Frequency of Benji's out-of-seat behavior during the fourth and fifth weeks of intervention.

- Characteristics of the individual child
- Teacher's consistent application of the intervention
- Child's understanding of the rules of time-out
- Characteristics of the time-out area
- Duration of time-out
- Evaluation of the effectiveness of the intervention

Characteristics of the Child

The practitioner must know the characteristics of the individual child before implementing a time-out intervention. For the acting-out, aggressive, group-oriented child, time-out may be very effective. Such children wish to be with the group and attended to by the teacher. Consequently time-out is not rewarding. However, for a withdrawn, passive, solitary child who is prone to daydreaming, time-out may be rewarding and would be contraindicated. These children may engage in their own little world while in the time-out area.

EXAMPLE   ■ Cheryl, a 6-year-old girl, is in Mr. Roy's class for behaviorally handicapped children. Cheryl is quiet, shy, and withdrawn; she frequently engages in daydreaming.

Mr. Roy reads about a new technique for behavior problems in a popular magazine. This technique was time-out. He decided to impose the intervention on Cheryl in an effort to force her to participate in class discussions and activities. He planned to put her in time-out each time she was inattentive in class.

Cheryl appeared to enjoy the opportunity to go to time-out for 3 minutes. Her rate of inattentiveness increased dramatically immediately after the intervention was implemented. She evidently appreciated the opportunity to legitimately participate in her dream world. ■

This example is a stark illustration of an abuse of time-out by its use with a child whose behavior was reinforced by the intervention.

EXAMPLE   ■ Richard, an 11-year-old boy in Ms. Jones' physical education class, was constantly arguing and fighting with his teacher and classmates about the rules of a game or how an activity should be conducted. This behavior occurred particularly when he was losing. Observation indicated that Richard truly enjoyed the activities and the company of his peers and Ms. Jones. However, the behavior was obtrusive and had to be eliminated for the sake of the group.

Ms. Jones selected time-out as a potentially effective intervention. Before the technique was imposed, it was decided that each time Richard started to argue or fight during PE, he was to be sent to time-out. The time-out was out of view but not out of hearing of class activities. Under these conditions Richard's disruptions were eliminated very rapidly. ■

Time-out in this situation was effective because Richard preferred to be with his classmates and teacher rather than in the less stimulating time-out area.

Teacher's Consistency of Application

If time-out is to be applied as an intervention with a particular child, it must be used with consistency over a predetermined period of time (Brantner & Doherty, 1983). Frequently teachers are inconsistent in their application of time-out. As a result, the child becomes confused, and the wrong behavior is reinforced. This situation is analogous to the confusion that results when a child is forced on Monday, Wednesday, and Friday to eat green vegetables under pain of death at the hands of Father, but on Tuesday and Thursday Father is not so insistent, and on the weekend at Grandma's house, the child does not have to eat green vegetables at all.

Child's Understanding of the Rules

Children should know specifically what behaviors are not acceptable in their classrooms. In addition, they should know the consequences of exhibiting the forbidden behaviors. If time-out is to be used as an intervention, the rules for time-out should be communicated to the children; they should be posted and reviewed frequently. The rules assist the teacher in trying to remain consistent and fair in the application of the intervention.

Time-out should never be used whimsically with children; that is, one day a child is sent to time-out for talking in class, the next day for chewing gum, the next day for not completing a homework assignment, and so on. Such misuse will confuse the child and reduce the effectiveness of the intervention.

When time-out is imposed on the behavior of very young children the teacher is often confronted with an additional problem. Frequently it is impossible to communicate verbally to such children the rules governing time-out and its imposition. In this situation it is necessary to initiate the program and demonstrate the intervention through implementation.

Time-out is not a technique that includes lecturing, reprimanding, or scolding before, during, or after the intervention. These techniques, although frequently used in everyday classroom exchanges, can provide unwanted reinforcement to the child. The teacher may wish to include a warning stage in the time-out procedures. When the inappropriate behavior occurs, the child may be redirected to the appropriate behavior. If within 10 or 15 seconds the child does not comply and return to task, then he or she is directed to time-out (Cuenin & Harris, 1985). Time must be taken to explain why time-out is warranted, but the explanation should be brief and explicit. Going to time-out should not be a matter for debate between child and teacher. As the program continues, these explanations need only be reminders of the rules and consequences of exhibiting certain behaviors. Nelson and Rutherford (1983) noted two problems when a child is forced to go to time-out: (1) the physical contact may unwittingly reinforce the child's inappropriate behavior, and (2) the teacher may simply be unable to physically control the child.

EXAMPLE ■ Ms. Smith selected time-out as an intervention to decrease Elmo's talking in class. Each time Elmo talked out of turn in class, Ms. Smith would grab him by the arm and drag him to the time-out area. There she would proceed to babble at him (rather incoherently) for about 10 minutes. She would always conclude with the statement, "Now, be quiet for two minutes." She would then proceed to stare at Elmo for two minutes. At the end of that time should would say, "Now, get back to your seat."

   Ms. Smith's intervention is an example of the improper use of time-out. The results were as expected:

1. Elmo continued to talk out in class because, although he was not particularly interested in Ms. Smith's lectures, he was pleased with his classmates' reactions to her behavior.
2. Ms. Smith's classroom group certainly enjoyed the circus.
3. Ms. Smith suffered from nervous tension.   ■

Characteristics of the Time-Out Area

Care must be taken in the selection of the time-out area. Teachers should avoid selecting an area that may appear nonreinforcing but is in effect reinforcing to children. For instance, placing a child in the corridor for time-out may be extremely reinforcing. In the hallway the child has an opportunity to communicate with everyone who passes. In addition, the child is provided with a legitimate opportunity to get out of the classroom and assignments.

   Another commonly used but generally ineffective area for time-out is the principal's office. The office has been demonstrated to be one of the most stimulating and reinforcing areas in the school for the majority of children. In the office the child has an opportunity to observe peaked parents, out-of-sorts mailmen, and anxious administrators in their natural human state. In addition, the child has opportunities to pick up the latest school news and gossip for dissemination among peers and teachers.

   Many administrators do not understand the concept of time-out, and on occasion the child is given various clerical tasks to perform in the office, such as stapling, folding, carrying messages, and making announcements. The child who is in time-out just happens to be available when a body is needed to do something; the reason for the child's presence in the office is not considered when the task is assigned. An investigation of the use of the office for time-out would probably reveal that it is a far more attractive alternative for the child than sitting in the classroom reading, writing, or doing math problems.

   The time-out area should be as nonreinforcing as possible and devoid of extraneous visual and aural stimulation. In most classroom settings it is not necessary to construct a time-out room, although this practice is followed in many special classes for severely disturbed children. A chair in an out-of-the-way corner of the classroom is adequate. In some settings, room dividers, screens, filing cabinets, or the backs of bookcases can be arranged to construct the walls of the time-out area. It is necessary to ensure that the area is supervised, safe, properly lighted, and ventilated. A chair may be placed in the time-out area. However, many children, especially young children, prefer to sit on the floor, and this practice should be permitted.

The area selected should be (1) away from high traffic, (2) away from doors and windows, (3) out of the other children's view, and (4) within view of the observer.

It is recommended that a chair be placed outside the area for the observer-supervisor. A paraprofessional can serve as observer-supervisor if properly instructed. However, in cases where a paraprofessional is not available for this duty, the area must be in a location that permits the teacher to observe it from his or her teaching station. Figure 5.4 is a diagram of a time-out area in a classroom.

Duration of Time-Out

Time-out loses its effectiveness as an intervention if a child is left in the setting for too lengthy or too brief a period of time (Harris, 1985; Brantner & Doherty, 1983). Time-out should be limited to approximately 2 minutes after the child has

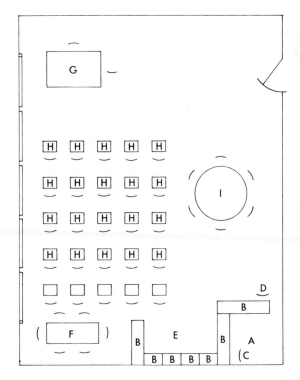

FIGURE 5.4
Classroom with time-out area. A, time-out area; B, bookcase; C, child's chair; D, supervisor's chair; E, library; F, science or game area; G, teacher's station; H, students' desks; I, discussion center.

quieted. Four or 5 minutes in time-out should be a maximum except under extraordinary circumstances. Never should a child remain in time-out for more than 10 minutes. Consistency in the duration of the time-out period is sought. It is strongly recommended that the teacher use an inexpensive, bell-type egg timer to ensure that the time limit of time-out is not violated. The timer alerts both teacher and child to the exact moment the time-out period expires. In addition, it reassures the child that the teacher is being fair in the application of the intervention.

Evaluation of Effectiveness

Records of time-out incidents should be recorded and analyzed by the teacher or parent. Teachers should prepare a log such as the one in Figure 5.5. A copy of this log is provided in the back of the text.

The log should include (1) the time the child was sent or escorted to time-out, (2) the time the child returned to the activity, (3) any incidents during time-out, (4) the activity taking place just before the child was sent to time-out, and (5) the activity to which the child returned after time-out.

The log should be posted on the exterior wall of the time-out area. The teacher or parent evaluates the overall effectiveness of the technique by studying the child's time-out record. In addition, the records, if closely analyzed, provide clues as to why time-out is an effective or ineffective intervention in a particular case.

EXAMPLE   ■   Mr. Sherman was recently called to a day school for severely disturbed boys to consult on the case of Hector, a 14-year-old student. When Hector enrolled in the school 2 years ago, he was exposed to time-out as a behavior control intervention. During the following 2 years, time-out was effective in modifying much of Hector's behavior.

The boy had progressed to a point of being sent to time-out on an average of only once each day. However, he had never progressed beyond this point. His daily disruption prohibited his integration into a regular classroom.

Fortunately, at the day school precise time-out records were maintained for all children and were available for study. An analysis of Hector's log indicated that he was in time-out each day immediately after the teacher announced that it was time for math. Although math time varied, it was discovered that Hector's disruptive time varied with it.

Mr. Sherman suggested that for Hector, time-out was more reinforcing than math; that is, it was the lesser of two evils. In an effort to test this hypothesis, Hector's math period was eliminated; Hector no longer went to time-out.

Hector's skill in math has progressed acceptably under the guidance of a tutor. The tutor assists him individually during regular math periods.   ■

It is highly recommended that the child return to the task that was interrupted by the time-out. Of course, the feasibility of the child's returning to the interrupted task will vary with the structure of the class schedule and activities. If the child is returned to and held responsible for the task being engaged in before time-out, the child learns that time-out cannot be used as a means of avoiding assignments

Time-out Log

Child _____

Supervisor _____

Date _____

Time		Behavior before time-out	Behavior during time-out	Behavior after time-out
Enters	Leaves			

FIGURE 5.5
Data log to be posted at time-out area.

149

he or she finds difficult or simply dislikes. This recommendation assumes that the assigned task is appropriate to the child's learning level and competency.

The following examples will further clarify the process of time-out.

EXAMPLES ■ Ms. Drake was confronted with the problem of Donald striking other children in the stomach. She was so distressed by this behavior that she was about to reciprocate in kind. Ms. Drake had tried every intervention she knew to change the behavior (and a few she didn't know she knew), but they only increased it.

At an in-service workshop, time-out as a technique to decrease inappropriate behavior was described. After absorbing the available knowledge about time-out and becoming somewhat comfortable with the concept, Ms. Drake implemented it in her classroom.

First, a set of "classroom rules of behavior" was presented to the children. Next, a time-out area was designed, and the concept of time-out was introduced and explained to the group.

The new rules included "Do not strike other children." Persons exhibiting this behavior would be in time-out for 3 minutes in an area located in a corner of the classroom. The area was screened off, devoid of visual stimuli, and unfurnished with the exception of a chair. A child in time-out could neither see nor be seen by classmates (Figure 5.4). After the rules were communicated and apparently understood by all members of the class, time-out was implemented.

When Donald struck another child, he was quietly escorted to the time-out area for 3 minutes. After sitting quietly in the area for that period of time, Donald was asked why he was sent to time-out. If his response indicated that he understood the reason, he was instructed to return to his regular seat. However, if his response indicated that he did not understand the reason for being sent to time-out, it was briefly explained to him. He was then instructed to return to his seat. After several repetitions of the time-out routine, both Donald and Ms. Drake became aware of the potency of the intervention.

Donald's baseline and intervention data are presented in Figure 5.6. ■

■ Mr. Seltz had used every method possible to decrease Shauna's unacceptable burping behavior in the classroom. Finally time-out was used as a technique to eliminate this behavior. Shauna was told that each time she burped in class she was to go to the time-out area for 2 minutes. Mr. Seltz reinforced Shauna with attention and praise whenever she performed appropriately in the class. The baseline and intervention data for the behavior are presented in Figure 5.7. The data clearly indicate that Shauna preferred to cease burping rather than be placed in time-out. ■

As indicated in the examples, time-out can work effectively if it is properly applied. When implementing a program, the new practitioner of behavior modification should adhere closely to the suggestions in this section.

Satiation

Satiation is the decreasing or elimination of an inappropriate behavior as a result of continued and increased reinforcement of the behavior. Satiation is a more common occurrence than is generally realized. Because it is so common, we are frequently unaware of its effect on our behavior.

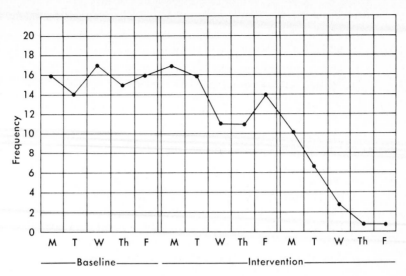

FIGURE 5.6
Frequency of Donald's striking behavior before and during the intervention.

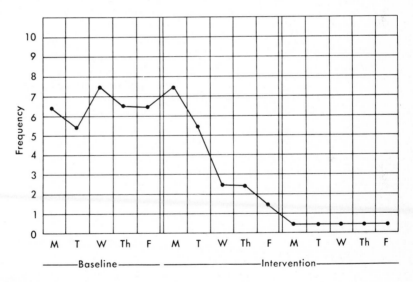

FIGURE 5.7
Frequency of Shauna's burping behavior before and during the intervention.

Many people engage in certain sports and recreational activities (golf, baseball, camping, cards, and the like) with such frequency and regularity that they become satiated; that is, they discontinue the activity.

Bob loved (not just liked, but loved) chocolate ice cream. He would snitch it from the freezer any time of the day or night. His wife, Louise, scolded and deprived him in an effort to decrease his intake. One day, with great ceremony, Louise presented

Bob with 2 gallons of chocolate ice cream. He was given ice cream at every opportunity, day and night, until he became satiated. Bob now prefers gelatin.

All of us have remembrances from our college days of the class hero who wished to gain immortality in the books on world records. This individual is the one who today hates bananas, pizza, blueberry pie, goldfish, raw eggs, frankfurters, and a score of other questionable edibles.

Perhaps everyone reaches the point of satiation in relation to some behavior. Grandma used to call this phenomenon "getting too much of good thing."

The continued and increased reinforcement of a behavior can result in a decrease in that behavior. The central factor that influences the effectiveness of satiation as an intervention is the reinforcement schedule.

As discussed in Chapter 2, a variable reinforcement schedule is more resistant to satiation than a continuous or fixed reinforcement schedule. Consequently the key to successful application of satiation as an intervention is *continuous or fixed reinforcement schedule*.

The following example will clarify the application of a satiation intervention in the classroom.

EXAMPLE ■ Charles, a student in Ms. Barker's classroom, borrowed paper without permission from his teacher's and classmates' desks. Ms. Barker wanted to decrease this behavior. She tried techniques such as reprimanding, parent counseling, and having Charles counseled by the school psychologist. Nothing appeared to work. The school psychologist suggested trying a satiation procedure. Ms. Barker was impressed and willing to try any technique that might prove successful. She decided to implement the satiation program.

She placed a ream of paper on her desk at the beginning of the school day. After the children had arrived and morning exercises were completed, Ms. Barker gave Charles three sheets of paper. Four minutes later she returned to Charles's desk and gave him three more sheets of paper; 4 minutes later Charles received three more sheets of paper and so on throughout the day. This process continued day after day until Charles's possession of paper lost its value to him. Charles began to tell Ms. Barker that he did not need or want any paper; he had more than he could use to complete his assignments for the next 6 months. Figure 5.8 presents the baseline and intervention data for Charles's behavior.

Charles's behavior was placed on a fixed reinforcement schedule. The behavior rapidly decreased because of satiation. ■

The process of satiation can be a very helpful tool in decreasing certain inappropriate classroom behaviors, such as pencil sharpening, putting paper in a wastebasket, getting drinks of water, and constantly requesting the time.

Punishment

Briefly discussed in Chapter 2, punishment is perhaps the most misunderstood and emotionally explosive of the behavior modification techniques. It is an intervention used to decrease or eliminate an inappropriate behavior.

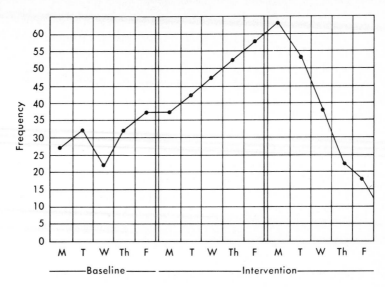

FIGURE 5.8
Frequency of Charles's "borrowing" behavior before and during the intervention.

There are two distinct forms of punishment that the teacher or parent may consider for application with students. As commonly understood and applied by parents and teachers, punishment is the *addition* of an aversive stimulus (something unpleasant) as a consequence of a behavior. Punishment of this form can be either physical or psychological. Examples are a spanking (physical punishment) or a scolding or reprimand, extra work, after school detention, or an undesirable additional task (psychological punishment).

The other form of punishment is the *subtraction* of something the child perceives as desirable. Examples are the taking away of television privileges, late bedtime hours, freedom to leave the house, or tokens and points.

The subtraction of previously earned tokens or points in the token economy intervention presented in Chapter 4 is called *response-cost.* In this situation students are informed that not only can they earn points for privileges and goods, but if they exhibit specific unacceptable behaviors, they can lose points. A specific number of points are subtracted from the total for each transgression. In a word, the child is punished for exhibiting specific inappropriate behaviors.

Punishment by deprivation or response-cost is generally considered less harmful to the child and more effective intervention than the addition of physical or psychological aversive stimuli.

The short-term effectiveness of punishment for decreasing behaviors is difficult if not impossible to dispute (Wood, 1978). Punishment is *effective* for obtaining short-term goals. However, other interventions such as extinction and ignoring the behavior are probably more effective for attaining permanent long-range changes.

Wood and Lakin (1978) presented several reasons for avoiding the use of punishment:

1. It does not eliminate but merely suppresses the behavior.
2. It does not provide a model for the desired acceptable behavior.
3. Aggression on the part of the practitioner presents an undesirable model.
4. The emotional results of punishment may be fear, tension, stress, or withdrawal.
5. The child's resulting frustration may result in further deviation.

In addition, physical punishment may result in physical harm to the child, although such harm is unplanned.

Punishment in the perception of the punished child is frequently associated with the punisher rather than with the unacceptable behavior. As a result, the punished child's reactions may be avoidance and dislike of the punisher rather than a change in behavior. Teachers who acknowledge that they are in effect behavioral models for their students will avoid assuming the role of punisher.

It may be helpful at this point to clarify some of the punishments that are frequently applied in school and homes. The following is a list of commonly used punishments.

☐   Denying participation in scheduled activities (games, field trips).
☐   Denying snacks (milk, cookies, candy).
☐   Physical punishment (paddlings, spankings, slaps).
☐   Verbal punishment (scoldings, reprimands, sarcasm, derogation, curses).
☐   Having the child stand apart from the others (in the corner, hallway).
☐   Having the child wear a sign ("I am a bad boy").

Members of the teaching profession seem to be very efficient in developing and applying harsh physical and psychological punishment. However, a variety of other methods of behavior management are available for the teacher's use. Punishment, especially harsh physical and psychological punishment, should not be used in schools or classrooms. "All reasonable positive alternatives should have been considered, if not actually tried before decision is made to use an aversive procedure" (Wood, 1978, p. 120).

If punishment is to be used, the teacher or parent should adhere to the following guidelines:

1. Specify and communicate the punishable behavior to the children by means of classroom rules for behavior.
2. Post the rules where the children can see them; review them with the group frequently.
3. Provide models of acceptable behavior.
4. Apply the punishment immediately.
5. Apply the punishment consistently, not whimsically.
6. Be fair in using the punishment (what is good for Peter is good for Pauline).
7. Impose the punishment impersonally. Do not punish when you are angry or otherwise out of self-control.

The following is an example of the misuse of punishment:

EXAMPLE ■ Paul, an 11-year-old boy in Ms. Woods's classroom was frequently punching other boys during recess. Ms. Woods told Paul he would receive two swats with the paddle each time he hit another child.

Paul went to morning recess and within 10 minutes had punched three children and the playground supervisor. Paul was returned to the classroom. Nothing was said or done about his behavior.

At about 2:30 PM, Mr. Brinks, the assistant principal, arrived at the classroom door. Paul was called into the hallway. Mr. Brinks struck him eight times with the paddle (two swats for each person). Ms. Woods observed the punishment as a witness.

After accomplishing this task, Mr. Brinks returned to his office without comment; Ms. Woods returned to the classroom without comment; Paul returned to his seat, crying and confused. ■

The absurdity of this example is that it happened at all and continues to happen.

EXAMPLES ■ In the Meyers' kitchen is a cookie jar for petty cash. On the first day of each month Mr. Meyer places $50 in bills and coins in the cookie jar. The rules for removing money from the jar are (1) anyone can take up to $5 at any time for legitimate reasons and (2) the purpose for which the money is used, the date and the borrower's signature are written on a slip of paper and put in the cookie jar.

At the end of each month Mr. Meyer totals the amounts of the slips. The total is seldom $50 because their teenage son, Herman, takes $15 to $20 without putting a slip in the jar.

The Meyers have discussed this behavior with Herman several times without effect. It was decided that the next time the behavior occurred Herman would no longer be allowed to take money from the petty cash fund. Herman considers his parents' action cruel and unusual punishment. However, he is complying with their wishes. ■

■ Mr. Sayers is a master at applying sarcasm and degradation. He is quick and devastating with his tongue, much to the discomfort of his students. His favorite epithets are "stupid," "dumbbell," "idiot," "meathead," and "dink."

One day Rosemary was clowning around in English class. This behavior greatly disturbed Mr. Sayers. He grabbed 17-year-old Rosemary by the arm, shook her, and called her a "dink." The girl was very embarrassed and began to cry. Encouraged by her reaction, Mr. Sayers added a few more names to the list and caused the other students to laugh.

This is an example of a teacher losing self-control and perhaps causing psychological damage to a student. Mr. Sayers was unaware, or so he claimed, of the contemporary meaning of "dink." However, Rosemary and her peers were very aware of its meaning. ■

The authors are irrevocably opposed to the use of corporal punishment, whether it is paddling, slapping, spanking, or using a cattle prod or electric wand. We are opposed to psychological punishment, which at minimum can erode the already fragile self-concept of the developing child. If punishment must be implemented, two forms are preferred: loss of privileges and reprimands (Shea & Bauer, 1987).

Loss of Privileges

Unlike the vast majority of interventions discussed in this text, loss of privileges is a negative behavior management intervention, though its results may be positive. Loss of privileges is also known as deprivation of privileges or response-cost, which was explained in the previous section. When the loss of privileges is applied, a portion of the child's present or future positive reinforcers are taken away following the exhibition of the target behavior.

This intervention is most effective when the privilege the child loses is a natural or logical consequence of the inappropriate behavior. For example, if a child refuses to work on assignments during class time, then the privilege of free time is lost. Likewise, if a child is late for the school bus, then he misses it. It is not always possible to impose natural consequences; thus, the teacher on occasion must impose an artificial consequence. In an artificial consequence, the relationship between the privileges lost and the behavior exhibited is arbitrary. It exists only because the teacher decides it will exist. Such artificial relationships must be carefully explained to the child.

When using loss of privileges the teacher has several guidelines to follow:

1. Be sure the child understands the relationship between the target behavior and the privilege to be lost.
2. Be sure the child knows the punishable behavior and the consequence of exhibiting it.
3. When possible use natural or logical consequences.
4. Apply the loss of privilege interventions fairly.
5. Avoid warning, nagging, or threatening.
6. Do not debate the punishable behaviors, the rules, or the punishment once these have been established.
7. Do not become emotionally involved. Don't feel guilty when the child loses a privilege. If the child knows the rules and the consequences of the behavior, then he or she has chosen to break the rule and suffer the consequences.
8. Be consistent.
9. Reinforce appropriate behavior; do not emphasize inappropriate behaviors only.

EXAMPLES ■ Patricia is head cheerleader at Saint Rudolph's High School. She greatly enjoyed leading cheers at basketball and football games. Patricia is also tardy for English class about 3 times a week. Her English teacher, Sister Mary, is very concerned that Patricia will fail the course if her attendance does not improve. Sister talked to the principal, Sister Sharon, and they agreed that Patricia would be deprived of the privilege of cheering at one game for each time she was tardy for English class. The rule was explained to Patricia and implemented. After missing two games during the next 3 weeks, Patricia's tardiness ended. ■

■ Thomas, a salesperson for a major computer software firm, owned a 1990 Benz 535SEL and loved to drive down the interstate highways at 80 and 85 miles per hour. He had been caught by the highway patrol on three occasions and fined. On the fourth occasion, the officer took away his driving privilege for 30 days. Thomas still enjoys driving fast but controls this urge. ∎

∎ Kevin, who is 17 years old, is allowed to stay out on Friday and Saturday nights until midnight. He consistently arrives home (and awakens his parents) at 1 or 2 o'clock in the morning. Needless to say, this behavior has caused many heated discussions. It is finally agreed by Kevin and his parents that for each minute he is late arriving home, 5 minutes will be subtracted from the curfew time on the next evening he goes out with his friends. After losing several hours during the course of the following few weeks, Kevin's behavior improved. ∎

Reprimands

Another form of punishment is the reprimand (Houten, 1980). To be reprimanded is to be scolded, "yelled at," "bawled out," or otherwise verbally chastised for exhibiting an inappropriate target behavior. Reprimands are useful when a child is engaging in behavior that necessitates immediate action because it is potentially harmful to self, others, or property.

It is suggested that reprimands be used selectively in response to specific behaviors. A reprimand should include a statement of an appropriate alternative to the inappropriate behavior.

The following are some guidelines for the effective use of reprimands:

1. Be specific. Tell the child exactly what inappropriate behavior is being reprimanded.
2. Reprimand the behavior, do not derogate the child.
3. Reprimand immediately.
4. Be firm in voice and physical demeanor.
5. If either the child or others may be harmed by the behavior, remove the child.
6. If necessary, back up the reprimand with loss of privileges.
7. Encourage the child to behave appropriately and include a statement of the appropriate behavior in the reprimand.
8. Be calm.
9. When it's over, it's over. Do not keep reminding the child of past inappropriate behavior; avoid embarrassing the child in the presence of peers and others. To this end, use nonverbal reprimands: shake your head "no," point your finger, frown, and so on.
10. Always observe the child's reaction to the reprimand to determine if it is aversive.

EXAMPLES ∎ Margie! Turn off the lathe. Do not turn it on again until you have put on your safety glasses and removed that loose scarf from your neck. Please review the safety rules. ∎

∎ Donald! Sit up straight and put your feet on the floor while you are typing. Proper posture will help your concentration and prevent back pain and physical discomfort in the future. ∎

- Mary! Put on your seatbelt. It is the law in Illinois and may save you from injury if we have an accident. ■

- Herm! Close the windows when you turn on the air conditioner. This will save electricity, which is very expensive. ■

Reinforcement of Incompatible Behaviors

At times it is necessary or desirable to decrease a behavior by systematically reinforcing a behavior that is in opposition to or incompatible with it. This intervention is called the process of reinforcing incompatible behaviors.

For instance, a teacher has two students in the classroom who are constantly bickering with each other. After analysis of the situation, it is proposed that the behavior would decrease if one of the students' seats were relocated to the opposite side of the room. The students are separated, and the behavior decreases.

The assumption underlying the intervention in this example is that the distance between the seats is incompatible with the bickering.

The effectiveness of this intervention is heavily dependent on the selection of the two truly incompatible behaviors (sitting apart and bickering).

EXAMPLE   ■ For a major part of the school year, Mr. Weber had been trying to decrease Wallace's random walking about the classroom. All efforts appeared to have been in vain. It seemed that the more effort Mr. Weber put forth to modify Wallace's out-of-seat behavior, the more frequent it became. Evidently the attention Wallace received from Mr. Weber for being out of his seat was reinforcing.

As a last resort Mr. Weber decided to attempt the technique of reinforcing incompatible behaviors. To remain in one's seat would be incompatible with walking about the classroom. Mr. Weber decided to positively reinforce Wallace's in-seat behavior and ignore his out-of-seat behavior. Initially Wallace resisted the program. However, after a short time the out-of-seat behavior decreased and was eventually eliminated. Figure 5.9 represents the data collected on Wallace's behavior.

There is no known explanation for the recurrence of Wallace's out-of-seat behavior on the sixteenth and seventeenth days of the intervention. One possible explanation is that since the target behavior had not been exhibited for 2 days, Mr. Weber acted as though the behavior had been eliminated. He may have altered his response to either the behavior he was reinforcing or the behavior he was ignoring. ■

The classroom teacher could probably think of a number of other situations wherein reinforcing an incompatible behavior might decrease target behavior.

EXAMPLES   ■ John cannot be looking at the teacher and looking out the window at the same time. ■

- Paul cannot be standing in line for lunch and writing on his chair at the same time. ■

- David cannot be mowing the lawn and watching television at the same time. ■

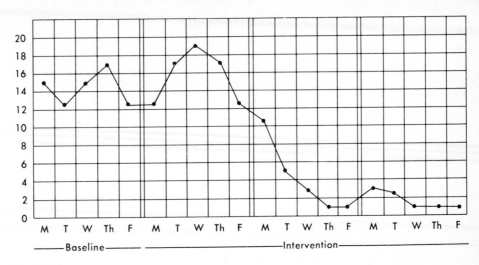

FIGURE 5.9
Frequency of Wallace's out-of-seat behavior before and during the intervention.

Desensitization

Desensitization, the process of systematically lessening a specific, learned fear or phobic reaction in an individual became a popular therapeutic technique in the second half of the 1970s. It was developed by Wolpe during the 1950s and 1960s.

> The desensitization method consists of presenting to the imagination of the deeply relaxed patient the feeblest item in a list of anxiety-evoking stimuli repeatedly, until no more anxiety is evoked. The next item of the list is presented, and so on, until eventually, even the strongest of the anxiety-evoking stimuli fails to evoke any stir of anxiety in the patient. It has consistently been found that at every stage of stimulus that evokes no anxiety when imagined in a state of relaxation will also evoke no anxiety when encountered in reality.*

As indicated by Wolpe, the process of desensitization has been demonstrated to be an effective technique when applied to individuals with fears and anxieties related to public speaking, school attendance, participation in large groups, water, animals, heights, flying, test taking, and the like.

The process of systematic desensitization, according to Wolpe, involves three phases or steps:

1. Training the subject in deep muscle relaxation
2. Constructing an anxiety-evoking hierarchy of stimuli
3. Counterposing relaxation and the anxiety-evoking stimuli

*From "The Systematic Desensitization Treatment of Neuroses" by J. Wolpe, 1961, *Journal of Nervous and Mental Diseases, 132,* pp. 189-203. Copyright 1961 by The Williams & Wilkins Co.

The importance of these three phases can not be overemphasized; they are interdependent.

The practitioner is *not* encouraged to apply systematic desensitization on the basis of the information provided in this text alone. Teachers and parents should study other sources and obtain the services of a behavior therapy consultant before implementing a desensitization intervention.

The following reports of research are presented to clarify the procedures and effects of systematic desensitization under various conditions with a variety of problems.

Kravetz and Forness (1971) reported an experiment with a 6½-year-old boy who was unable to verbalize in the classroom. Psychiatric and medical reports did not reveal any known reason for his not talking in the classroom. The child's school progress was poor; however, test results indicated that he had above-average potential. A desensitization intervention of 12 sessions (2 per week) was implemented to reduce the child's fear of speaking in class.

The anxiety-evoking stimulus hierarchy used in this study is presented here:

1. Reading alone to investigator;
2. Reading alone to roommate;
3. Reading to two classroom aides (repeated);
4. Reading to teacher and classroom aides (repeated);
5. Reading to teacher, classroom aides, and small group of classroom peers (repeated);
6. Reading to entire class;
7. Asking question or making comment at weekly ward meeting when all patients, teachers, and staff were present.*

The reader should note that steps 3, 4, and 5 were repeated during the behavior process. This desensitization program, combined with positive reinforcement, was successful in helping the boy overcome his fear of verbalizing in the classroom.

Deffenbacher and Kemper (1974) applied systematic desensitization in a program to reduce test-taking anxiety in 28 junior high school students. The group was composed of 12 girls and 16 boys. All of the students had been referred by either a counselor, their parents, or a teacher. The test-taking anxiety-evoking stimulus hierarchy used with these students included:

☐ You are attending a regular class session.
☐ You hear about someone who has a test.
☐ You are studying at home. You are reading a normal assignment.
☐ You are in class. The teacher announces a major exam in 2 weeks.
☐ You are at home studying. You are beginning to review and study for a test that is a week away.

---

*From "The Special Classroom as a Desensitization Setting" by R. Kravetz and S. Forness, 1971, *Exceptional Children, 37*, pp. 389-391. Copyright 1971 by The Council for Exceptional Children.

□ You are at home studying, and you are studying for the important test. It is now Tuesday and 3 days before the test on Friday.

□ You are at home studying and preparing for the upcoming exam. It is now Wednesday, 2 days before the test on Friday.

□ It is Thursday night, the night before the exam on Friday. You are talking with another student about the exam tomorrow.

□ It is the night before the exam, and you are home studying for it.

□ It is the day of the exam, and you have 1 hour left to study.

□ It is the day of the exam. You have been studying. You are now walking on your way to the test.

□ You are standing outside the test room talking with other students about the upcoming test.

□ You are sitting in the testing room waiting for the test to be passed out.

□ You are leaving the exam room, you are talking with other students about the test. Many of their answers do not agree with yours.

□ You are sitting in the classroom waiting for the graded test to be passed back by the teacher.

□ It's right before the test, and you hear a student ask a possible test question which you cannot answer.

□ You are taking the important test. While trying to think of an answer, you notice everyone around you writing rapidly.

□ While taking the test you come to a question you are unable to answer. You draw a blank.

□ You are in the important exam. The teacher announces 30 minutes remaining but you have an hour's work left.

□ You are in the important exam. The teacher announces 15 minutes remaining but you have an hour's work left.*

The desensitization treatment consisted of eight sessions (one per week) in groups of two to five students. The intervention effectively reduced test-taking anxiety.

Desensitization is a potent intervention that can be applied in a modified form by the teacher in the classroom. However, if desensitization is to be applied in the classroom, the following conditions must exist:

1. The teacher must have a positive interpersonal relationship with the child. The child must trust the teacher and be free to express fears in the teacher's presence.
2. The teacher must construct an anxiety-evoking stimulus hierarchy.
3. The teacher must be willing (and have adequate time) to accompany the child in the progression from the least to the most anxiety-evoking stimulus in the hierarchy.

*From "Systematic Desensitization of Test Anxiety in Junior High Students" by J. Deffenbacher and C. Kemper, 1974, *The School Counselor, 21,* pp. 216-222. Copyright 1974 by the American Personnel and Guidance Association. Reprinted with permission.

Under normal classroom conditions the desensitization process is time consuming. The teacher must be consistent and patient in the application of this intervention. It may be necessary to repeat some of the specific anxiety-evoking situations until their effect on the child has been eliminated.

EXAMPLES ■ David, a 5-year-old boy in Ms. Philly's class for children with behavior problems, was afraid of dogs. Whenever the boy saw a dog, he would crawl under the nearest object or person and scream until the animal disappeared from view.

This behavior made it impossible for David to go out on the playground during recess with his peers, to walk to and from school, or to play outdoors in his neighborhood.

Desensitization was suggested as a possible intervention. Ms. Philly thought it was an excellent idea but suggested that implementation be deferred until she knew David better. A stimulus hierarchy was constructed, but the intervention was held in abeyance until 3 months after the beginning of the school year.

The following anxiety-evoking stimulus hierarchy was used to reduce David's fear of dogs:

1. Pictures of dogs were hung on the walls of the classroom. The pictures were initially placed as far away from David's desk as possible. As desensitization continued, they were moved nearer to David.
2. Pictures of dogs were observed by David in motion pictures and filmstrips.
3. Pictures of dogs were affixed to David's desk and notebook covers.
4. David observed dogs playing in the school yard from his classroom window.
5. David observed dogs playing in the school yard from the door of the school.
6. David observed dogs playing in the school yard as he stood at a distance that was systematically decreased.
7. David permitted dogs to walk past him in the school yard.

At *no time* during the desensitization process was David encouraged to touch or pet a dog. This precaution was taken simply because *some* dogs do bite *some* children.

During the desensitization process, Ms. Philly removed David from an anxiety-evoking situation whenever he manifested the slightest discomfort. The lessening of David's fear permitted him to tolerate dogs and to increase his interactions with his peers in the school yard and neighborhood. ■

■ Keith, an 8-year-old third-grade student, was enrolled in summer camp. Keith had a fear of water. Swimming lessons were a part of the camp program. Although swimming was not mandatory, it was encouraged. At the first suggestion of swimming or going to the pool, Keith would have a temper tantrum of considerable magnitude.

It was decided that Keith should overcome this irrational fear. The staff concluded that systematic desensitization would be an effective intervention.

The following stimulus hierarchy was constructed and applied during desensitization:

1. Swimming was announced to the group and discussed with Keith's peers. Keith did not attend swimming lessons but watched his peers, who were very happy and excited, get on the bus and depart for swimming.
2. Keith rode the bus to the pool and waited outside the building.
3. Keith rode the bus to the pool and waited outside the locker room.

4. Keith entered the locker room, put on his trunks, and remained in the locker room.
5. Keith, in trunks, observed the lesson from the pool observation room.
6. Keith observed the lesson from the poolside (approximately 10 feet from the water).
7. Keith observed the lesson from the edge of the pool.
8. Keith observed the lesson while sitting on the edge of the pool with his feet in the water.
9. Keith stood in the pool with his hands on the edge of the pool.
10. Keith walked in the shallow end of the pool with his hands on the edge of the pool.

Throughout this procedure Keith was accompanied by his counselor, who provided positive reinforcement. As a result of this process and within 3 weeks, Keith began his swimming lessons. After 3 years it was noted that the fear had not returned. Keith is an excellent swimmer. ■

SUMMARY

In this chapter some techniques frequently used to decrease behaviors are discussed.

Extinction is the discontinuation or withholding of the reinforcer of a behavior that has previously reinforced that particular behavior. The technique is based on the principle that if the reinforcer is taken away, the probability of recurrence of the behavior is decreased.

The second technique, time-out, is a frequently misunderstood behavioral intervention. Time-out is the removal of a child from an apparently reinforcing setting to a presumably nonreinforcing setting for a specified and limited period of time. Six factors related to the effectiveness of time-out are (1) the characteristics of the individual child, (2) the consistency of application by the teacher, (3) the child's understanding of the rules, (4) the characteristics of the time-out area, (5) the duration of time-out, and (6) the evaluation of the effectiveness of the intervention.

Satiation is the decreasing or elimination of an inappropriate behavior as a result of continued and increased reinforcement of that behavior. This intervention is effective for decreasing behaviors such as "borrowing" materials and dominating time.

Punishment, the most familiar of the interventions discussed, is the addition of an aversive stimulus or the subtraction of a desired reinforcer or privilege as a consequence of behavior. There are a number of serious concerns associated with the use of punishment. The major problem with the use of punishment to modify behavior is that punishment does not eliminate inappropriate behavior; it only suppresses the behavior. Punishment should be used very infrequently, if ever, in the school. Reprimand and loss of privileges are discussed as useful forms of punishment.

The reinforcement of incompatible behaviors involves systematically reinforcing a behavior that is in opposition to or incompatible with the target behavior. The effectiveness of this technique depends greatly on the pairing of incompatible behaviors.

Desensitization is the process of systematically lessening a specific fear in an individual.

PROJECTS

1. Joanie, a girl in Ms. Jewel's classroom, is constantly asking, "What time is it?" She requests the time about 15 times per day. The teacher considers this to be an attention-getting behavior and wishes to eliminate it. She usually responds to Joanie's request by telling her the time. Using this example, design four interventions for eliminating the behavior using the following processes:
   a. Extinction   c. Satiation
   b. Time-Out   d. Reinforcement of incompatible behaviors
2. Write a brief essay (250 words or more) emphasizing the pros and cons of punishment in the school.

REFERENCES

Brantner, J. P., & Doherty, M. A. (1983). A review of time-out: A conceptual and methodological analysis. In S. Axelrod & J. Apsche (Eds.), *The effects of punishment on human behavior* (pp. 87-132). New York: Academic Press.

Cuenin, L. H., & Harris, K. R. (1986). Planning, implementing, and evaluating time-out interventions with exceptional students. *Teaching Exceptional Children, 18*(4), 272-276.

Deffenbacher, J., & Kemper, C. (1974). Systematic desensitization of test anxiety in junior high students. *The School Counselor, 21,* 216-222.

Foxx, R. M., & Shapiro, S. T. (1978). The time-out ribbon: A nonexclusionary time-out procedure. *Journal of Applied Behavior Analysis, 11,* 125-136.

Hall, R. V., & Hall, M. C. (1980a). *How to use planned ignoring.* Austin TX: Pro-Ed.

Hall, R. V., & Hall, M. C. (1980b). *How to use time-out.* Austin, TX: Pro-Ed.

Harris, K. R. (1985). Definitional, parametric, and procedural considerations in time-out interventions and research. *Exceptional Children, 51*(4), 279-288.

Houten, R. V. (1980). *How to use reprimands.* Austin, TX: Pro-Ed.

Kravetz, R., & Forness, S. (1971). The special classroom as a desensitization setting. *Exceptional Children, 37,* 389-391.

Lewellen, A. (1980). *The use of quiet rooms and other time-out procedures in the public school: A position paper.* Mattoon, IL: Eastern Illinois Area of Special Education.

Nelson, C., & Rutherford, R. (1983). Time-out revisited: Guidelines for its use in special education. *Exceptional Education Quarterly, 3,* 56-67.

Powell, T. H., & Powell, I. Q. (1982). Guidelines for implementing time-out procedures. *The Pointer, 26,* 18-21.

Salend, S. J., & Gordon, B. D. (1987). A group-oriented time-out ribbon procedure. *Behavioral Disorders, 12*(2), 131-137.

Shea, T. M., & Bauer, A. M. (1987). *Teaching children and youth with behavior disorders.* Englewood Cliffs, NJ: Prentice-Hall.

Wolpe, J. (1961). The systematic desensitization treatment of neuroses. *Journal of Nervous and Mental Diseases, 132,* 189-203.

Wolpe, J. (1974). *The practice of behavior therapy* (2nd ed.). New York: Pergamon Press.

Wood, F. H. (1978). Punishment and special education: Some concluding comments. In F. H. Wood & D. C. Lakin (Eds.), *Punishment and aversive stimulation in special education: Legal, theoretical and practical issues in their use with emotionally disturbed children and youth* (pp. 119-122). Minneapolis: University of Minnesota.

Wood, F. H., & Lakin, K. C. (1978). The legal status and use of corporal punishment and other aversive procedures in schools. In F. H. Wood & K. C. Lakin (Eds.), *Punishment and aversive stimulation in special education: Legal, theoretical and practical issues in their use with emotionally disturbed children and youth* (pp. 3-27). Minneapolis: University of Minnesota.

Zabel, M. K. (1986). Time-out use with behaviorally disordered students. *Behavioral Disorders, 12*(1), 15-21.

CHAPTER SIX

Psychodynamic Behavior Management

Jack, a 13-year-old seventh grader, is enrolled in Mr. Bird's junior high resource room for students with adjustment difficulties.

Jack functions well in the academic areas. He performs above grade level in all subjects. However, his social behavior is creating difficulties for Jack, his classmates, and his teachers. Jack's unacceptable social behaviors have caused him to be ignored by some students, overtly rejected by others, and used as a scapegoat by a few.

Essentially Jack believes he is unacceptable to (unwanted by) his peers. He appears to believe that others are making fun of him or rejecting him when they are being overtly friendly. When Jack feels he is being rejected, he immediately attempts to escape his discomfort. He escapes by putting his head in his lifttop desk and closing the top, placing an open book over his face, placing his backpack over his head, walking the hallways sideways with his face to the wall, and so on.

Mr. Bird recognizes that eventually this behavior will affect all facets of Jack's functioning, including academics. Mr. Bird realizes that he is not a trained psychotherapist. However, he wishes to assist Jack in a practical manner with his unacceptable overt social behavior in the classroom and school.

Mrs. Lietner, a sixth-grade teacher, is watching 12-year-old Wendell and his classmate, Tommy, shooting baskets in the schoolyard. They are playing "21," and Tommy is winning 16 to 10.

Suddenly and for no observable reason, Wendell throws the basketball in Tommy's face with great force. When Tommy recovers, he begins to chase Wendell. Wendell runs around the playground for a few minutes and then begins to climb over the fence with Tommy in hot pursuit. As Wendell climbs the fence, his shirt catches on a wire and tears. He immediately runs to Mrs. Lietner and reports that Tommy tore his shirt.

Mrs. Lietner calls both boys to her side. Each is asked to review the incident. They are encouraged to verbally reconstruct the game, Wendell's throwing of the basketball into Tommy's face, the chase, fence climbing, and the torn shirt. During the discussion it becomes apparent to Mrs. Lietner that Wendell fails to see any connection between his behavior, Tommy's behavior, and the torn shirt.

The teacher recognizes that this incident is similar to many others in which Wendell has been involved throughout the year. He appears either unable or unwilling to perceive the relationship between his actions and their consequences.

Mrs. Lietner recognizes her need for a behavior management intervention to assist Wendell.

Several behavior management interventions derived from the psychodynamic model are presented in this chapter. Four categories of interventions are discussed. These are counseling techniques, the expressive media, behavior influence techniques, and social skills curriculum. The counseling techniques discussed are the life-space interview and reality therapy. The expressive media include free play, puppetry, role playing and psychodrama, creative movement, dance and physical activities, music, the written word, the spoken word, bibliotherapy, art therapy, and others. The behavior influence techniques reviewed are planned ignoring, signal interference, proximity control, interest boosting, tension reduction through humor, hurdle helping, program restructuring, support from routine, direct appeal, removing seductive objects, antiseptic bouncing, and physical restraint. Also presented in this chapter is a discussion of the psychoeducational model.

Several important psychodynamic interventions employed by professionals in the mental health disciplines are not presented in this text because of their complexity and special training requirements. These include individual and group psychotherapy, directive and nondirective counseling, psychoanalysis, and family therapy.

Before studying the remainder of this chapter, the reader is urged to review the theoretical framework underlying the psychodynamic model presented in Chapter 1.

CHAPTER OBJECTIVES

After completing this chapter, you will be able to do the following:

1. Define the operational principles underlying the psychoeducational model.
2. Describe and exemplify the application of life-space interviewing and reality therapy.
3. Understand the application of the expressive media in behavior management.
4. Explain the application of the behavior influence techniques in the management of behavior.
5. Characterize the application of social skills curriculum.

Psychoeducational Model

A broad perspective for the education and management of children is the *psychoeducational model*. Originally the psychoeducational model was closely associated with the teaching strategies classified as psychoanalytic-psychodynamic (Berkowitz and Rothman, 1967; Peter, 1965; Morse, 1985).

According to Long and others (1980), however, the psychoeducational approach is a general term that is representative of a theory, method, or viewpoint on the education of troubled children. As a generic term it includes a variety of psychological and educational approaches to helping such children and youth (Nichols, 1984; Fink, 1988). It is this model with which the many interventions detailed in this chapter appear to be most compatible.

The psychoeducational model as interpreted by Long, Morse, and Newman follows:

> To give this concept some substance, the following operating principles are considered basic to the psychoeducational approach. We believe:
>
> 1. Cognitive and affective processes are in continuous interaction.
> 2. Accepting the existence of mental illness, our task is to describe the pupil in terms of functioning skills that highlight areas of strength and pinpoint areas of weakness for remediation.
> 3. The psychoeducational process involves creating a special environment so that initially each pupil can function successfully at his present level.
> 4. Given this specialized environment, each pupil is taught that he has the capacity and resources to function appropriately and successfully.
> 5. Understanding how each pupil perceives, feels, thinks, and behaves in this setting facilitates educational conditions for optimal behavioral change.
> 6. There are no special times during the school day. Everything that happens to, with, for, and against the pupil is important and can have therapeutic value.
> 7. Emotionally troubled pupils have learned a vulnerability to many normal developmental tasks and relationships such as competition, sharing, testing, closeness, etc. As teachers, we are responsible for awareness of these areas and for modifying our behavior in appropriate fashion.
> 8. Emotionally disturbed pupils behave in immature ways during periods of stress. They will lie, fight, run away, regress, and deny the most obvious realities. We can anticipate immature behavior from children in conflict; our hope for change is to expect mature behavior from adults.
> 9. Pupils in conflict can create their feelings and behaviors in others; aggressive pupils can create counter-aggressive behaviors in others; hyperactive children can create hyperactivity in others; withdrawn pupils can get other children and adults to ignore them; passive-aggressive pupils are effective in getting others to carry their feelings for days. If a child succeeds in getting the adult to act out his feelings and behavior, he succeeds in perpetuating his self-fulfilling prophecy of life, which in turn reinforces his defenses against change.
> 10. Emotionally troubled children have learned to associate adult intervention with adult rejection. One staff goal is to reinterpret adult intervention as an act of protection rather than hostility. The pupil must be told over and over again that adults are here to protect him from real dangers, contagion, psychological depreciation, etc.
> 11. We are here to listen to what the pupil says, to focus on what he is feeling.
> 12. We are to expect and accept a normal amount of hostility and disappointment from pupils and colleagues.
> 13. Pupil's home and community life is an important source of health that must be considered by any remedial process. However, if all attempts fail, the school becomes an island of support for the pupil.
> 14. We must demonstrate that fairness is treating children differently. Although group rules are necessary for organizational purposes, individualized expectations are necessary for growth and change.

15. Crises are excellent times for teachers to teach and for pupils to learn.
16. Behavioral limits can be a form of love, i.e., physical restraint can be a therapeutic act of caring for and protecting pupils.
17. Teaching pupils social and academic skills enhances their capacity to cope with a stressful environment.
18. Pupils learn through a process of unconscious identification with significant adults in their lives. This means the teacher's personal appearance, attitudes, and behavior are important factors in teaching which must be evaluated continuously.*

It is within the context of this psychoeducational model and the psychodynamic model presented in Chapter 1 that the counseling, behavior influencing, expressive media interventions, and social skills curriculum discussed in this chapter take on their significance. The reader is urged to study both models with great care.

Counseling Techniques

Teachers frequently limit their ability to help children with behavior problems by excluding various counseling and other psychoeducational interventions that are available to them (Nichols, 1986). Many of the methods discussed in this chapter are frequently not applied by teachers because these methods have traditionally been seen to be within the purview of the psychologist, psychiatrist, counselor, and social worker. However, the methods presented here have been carefully selected and explained to enable the teacher to apply them to students with behavior problems. Methods that require specialized training are noted.

Life-Space Interview

The life-space interview is a here-and-now intervention built around a child's direct life experience. It is applied by a teacher perceived to be significant in the child's life-space. The interviewer has a definite role and power influence in the child's daily life. The life-space interview technique is imposed to structure an incident in the child's life to enable the child to solve the problems confronting him or her. The interviewer's role is facilitator.

According to Redl (1959), the life-space interview technique may be applied for either of two purposes: clinical exploitation of life events or emotional first aid on the spot.

In the first situation, *clinical exploitation of life events,* the interviewer uses an actual incident to explore with the child habitual behavioral characteristics. This is an effort to use the incident to attain a long-range therapeutic goal previously established for the child by a clinical or individualized educational program team.

---

*From *Conflict in the classroom,* 3rd ed., by Nicholas J. Long, William C. Morse, and Ruth G. Newman. © 1976 by Wadsworth Publishing Company, Inc. Reprinted by permission of the publisher.

When the life-space interview technique is employed for the exploitation of life events, the interviewer assists the child in increasing conscious awareness of distorted perceptions of existing realities, pathological behavioral characteristics, hidden social and moral values and standards, or reactions to the behaviors and pressures of the group. The interviewer uses the technique to discuss with the child more personally productive and socially acceptable means of solving problems. This particular application of the life-space interview requires training and experience.

EXAMPLE   ■   Jack, who was introduced to the reader at the beginning of this chapter, is an excellent example of the application of the life-space interview of the clinical exploitation of life events. Jack's bizarre methods of escaping from what he perceived to be rejections were habitual behavioral characteristics. The unacceptable behavior was repeated several times each day.

The staff discussed and agreed that life-space interviewing was an appropriate intervention in Jack's case. Each time Jack engaged in the behavior, he was immediately removed from the setting in which the behavior occurred by a supportive teacher.

The incident was verbally reconstructed and discussed, and a plan for a more acceptable response by Jack to a peer's smile, wave, and so on, was agreed on by Jack and the supportive teacher. Jack returned to the setting in which the behavior was manifested and continued his daily schedule.

Over time and after many life-space interviews, Jack increased his capacity to differentiate between social acceptance and rejection.   ■

The life-space interview technique also provides a child *emotional first aid on the spot* at times of stress. The purpose of the life-space interview technique in on-the-spot first aid is to assist the child over a rough spot in the road in order to continue an activity. The interview is imposed to (1) reduce the child's frustration level, (2) support the child in emotionally charged situations, (3) restore strained child-teacher and child-child communications, (4) reinforce existing behavioral and social limits and realities, or (5) assist the child in efforts to find solutions to everyday problems of living and emotionally charged incidents, such as fights and arguments.

EXAMPLE   ■   John and Thomas, both 11-year-old fifth-grade students, were on a camping trip with their teacher and classmates. The boys were in the process of erecting their two-person tent before the evening meal.

During the process of erecting the tent, John shouted at Thomas: "Come on, stupid. Get the stakes in right. Boy, am I sick of you. You're slow. Hurry up. I'm hungry. We can't eat until you get this dumb tent up."

Thomas proceeded to tell John: "Do it yourself, big mouth. I don't care if I ever eat. Besides I'm not sleeping in there with you anyway."

Both boys were extremely frustrated after a long day of backpacking. They began fighting.

Mr. Wise recognized that *emotional first aid on the spot* by means of a life-space interview was needed. He stopped the fight and allowed the boys to calm down before beginning the interview. During the interview each boy reconstructed the incident as he perceived it, listened to Mr. Wise's perception of the incident, and agreed to try again with a specific plan of action. The tent was erected quickly, and the evening meal was eaten.   ■

As in any counseling situation, the application of the life-space interview is dependent on a variety of variables: the purpose and goal, the specific environment, the training and experience of the teacher, and especially the child and the particular problem or difficulty.

The application of the life-space interview technique in the school is a decision involving all members of the team responsible for the child. When the technique is adopted for use, it should be used with consistency by all personnel under the supervision of trained and experienced professionals.

Fagen (1981) outlined a series of steps that occur during the life-space interview. This is not a rigid series of steps; on occasion during an interview, some steps are omitted and others reordered.

Generally the interview begins as a result of a specific incident in the individual's (or group's) actual life-space. The interviewer encourages those involved in the incident to state their personal perceptions of the occurrence. At this time the interviewer must determine if this is an isolated happening or a significant part of a recurring theme.

The interviewer *listens* to those involved in the incident as they reconstruct it, accepting their feelings and perceptions without moralizing or attacking. Although individual perceptions of the incident are accepted, the interviewer may suggest alternative perceptions for consideration.

The interview process then moves into a resolution phase. This phase should be nonjudgmental in tone. Many conflicts and confrontations are resolved at this point, and the interview is terminated.

However, if the problems are not resolved, the interviewer may offer his or her view of the happening as it is related to the situation in which the individual or individuals find themselves. Finally, those involved and the interviewer develop an acceptable plan to deal with the present problem and similar problems in the future.

Several guidelines for interviewer behavior have been offered by Brenner (1969):

1. *Be polite.* If you do not have control of your emotions, do not begin the interview.
2. Sit, kneel, or stand to *establish eye contact.* Talk with, never at, the individual being interviewed.
3. When you are unsure of the history of the incident, investigate. *Do not conduct an interview on the basis of second- or third-hand information or rumors.*
4. *Ask appropriate questions* to obtain a knowledgeable grasp of the incident. However, do not probe areas of unconscious motivation; limit the use of "why" questions.
5. *Listen to the individual* and attempt to comprehend his or her perception of the incident.
6. Encourage the individual to ask questions. Respond to the child's questions appropriately.
7. When the individual is suffering from apparent shame and/or guilt as a result of the incident, *attempt to reduce and minimize these feelings.*
8. *Facilitate the individual's efforts to communicate* what he or she wishes to say. If the individual is having difficulty in this area, provide help.

9. *Work carefully and patiently* to develop a mutually acceptable plan of action for immediate or future implementation.

Reilly, Imber, and Cremins (1978) and DeMagistris and Imber (1980) researched the effectiveness of the life-space interview in educational settings. In the former study, researchers found that in the resource room, the interview decreased inappropriate behavior. In the second study, conducted in a self-contained special class with eight disturbed boys, researchers found academic performance improved and inappropriate behavior decreased. Naslund (1987) reported a study conducted at the Rose School in Washington, D.C. using the life-space interview technique with 28 elementary school-age students with emotional disturbances. The study was in a crisis intervention program that applied the life-space interview as a basic intervention strategy. The study focused on frequency of use, reasons for referral, type of interview, and changes in these factors over an academic year. Naslund stated the results were significant. Caution should be exercised in generalizing the findings of these studies due to sample limitations and research design. A comprehensive discussion of the purpose, application, and effectiveness of the life-space interview is found in a special issue of *The Pointer* (Long & Fagen, 1980).

Reality Therapy

In his 1965 and 1969 publications, Glasser offers a unique perspective on mental health and the treatment of mental illness. His thesis is a departure from traditional Freudian and neo-Freudian theoretical frameworks that mental health is a state of contentment and mental ill health is a state of discontent. From the reality therapy point of view, mental health is the ability to function competently in the environment, whereas mental illness is incompetence.

An individual in need of psychiatric assistance is unable to fulfill essential psychological needs. The objective of reality therapy is to lead the individual toward competent functioning in the environment. This technique is designed to help the individual grapple successfully with the tangible and intangible aspects of the real world and as a result be able to fulfill personal needs.

According to Glasser (1965), human beings have two basic psychological needs: (1) to love and be loved, and (2) to feel worthwhile to self and others.

To feel worthwhile to self and others, an individual must maintain satisfactory standards of behavior. The individual who fails to maintain acceptable standards suffers pain or discomfort. This discomfort is *mental illness,* that is, lack of responsible involvement with significant others in the environment. A mentally ill person desiring to return to the state of mental health, that is, responsible and competent functioning, must have someone whom he or she genuinely cares about, and the person must believe that the feeling is mutual. In 1984, with the development of his theory, Glasser identified five basic needs—one is physiological and the others are psychological. These needs are (1) survival, (2) love and belonging, (3) power, (4) freedom, and (5) fun.

In reality therapy, the process of therapy and the process of teaching are identical. The therapist's or teacher's primary objective is to teach the mentally ill person responsible behavior. Responsibility is the ability to fulfill one's personal needs in a manner that does not deprive other individuals of their ability to fulfill their personal needs.

According to Glasser's thesis, learning to be a responsible person is not a natural developmental process. Individuals are taught to be responsible through involvement with responsible and significant others. This involvement with others includes love and discipline. The majority of individuals learn to be responsible from loving and disciplining parents or guardians and others, such as teachers.

In summary, reality therapy is the process of teaching an irresponsible individual to face existing reality, to function responsibly, and, as a result, to fulfill personal needs.

For the mentally ill individual, the therapeutic process includes:

☐ Involvement with an acceptable person who is perceived by the mentally ill person as caring about him or her. The quality of the involvement must be sufficient to permit the ill individual to face existing reality and begin to view personal behavior as irresponsible.
☐ A therapist who is accepting of the individual and maintains involvement with the individual while rejecting irresponsible behavior.
☐ The learning of responsible means of fulfilling personal needs in reality. This learning process is a cooperative activity that may include direct instructions, discussions, conversations, and planning sessions relative to any element of the individual's present life-style.

Reality therapy processes assume that the therapist is an acceptable and accepting person. The therapist, who may be a teacher, is also assumed to be appropriately trained and experienced in reality therapy techniques.

In an educational program reality therapy's goal is to guide individuals toward more responsible behavior. This goal is attained by means of the reality therapy interview.

Guidelines for teachers engaged in the interview are as follows:

1. Be personal. Demonstrate that you are a person who cares about the individual and who is interested in his or her welfare.
2. Focus the therapeutic process on present behavior, not on past behavior. Accept the individual's expressed feelings, but do not probe into unconscious motivation. Ask "what," "how," and "who" questions. Limit the asking of "why" questions.
3. Do not preach, moralize, or make value judgments about the individual's behavior.
4. Help the individual formulate a practical plan to increase responsible behavior. Planning is a cooperative effort.
5. Encourage the individual to overtly make a commitment to the mutually agreed-on plan.

6. Do not accept excuses for irresponsible behavior. When a plan fails or cannot be implemented, develop another.

7. Do not punish the individual for irresponsible behavior. Allow the individual to realize the logical consequences of irresponsible behavior unless the consequences are unreasonably harmful.

8. Provide emotional support and security throughout the therapeutic process.

Because it is primarily verbal in nature, reality therapy is perhaps most appropriately used with upper elementary school children and adolescents who are capable of carrying on meaningful verbal transactions with others.

EXAMPLE ■ Kyle, a tenth-grade student at Greenwood High School, had superior academic potential. However, he was failing several subjects. It became evident that Kyle's future relative to graduation and college was being affected by his behavior.

Mr. Germaine, Kyle's favorite teacher, decided he must help the young man. He did not want Kyle to jeopardize his future. Mr. Germaine decided to use the reality therapy approach with Kyle. After all, he and Kyle were friends; he cared about the young man; and he knew Kyle could improve with help.

In their first session it was found that Kyle would not work in any subject areas if he did not like the teacher. If the teacher was too demanding, unfriendly, and so on, Kyle just gave up—he refused to study.

Kyle recognized that his behavior was only harmful to himself. He and Mr. Germaine developed a plan of action. During the next few months they met regularly to monitor Kyle's progress. Kyle learned to accept responsibility for his behavior. His grades improved dramatically. ■

Glasser (1969) and Heuchert (1989) suggested reality therapy principles for application with classroom groups. In an effort to reduce the emphasis in schools on competition and achievement, he proposed reality therapy meetings to teach decision making, social responsibility, and cooperation. These purposes are accomplished through social-problem-solving, open-ended, and educational-diagnostic meetings. The social-problem-solving meeting is focused on individual and group problems in classroom and school. Open-ended meetings are discussions of any thought-provoking questions related to the members of the group or the group itself. Educational-diagnostic meetings focus on the content of the educational program in which the group is involved.

Few studies of the effect of reality therapy have been conducted. In general, studies lack experimental rigor and yield mixed results. Cook [(1972) in Shearn & Randolph, 1978] reported no significant changes in positive or negative behaviors of sociometrically underchosen adolescents exposed to reality therapy. Hawes [(1970) in Shearn & Randolph, 1978] reported significant gains in the self-concept of black children in reality therapy. However, Glick [(1968) in Shearn & Randolph, 1978] reported no significant changes in self-concept and self-responsibility of emotionally disturbed boys in residential school. However, significant changes in self-esteem were reported.

Scheaf [(1972) in Shearn & Randolph, 1978] noted no significant changes in the reading achievement of delinquents involved in reality therapy. Shearn and Randolph (1978), using a four-group experimental design, studied the effects of reality therapy on the task-oriented behaviors and self-concept of fourth-grade students; results were not significant. In a follow-up study of adolescents who had successfully left a facility using reality therapy and contingency management procedures, most of the students were found to be moderately successful young adults; only one of the 18 subjects returned to the facility and only four were unemployed 2 to 4 years after leaving the program, despite substantial deficits in academic skills (Leone, 1984).

Classroom Conference

McIntyre (1987) developed a method of classroom conferencing specifically designed for teachers of students with behavioral problems. The "long talk" is an easily implemented classroom conferencing procedure and is especially responsive to a variety of interpersonal interaction and counseling styles. The "long talk" is applied to help students analyze their behavior and develop better self-control.

The steps in classroom conferencing are meet, review, discuss respect, discuss typical behavior, devise another response, and reconvene.

The teacher should **meet** privately with the student as soon as possible after the behavioral incident. During the conference, the student is requested to **review** the incident. The teacher should clarify the student's perception to assure that both student and teacher are discussing a common perception. The teacher may make corrections in the student's perception on the basis of first-person knowledge of the incident. Next, the teacher and student **discuss respect** to clarify what actions and feelings resulting from the incident were right and wrong and whose rights and privileges were violated. Student and teacher **discuss typical behavior** during the next step of the conferencing process. The student is helped to see the inappropriateness of the behavior and is informed that it is unacceptable.

In the fifth step, student and teacher **devise another response**. The student is requested to suggest alternative ways of responding in like and similar situations in the future. All suggested alternatives are accepted and written on paper. The student is asked to select the alternative he or she will use in the future. The alternative's use in various situations is discussed. The pros and cons of the alternative are discussed. If the alternative that the student selects is unrealistic, he or she is requested to select another. The teacher may assist students who are unable to generate alternatives.

In the final step, student and teacher **reconvene** to review student progress and performance and engage in further planning, as necessary. Behavior change takes time, and a series of conferences is often necessary.

Expressive Media

The expressive media refers to interventions that encourage and permit children to express personal feelings and emotions in creative activities with minimal constraints.

All human beings have feelings and emotions that must be expressed in some manner if mental health is to be maintained. A child's feelings and emotions, positive and negative, can be expressed verbally and physically. Frequently children (and adults) unconsciously express their feelings and emotions in socially unacceptable ways. This can result in conflicts with others and may have negative impact on the individual's self-concept.

The expressive media, applied in an appropriate environment and under competent guidance, can be an acceptable and legitimate means for expressing positive and negative feelings and emotions. Adults frequently reduce personal stresses and frustrations in verbal exchanges with trusted friends and relatives or by means of avocations, hobbies, games, projects, trips, sports, vacations, and so on. For children, who are generally less capable in verbal communications and less in control of their personal life-style, the expressive media are an opportunity to reduce stresses and frustrations without danger of conflict with others.

The media can provide many benefits for children. Not only are they beneficial in the affective domain, but they provide a variety of cognitive and psychomotor learning benefits.

If the media are to be used as a behavior management technique, the child must be provided with opportunities to find a personally satisfying medium of expression. The individual must be provided with consistent, repeated opportunities to express feelings and emotions through the chosen medium.

Cheney and Morse (1972) summarized the value of the expressive media for children as follows:

> This group of interventions supports and develops the child's expressive abilities. Such techniques serve to mobilize the child's internal resources in a number of ways: they facilitate involvement through activity rather than retreat and withdrawal; they provide acceptable channels for cathartic release; they serve as means of both externalizing the child's conflicts and communicating his feelings about them to others (though both the signal and response may be nonverbal, and nonconscious and not discussed); many of the expressive media seem to embody inherent "therapeutic" qualities. For children with verbal inhibitions the whole "language" may be nonverbal. (p. 352)

Axline (1947) suggested several principles for play therapy that are applicable by teachers using the expressive media. The therapist must develop a warm relationship, built on accepting the child exactly as he or she is. The therapist establishes a feeling of freedom in the relationship, so that the child expresses his or her feelings. The therapist must be sensitive to the feelings of the child and reflect those back to facilitate insight. The relationship is built on respect and a belief that the child can change his or her behavior. The only limits established in this setting are those necessary to assist the child in becoming aware of responsibility in his or her relationships.

When using the expressive media for therapeutic purposes, the individual's activities should not be prescribed, though some limitations and structure in their application relative to time, place, specific media, and behavioral extremes are necessary.

Minimal limits must be established and communicated to the child either verbally or by demonstration (Ginott, 1959). These limits involve (a) time, (b) the use and location of materials and equipment, (c) the prevention of the destruction of facilities, equipment and materials, and (d) restrictions to ensure the safety of the child and the teacher.

Free Play

Play therapy as described by Axline (1947) is difficult, if not impossible, to initiate in the classroom because of (1) restrictions inherent with the classroom setting, (2) the traditional role of the teacher, and (3) the teacher's lack of training in play therapy.

However, free-play sessions can be provided for individuals or groups. If a free-play program is instituted, sessions should be scheduled with regularity. Play materials and equipment, located in the designated free-play area, should be "primitive" or basic materials that the child or group can use to create an environment in which to express feelings and emotions. Complicated toys and games, although entertaining, may restrict the child's creative activities. These complex items often require the child to be passive rather than active during the sessions.

In a free-play session, the child is invited to play with any of the materials in the play area and is encouraged to select materials of interest. Activity is only restricted by the limits previously discussed. The teacher's role is that of observer and activity facilitator.

EXAMPLE   ■   Elmer, a 6-year-old severely emotionally disturbed child, is assigned full-time to Mr. Parker's special class. Elmer is severely withdrawn. He is unable to interact verbally and nonverbally with Mr. Parker and his classmates. He spends his days quietly sitting at his desk unless physically moved from activity to activity and location to location.

Mr. Parker believes that a daily 30-minute free-play period might decrease Elmer's withdrawal. Mr. Parker believes that if Elmer will begin playing with the objects in the free-play area of the classroom, he will, in time, begin relating to his classmates and teacher.

During the first several sessions of free play, Mr. Parker, with great enthusiasm, demonstrates to Elmer the use of the various play objects and manually guides Elmer through simple activities. Elmer is introduced to the sandbox, watertable, doll house, tools, dishes, toy animals, trucks and cars, and so on.

After several weeks of free play, Mr. Parker observes that Elmer is quietly and carefully manipulating some of the toys without encouragement. He is particularly interested in the dolls, doll house, hammer, and pegboard.

As the months progress, Elmer begins playing and talking with the toys with vigor. Before the end of the school year, Elmer is silently playing with one of his classmates and occasionally talking to Mr. Parker. ∎

Puppetry

Puppets may help children express feelings and emotions. Many children who cannot or will not communicate with others directly will do so through a puppet.

Many language development and affective education programs have successfully implemented puppetry into their programs. Perhaps the child feels safe and secure in the world of puppets, which can be manipulated and managed to express personal needs and moods.

Experience in clinical, classroom, and camp settings has demonstrated that sophisticated puppets and puppet stages are unnecessary. Simple hand puppets, which often are created and constructed by the children and may be personal possessions, are effective (D'Alonzo, 1974). The puppet stage may be a tabletop and a cardboard box decorated by the children.

Children enjoy not only playing spontaneously with the puppets but also creating and producing puppet shows. Children who are not involved directly in the puppet show can profit from this activity. They respond and converse with the puppet being manipulated by a teacher or peer.

EXAMPLE ∎ Mary Lou, a shy kindergarten student, was unable to communicate verbally with her classmates and teacher during the first 3 months of the school year. Mary Lou was not a disruptive child, she was always smiling and cheerful, followed directions, and completed all tasks not requiring verbalization. Her mother reported that she was very verbal at home. In addition, Mary Lou's mother said that her daughter enjoyed kindergarten.

Mrs. Holtz, the kindergarten teacher, believed the puppet play might help Mary Lou overcome her shyness. Mary Lou and her teacher worked together to make and decorate personal puppets. When the puppets were complete, Mrs. Holtz and Mary Lou held semi-private play sessions for 15 minutes each day. After several days Mary Lou's puppet began talking to Mrs. Holtz's puppet. As other children joined the puppetry group, Mary Lou's puppet cautiously talked to other puppets. Before the Easter break arrived, Mary Lou was very talkative in school. Her puppet was seldom used. ∎

Role Playing and Psychodrama

Role playing and psychodrama are potentially valuable therapeutic interventions for use with children. Psychodrama was originally developed for therapeutic purposes by Moreno (1946). These techniques are based on the assumption that individuals may gain greater understanding of their behavior if they act out various aspects of their lives (Newcomer, 1980). Warger (1985, 1987) recommends creative drama for children whose play development may be slow as a consequence of a handicapping condition. It is an excellent method for enhancing skills critical to learning and developing social skills, and it can be readily individualized.

According to Raths and others (1966), role playing can assist an individual in the clarification of feelings and emotions as they relate to existing reality in three ways:

1. It can focus on real occurrences. An incident may be reenacted and the participants told to attend to the feelings aroused, or an incident may be reenacted with the participants changing roles and attending to the feelings aroused by these new roles. An individual may be directed to deliver a soliloquy to recreate an emotionally loaded event. Emphasis here is on expressing feelings that were hidden or held back when the event first occurred.
2. It can focus on significant others. The individual may portray a significant person in his or her life about whom a great amount of conflict is felt.
3. It can focus on processes and feelings occurring in new situations. Directions for this type of role playing may be very specific, with the participants provided with special characters and actions, or directions may be vague, allowing the participants to form their own characters.

Role playing and psychodrama techniques have been incorporated into several social skills and affective education programs concerned specifically with the learning of values and standards.

EXAMPLE   ■ Thomas, a 15-year-old tenth grader, was extremely overweight. He was the class scapegoat. His classmates were constantly making fun of his size. They called him "porky," "fatso," "pig," "slob," "tubby," and so on. Each day someone came up with a new name to call him.

Thomas was a sensitive person, and whenever he was called a name, he withdrew. Frequently the teacher saw tears in his eyes.

Mrs. Minup was very concerned about Thomas's mental well-being and his classmates' lack of consideration and compassion for Thomas and other children who were different. She believed that role playing might be a method of helping the whole class, including Thomas, gain insight into their behavior.

Without including obesity, Mrs. Minup conducted a series of role-playing activities with the class. The students role played their reactions and feelings to roles concerned with height, complexion, race, religion, and so on.

As the students began to empathize with the feelings of the characters they were role playing, Thomas became more accepted and less a target of their hurtful behavior. ■

Drama, as a therapeutic technique, can be used with students for several purposes in the education setting (Newcomer, 1980; Necco, Wilson, & Scheidmantel, 1982; Creekmore & Madan, 1981). Among these are the following:

□ To assist in finding solutions, making decisions, and assuming responsibility for personal social-emotional problems.

□ To assist in affective education, increase feelings and emotions, and improve communication skills.

□ To assist in solving problems associated with normal child and adolescent development.

□ To facilitate group cohesiveness.

□ To facilitate experimentation with adult roles.

□ To aid in the conceptualization of abstracts in subject matter such as language, science, etc.

□ To offer entertainment and recreation opportunities.

□ To offer the teacher opportunities to observe students in various situations.

Newcomer (1980) cautions teachers to apply drama therapy with care. Student preparation includes a clear understanding of the purpose, objectives, and benefits of drama. Rules and regulations should be explained. Participation is always voluntary and devoid of personal criticism.

Creative Movement, Dance, and Physical Activities

As a therapeutic intervention, creative movement, dance, and other physical activities have the capacity to assist children in expressing their feelings and emotions in an acceptable manner (Chace, 1958). This can be accomplished in a variety of ways, such as by imitating nature or animals or by expressing the feelings of others or expressing personal feelings under varying circumstances. During creative movement sessions the child can express past, present, and even future feelings and emotions. These activities encourage the child to externalize personal feelings and begin to deal with them.

Movement activities can be conducted with or without music (Hibben & Scheer, 1982). On occasion, voices, hand clapping, feet stamping, recorded environmental sounds, and rhythm instruments are used to facilitate sessions.

EXAMPLE ■ At Camp R&R it was noticed by the staff that the preteen group known as the "cool persons" was the most "uptight" of all the groups. Children in this group appeared afraid to "let go," to have a good time, or to relax. They appeared concerned about making mistakes in front of their peers.

Ms. Taphorn, a dance enthusiast, suggested that a daily early morning session of creative movement might relax the group and develop cohesiveness. During the sessions, in which Ms. Taphorn and the staff participated, the group became trees, grass, wind, rain, sun, and flowers. They acted out sadness, happiness, joy, sorrow, excitement, fear, and so on.

Within a few days, the "cool persons" were acting as "happy cool persons." The campers began to relax and enjoy each other's company. ■

In a research brief, Zabel (1988) suggested that available research tends to support physical exercise as an adjunctive therapy. Physical activities have been used to provide both aerobic activity and therapeutic restructuring of the environment (Lane, Bonic, & Wallgren-Bonic, 1983). Group "walk-talks" have demonstrated the production of healthy levels of fatigue and improve peer relationships among adolescents (Lane et al., 1983). Daily jogging programs have decreased disruptive behaviors among behavior disordered children (Allen, 1980; Hoenig, Shea, & Bauer, 1986). Anderson (1985) reported positive effects from the "A.M. Club," a jogging club for junior high school students with behavioral disorders. Evans, Evans, Schmid, and Pennypacker (1985) studied the relationship between jogging and touch football and specific behaviors in adolescents with behavioral disorders. The data indicated that a decrease in talk-outs and an increase in problems completed were associated with vigorous exercise. Yell (1987) studied the effects of jogging on the talk-outs and out-of-seat behavior of elementary school students with behavioral disorders. A decrease in the inappropriate behaviors following jogging was found in five of six students.

Music

It is an accepted fact in contemporary society that people are affected by music. We are exposed to mood-modifying music in restaurants, factories, supermarkets, department stores, banks, and so on. Presumably this music has some effect on our behavior and moods (Roter, 1981).

Music is applied as a therapeutic intervention for children in several ways (Purvis & Samet, 1976; Lament, 1978):

1. Children enjoy listening to recordings.
2. Music is an effective tool for reducing excitement and activity levels after high-interest, strenuous activities.
3. Young people enjoy producing music. Although every child cannot successfully learn to play a piano or guitar, most children can learn to enjoy singing and participating in a rhythm band.

Through music, children can express feelings and emotions in an acceptable way.

EXAMPLE ■ Mr. Binckly used music for two purposes in his class for behavior-disordered acting-out elementary school boys. Music was used (1) to calm the group after vigorous outdoor activity, and (2) to allow the group to express pent-up energy and aggression.

After outdoor activities the class devoted 5 minutes to sitting quietly and listening to calming music. Mr. Binckly found this an excellent way to help the group make the transition from recess and physical education to academics.

In addition, Mr. Binckly used music to channel the students' energy after a test or long period of seatwork. On such occasions the group would sing a few songs. No effort was made to perfect the technique. ■

Music as therapy has several advantages for children. It encourages personal freedom and interpretation, and provides "a unique personal experience that has its own meaning for each individual" (Thursby, 1977, p. 77). Music responds to the needs of individuals within a broad range of ages, intellectual abilities, social and educational experiences, and emotional characteristics. Music encourages self-subordination through cooperation and encourages self-discipline and self-directed behavior (David and Newcomer, 1980).

In a discussion of the advantages of music as an integral component of the Developmental Therapy curriculum for severely emotionally disturbed children, Wood (1976) suggested that for such children: "Communication must be established as a basis for trust if there is to be subsequent growth; and of all the ways to communicate, perhaps music is the most universal . . . Whatever form the disturbance takes, and whatever the age of the child, there is a way to reach each child through music in order to begin the gradual movements toward healthier responses" (p. vii).

Michel (1976) suggested that music therapy techniques may be of assistance even though a trained music therapist is not available. Music can be used by the teacher as part of a child's education program, as an adjunct to daily programming, and to teach specific subject matter (Duerksen, 1981). As part of a child's education, music may be used for the following purposes (Lament, 1978; Hibben & Scheer, 1982; Ferolo, Rotatori, Macklin, & Fox, 1983; Ferolo, Rotatori, & Fox, 1984; David & Newcomer, 1980):

☐ To facilitate cognitive development, through increasing abstract thinking, increasing attending, and providing practice for conceptual skills.
☐ To facilitate affective development and social skills and encourage social interaction.
☐ To increase psychomotor skills, coordination, body image, position in space, movement skills, and auditory and visual discrimination.
☐ To assist in the development of self-concept, to develop self-reliance, and to provide an opportunity to be successful.
☐ To provide creative experiences and increase expressive skills, and to provide an expressive outlet for "blowing off steam."

There are several adjunctive uses of music in the educational setting (Duerksen, 1981; David & Newcomer, 1980). Music may be used to manage the behaviors of individuals and groups, to produce a relaxing atmosphere, or to serve as a distraction for children and youth with behavior disorders. Musical activities may serve to motivate students: They can be used as reinforcement for improved behavior, completed work, or other target behaviors. Because it is nonverbal, music may serve both as a form of communication and an aesthetic outlet for some children and youth with behavior disorders.

Music may also be used to teach subject matter (Duerksen, 1981; Thursby, 1977). For instance, it can provide musical background and context for academic subject areas. In nonacademic areas music can also be used to inspire creative writing, art, and story telling.

In whatever its applications, it is important to remember that the goals of music therapy are not to teach specific musical skills and knowledge but to assist the student in reaching nonmusical developmental goals.

The Written Word

Few studies have been conducted on the therapeutic benefit of writing as an intervention for children, although writing has been repeatedly demonstrated to be a useful therapeutic intervention for adults. It seems logical that children can express personal feelings and emotions through written communications. By writing and at times sharing with others that which is written, it is possible to externalize personal conflicts and frustrations (Levinson, 1982).

"The written word is a modality for self-expression, self-exploration, and problem solving. Through story writing, students reveal their perceptions, attitudes, coping skills and problem-solving strategies. Story-writing tales can be structured to encourage students to explore the decision-making process and identify behavioral alternatives and consequences" (Dehouske, 1982, p. 11).

Writing for therapeutic benefit is not concerned with any particular format. Concern is focused entirely on content. The written forms may include poetry, stories, essays, articles, books, journal entries, and so on.

EXAMPLE   ■   For a teenager, Michael had several serious problems on his mind. He was not only concerned about himself and his future, but he was concerned about his parents, who were separated and considering divorce.

Michael had great difficulty talking about his problems to anyone, including parents, teachers, and friends. The school counselor suggested that Michael might keep a journal in which he could write about his concerns and his feelings. The counselor told Michael not to be concerned about spelling, grammar, hand-writing, and so on—just write what he wished. The counselor offered to discuss these writings with Michael if and when Michael wished.

Michael wrote a daily journal. He did not discuss the content with the counselor but did report that it helped to write about his problems and reread his daily entries.   ■

The Spoken Word

Although many children are not developmentally or emotionally prepared to enter formal verbal psychotherapy, they frequently enjoy and profit from communicating verbally. Communications may take the form of group story-telling sessions or conversations and discussions with teachers. In each of these the child is encouraged to express feelings and emotions.

EXAMPLE ■ Mr. Blackside believed a special camp was a setting in which emotionally disturbed campers could express their feelings.

It was suggested that the campers' aggressions, in part, could be channeled into evening campfire discussions and story-telling sessions. During these sessions the campers were encouraged to review the day's activities. They were encouraged to discuss their arguments, fights, and hurt feelings. ■

Newcomer (1980) suggests the therapeutic benefit of the spoken word is greatest if creative, original materials are emphasized. The teacher helps the children create stories and cast themselves as characters in the story. The story may be acted out by the children with emphasis on the affective content.

Bibliotherapy

Bibliotherapy is an indirect intervention that uses the interaction between the reader and literature for therapeutic purposes. It is a tool for helping children deal with their problems through reading literature about characters who possess problems similar to their own (Adderholdt-Elliott and Eller, 1989). This intervention can be applied with children and youth to encourage them to fulfill their needs, relieve pressures, and improve mental and emotional well-being (Russell and Russell, 1979).

For bibliotherapy to be effective, the child must be able to read, motivated to read, and be exposed to appropriate materials. Literature, which is selected by the teacher and child, focuses on the child's needs, is at the appropriate level, is realistic, and accurately represents the characters in the story (Cianciolo, 1965). Adderholdt-Elliott and Eller recommend using bibliotherapy with students who are gifted.

Hoagland (1972) indicates that bibliotherapy works as a three-phase process. First, the children identify themselves in the literature—they must perceive themselves as a part of the story or as a character. Second, children become emotionally involved in the story and the problem it presents. Finally, they arrive at a greater understanding of themselves and their problems by identifying with the characters or situations in the story. Halsted (1988) noted three elements in the bibliotherapy process: identification, catharsis, and insight.

Learning activities used to facilitate bibliotherapy include:

1. Writing a summary of the book for discussion.
2. Dramatizing, role playing, or presenting skits or puppet shows about the message in the literature.
3. Making art works that represent characters and situations in the literature.

Though more research is needed on the effects of bibliotherapy, Schrank and Engels (1981), in a review of the extant research, concluded that it was an effective intervention.

Harms, Etscheidt, and Lettow (1986) suggested the use of poetry as an aid to helping children recognize and explore their feelings and emotions. Poetry is generally brief and concise, and it explores a broad range of topics and events. It can help the child in several ways: creating mental images, responding to varied perspectives, reciting, exploring rhythmic activity, and enacting stories. Children can also express their feelings and emotions by writing poetry.

Art Therapy

Art productions, from the young child's scribbling to the young adult's realistic drawings and paintings, are expressions of self. Art as a therapeutic treatment medium is a growth-oriented experience that benefits children in many ways: communication, socialization, creativity, self-expression, self-exploration, and manipulation of the environment (Williams and Wood, 1977).

Children should be afforded opportunities to express their feelings and emotions through the two-dimensional arts. These productions may be finger paintings, pencil drawings, water colors, oil, tempera, and so on. Teachers should remember that their personal perceptions of the form and content of a child's art production are secondary. The important element is the child's perceptions and feelings.

The three-dimensional arts are more limited than the two-dimensional arts for classroom use because of the nature of the materials and equipment. They are, nevertheless, valuable therapeutic tools. In three-dimensional art forms the child can externalize feelings and emotions through the manipulation of clay, plaster, sand, wood, plastic, and a variety of other materials. Arts and crafts projects are included in this group of therapeutic interventions.

Omizo and Omizo (1988) implemented an art therapy program for adolescents with learning disabilities. The intervention consisted of 12 sessions of 45 to 60 minutes within a 6-week period. Students, under the guidance of their teachers, engaged in activities using common art materials (crayons, clay, paint). In interviews at the conclusion of the program, teachers reported students were better behaved; and they behaved in ways indicating enhanced self-esteem. The teachers reported that they enjoyed working with students in art therapy, and that they themselves felt better as well.

EXAMPLE ■ Mrs. Fingerling believed that children would express their feelings and emotions through the two- and three-dimensional art forms if encouraged to do so. She established an art center in the classroom. The center included the materials and equipment needed for painting with various media, drawing, sculpting, molding, and so on. She scheduled 45 minutes of art activities 3 days each week. The period was scheduled at the end of the day so those children wishing to continue their work could remain for an extra few minutes. To introduce the program, Mrs. Fingerling systematically demonstrated the use of various media. Each child was encouraged to choose his or her medium. They were encouraged to experiment and produce objects meaningful to them. ■

Photography and Videotaping

A long dormant, but recently revitalized, therapeutic method is phototherapy (DMHDD, 1980). Minner (1981) suggested photography as an adjunctive therapy for children with behavioral disorders and other handicapping conditions. This media is useful not only for its therapeutic benefit but also to stimulate creativity. Minner suggested two activities in which photography can be used effectively: a slide-tape presentation and a visual arts gallery. Both activities are responsive to individualization.

Production of a slide-tape presentation involves several steps:

1. Selecting a topic. This can be a collaborative activity involving students and teacher.
2. Taking photographs, which involves selecting specific subjects and learning to operate the camera, lights, meter, and other equipment.
3. Preparing the script, which involves arranging the slides, writing the script, selecting and recording music, taping the script, and operating the equipment.

The school or classroom visual arts gallery, another beneficial outcome of photography, can include unusual and creative photographs that are framed and titled and may be changed periodically or seasonally to project special themes. Students may share the gallery—which may be in the classroom or in another location in the school—with peers, teachers, administrators, and parents.

Raschke, Dedrick, and Takes (1986) suggested videotape feedback as a therapeutic tool. Videotaping can be used to help students with behavioral problems become more aware of their behavior and develop more appropriate ways of interacting. They suggest three techniques: behavioral rehearsal, self-control training, and reality replay.

Behavioral rehearsal engages the student in role-playing simulations of situations involving interpersonal relations. Playback sessions are devoted to teacher and student analysis of the tape and discussion. Through discussion, the student is helped to grow in understanding of behavior, its antecedents and consequences, and alternative ways of behaving.

Self-control training using videotape feedback can be helpful in the areas of on-task behavior, disruptive behavior, and academic productivity. Using feedback, students can be trained in self-assessment, self-monitoring, and self-reinforcement. Reality replay can be a valuable therapeutic tool for students who are unable to see the antecedents and consequences of their behavior. During playback, the students can clearly see both their appropriate and inappropriate behaviors and its antecedents and consequences. They may become aware of the coping mechanisms they use to justify or rationalize their behavior and discuss more appropriate and productive coping mechanisms.

Teachers are cautioned to use videotape feedback in a nonjudgmental manner with students.

Pet-Facilitated Therapy

Pets have been used in a variety of settings to facilitate therapeutic goals. Pet-facilitated therapy has been applied with children with emotional disturbances, children with physical handicaps, geriatric patients, depressed veterans, and psychiatric patients. A variety of animals have been used in therapy including dogs, cats, rabbits, and horses. Other common classroom pets may be used in the program.

Polt and Hale (1985) described a pet-facilitated therapy program with developmentally delayed children at the Hope Center in Denver. A dog and a cat were co-therapists in the program. The goals of the program were to give children experience with animals, and their needs and care, and to respond to the individual child's therapeutic goals. Among the individual goals sought in the Hope Center program were (a) overcoming fear of animals, (b) increasing self-confidence, (c) developing nurturing skills, (d) improving reality orientation, (e) increasing self-esteem, and (f) learning to cooperate with others.

To implement a pet-facilitated therapy program, several steps must be taken. First, staff commitment to the program is sought in a meeting that encourages the expression and discussion of questions and concerns. Parents should participate in this meeting and their permission for their child's participation must be obtained. Next, animals must be selected with great care. Obedience-trained, people-oriented, docile animals are used in the program. Both individual and group program goals should be developed. The individual goals should be developed in response to the child's individualized education program. At least weekly sessions should be scheduled; more frequent sessions are desirable.

Behavior Influence Techniques

Psychodynamic theorists and practitioners recognize that many of the counseling and expressive arts techniques do not immediately change unacceptable behaviors to acceptable behaviors. Techniques of behavior management are needed that can be implemented to interfere with on-going unacceptable behaviors in the classroom, resource room, school, or playground.

Teachers have a responsibility to interfere with behaviors when they:

- Present a real danger.
- Are psychologically harmful to the child and others.
- Lead to excessive excitement, loss of control, or chaos.
- Prohibit the continuation of the program.
- Lead to destruction of property.

- Encourage the spread of negativism in the group.
- Provide opportunities to clarify individual and group values, standards, and social rules.
- Lead to conflict with others outside the group.
- Compromise the practitioner's mental health and ability to function.

Redl and Wineman (1957) suggested 12 behavior management interventions, compatible with psychodynamic framework, for the management of surface behaviors. The work of Redl and Wineman has been expanded on by Long and Newman (1961, 1965) and Shea and others (1974). The behavior influence techniques are planned ignoring, signal interference, proximity control, interest boosting, tension reduction through humor, hurdle helping, program restructuring, support from routine, direct appeal, removal of seductive objects, antiseptic bouncing, and physical restraint.

Planned Ignoring

At one time or another most children engage in unacceptable behavior in an effort to gain the attention of their classmates, teacher, and parents. These unacceptable behaviors are legion in number and may include pencil tapping, body movements, hand waving, whistling, snorting, desk top dropping, book dropping, and so on. Such behavior, although relatively benign, is annoying to others.

Planned ignoring may be used to eliminate many of these behaviors. The teacher using this technique simply ignores the disruptive behavior. No response is made when the behavior occurs. It is generally true that when attention-seeking behaviors are ignored, they become nonfunctional and decrease in frequency.

Signal Interference

There are a variety of nonverbal techniques that a teacher may use to interfere with unacceptable behaviors. Nonverbal techniques or signals, such as eye contact, a frown, finger snapping, toe tapping, book snapping, light flicking, and so on, can alert a child or group to their unacceptable behavior. Often nonverbal behavior influence techniques help the disruptive child "save face" with his or her peers, and thus the disruption is not escalated. They also save the shy child from unnecessary embarrassment.

Conversely, nonverbal signals can be used to reinforce acceptable behaviors in the classroom.

Proximity Control

Very frequently the proximity of an authority figure (teacher, parent, police officer) results in the discontinuation of unacceptable behaviors. Even college professors find it useful to walk about the classroom in an effort to reduce the level of conversation and side comments.

In addition, proximity can have a positive effect on children experiencing anxiety and frustration. The physical presence of a teacher or parent available to assist has a calming effect on troubled children.

Interest Boosting

All persons become bored with routine and difficult tasks. Interest tends to wane with time. The teacher who observes a child losing interest or becoming bored with a task should make an effort to boost the child's interest. This may be accomplished by offering to help, noting how much work has been accomplished, noting how well done the completed part of the task is, discussing the task, and so on. Interest boosting may help the child reorganize a task and mobilize his or her energies to complete it.

Tension Reduction through Humor

Humor has been used to reduce tension, frustration, and anxiety for as long as human beings have been laughing. Children, quite naturally, become tense when engaged in significant tasks. The prudent teacher will apply humor in an effort to help children relax and place their tasks in perspective when they become frustrated. A joke or a humorous comment will frequently reduce tension. Caution must be used to be sure the humor is not harmful to any individual.

Hurdle Helping

Hurdle helping is a technique applied to assist a student who is experiencing difficulty with a specific task. Hurdle helping may simply be an encouraging word from the teacher, an offer to assist with a specific task, or the making available of additional materials and equipment. Help is provided before the child becomes disruptive or simply gives up on the assignment.

Program Restructuring

Occasionally teachers, especially new teachers, are so committed to a lesson, task, or schedule that they will continue regardless of student response. Prudent teachers are sufficiently observant to recognize when a lesson or activity is going poorly; they are flexible. Before the class becomes disruptive or loses all interest, the teacher either restructures the lesson or postpones it until a more appropriate time.

Support from Routine

All persons, including children, like to know their daily schedule. We appreciate being able to plan our day and knowing where, when, why, and with whom we will be at various times. It appears to be especially important to children with behavior problems that they be provided with a schedule and a routine.

The teacher is wise to announce and post the day's schedule in the classroom. Changes in the schedule should be announced in advance, if possible. The children should be reminded of future special events. It is equally important to post and review classroom rules.

Direct Appeal

Many times during an unacceptable behavior incident, the teacher can quickly and effectively resolve the problem through direct appeal to the students' sense of fairness. The direct appeal is derived from the following:

1. The teacher's personal positive relationship with the individual or group.
2. The consequences that will result if the unacceptable behavior continues.
3. The effect of the behavior on the student's peers.
4. The teacher's authority over the student and group.

Many teachers neglect this approach to influencing behavior in favor of more indirect interventions. They neglect to simply and forcefully state, "Stop this behavior because . . ."

Removal of Seductive Objects

Frequently misbehavior occurs because the student has available some object of attention that is distracting. Young children bring small toys, games, and other objects to the classroom that distract them. Older children are distracted by books, magazines, combs, keys, and so on. When the teacher finds that these objects are keeping the child from the assigned task, the objects should be confiscated until after class or school. The confiscation should be kind and firm. Discussion is not necessary. It is more effective if children are trained to routinely store such objects in an appropriate place before school and until it is time to use them.

Antiseptic Bouncing

When a student becomes agitated and frustrated with an activity and before he or she is physically or verbally disruptive, it is prudent to remove the student from the work setting. This removal is called antiseptic bouncing. It is viewed as a positive behavior influence technique and not as a punishment. Antiseptic bouncing, properly applied, provides the student with an opportunity to avoid embarrassment, calm down, reorganize thought, and begin the task anew.

Physical Restraint

Perhaps no children are more concerned with their physical and emotional well-being—and perhaps their continued existence—than children who have lost control of themselves in a tantrum. These children feel totally and absolutely helpless. They simply cannot control their physical and verbal behaviors. On such an occasion physical restraint is necessary. The child is held until calm. The teacher communicates physically and verbally to the child in a calm voice or whisper. The teacher communicates to the child "You are safe; I will protect you; I will not let you harm yourself." After the child regains control, the teacher may wish to discuss the incident with the child. They may plan ways the child can avoid similar problems in the future. Due to the controversy in the 1980s surrounding the use of physical restraint and physical contact with children, it is prudent to discuss the use of such methods with the school administrator and ascertain school and district policies with regard to their use. Parental permission must be obtained if physical restraint is to be used to manage children's behavior.

The behavior influence techniques discussed in this section are effective in the control of directly observable behaviors. They should be a part of the behavior management method of all teachers. The techniques are most effective when used with consistency.

Social Skills Curriculum

Often students with behavior problems are viewed by peers, teachers, parents, and others as socially incompetent. They engage in behavior excesses such as cursing, shouting, arguing, and disrupting. They either have not had the opportunity to learn or have not learned, when given the opportunity, appropriate social skills (Carter & Sugai, 1989).

A social skills curriculum is designed to help students focus on increasing their awareness and understanding of personal emotions, values, and attitudes through educational activities (Edwards & O'Toole, 1985; Epanchin & Monson, 1982; McGinnis, Sauerbry, & Nichols, 1985). These activities lead to improvement of the students' interpersonal problem-solving skills. Neel (1988) suggests that social skills training would better prepare all children to live in our complex society.

Goldstein, Spafkin, Gershaw, and Klein (1983) list fifty social skills in six categories needed by children and youth to enhance their social functioning. These skills are listed in Table 6.1.

TABLE 6.1
Social skills by skill groups

Group I.   Beginning Social Skills
1. Listening
2. Starting a conversation
3. Having a conversation
4. Asking a question
5. Saying "thank you"
6. Introducing oneself
7. Introducing other people
8. Giving a compliment

Group II.   Advanced Social Skills
9. Asking for help
10. Joining in
11. Giving instructions
12. Following instructions
13. Apologizing
14. Convincing others

Group III.   Skills for Dealing with Feelings
15. Knowing one's feelings
16. Expressing one's feelings
17. Understanding the feelings of others
18. Dealing with someone else's anger
19. Expressing affection
20. Dealing with fear
21. Rewarding oneself

Group IV.   Skill Alternatives to Aggression
22. Asking permission
23. Sharing something
24. Helping others

25. Negotiating
26. Using self-control
27. Standing up for one's rights
28. Responding to teasing
29. Avoiding trouble with others
30. Keeping out of fights

Group V.   Skills for Dealing with Stress
31. Making a complaint
32. Answering a complaint
33. Showing sportsmanship after the game
34. Dealing with embarrassment
35. Dealing with being left out
36. Standing up for a friend
37. Responding to persuasion
38. Responding to failure
39. Dealing with contradictory messages
40. Dealing with an accusation
41. Getting ready for a difficult conversation
42. Dealing with group pressure

Group VI.   Planning Skills
43. Deciding on something to do
44. Deciding what caused a problem
45. Setting a goal
46. Deciding on one's abilities
47. Gathering information
48. Arranging problems by importance
49. Making a decision
50. Concentrating on a task.

(From "Structures Learning: A Psychoeducational Approach for Teaching Social Competencies" by A. P. Goldstein, R. P. Spafkin, N. J. Gershaw, and P. Klein, 1983. *Behavioral Disorders,* 8(3), pp. 161-162. Copyright 1983 by *Behavioral Disorders.* Reprinted by permission.)

The social skills curriculum most compatible with the psychoeducational framework discussed previously in this chapter is the "Psychoeducational Curriculum for the Prevention of Behavioral and Learning Problems" (commonly referred to as the "Self-Control Curriculum") by Fagen, Long, and Stevens (1975). The self-control curriculum was designed as a preventive intervention for use with all children.

This curriculum is based on the assumption that a common denominator for disruptive behaviors of children with behavior and learning problems is a lack of self-control. To function effectively, children must develop the capacity to control their behavior, even when frustrated. Self-control is defined as "one's capacity to direct and regulate personal action (behavior) flexibly and realistically in a given situation" (Fagen & Long, 1976). An important objective of the curriculum is the

TABLE 6.2
The self-control curriculum: overview of curriculum areas and units

Area	Curriculum Unit
Selection	1. Focusing and concentration 2. Mastering figure-ground discrimination 3. Mastering distractions and interference 4. Processing complex patterns
Storage	1. Developing visual memory 2. Developing auditory memory
Sequencing and ordering	1. Developing time orientation 2. Developing auditory-visual sequencing 3. Developing sequential planning
Anticipating consequences	1. Identifying feelings 2. Evaluating consequences
Appreciating feelings	1. Identifying feelings 2. Developing positive feelings 3. Managing feelings 4. Reinterpreting feeling events
Managing frustration	1. Accepting feelings of frustration 2. Building coping resources 3. Tolerating frustration
Inhibition and delay	1. Controlling action 2. Developing part-goals
Relaxation	1. Developing body relaxation 2. Developing thought relaxation 3. Developing movement relaxation

(From *Teaching Children Self-Control: Preventing Emotional and Leaning Problems in the Elementary Schools (p. 77)* by S. A. Fagan, N.J. Long, and D.J. Stevens, 1975, Columbus, OH: Merrill Publishing Co. Copyright 1975 by Merrill Publishing Co. Reprinted by permission.)

reduction of students' anxiety over losing self-control by increasing the skills and confidence they have in the ability to regulate their impulsive behavior. Morse (1979) indicated that the self-control curriculum advocates inserting a cognitive pause between an impulse and its expression. It trains students to use cognitive processes to balance personal behavioral options in terms of their experiences and goals.

Skillful self-control depends on the integration of eight skills clusters. These skill clusters, in turn, are composed of several specific skills. The clusters and skills are presented in Table 6.2.

In the curriculum, the learning of each specific skill is accomplished through a variety of activities. Through learning the skills in the eight clusters, the authors predict growth in the student's capacity to direct and regulate personal action in given situations. Activities that make up the curriculum include games, role playing, lessons, and discussion. Activities are implemented in small, developmental steps and include positive feedback. Short, regular training sessions are advised. Andersen, Nelson, Fox, and Gruber (1988) suggested procedures for integrating a social skills curriculum with cooperative learning and structured learning teaching methods.

There are a variety of social skills and affective education curricula available in the literature. The practitioner must give careful consideration to the appropriateness of a particular program for the children for whom it is to be applied. Schumaker, Pederson, Hazel, and Meyen (1983) suggest five questions for practitioners to address when selecting a social skills curriculum:

1. Does the curriculum promote social competence?
2. Does the curriculum accommodate the learning characteristics of the students for whom it is to be applied?
3. Does the curriculum target the social skills deficits of the students for whom it is to be applied?
4. Does the curriculum provide training in situations as well as in skills?
5. Does the curriculum include instructional methodologies found to be effective with the population of students for whom it is to be applied?

Carter and Sugai (1989) developed a comprehensive procedure for the analysis of a social skills curriculum. Analysis includes giving consideration to instructional strategies, grouping, individualization, cost-effectiveness, instructor training, field test results, student assessment and evaluation, and maintenance and generalization training. These authors designed a useful curriculum analysis checklist and decision making grid.

Nelson (1988) notes that research indicates that a social skills curriculum does promote the acquisition of socially appropriate behaviors by students with exceptionalities. However, there is little research evidence that social skills instruction is effective over time and across settings.

SUMMARY

In this chapter, a variety of behavior management interventions derived from psychodynamic theory are discussed. Attention is given to the psychoeducational model; a broad perspective applied to the management and education of children. Two counseling techniques, life-space interviewing and reality therapy interviewing for use by teacher, with minimal training, are discussed in detail.

The expressive media are presented as indirect behavior management interventions. The expressive media include free play, puppetry, role playing and psychodrama, creative movement and dance, music, the spoken and written word, bibliotherapy, art therapy, and others. They are recommended as therapeutic interventions that encourage children to express their positive and negative feelings and emotions in an acceptable manner.

Several behavior influence techniques are discussed as interventions teachers may wish to apply when a student's surface behavior interferes with daily function.

(These interventions *must* be applied in circumstances that endanger the student, teacher, peers, and property.) The chapter concludes with a discussion of social skills curriculum that may be applied to instruct students in socially appropriate behaviors.

In the next chapter, attention is focused on interventions derived from environmental and biophysical theories.

PROJECTS

1. Write a brief essay (300 words) on the advantages and disadvantages of the psychodynamic behavior management interventions.
2. Conduct a life-space interview with a classmate. Invite your other classmates to evaluate your performance.
3. Conduct a reality therapy interview with a classmate. Invite your other classmates to evaluate your performance.
4. Conduct a library research study of one of the expressive media as a behavior management intervention. Report your finding in a formal presentation to your classmates.
5. Discuss the advantages and disadvantages of the behavior influence techniques for the teacher.
6. Research the literature on self-control curriculum and report your findings to your class.

REFERENCES

Adderholdt-Elliot, M., & Eller, S.H. (1989). Counseling students who are gifted through bibliotherapy. *Teaching Exceptional Children, 22*(1), 26-31.

Allen, J. I. (1980). Jogging can modify disruptive behaviors. *Teaching Exceptional Children, 12*(2), 66-70.

Andersen, M., Nelson, L. R., Fox, R. G., & Gruber, S. E. (1988). Integrating cooperative learning and structured learning: Effective approaches to teaching social skills. *Focus on Exceptional Children, 20*(9), 1-8.

Anderson, E. (1985). A. M. Club. *Teaching: Behaviorally Disordered Youth, 1,* 12-16.

Axline, V. M. (1947). *Play therapy.* Boston: Houghton Mifflin Co.

Berkowitz, P. H., & Rothman, E. P. (Eds.). (1967), *Public education for disturbed children in New York City.* Springfield, IL: Charles C. Thomas.

Brenner, M. B. (1969). Life space interviewing in the school setting. In H. Dupont (Ed.), *Educating emotionally disturbed children.* New York: Holt, Rinehart & Winston.

Carter, J., & Sugai, G. (1989). Social skills curriculum

analysis. *Teaching Exceptional Children, 22*(1), 36-39.

Chace, M. (1958). Dance in growth or treatment settings. *Music Therapy, 1,* 119-121.

Cheney, C., & Morse, W. C. (1972). Psychodynamic interventions in emotional disturbance. In W. C. Rhodes & M. L. Tracy (Eds.), *A study of child variance: Vol. 2. Interventions.* Ann Arbor: The University of Michigan Press.

Cianciolo, P. J. (1965). Children's literature can affect coping behavior. *Personnel and Guidance Journal. 43*(9), 897-903.

Cook, J. H. (1972). *The effects of small group counseling on the classroom behavior of sociometrically underchosen adolescents.* Unpublished doctoral dissertation, University of Georgia. (Discussed in Shearn & Randolph, 1978).

Creekmore, N. N., & Madan, A. J. (1981). The use of sociodrama as a therapeutic technique with behavior disordered children. *Behavioral Disorders, 7*(1), 28-33.

D'Alonzo, B. (1974). Puppets fill the classroom with

imagination. *Teaching Exceptional Children,*
6(3), 141-144.

David, D., & Newcomer, P. L. (1980). Art and music
therapy. In P. L. Newcomer (Ed.), *Understanding*
and teaching emotionally disturbed children
(pp. 391-408). Boston: Allyn & Bacon.

Dehouske, E. J. (1982). Story writing as a problem
solving vehicle. *Teaching Exceptional Children,*
15(1), 11-17.

DeMagistris, R. J., & Imber, S.C. (1980). The effects
of life space interviewing on the academic and
social performance of behavior disordered
children. *Behavioral Disorders, 6*(1), 12-25.

Department of Mental Health and Developmental
Disabilities, State of Illinois (1980). Photo therapy:
Old technique reappears as a new tool. *Feelings,*
5(1), 3-4.

Duerksen, G. L. (1981). Music for exceptional
students. *Focus on Exceptional Children, 14*(4),
1-11.

Edwards, L. L., & O'Toole, B. (1985). Application
of self-control curriculum with behavior disordered students. *Focus on Exceptional Children,*
17(8), 1-8.

Epanchin, B. C., & Monson, L. B. (1982). Affective
education. In J.L. Paul & B.C. Epanchin (Eds.),
Emotional disturbance in children: Theories
and methods for teachers. Columbus, OH:
Merrill.

Evans, W. H., Evans, S. S., Schmid, R. E., &
Pennypacker, H.S. (1985). The effects of exercise
on selected classroom behaviors of behaviorally
disordered adolescents. *Behavioral Disorders,*
11(1), 42-51.

Fagen, S. A., & Long, N. J. (1976). Teaching children
self-control: A new responsibility for teachers.
Focus on Exceptional Children, 7(8), 1-10.

Fagen, S. A., Long, N. J., & Stevens, D. J. (1975).
Teaching children self-control: Preventing
emotional and learning problems in the
elementary school. Columbus, OH: Merrill.

Fagen, S. A. (1981). Conducting an LSI: A process
model. *Pointer, 25*(2), 9-11.

Ferolo, M. A., Rotatori, A. F., & Fox, R. (1984).
Increasing visual attention by music therapy
programming for sensory stimulation with
profoundly retarded children. *ICEC Quarterly,*
33(2), 17-21.

Ferolo, M. A., Rotatori, A., Macklin, F., & Fox, R.
(1983). The successful use of behavior modification in music therapy with severely/pro-
foundly retarded people. *ICEC Quarterly, 32*(2),
30-34.

Fink, A. H. (1988). The psychoeducational philosophy: Programming implications for students
with behavioral disorders. *Behavior in Our*
Schools, 2(2), 8-13.

Ginott, H. G., (1959). The theory and practice of
therapeutic interventions in child treatment.
*Journal of Consulting Psychology, 23,*160-166.

Glasser, W. (1965). *Reality therapy: A new*
approach to psychiatry. New York: Harper &
Row.

Glasser, W. (1969). *Schools without failure.* New
York: Harper & Row.

Glasser, W. (1984). *Control theory.* New York: Harper
& Row.

Glick, B. H. (1968). *The investigation of changes*
in self-concept, social self-esteem, and aca-
demic self-responsibility of emotionally dis-
turbed boys who participate in open-ended
classroom meetings. Unpublished doctoral
dissertation, Syracuse University. (Discussed in
Shearn & Randolph, 1978.)

Goldstein, A. P., Spafkin, R. P., Gershaw, N. J., &
Klein, P. (1983). Structures learnings: A psychoeducational approach for teaching social competencies. *Behavioral Disorders, 8*(3), 161-170.

Halsted, J. W. (1988). *Guiding gifted readers.*
Columbus, OH: Ohio Psychology Publishing.

Harms, J. M., Etscheidt, S. L., & Lettow, L. J. (1986).
Extending emotional responses through poetry
experiences. *Teaching: Behaviorally Disor-*
dered Youth, 2, 26-32.

Hawes, R. M. (1970). *Reality therapy in the*
classroom. Unpublished doctoral dissertation,
University of the Pacific. (Discussed in Shearn
& Randolph, 1978).

Heuchert, C. M. (1989). Enhancing self-directed
behavior in the classroom. *Academic Therapy,*
24(3), 295-303.

Hibben, J., & Scheer, R. (1982). Music and
movement for special needs children. *Teaching*
Exceptional Children, 14(5), 171-176.

Hoagland, J. (1972). Bibliotherapy: Aiding children
in personality development. *Elementary English,*

15, 390-394.

Hoenig, G. K., Shea, T. M., & Bauer, A. M. (1986). Jogging and children with behavior disorders: Effects on self-doubting and aggressive behaviors. *ICEC Quarterly, 36*(4), 16-21.

Lament, M. M. (1978). Reaching the exceptional student through music in the elementary classroom. *Teaching Exceptional Children, 11*(1), 32-35.

Lane, B., Bonic, J., & Wallgren-Bonic, N. (1983). The group walk-talk: A therapeutic challenge for secondary students with social-emotional problems. *Teaching Exceptional Children, 16*(1), 12-17.

Leone, P. (1984). A descriptive follow-up of behaviorally disordered adolescents. *Behavioral Disorders, 9*(3), 207-214.

Levinson, C. (1982). Remediating a passive aggressive emotionally disturbed pre-adolescent boy through writing: A comprehensive psychodynamic structured approach. *The Pointer, 26*(2), 23-27.

Long, N. J., & Fagen, S. A. (Eds.) (1980). *The Pointer, 25*(2).

Long, N. J., Morse, W. C., & Newman, R. G. (1980). Milieu therapy. In N. J. Long, W. C. Morse, & R. G. Newman (Eds.), *Conflict in the classroom: The education of emotionally disturbed children* (4th ed.). Belmont, CA: Wadsworth Publishing Co.

Long, N. J., & Newman, R. G. (1965). Managing surface behavior of children in school. In N. J.Long, W. C. Morse, & R. G. Newman (Eds.), *Conflict in the classroom: The education of emotionally disturbed children*. Belmont, CA: Wadsworth Publishing Co.

Long, N. J., & Newman, R. G. (1961). A differential approach to the management of surface behavior of children in school. *Bulletin of the School of Education, 37*, Indiana University.

McGinnis, E., Sauerbry, L., & Nichols, P. (1985). Skill-streaming: Teaching social skills to children with behavior disorders. *Teaching Exceptional Children, 17*(3), 160-167.

McIntyre, T. (1987). Classroom conferencing: Providing support and guidance for misbehaving youth. *Teaching: Behaviorally Disordered Youth, 3*, 33-35.

Michel, D. E. (1976). *Music therapy: An introduction to therapy and special education through music.* Springfield, IL: Charles C. Thomas

Minner, S. (1981). Using photography as an adjunctive and creative approach. *Teaching Exceptional Children, 13*(4), 145-147.

Moreno, J. L. (1946). *Psychodrama.* Beacon, NY: Beacon House.

Morse, W. C. (1979). Self-control: The Fagen-Long curriculum. *Behavioral Disorders, 4*, 83-91.

Morse, W. C. (1985). *The education and treatment of socioemotionally impaired children and youth.* Syracuse, NY: Syracuse University Press.

Naslund, S. R. (1987). Life space interviewing: A psychoeducational intervention model for teaching pupils insight and measuring program effectiveness. *Pointer, 31*(2), 12-15.

Necco, E., Wilson, C., & Scheidmantel, J. (1982). Affective learning through drama. *Teaching Exceptional Children, 15*(1), 22-24.

Neel, R. S. (1988). Implementing social skills instruction in schools. *Behavior In Our Schools, 3*(1), 13-18.

Nelson, C. M. (1988). Social skills training for handicapped students. *Teaching Exceptional Children, 20*, 19-23.

Newcomer, P. L. (1980). *Understanding and teaching emotionally disturbed children.* Boston: Allyn & Bacon.

Nichols, P. (1984). Down the up staircase: The teacher as therapist. In J. Grosenick, S. Huntze, E. McGinnis, & C. Smith (Eds.), *Social/affective interventions in behavioral disorders.* Des Moines: State of Iowa Department of Public Instruction.

Nichols, P. (1986). Down the up staircase: The teacher as therapist. *Teaching: Behaviorally Disordered Youth, 2*, 1-13.

Omizo, M. M., & Omizo, S. A. (1988). Intervention through art. *Academic Therapy, 24*(1), 103-106.

Peter, L. J. (1965). *Prescriptive teaching.* New York: McGraw Hill Book Co.

Polt, J. M., & Hale, C. (1985). Using pets as "therapists" for children with developmental disasbilities. *Teaching Exceptional Children, 17* (3), 218-222.

Purvis, J., & Samet, S. (1976). *Music in developmental therapy.* Baltimore: University Park Press.

Raschke, D., Dedrick, C., & Takes, M. (1986). Videotape feedback as a therapeutic tool. *Teaching: Behaviorally Disordered Youth, 2,* 14-19.

Raths, L.E., Harmin, M., & Simon, S.B. (1978). *Values and teaching.* Columbus, OH: Merrill.

Redl, F. (1959). The concept of the life space interview. *American Journal of Orthopsychiatry, 29,* 1-18.

Redl, F., & Wineman, D. (1957). *The aggressive child.* New York: The Free Press.

Reilly, M. J., Imber, S. C., & Cremins, J. (1978). *The effects of life space interviews on social behaviors of junior high school special needs students.* Paper presented at the 56th International Council for Exceptional Children, Kansas City.

Roter, J. (1981). Music a therapeutic intervention for emotionally disturbed youth. In F. H. Wood (Ed.), *Perspective for a new decade: Education's responsibility for seriously disturbed and behaviorally disordered children and youth.* (pp. 154-162). Reston, VA: Council for Exceptional Children.

Russell, A. E., & Russell, W. A. (1979). Using bibliotherapy with emotionally disturbed children. *Teaching Exceptional Children, 11,* 168-169.

Scheaf, W. A. (1972). *The effects of paired learning and Glasser-type discussions on two determinants of academic achievement and on reading achievement of male delinquents.* Unpublished doctoral dissertation, Case Western Reserve University. (Discussed in Shearn & Randolph, 1978.)

Schrank, F., & Engels, D. (1981). Bibliotherapy as a counseling adjunct: Research findings. *Personnel and Guidance Journal, 60*(3), 143-147.

Schumaker, J. B., Pederson, C. S., Hazel, J. S., & Meyen, E. L. (1983). Social skills curricula for mildly handicapped adolescents: A review. *Focus on Exceptional Children, 16*(4), 1-16.

Shea, T. M., Whiteside, W. R., Beetner, E. G., & Lindsey, D. L. (1974). *Microteaching module: Behavioral interventions.* Edwardsville: Southern Illinois University.

Shearn, D. F., & Randolph, D. L. (1978). Effects of reality therapy methods applied in the classroom. *Psychology in the Schools, 15,* 79-83.

Thursby, D. D. (1977). Everyone's a star. *Teaching Exceptional Children, 9*(3), 77-78.

Warger, C. L. (1985). Making creative drama accessible to handicapped children. *Teaching Exceptional Children, 17*(4), 288-293.

Warger, C. L., & Weiner, B. B. (Eds.), (1987). *Secondary special education: A guide to promising public school programs.* Reston, VA: Council for Exceptional Children.

Williams, G. H., & Wood, M. M. (1977). *Developmental art therapy.* Baltimore: University Park Press.

Wood, M. M. (1976). Foreword. In J. Purvis & S. Samet (Eds.), *Music in developmental therapy* (pp. vii-viii). Baltimore: University Park Press.

Yell, M. L. (1988). The effects of jogging on the rates of selected target behaviors of behaviorally disordered students. *Behavioral Disorders, 13*(4), 273-279.

Zabel, R. H. (1988). Research in brief. *Behavior in Our Schools, 2*(3), 9.

CHAPTER SEVEN

Environmental and Biophysical Behavior Management

Jack and his gang were loitering near the front door of Hooverville High School planning their Monday morning activities. By general consensus their target for the day was to be Marcie Meek. Jack conducted a discussion during which the group of five boys decided how to make life miserable for Marcie. They agreed to whistle and catcall at her in the corridors. They were going to tell everyone they met that Marcie was "easy." Finally, every time she was called on during class, they would grumble and sigh.

Jack and the gang were of considerable concern to the whole school population, especially to Mr. Whiteburn, assistant principal for discipline. It appeared that Jack and his friends selected a different student or teacher each day as a target for their hostility. Each of the boys had been referred to Mr. Whiteburn several times during the year for disciplining. He had punished them, individually and as a group, many times without success. He had even called their parents.

Although the group's behavior was disruptive, it was not severe enough to result in expulsion or suspension.

Mr. Whiteburn knows that the group's behavior must be redirected from negative to positive goals before the boys become involved in a serious incident. He must seek out a means to help the gang plan and carry out appropriate activities.

Six-year-old John was being observed by the first-grade teacher, Mrs. Prime. As she observed John, he climbed over the worktable, ran to the toy box, and threw several blocks, trucks, and dolls on the floor. Next John ran around the room touching each child and the four walls.

After this he returned to his seat at the worktable, grabbed his crayon, and scribbled on his work sheet for about 10 seconds. While he was scribbling, John was wiggling in his chair and tapping his feet.

Suddenly John fell to his hands and knees and began crawling to the toy box. He climbed into the box and threw the remaining toys on the floor. Having accomplished this, John returned to the worktable. John's hyperactive behavior continued throughout Mrs. Prime's 1-hour observation session.

That afternoon, in discussion with John's mother and preschool teacher, Mrs. Prime learned that John's behavior during the observation session was typical of his behavior at home and in preschool. Both the preschool teacher and his mother reported using a variety of behavior modification interventions without success. John appeared unable to control his activity; he appeared driven.

Mrs. Prime knew she must have some assistance if John were to attend her first grade class. He simply could not succeed in school unless his behavior was controlled.

In this chapter a variety of behavior management interventions derived from environmental and biophysical theories are reviewed and exemplified. The environmental behavior management interventions include child-centered, environment-centered, child-environment-centered and interface-centered strategies. Other environmental interventions include strategies related to group composition and processes, the classroom setting, and class meetings. The antecedents of effective management and inschool suspension, suspension, and expulsion are also discussed in the first section of this chapter. The section concludes with a review of milieu therapy and the levels system.

The second section of this chapter is devoted to a discussion of biophysical strategies such as prenatal and postnatal care, nutrition, medication, diets, and so on. This section concludes with discussion of the educator's role in biophysical interventions.

It should be noted that, for the most part, environmental interventions focus attention on the manipulation of groups and the environment rather than on individual students.

Several environmental and biophysical interventions employed by professionals in the medical and mental health disciplines are not presented in this chapter because of their complexity and the special training requirements necessary for implementation. The reader is urged to review the theoretical frameworks underlying the environmental and biophysical models presented in Chapter 1 before studying this chapter.

It should be noted that the educator has limited direct involvement in the diagnosis, prescribing, implementation, and evaluation of biophysical interventions.

CHAPTER OBJECTIVES

After completing this chapter, you will be able to do the following:

1. Differentiate among child-, environment-, child-environment-, and interface-centered environmental interventions.
2. Discuss group composition and process, discussion groups, and class meetings.
3. Describe and exemplify the several antecedents to effective management.
4. Explain milieu therapy.
5. Design a levels system.
6. Define expulsion, suspension, and inschool suspension.
7. Characterize the several biophysical interventions.
8. Understand the educator's role in biophysical intervention.

Environmental Interventions

In varying degrees, the interventions discussed in this section focus attention on the child's environment as the locus of the behavior problem. There are four groups of environmental interventions; these are distinguished from one another by the degree of emphasis placed on the individual's environment for the purposes of intervention.

According to Rhodes and Gibbens (1972) and Wagner (1972), these groups are as follows:

1. Child-centered interventions, which focus almost exclusively on the child.
2. Environment-centered interventions, which focus almost exclusively on the environment.
3. Child-environment-centered interventions, which focus on both the child and environment.
4. Interface-centered interventions, which focus on the exchange patterns between the child and the environment.

The distinctions among these classifications are blurred; the degree of emphasis focused on the child, the environment, and the relationship between them is not clear-cut. Wagner, however, made an attempt to place the environmental interventions on a continuum ranging from primary emphasis on the child to primary emphasis on the environment.

Child-Centered Interventions

Among the child-centered interventions, which are primarily concerned with accommodating the child to the environment, are the following.

Remedial Programs Aimed at Psychomotor, Cognitive, and Affective Learning. These interventions include programs in gross and fine motor coordination, perceptual training, academic education, and affective education, among others. The activities normally conducted in special education rooms or by itinerant teachers are excellent examples of child-centered interventions as applied in the school.

Natural Community Interventions. Although few if any opportunities exist for this type of intervention in this century, the general goal of these interventions is the placement of an individual in a natural community setting where behavior is changed by naturally occurring processes inherent in community living (Byrne, 1869; cited in Wagner, 1972). Terez (1986) reports that the natural community intervention strategy remains viable in Belgium in the town of Geel. The Geel Family Care system serves approximately 870 patients living in 660 families in the community.

The natural community intervention was one of the objectives of the community mental health movement that began in the 1960s and continues to the present in the United States. During this period many mentally ill and mentally retarded persons were returned to live in the community with the hope that a natural environment would have a therapeutic effect on their behavior.

Artificial Community Interventions.   Aimed at the child, these interventions involve the development and systematic manipulation of an artificial community (commune, collective, or residential center) to modify the child's behavior. There are many examples of artificial community interventions in contemporary society. These include halfway houses, community living centers, residential schools, and so on.

Artificial Group Interventions.   These interventions involve attempts to change the child in the home community by means of an artificial group. This approach is used frequently in delinquency rehabilitation programs. Groups are organized to maintain and change the individual in the community. The group provides the individual with social and psychological support as well as guidance and direction. Contemporary examples of artificial group interventions include the Guardian Angels and similar positively oriented street gangs as well as the Scouts, Big Sisters, Big Brothers, and so on.

Environment-Centered Interventions

Among the environment-centered interventions, which are primarily focused on changing the child's environment, are the following.

Family Environment Interventions.   Aimed at the child's family unit, these interventions are accomplished primarily by training and education in child rearing, behavior management, and family living. Family counseling and therapy are often included in this intervention.

School Environment Interventions.   Aimed at modifying the school environment and thus increasing the child's probability of success and acceptance, these interventions are accomplished through in-service teacher training, consultation, and the like.

Child-Environment-Centered Interventions

Child-environment-centered interventions, which focus on both the child and the environment, include the following.

Natural Group in Urban Environment Interventions. These interventions involve the manipulation and redirection of existing natural groups, such as street gangs. The gang is redirected from primarily destructive effects on the community to constructive effects. The natural group in the urban environment intervention is similar to the artificial group intervention noted earlier.

Child-School-Environment Interventions. In these interventions the focus is on the remediation of the child's behavior and learning and on the environment's responsiveness to the child (Weinstein, 1968). Child-school-environment interventions are best exemplified by the Re-Ed Schools and similar schools that focus attention on all facets of the child, his or her behavior, the family, the school, residential care unit, and the community.

Interface-Centered Interventions

These interventions are aimed at modifying the reciprocal relationship between the child and the environment, including persons in the environment. The focus is on assessing and changing the quality of individual-environment transactions. Emphasis is on specific problem areas.

Examples of these interventions include (1) training students in behavior modification techniques that they apply in school with teachers and peers, and (2) evaluating and modifying a specific problem interface in which a student is functioning ineffectively.

Group Composition

Several behavior management interventions are closely associated with classroom and activity groups. Some specific management techniques employed as a part of these environmental interventions are discussed in Chapter 6 as counseling techniques (under that heading) and throughout this text as behavior modification interventions. However, when the group is a significant part of a child's overall behavior management program, two important topics must be considered in the selection and imposition of these management techniques: group composition and group processes.

Grouping children on the basis of school records and admission data is an important but difficult task. It is a process that of necessity involves the cooperation of all persons familiar with the children.

Among the variables to be considered during the grouping process are (1) age, (2) sex, (3) interests, (4) handicapping conditions, if any, (5) personality traits, (6) the degree, intensity, and kind of behavior problems, if any, and (7) group experiences and skills. When grouping children, an effort is made to avoid extremes in group composition while at the same time attempting to form a "balanced" group. In the organization of groups, the adult members of the group, such as the teacher and paraprofessional, are considered group members.

Extremes in group (and subgroup) composition are avoided when

1. Children of greatly different ages are not placed in the same group.
2. Children without common interests are not placed in the same group.
3. An individual is not placed in a group that lacks a like-sex peer.
4. A child with a severe handicap is not placed in a group of nonhandicapped or mildly handicapped children if the placement prohibits either from participating in important activities. However, if adequately trained personnel are available to assist, the curriculum can be modified and this potential limitation circumvented.
5. Children with potentially conflicting personality traits and behavior problems are not placed in the same group.
6. An unskilled child is not placed in a group composed of individuals who are highly skilled and experienced in group processes. This placement is only permissible if the group members, including the adults, are aware of the child's lack of skill and experience in groups and agree to facilitate the child's integration.
7. An individual who is neither ready nor willing to participate in group activities is not placed in a group environment. Reference here is to children with severe behavior and learning problems who lack skills needed for meaningful group participation. Frequently these individuals remain in the group but do not become "functioning" members.

Grouping is a difficult process because the staff must deal with intangible variables that defy precise measurement. However, the group can have a positive impact on student behavior. Using a nonintrusive management technique to control acting-out behavior, Stainback, Stainback, Etscheidt, and Doud (1986) reaffirmed the belief that peer modeling affects student behavior. They studied the differences in the acting-out behavior of a student in a well-behaved group and in a disruptive group. They noted a significant decrease in acting-out behavior in the well-behaved group.

Group Process

The group process itself can be of therapeutic benefit to some children. Loughmiller (1965) used self-governing, problem-solving groups in the camp setting. Also applicable in the school setting, these groups are set up to expose students to a wide range of successful interpersonal experiences. These experiences encourage participation, responsibility, and cooperation in activities.

In this intervention, children and teachers are responsible for their daily activities within predetermined limits established by the administration. The members find themselves in a situation where majority rule prevails. Each individual is responsible for his or her personal behavior and for the behavior of the group (Shea, 1977).

Some limits on the group's behavior and activities are imposed by an administrator or other nongroup authority figure rather than by the teacher, who is a member of the group. However, the group members may impose, by means of majority rule, additional limits on behavior and activities. The limits imposed by the administrator are few in number and are concerned with dining and work schedules, attendance at assemblies, transportation, health, safety, and the like. These limits must be imposed by the administration if it is to meet its responsibilities to the members of the group.

Any social cosmos requires certain routines (Morse and Wineman, 1957). Without routines, limits, and prescribed ways of behaving, anarchy would result and the group would disintegrate. Thus the group, as a group, decides (1) the limits to be set on social interaction, (2) how extreme behaviors are to be managed if they occur, (3) how activities and schedules of events are to be developed and executed, (4) who is to be responsible for various phases of daily living, and (5) how problems and conflicts are to be resolved.

The problem-solving process becomes a part of the group's daily life. When conflicts or unfamiliar problems occur that prohibit the group from attaining its immediate goals, problem solving is initiated. During the problem-solving process, the group attempts to develop alternative solutions to the circumstances confronting them. The members have two major tasks: (1) identifying and clarifying their problem, and (2) discussing (evaluating) and agreeing on one or more solutions to the problem. The agreed-upon solution can be imposed either immediately or in similar situations in the future. In addition to these tasks, the members of the group must deal with the positive and negative social-emotional behaviors that naturally occur during the problem-solving process.

Morse and Wineman (1957) recommended the application of life-space interview techniques in the group on a regular and emergency basis. Discussed in Chapter 6 as a counseling technique, the life-space interview may focus on a variety of critical group-process issues:

- Existing social realities that prohibit group desires
- Existing defense or coping mechanisms that the group and its members unconsciously apply for protection against those who are not members of the group
- Techniques for application by the members to admit mistakes, misdeeds, and asocial behaviors
- Ways to use the group as a setting in which emotions and frustrations may be expressed and the limits on such expression
- Ways to strengthen the group's and the individual members' self-concept, especially after conflicts, frustrations, and failures
- Procedures for identifying, clarifying, and agreeing to mutually acceptable solutions to common problems

As a group member, the educator's role is important if group behavior management interventions are to be effectively applied in the classroom and school. The teacher must be a model of "give and take" democratic leadership and must be willing to permit the members of the group to make meaningful decisions, implement programs, and realize the consequences of their actions.

The teacher allows the logical consequences of the group's decisions and actions to occur. At the same time, however, the teacher protects the group from repeated or excessive failure and individual members from physical and psychological harm.

Discussion Groups

Anderson and Marrone (1979) described the use of therapeutic discussion groups in public school classes for emotionally disturbed students. As a result of 12 years of experience with more than 6,000 children, they concluded " . . . we cannot imagine a program for emotionally handicapped students that would not fit the proven, cost-effective methodology of therapeutic discussion groups in the classroom" (p. 15).

After a period of experimentation during which students were involved in individual therapy, therapeutic discussion groups, or nontherapeutic treatment, it was concluded that the group model benefited the children and teachers in several ways. Teachers benefited by receiving support through teamwork with mental health professionals. In addition, they received training in psychodynamic theory and techniques that enhanced their understanding of student behavior. For students, the group provided structured time for communication and affective education. The goal of the therapeutic discussion groups was to change behavior. Through the group, appropriate student behavior could be reinforced and empathy, concern, and caring encouraged. Group discussion also increased the opportunities for early intervention with children who had potential problems. Group techniques were applied successfully with psychotic, passive aggressive, and depressed children.

When implemented, group sessions of 30 to 60 minutes are conducted weekly with the psychologist or psychiatrist, teacher, paraprofessional, and social worker present. The group sits in a circle, and meeting length varies according to the age and needs of the children. Pre- and post-meeting sessions are conducted by the mental health consultant with the teacher to evaluate the session and to discuss concerns, needs, and behaviors of the children. Group sessions then become a standard part of each student's program.

Anderson and Marrone suggest the following group discussion guidelines:

1. Children may speak on any topic. Physical aggression and obscene language are inappropriate.
2. Confidentiality is stressed.
3. Discussion may be initiated or facilitated by centering on a specific student interest, need, positive behavior, or similar topic.
4. After several weekly meetings, when the team has an understanding of each student's needs, the following therapeutic progression is applied:
   a. Help each student recognize his or her ineffective behavior.
   b. Help the student explore and recognize the feelings behind the ineffective behaviors.

    c. Identify the source of the feelings.

    d. Connect these feelings with the student's actions and their consequences.

    e. Facilitate the student's commitment to change.

    f. Plan alternative behaviors with the student.

    g. Support the student's efforts to change.

    h. Recognize the new behavior and encourage it.

There are several prerequisites for the successful implementation of groups in the public schools. Anderson and Marrone maintain that a belief in the use of therapeutic discussion groups and administrative support are essential. The program must also have a competent mental health consultant (psychiatrist, clinical psychologist, case worker, counselor) who accepts the team concept.

Class Meetings

Class meetings can be instituted as a part of the normal classroom procedure. Meetings can be called to deal with the common problems of living and learning in a group setting. Over a period of time the members of the class learn, with guidance, to seek solutions to problems through verbal transactions with peers and the teacher. During class meetings, members grow in understanding of themselves and others. They learn to conceptualize problems from another's point of view. Coleman and Webber (1988) recommended working with adolescents in groups to reduce teacher-student conflicts and to enhance student self-control.

Three kinds of meetings for classroom application have been suggested by Harth and Morris (1976) and Morris (1982).

Open Meeting. This meeting is called to permit an individual to express covert feelings. The individual is given an opportunity to state to the group the frustrations and feelings that the individual believes are the result of another member's actions. This other member, or antagonist, may be a peer or the teacher. Any member of the group may request an open meeting. The session is generally conducted by a peer.

EXAMPLE ■ Billy's ninth-grade class was responsible for planning and conducting the all-school assembly for the Christmas holiday. It was the most important activity of the school year for the class. Each member of the class had a role to play in the program.

Unfortunately for Billy, he was absent from school with the flu on the day his class planned the program. Neither the teacher nor his fellow students remembered to assign a function to Billy. Consequently he was very frustrated and angry. He was angry with the teacher and his peers. He was hurt and sad because he was a forgotten person. After all, it was not his fault that he got the flu and his mother made him stay at home.

Billy's teacher, Mr. Jetro, had always suggested to his students that if they had a concern about the group, they should request a class meeting. At the meeting they could express and discuss their concern with the group.

Billy asked Mr. Jetro for a meeting. At the meeting he stated his personal concerns. As a result of his action, Billy not only was assigned a role in the assembly but also was given an apology by the program chairperson and teacher for their oversight. ■

Problem-Solving Meeting. This meeting is focused primarily on potential problems. It may be called by any member of the class. Topics include such items as tardiness, disorganization, lack of follow-through on previous commitments, group responsibilities, distractions in the classroom, lack of time to complete assignments, and the like. During the meeting, a solution to the problem is sought by the group. The agreed-upon solution is implemented.

EXAMPLE   ■ Mr. Kaat always tells his senior honors German classes that if they are honestly overburdened by the class assignments they may request a class meeting to discuss the problem. On one particular occasion, Mr. Kaat assigned the class a 10-page technical translation and a term paper just 3 days before midyear examinations. The students believed they were severely overburdened and would as a result do inadequate work on translation, term paper, and examinations. They were also concerned about having sufficient time to prepare for their other examinations.

A problem-solving meeting was called at which a more realistic schedule was agreed to by Mr. Kaat and the class.   ■

Decision-Making Meeting. This meeting focuses primarily on program and curriculum decisions. It gives the program direction: What is to be done? How is it to be accomplished? Where? When? Who is responsible? Why? The decision-making meeting is an excellent medium for involving all members of a class in the curriculum-planning.

EXAMPLE   ■ Mrs. Picoff was faculty advisor for the Blaskit Island High School Future Teachers Society. She was very concerned about the group's future because of lack of interest on the part of the members. The principal had told her that he was considering disbanding the group because they did not plan or complete any projects of benefit to the school or community.

Mrs. Picoff called the officers and members of the group together for a problem-solving meeting. At the meeting she presented the problem confronting the group. As a consequence, the members planned an annual schedule, assigned responsibilities to various members, and established a feedback mechanism to ensure that each person met his or her responsibilities.   ■

These class meetings are designed to find practical solutions to real problems. In addition, the class meeting intervention has significant potential as a preventive technique if consistently and appropriately applied.

Antecedents of Effective Management (Organizing for Instruction)

The effective classroom is planned and organized to facilitate instruction and behavior management. Prior to beginning the school day or year, the teacher must take into consideration a broad range of factors to enhance the probability that learning will occur in the classroom. Among those factors that must be given consideration are space utilization and storage, including procedures for the use of classroom and nonclassroom space, facilities, materials, and equipment. The teacher must develop procedures for individual, small, and whole group activities; beginning and ending the school day or period; transitions; housekeeping; interruptions; visitors; fire drills; and various other activities. The teacher must consider classroom rules for behavior and develop schedules. Cues or prompts to be used in the classroom should also be planned.

The more thoroughly a classroom facility and program are planned, the greater the probability of success for both children and teacher. This section is devoted to an overview of the antecedents to effective instruction and classroom management. The suggestions presented are general and must be modified to respond to the needs of a particular classroom situation.

Space, Materials, and Equipment. Teachers begin the school year by planning for the use of the space, materials, and equipment that they have been assigned. They must give consideration to the use of the space shared with others such as hallways, lunchroom, playground, library, and music room (Evertson, Emmer, Clements, Sanford, Worsham, & Williams, 1981).

Walls, Ceilings, and Bulletin Boards. These are valuable spaces that can be used to display a variety of materials such as schedules, rules, seasonal and topical items, calendars, study assignments, housekeeping assignments, charts, maps, and so on. It is prudent not to overdecorate; space should be reserved for student work and current items. Students can profit from helping to plan displays for bulletin boards. Materials displayed on walls, ceilings, and bulletin boards should be changed periodically so that students will not become desensitized to it.

Floor Space. The use of floor space will vary with the size of the room, the number of students and their characteristics, and the activities to be conducted. The room must be arranged to assure that the teacher can observe all areas in which students will be working and to assure that the students will be able to see the teacher and work materials that the teacher is using for instruction. Student desks and tables should be arranged away from high traffic areas. If tables are used instead of desks or in addition to desks, then space for storage of student materials must be planned. Space must be planned for individual, small group, and whole group activities. If learning centers (reading, mathematics, science) are used, then space must be planned to include these areas. Centers that generate a high degree of activity and noise should not be located near centers that require a high degree of student concentration. All needed materials and equipment should be located in the appropriate center.

The teacher must plan where common items such as plants, pet cages, fish tanks, bookcases, and storage cabinets will be located in the classroom. The teacher's desk, file, and other equipment must be located where they are easily accessible yet do not interfere with activities. Every effort should be made to maintain traffic lanes in the classroom; this will prevent confusion as students move about the room. If the classroom is serving students with physical handicaps, free traffic lanes must be maintained and space organized to assure accessibility.

Storage Space. There are various kinds of supplies, materials and equipment used in the classroom—everyday supplies and materials; infrequently used supplies and materials; student supplies and materials; and teacher supplies and materials, as well as the personal items of students and teacher. The teacher must plan for their storage and use.

Everyday supplies and materials such as pencils, paper, ditto masters, and chalk should be stored in an easily accessible location. The teacher may wish to locate these items where they are available to students. Students' instructional materials such as texts, workbooks, dictionaries, and study guides may be stored in students' desks, bookcases, or filing trays and cabinets. Infrequently used items such as seasonal and topical materials should be stored in the back of cupboards. Equipment such as overhead projectors, record players, and movie projectors should be stored in a safe place when not in use but accessible to electrical outlets. Students should have a private place to store personal items such as clothing, gym shoes, lunch boxes, and prized possessions. The teacher must have private space for his or her briefcase and other personal items as well as personal instructional materials and equipment.

Procedures. The teacher is responsible for developing a variety of classroom and nonclassroom procedures designed to assure that student will learn and behave effectively and efficiently. The teacher must be sure that these procedures are compatible with school policy.

Student Use of Classroom Space and Facilities. Procedures should be established to facilitate the care of students' desks and storage areas. Procedures are established for the number of students permitted in various areas of the room at one time and for the use of the drinking fountain, sink, pencil sharpener, restroom, and other shared facilities within the classroom. Procedures for the use and care of common and personal instructional materials must be developed, and procedures should be made with regard to students' and teacher's personal space and possessions.

Student Use of Nonclassroom Space and Facilities. Procedures should be developed for the use of nonclassroom space and facilities such as restrooms, drinking fountains, offices, library, media room, resource rooms, and others areas. Procedures must be developed for students leaving the classroom and the movement of individual students and groups of students throughout the school building. Playground activities procedures must be developed. These procedures should facilitate fair play and safety and maximize enjoyment. Special procedures are frequently needed for the lunchroom because of the large number of students in the facility and the limited time available to eat.

Whole Group, Small Group, and Individual Activities. Procedures for a variety of individual, small group, and whole group activities must be established by the teacher. Procedures are developed for the conduct of discussions, the answering of questions during class, talking among students, out-of-seat behavior, and so on. Students should be instructed about the cues and prompts the teacher will use to attain student attention. Procedures are developed for making assignments to work groups, assigning homework, distributing supplies and materials, turning in work, returning assignments, and completing missed assignments. Students should know what they are expected to do when they have completed a task and have unscheduled time available.

Small group activities require procedures. Students must know the cues the teacher uses to begin and end small group activities, what materials to bring, and behavioral expectations. Students who are not in a particular small group must know what is expected of them during other students' small group activities.

Students working individually must know how to obtain their work, where they are to work, what work to do, how to signal for assistance, and what to do when their work is complete.

Teachers are prudent to establish standard procedures for beginning and ending the school day or period. Students should know what behaviors are appropriate and inappropriate during this time. Students should know the procedures for reporting after an absence, tardiness, and early dismissal. It is important to begin and end the day on a positive note.

Procedures are developed for the selection and duties of classroom helpers. These activities should be shared by all students. Finally, procedures should be established for conduct during classroom interruptions and delays, for fire, tornado, and earthquake drills and other infrequent and unplanned occurrences.

Rules. Rules of behavior are needed in all classrooms. According to Joyce, Joyce, and Chase (1989), a rule is "the specification of a relation between two events and may take the form of instruction, direction, or principle." Students follow rules to obtain reinforcers. These reinforcers may be artificial (grades, points, free time) or natural (getting the correct answer, praise, self-satisfaction). Teachers use various kinds of rules to organize the classroom instruction and conduct. Rules usually are designed to apply to those activities and occurrences that are not governed by classroom and nonclassroom procedures discussed in the previous section.

Rules should be few in number. They should be brief and understandable to the students and positively stated. They should communicate expectations rather than prohibitions. However, it may be necessary to state rules that prohibit specific behaviors.

Rules are best developed through the collaborative efforts of students and teacher. When students are involved in developing rules, the rules become "our rules" rather than "the teacher's rules." When rules are set collaboratively, they may be changed only through discussion and consensus (Cheney, 1989). Rules should be posted in a highly visible location in the classroom and reviewed with the students frequently

(Blankenship, 1986). At the beginning of the school year, the rules should be reviewed daily.

The teacher must give students repeated examples of the behaviors that a student demonstrates when following the rules. The function of a rule is to encourage appropriate behavior and prevent inappropriate behavior. Teachers are responsible for enforcing classroom rules with fairness and consistency (Rieth & Evertson, 1988). Rules are not made to aid the teacher in catching students acting inappropriately.

Four or five rules are more than adequate to govern classroom behavior. They should be general—but not so general as to be meaningless. Rules must be sufficiently objective to be exemplified by the teacher. Examples of general rules are the following:

- Be polite and helpful.
- Keep your space and materials in order.
- Take care of classroom and school property.

Some teachers have certain highly specific rules. Examples of specific rules are the following:

- Raise your hand before speaking.
- Leave your seat only with permission.
- Only one person in the restroom at a time.

Such specific rules should be few in number and carefully explained to the students.

Joyce, Joyce, and Chase (1989) remind teachers that students whose behavior is rule-governed (under the control of reinforcers) may become insensitive to environmental conditions that make rule-following inappropriate. To prevent the development of environmental insensitivity due to rule-following, they suggest that students (1) be exposed to contingencies incompatible with specific rules, (2) be provided various tasks for meeting the objective of the rule, (3) be exposed to natural contingencies for appropriate classroom behavior, and (4) be overtly aided to make transitions from rule-governed behaviors that were in effect in previous environments.

Cuing. Cuing is the process of using symbols to communicate essential messages between individuals. The use of cuing reduces interruptions in on-going classroom activities, and the symbols facilitate structure and provide routine (Legare, 1984; Olson, 1989). Cuing is a proactive, preventive behavior management intervention (Slade & Callaghan, 1988).

There are various cues or help signs that can be used in the classroom. Such cues are most effective if developed collaboratively by students and teacher at the beginning of the school year.

Among the many cues that may be implemented are the following:

- Students place a sign or flag in a holder on their desks when assistance is needed.

- Students write their name on the chalkboard when help is needed.
- Students take a ticket (as in the supermarket deli) when help is needed.
- Students use a heavy cardboard symbol such as the letter "R" for restroom, "P" for pencil, or "W" for water in place of frequently asked questions.
- Teachers use a traffic signal to control noise levels (red = too loud, yellow = caution, green = noise level is OK).
- Teachers turn on or off the lights to signal the beginning and end of activities.

In addition, teachers may use body language, hand signals, smiles or frowns, and schedules as cues (Rosenkoetter & Fowler, 1986). The design and use of cues is limited only by imagination. Of course, cues should not be used in lieu of appropriate verbal communication.

Transitions. Transitions are the movement from one activity to another. According to Rosenkoetter and Fowler (1986), transitions are complex activities that frequently result in classroom disruptions. They should be carefully planned to minimize the loss of instructional time. Effective transitions teach children self-management skills.

In a study of 22 classes (15 regular and 7 special education) for young children (4 and 5 years old), Rosenkoetter and Fowler found that on average, 18% of the school day was devoted to transitions. Special education and regular education classes differed with regard to the management of transitions. Regular teachers used more cues than special teachers. Special teachers used children's names as cues; regular teachers used group names. Individual cues in the regular classes were rare; when special teachers used group cues, they would follow with individual cues. Special teachers employed one- or two-step directions; regular teachers employed three- or four-step directions. Special teachers often used proximity control. It was noted that in the special class, children were frequently not held responsible for their materials and were not taught group movement.

The authors discussed the implications of these differences for the mainstreaming of children from special to regular classes. They suggested several guidelines for special teachers wishing to facilitate transition behaviors:

- Visit the mainstream class to determine transition rules.
- Plan for transitions and use shaping to assist in the learning of appropriate behavior.
- Evaluate existing transition behaviors to determine if students need more or less assistance.
- Move from individual to group cues.
- Use a variety of cues.
- Teach lining up and moving in line behaviors.
- Teach children how to ask for assistance.

Teachers may use the following activities to facilitate transitions (Shea & Bauer, 1987):

- ☐ Model appropriate transition behaviors.
- ☐ Signal or cue the beginning and ending of activities.
- ☐ Remediate transition difficulties such as slowness and disruptiveness.
- ☐ Observe student performance during transitions and, if the student is having difficulties, repeat the rules and practice until they are firmly established behaviors.
- ☐ Reinforce quick and quiet transitions.

Effective transitions are essential to maximize engaged time in the classroom.

Schedules. Scheduling is an important teacher function. Rosenshine (1977) found that student learning increases when teachers allocate considerable time for instruction and maintain a high level of task engagement. To develop an effective schedule, two important variables are considered: allocated time and engaged time (Shea and Bauer, 1987). Englert (1984) describes allocated time as the amount of time scheduled for a specific subject or activity. Engaged time is the amount of time the students are actually participating in the subject or activity. To increase engaged time, teachers must plan the schedule with care, beginning and ending activities on time, facilitate transitions from activity to activity, and assign scheduled activities as a first priority rather than engaging in spontaneous, alternative activities (Englert, 1984).

Scheduling is a dynamic process—a continuous and creative activity (Gallagher, 1988). Schedules must be revised throughout the school year in response to emerging student needs and changing behaviors, as well as the demands of the curriculum. The two most important kinds of scheduling to the teacher are overall program scheduling and individual program scheduling.

Schedules are based on individual and group priorities. After the teacher determines priorities, available time, personnel, and materials must be fitted into those priorities. Shea and Bauer (1987) suggested the following step-by-step process for schedule development:

1. Using each student's individualized education program or personal educational records as a data base, complete a 3-by-5-inch index card for each goal for each student. On the card, write the student's name, current level of functioning, and short-term objectives with reference to the goal.
2. Group students by sorting the cards by goals and functional levels.
3. Choose a specific schedule format. Reproduce the schedule format on a standard sheet of paper. In the left-hand column, write the time periods available for scheduling.
4. Write the "given" activities (lunch, recess, art, music, speech therapy) in the schedule. A resource room teacher must write in the "givens" imposed by other teachers' schedules. Write in the times needed for transitions. Write in the times needed for data recording, communicating with others, and preparing for instruction.
5. Write group activities on the schedule. Adjust these until there are no conflicts with other scheduled activities.

6. Review and discuss the proposed schedule with others serving the students (regular or special teachers, therapists, parents) to minimize conflicts.
7. Establish procedures for periodically evaluating the schedule.

Two common schedule formats are the Premack principle schedule and the distributed duties schedule. The Premack schedule is based on the presumption that behaviors that occur frequently can be used as reinforcers for less frequently occurring behaviors. This principle is known as "Grandma's Law" or "If you eat your green beans then you can have your ice cream." To apply this principle to scheduling, the teacher first marks each scheduled period of time with a plus (+) or a minus (−) sign. The plus mark denotes behaviors that naturally occur at a high frequency level, and the minus sign denotes those that do not. It is suggested that the day begin and end with positive activities. The following is a partial schedule based on the Premack principle:

+ 9:00   Free-time to play quietly with classroom toys, talk to friends, or read.
− 9:10   Return to seats for individual study during attendance, lunch count, so on.
+ 9:15   Circle or sharing time
− 9:35   First reading group, individual study
+ 9:55   Transition time, drinks, restroom
− 10:00   Second reading group, individual study
+ 10:20   Recess

The distributed-duties schedule (Bauer, 1980) is useful in programs in which paraprofessionals, volunteers, and other personnel are available to meet the need of students. To use this schedule format, students are grouped homogeneously by functional level and individual goals and objectives. Next, they are grouped into the same number of groups as there are personnel available to work with them during a given period of time. Each person assumes responsibility for a group's instruction during his or her available time periods. Personnel are usually assigned to groups on a rotating basis, as shown on this partial schedule:

	Group A Jim/Betty/Mary	Group B Tara/Elmer/Mable	Group C John/Tom/Dolores
9:00		all students—group meeting	
9:20	spelling	reading	reading
9:40	numbers	basic concepts	math
10:00	reading	language arts	independent***
10:20		all students—recess	
10:40	music*	language arts**	spelling

* Betty to speech therapy
** Elmer to 3rd grade
*** John to psychologist

Staff Assignments

	Annie B	Pam E	Bill W
Group A	9:00—10:00	10:00—12:00	P.M.
Group B	10:00—12:00	P.M.	9:00—10:00
Group C	P.M.	9:00—10:00	10:00—12:00

Another variable considered when developing schedules is the length of time of the activity periods. As a rule, it is more effective to begin the school year with brief activity periods and gradually lengthen them as the year progresses; the students then learn the schedule and become involved in the learning process.

Milieu Therapy

Milieu therapy is a clinical concept, and although it varies in ease of application, it can be applied in any setting in which children function. In varying degrees this intervention can be applied in residential settings, day school, special classrooms, regular classrooms, and camp settings.

According to Long and others (1980), "Milieu implies the total environment a child lives in, the whole culture that surrounds him, in other words, everything that is done to, with, for, or by an individual in the place where he finds himself."

According to Redl (1959), a specific milieu is not "good" or "bad" for an individual in itself; its effects on the person or group are dependent on their needs in interaction with the milieu. Redl further indicated that no single aspect of the environment is more important than any other aspect. The importance of the various discrete aspects of the environment are dependent on the needs of the individual or group living in that particular setting.

Because it is not possible, a priori, to design with certitude a therapeutic milieu for an individual, milieu therapy is a continuous process throughout the child's placement in a particular setting. The staff must be constantly alert to the impact of the milieu on the individual and adjust it when necessary. Although these adjustments may appear simple when presented in a written statement, such environmental manipulations are difficult tasks requiring personnel who are observant and sensitive to the needs of the individual and the group.

Redl (1959) identified several critical elements in the milieu; these elements are presented here as questions that persons responsible for a particular milieu must ask themselves:

☐ *Social structures:* What are the roles and functions of various individuals and groups in the milieu? What is the role of the therapist? Of the teacher? Of the administrator? Of the children? Are staff members parent surrogates? Are they like brothers and sisters? Are they confidants? Are they friends? Are they authority figures? Are they servants? Who is in charge here? Staff? The children? Administrators? No one? Are there open or closed communication channels between staff and children? Between children and staff? Among staff personnel? Among the children?

☐ *Value systems:* What values and standards are consciously and unconsciously being communicated among and between the children and staff? Sympathy? Empathy? High expectations? Low expectations? Like? Dislike? Acceptance? Rejection? Trust? Mistrust?

☐ *Routines, rituals, and regulations:* Are routines, rituals, and behavioral regulations and limits facilitating or frustrating the goals of a program for the individual?

☐ *Impact of group processes:* What is the impact of the natural group processes on individuals and subgroups? On the total group? Are individual group members cast in the role of a leader? A follower? An antagonist? A scapegoat? An isolate? A mascot or pet? A clown? Can the individual at his or her present stage of development function effectively in a group setting such as this milieu provides?

☐ *Impact of the individual's psychopathological characteristics:* What are the effects of behaviors on the individuals themselves and on others? Are these effects positive? Are they negative? Do they result in aggression? In withdrawal? In respect? In pity? In fear?

☐ *Personal attitudes and feelings:* What are the staff's attitudes and feelings toward each other and the children? What is the impact of these attitudes and feelings on their behavior and on the behavior of others (staff and children)? Is the impact positive? Is it negative? Is it neutral? Is it productive? Is it destructive?

☐ *Overt behavior:* Regardless of the individual's intentions, what are group members really doing to each other? What is their overt behavior? Is their relationship helpful? Is it harmful? Is it supportive? Is it personal? Is it vindictive?

☐ *Activities and performance:* Is the activity program, including its structure, designed to facilitate the developmental process? Is it productive? Is it constructive? Is it busywork? Is it tedious? Is it frustrating? Is it boring? Is it wasteful? Is it negative? Is it destructive?

☐ *Space, equipment, time, and props:* Are space, equipment, time, and props available to adequately conduct the activities in the program?

☐ *Effects of the outside milieu:* What is the effect of information, visits, news, telephone calls, and the like, from persons on the outside on the individual or group?

☐ *Effects of the nonimmediate milieu:* What are the effects of parents, administrators, nurses, physicians, housekeepers, cooks, and others on the individual or group?

☐ *Limits and enforcement:* Are the behavioral limits within which the individual and group must function established? Are these limits reasonable? Are they enforced? Are they enforced consistently and fairly? How are extremes of behavior handled?

☐ *Program responsiveness:* Is the total milieu adequately and objectively monitored to ensure recognition of nontherapeutic elements? Is the structure of the milieu sufficiently flexible and responsive to allow and encourage modification to reduce or neutralize nontherapeutic elements?

The questions listed under each of the preceding variables that compose a milieu may be systematically responded to by educators wishing to evaluate the therapeutic quality of the program in which they teach.

The therapeutic milieu in any setting, residential or day, must be continuously monitored, discussed, evaluated, and manipulated for the benefit of the child.

Levels Systems

A levels system is an organizational framework designed to shape students' social, emotional, and academic behaviors (Bauer, Shea, & Keppler, 1986). Rather than an intervention technique or strategy derived from a single theoretical perspective, a levels system offers a structure within which various interventions may be applied. The interventions implemented in a levels system range in theoretical construct from behavior modification (token economy, positive reinforcement, contingency contracts) to psychodynamic (social-skills curriculum, group and individual counseling, expressive media interventions). The selection of the interventions is based on the practitioner's skills and the functioning level of each student concerned.

The purpose of a levels system is to increase student responsibility for personal, social, emotional, and academic performance. A student's progress through the various levels is dependent on his or her measurable behavior and achievement. As the student progresses through the levels, the behavioral expectations and privileges change (Bauer & Shea, 1988).

Levels systems originated in residential settings. In 1971, the Holy Cross Program (New York City) used a levels system in an adolescent substance abuse program. A 4-level system including a token economy was used to provide students with positive reinforcement and frequent feedback about their performance, to increase their tolerance for delayed gratification, and to develop their reliance upon self as a source of reinforcement (Coughlan, Gold, Dohrenwend, & Zimmerman, 1973). Levels systems have also been applied with incarcerated adolescents (Reid, 1979) and in residential treatment facilities (Rosenstock & Levy, 1978; Mitchell & Cockrum, 1980; Gable & Strain, 1981).

The few classroom adaptations reported in the literature appear to be derived from institutional systems. Gersten (in Swanson & Reinert, 1984) described demonstration classrooms for adolescents at the University of Northern Colorado in which a 5-level system was applied. Recently, levels systems have been suggested for application during the process of phasing out token economies without interrupting student progress (LaNunziata, Hunt, & Cooper, 1984). Mastropieri, Jenne, and Scruggs (1988) developed a levels system for application in a special education high school resource program. They found that existing literature suggests that levels systems facilitate student self-reinforcement and self-management, the durability and generalization of intervention gains, and the fading of other management structures such as a token economy.

To demonstrate this approach to behavior management, this section presents two levels systems that have been used in the public school setting. This first is designed for application with elementary and junior high school students, the second with high school students. The discussion of levels systems concludes with several guidelines for practitioners wishing to design a levels system appropriate for the students and environment in which they work.

CCSEC System

The Clark County Special Education Cooperative Day Treatment Program (CCSEC, Jeffersonville, Indiana) levels system is designed to facilitate the return of elementary and junior high school students from residential treatment centers to public school special education services. On entry into the program, the students are generally too severely impaired to profit from education services in the local school district. The levels system is individualized for each student on the basis of the annual goals and short-term objectives written in the student's individualized education plan. The system consists of four levels plus a disciplinary level. The expectations, privileges, and requirements for each level are presented in Table 7.1. Students are responsible for monitoring their behavior with teacher assistance. A staff meeting is conducted each week to review each student's performance and to revise individual expectations. Level changes made at these meetings will go into effect the following week.

Students who fail to meet the requirements of their current level return to the next previous level for a 1-week probationary period. During probation, if a student earns 80% of the possible available points, then he or she returns to the higher level. Each level has a minimum length of stay regardless of student behavior. Ground or Disciplinary Level offenses include running away, physically abusing staff and peers, destroying property, setting off the fire alarm, possession of weapons or drugs, and so on. The number of points the student must earn to return from Ground Level to the previous level varies as indicated in Table 7.1.

PALS

The Personal Adjustment Level System (PALS, Hinsdale Illinois South High School), a 5-level system for secondary students, is designed to increase self motivation and academic achievement. The goal of the system is reintegration into the mainstream of regular education. Small group and individual counseling sessions are an intregal part of the program. All students on Levels 1 through 4 are required to attend group sessions. Students who fail to attend the group remain at Day 1 of their present levels. Unlike the Clark system, initial level placement is determined by a student support team. Like the Clark system, there are minimum lengths of stay at each level. Students can earn bonus days for appropriate behavior or lose days for suspension and inappropriate behavior. Requirements and incentives for PALS levels are presented in Table 7.2.

The levels systems presented here demonstrate the diversity of this approach to managing students' behavior. Analysis indicates that both systems provide a framework within which various therapeutic interventions and behavior management strategies can be applied. Though they differ in specifics, each system contains (a) a description of each level, (b) criteria for movement from one level to another, and (c) specific behaviors, expectations, restrictions, and privileges for each level. Typically, levels systems are comprised of four to six levels. There is considerable variation in the criteria for movement from level to level. All levels systems have a procedure for evaluating student fulfillment of expectations. This procedure may be a point system, a group meeting of staff and/or students, or minimum stay guidelines.

Designing a Levels System

Practitioners wishing to design a levels system will find the following guidelines helpful.

Step 1: Determine the usual entry-level behaviors of the student population. For example, students entering the Clark program generally fail to (a) initiate assignments when requested, (b) attend to tasks more than half the time, and (c) interact appropriately with peers or adults.

As an alternative, an "assessment level" may be written into the system. During a brief (several day) assessment period, a student's functioning can be evaluated and compared to the expectations for the various levels. Then the student may be placed at an appropriate level rather than being required to progress through levels that are inappropriate to the student's present functioning.

Step 2: Determine the terminal behavior expectations for the students. For the Clark students, these expectations are the same as the social, academic, and behavioral expectations for the students entering public school systems. Expectations should be expressed positively ("If you are on time, you will be awarded two points.") as opposed to ("If you are late, you will lose two points.").

Step 3: List at least two but no more than four sets of behavioral expectations of approximately equal distance between the expectations listed in Steps One and Two. In the Clark program, for example, two sets of expectations were developed in the academic area. Between initiating assignments on command and meeting the criteria established by public school teachers, there are criteria that focus on beginning and completing assignments within specified time limits, i.e., working on a task for increasing time increments.

Step 4: Write the sets of graduated expectations on separate sheets of paper. Label them "Level One" through "Level Four."

Step 5: Consider including a Disciplinary or Ground Level. If such a level is appropriate for the students, describe expectations for this level on a separate sheet of paper. In the Clark system, Ground Level expectations are the same as expectations for the level below the one the student was on when he or she committed the offense.

TABLE 7.1
CCSEC levels systems

	Level I	Level II	Level III	Level IV (transition)	Ground Level
Minimum Length of Stay	9 weeks	12 weeks	15 weeks	9 weeks (transition)	3-5 days
Requirements for Maintaining Level Status		80% of possible points. (4 out of every 5 days)	80% of possible points (4 out of every 5 days)	Meets criteria established by public school SEH teachers	
Requirements for Advancing to Next Level	90% of possible points for 45 out of 60 days. No more than 10 Time-Outs	90% of possible points for 60 out of 72 days. No more than 6 Time-Outs.	90% of possible points for 75 out of 90 days. No more than 5 Time-Outs.	Meets criteria established by public school SEH teachers.	Level I: 70% pos. pts. Level II: 80% pos. pts. Level III: 85% pos. pts. Level IV: 90% pos. pts.
Academic Expectations	Starts assignments on command. During weeks 1-5, on task for 15 min. out of each ½ hour. Weeks 6-9, on task for 20 min. out of each ½ hr. (not necessarily consecutively)	Starts & completes assignments within specified time. On-task behavior: Weeks 1-4: 20 min. Weeks 5-8: 25 min. Weeks 8-12: 30 min.	Starts and completes assignments within specified time. Stays on task for 30 minutes at a time.	Meets criteria established by public school SEH teachers.	Same expectations for level below the one student was on prior to offense resulting in Ground Level placement.
Behaviorial Expectations	Discusses individual goals & class rules with teacher daily. Demonstrates effort to achieve them.	Independently states individual goals and class rules daily and demonstrates effort to achieve them.	Independently states individual goals & class rules daily & demonstrates effort to achieve them. Involved in process of determining individual goals for him/herself.	Meets criteria established by public school SEH teachers.	States reasons for GL placement and alternative strategies. Same expectations for level below the one student was on prior to offense resulting in GL placement.

TABLE 7.1
Continued

	Level I	Level II	Level III	Level IV	Ground Level
Social Skills Expectations	Interacts appropriately with 1 peer at a time with adult supervision. Accepts compliments appropriately. Interacts appropriately with adults.	Interacts appropriately with 2 or more peers at a time with adult supervision. Compliments him/herself & others at least once a day. Contributes to discussions in daily class meetings.	Interacts appropriately with 2 or more peers without adult supervision. Compliments him/herself & others at least twice a day. Verbally encourages peers to interact appropriately. Attempts to solve conflicts before asking for help.	Meets criteria established by public school SEH teachers.	Same expectations for level below the one student was on prior to offense resulting in Ground Level placement.
Privileges	Free time in classroom. Special activities determined by teacher.	Unescorted restroom and drink breaks and to and from bus. Setting table for lunch. Special Level II purchases in point store. Using computer during free time. Field trips. Purchasing soft drinks & snacks at specified times. Special activities determined by teacher. Playing Atari once a day with supervision.	Lunch in hospital cafeteria once a week. Running errands within building. Playing Atari in office. Special field trips. Special Level III purchases in point store.	Full time placement in public school SEH class. After a 9-week transition period, mainstreaming will be considered by Case Conference Committee.	Free time earned at teacher's discretion. Scheduled restroom breaks with direct supervision. Eat lunch at separate table. Privilege of using tape recorder, computer, record player, etc. is revoked.

(Adapted from Clark County Special Education Cooperative Day Treatment Program Levels System. Adapted by permission.)

TABLE 7.2
PALS

Length of Stay	Requirements	Incentives
Level I 20 days (or as contracted w/ teacher)	Personal goal-setting conference. Personal IEP conference. Learn school rules, PALS rules, daily routine. Log in journal daily. Keep record of assignments. Participate in weekly group therapy. Maintain appropriate behavior 70% of the time. Completion of 65% of assignments. Participate in required class activities. Document "helping others" project on a weekly basis. Maintain stable attendance. Progress on 60% of IEP goals. Contained for all classes except PE. Pass 75% of classes.	In-school field trips. One cafeteria pass per week. Off-campus lunch with teacher. Break time with teacher. Bonus days. Free time in class. Food privileges in classroom.
Level II 30 days	Log in journal three times each week. Personal IEP conference to review objectives and program. Participate in weekly group therapy. Complete 75% of assignments. Maintain appropriate behavior 75% of the time. Participate in required class activities. Attend regular class for 1-3 classes. Maintain stable attendance. Progress on 75% of IEP goals. Pass all classes.	In-school field trips. Bonus days. Two cafeteria passes per week. Two off-campus lunches with the teacher. Free time in class.
Level III 40 days	Log in journal weekly. Participate in weekly group therapy. Completion of 85% of weekly assignments. Maintain appropriate behavior 90% of the time. Integration into four academic classes and P.E. Document "helping others" project. Maintain stable attendance. Progress on 90% of IEP goals. Passing all classes. Participate in required class activities.	Three cafeteria passes per week. Up to four outside lunches with the teacher. Food privileges in classroom. In-school field trips. Outside field trips. Bonus days. Free time in classroom.

TABLE 7.2
Continued

Length of Stay	Requirements	Incentives
Level IV 50 days	Maintain stable attendance. Complete 90% of all assignments. Maintain appropriate behavior 90% of the time. Integrated for all classes. Passing all classes. Progress on 100% of IEP goals to criteria. Contact with special teacher daily.	Free time in class. Cafeteria passes. Off-campus lunch and breakfast with the teacher. Food privileges in classroom. In-school field trips. Outside field trips. Bonus days.
Level V (Exit) 25 days	No progress notes from regular teachers. Passing all classes. Integrated into all classes. Maintain appropriate behavior 100% of the time. Maintain stable attendance.	*Student is monitored only. Beginning at day 15, special teacher begins arrangement for permanent regular educational placement.

(Adapted from Personal Adjustment Level System, Hinsdale Illinois South High School. Adapted by permission.)

Step 6: Determine the privileges appropriate for students beginning the program, i.e., Level 1. The students in the Clark program require continuous supervision when initially admitted; thus, privileges are restricted to free time in the classroom and supervised activities.

Step 7: Determine the privileges appropriate for students preparing to terminate the program, i.e., at the highest level. For the students in the Clark program, the terminal privileges are those normally available to students with behavior disorders in the public schools.

Step 8: For each level in Step Three, list appropriate privileges evenly distributed among the levels. Remember to reduce the amount of direct supervision provided for the students as they progress through the levels.

Step 9: Next, consider the following questions to determine the length of stay for each level and movement among levels:

a. Will a minimum length of stay be required at each level?

b. How frequently will a student's status be reviewed? Weekly or biweekly meetings to review placement may be appropriate.

c. Who will review a student's status? Involving students in the evaluation process can be beneficial. Student involvement encourages the development of self-control and decision-making skills. Involving other students provides positive peer support, which is particularly beneficial at the secondary school level.

d. What level of appropriate behavior will be required to remain at the various levels?

e. What self-monitoring and teacher monitoring procedures are needed?

Step 10: Determine the appropriate communication systems among staff, parents, and students. A successful levels program requires frequent, positive communication. Communications may be facilitated by group meetings, individual conferences, written notes, or forms.

Step 11: Determine needed augmentive systems. It may be desirable within the levels system to use various augmentive systems such as contingency contracts or a token economy.

Caution should be exercised in planning and implementing a levels system. Expectations should be expressed positively. For example, rather than "stops hitting," the same expectation can be expressed positively by saying "keeps hands to self." The latter statement is not only positive but suggests to the student the appropriate alternative behavior.

If a Disciplinary or Ground Level is included in the system, then offenses and their consequences should be reasonable, carefully explained, and fairly administered.

The number of days at each level should be realistic. The student should not be required to remain at a level for so many days that he or she becomes frustrated and begins to resist or "drop out" of the system.

A behavior expectations checklist, such as the one presented in Table 7.3, may be developed for each level. The checklist presented in Table 7.3 is designed for use with Level III of PALS. The checklist is reviewed frequently by student and teacher. It is a reminder to the student of his or her duties, responsibilities, expectations, and consequences. In addition, the checklist is an excellent guide for use in student-teacher conferences.

Rosenberg (1986) cautions that simply putting a system in place is not enough; a periodic, brief review of the rules maximizes the effectiveness of a management system.

A significant benefit of a levels system is that its structure and routine provide security for students. The system provides workable limits with a theoretical flexibility that allows a levels system to respond to individual and group needs.

The advantages of a levels system parallel those of the positive peer culture (Carducci, 1980): (1) it delivers the teacher from the embattled "me against them" position, (2) it encourages the teacher to respect the strengths and abilities of the students, (3) it lends itself to specific classroom approaches such as grouping, students helping students, and individualized interventions, and (4) it provides a means for dealing with students' defense mechanisms such as projection and rationalization by placing the responsibility for personal behavior on the student.

Expulsion, Suspension, and Inschool Suspension

Recently, disciplinary removal through expulsion, suspension, and inschool suspension has been discussed in the literature as it applies both to students with exceptionalities and to regular students. There is considerable controversy surrounding the use of these behavior management procedures. Several court decisions impact on their use with regular and special education students.

TABLE 7.3
Behavior expectations checklist

REQUIREMENTS

_____	1. Weekly journal entry
_____	2. Weekly group therapy
_____	3. Complete 85% of assignments
_____	4. Appropriate behavior 90% of time
_____	5. Integrated for four classes and PE
_____	6. Document "helping others" project
_____	7. Maintain attendance
_____	8. Progress on 90% of IEP goals
_____	9. Pass all classes
_____	10. Participate in all required class activities

Beginning date:

Projected completion date:

Special Notes:

Student's signature: _____

Teacher's signature: _____

Hindman (1986) and Center and McKittrick (1987) define expulsion as the removal of a student from school for more than 10 days and suspension as the removal of a student from school for no more than 10 days. Inschool suspension is the removal of a student from regular or special education class but not from the school.

"Generally so long as students' constitutional rights are not infringed upon (*Tinker v. Des Moines,* 1969), and discipline is meted out with appropriate procedural due process (*Goss v. Lopez,* 1975), school officials' handling of student discipline has not been altered through the judicial process" (Bartlett, 1988a, 1988b). The message in this quote is applicable to students in the regular class and general school population. However, as a consequence of various court decisions, it is not always applicable to students in special education (Shea, Bauer, & Lynch, 1989).

The implementation of expulsion with students with handicapping conditions is limited by Public Law 94-142 (Morris, 1987). Except in circumstances in which the student is a threat to the life and well-being of self or others, students with handicapping conditions may be expelled or suspended only if the following criteria are met: (a) the procedures are included as disciplinary options in the student's IEP, (b) the procedural requirements of Public Law 94-142 are adhered to, and

(c) the use of the procedure does not result in a permanent cessation of educational services (Grosenick et al., 1982). In most circumstances, expulsion is considered a change in educational placement and cannot be imposed on students with handicaps.

According to the U.S. Supreme Court, suspension is considered to be not only a necessary tool to maintain order in school, but also a valuable educational device. Short-term suspension is permitted if the behavior for which the student is suspended is not directly linked to the handicap. In this situation, the suspension is not considered a change in educational placement. However, the linkage between the handicap and the behavior must be established or not established prior to the imposition of the suspension unless the student is dangerous to self or others. However, the general 10-day rule applies, and parents must be notified and agree to the suspension.

Center and McKittrick (1987) offer guidelines for those establishing school policy on expulsion and suspension. Policy should include clearly defined expectations for student behavior. Behavioral expectations are generally presented in a policy handbook and is made available to administrators, teachers, parents, and students. The handbook should include the rules, the consequences for violation, and the student's due process rights. A standard procedure should be developed and implemented consistently in all cases in which expulsion and suspension may be considered as disciplinary options. The imposition of these disciplinary procedures is a team process and should never be done unilaterally.

Inschool suspension has not been tested in the courts, and its use with both nonhandicapped and handicapped students is becoming more frequent in schools. Center and McKittrick suggest that school policies established for expulsion and suspension be used for inschool suspension.

Inschool suspension has several advantages over expulsion and suspension:

□ It eliminates the probability that the student will be unsupervised during the school day.
□ As a form of segregation of the general school population, it decreases the probability of disruption in the school.
□ With an effective learning program, it can be a useful educational experience.

Those wishing to implement an inschool suspension program must develop policies, curriculum, and management guidelines. The following is a summary of policies suggested by Center and McKittrick:

□ The 10-day rule should be applied.
□ Age range among students should be no more than 3 years or 3 grades.
□ A maximum enrollment should be set, perhaps 12 to 15 students. An experienced and qualified teacher should be assigned to each group.
□ Specific criteria should be set for assignment to the program.
□ Placements should be for a predetermined and specific period of time. The placement period should be uniform for particular offenses.
□ Placement should begin on a specific day of the week.

- Students should be required to meet specific criteria for return to their regular school program.
- Failure to successfully complete inschool suspension should result in a hearing to consider other disciplinary procedures.
- Policy should be established for multiple placements within a school year.
- Acceptance or continuation of participation in other school programs (special groups, co-curricular activities, special studies) should be contingent upon successful participation in the program.

Inschool suspension should not a viewed as simple detention. Students should not be allowed to sit passively for an hour a day for several days and then return to their regular program. Inschool suspension should be a valuable learning experience. There are two general approaches to curriculum in the inschool suspension program. The student may continue studying his or her regular curriculum. This approach is frequently difficult and requires the regular and inschool suspension teachers to coordinate their activities. It is particularly difficult in the secondary school where a student may be instructed by many teachers. This approach requires the inschool suspension teacher to be familiar with a broad range of curriculum.

The other approach to inschool suspension curriculum is the stand-alone curriculum, which includes two options: the learning skills program and the functional academics program. In the learning skills program, the student studies generic learning strategies such as listening skills, reading skills, study skills, and time management. In the functional academics program, the student studies daily living skills or work skills (budgeting, interviewing for a job, using credit, maintaining home and auto).

The inschool suspension program must include a behavior management program. Management should be positive and emphasize appropriate interpersonal and work skills. It could be a multi-purpose token economy such as that presented in Chapter 4.

The effectiveness of any inschool suspension program is greatly dependent on the teacher assigned to the program. The teacher must be a highly skilled instructor and behavior manager and must be able to relate positively and productively with students.

Biophysical Interventions

In this section several biophysical interventions about which educators should have knowledge are discussed. These include several preventive and curative techniques, such as genetic counseling, proper nutrition, general and specialized physical examinations, medication, and others.

In the majority of these interventions, the educator plays an important supportive role to that of the physician and other medical personnel. Consequently an analysis of the educator's functions in referral, collaboration and reporting, the modification of classroom structure and curriculum content, the obtaining of permission to administer medication, and the safeguarding and administering of medication is presented as a conclusion to the discussion of the biophysical behavior management interventions.

In addition to the educator's "need to know," the biophysical techniques are reviewed because the probability exists that some of the behavior problems of children are a direct result of biophysical or biophysical-environment interactions. In addition, the social-emotional (secondary) effects of many biophysical handicaps on the individual's life-style are of direct concern to educators.

The biophysical frame of reference implies that the source of an individual's behavior problem is an organic defect. There are two known causes of biophysical defects in unborn and newborn children: environment and heredity. Environmental factors of special importance to the health of the child are maternal factors (metabolic disorders, maternal age, and number and frequency of pregnancies) and factors that affect the mother during pregnancy (viral diseases and infections, venereal disease, drugs, alcohol, tobacco, diet, and injuries). In addition, the larger environment may have an effect on the child as a consequence of pollution, radiation, and the like.

Heredity, or the transmission of the characteristics or traits of the parents to the child, is a factor in some birth defects. Hereditary characteristics are transmitted from parents to child by means of the chromosomes. Chromosomes are present in every human cell, including the ovum and sperm. Chromosomes are composed of genes—the units of heredity. The inherited characteristics of a child are determined by the composition and manner in which the gene-carrying chromosomes from the parents combine at the time of conception. There are approximately 3900 disorders known to be caused by genetic defects (*Exceptional Parent,* 1987). Among the most commonly known disorders are Down syndrome, sickle cell disease, cystic fibrosis, and hemophilia. Because genetic disorders are permanent, chronic, and complex, they tend to evoke labeling. As a consequence, they impact on the lifestyle of both the individual and the family (Costello, 1988).

It is generally agreed that birth defects are best reduced or controlled by preventive, rather than curative, techniques. Among the curative interventions available are chemical regulation, corrective surgery, and rehabilitation through training.

Chemical regulation includes such familiar interventions as medication and diet. Corrective surgery is frequently effective in reducing the debilitating effects of clubfoot, cleft lip and palate, and some vision, hearing, and speech problems, among others. Cosmetic surgery is a valuable aid in reducing the effects of observable deformities on the individual. Rehabilitation and training services have a significant positive impact on the life of the mentally retarded, blind, deaf, mute, physically handicapped, learning-disabled, or behavior-disordered individual.

Several biophysical interventions are discussed in the sections that follow.

Genetic Counseling

Both the individual with the genetic condition and the family are greatly impacted by the diagnosis of a biophysical defect. They have many questions with regard to the individual's lifestyle in both the present and the future, the implications of the disorder for them and their offspring, as well as the practical issues of service and finance (Costello, 1988).

Genetic counseling involves providing an estimate of the probability of the occurrence of a disease or defect for a particular unborn individual (Kameya, 1972). The major goal of genetic counseling is the prevention of birth defects. The genetic counselor cannot predict with exactitude the occurrence of a defective child but can predict the probability of occurrence of some abnormalities in the offspring of specific parents and parents-to-be.

As a consequence of its capacity to predict the probability of birth defects, genetic counseling has raised some important ethical issues in contemporary society:

☐ Should a defective child be aborted?
☐ Do parents have an inalienable right to knowingly produce a defective child?

It should be remembered that the genetic counselor provides medical information on the *probabilities* that a defective child will be born. The counselor is *not* the ultimate decision maker. The parents must make the final decision concerning the unborn child.

Prenatal Care

Prenatal care involves a variety of examinations and interventions designed to ensure that the unborn child develops normally in a healthy environment. By means of prenatal care, the parents and physician can not only determine the growth and development patterns of the unborn child but also are in a position to immediately intervene if there are indications of problems. Prenatal care includes consideration of the mother's diet, exercise, and personal hygiene as well as the emotional status of both parents, especially the mother.

Postnatal Care

Postnatal health care is essential for the continued health and well-being of every child. There is in our society a high risk of injury, illness, and infection during childhood and adolescence. All children should be examined by a physician at least annually. Conscientious health care permits the family physician and parents to guide the child through the developmental years and to recognize and intervene if abnormalities develop. Postnatal care includes vision, hearing, and dental care.

Medical Examinations

Differential diagnoses among children with behavior disorders, minimal brain damage, hyperkinesis, a specific learning disability, and similar syndromes require a thorough medical examination. And, because there is no single test or combination of tests that conclusively rules out organic disease, the full physical evaluation includes a variety of tests.

For example, the ideal evaluation for a suspected hyperactive and/or hyperanxious child is a collaborative effort by the parents, teachers, school psychologist, and physician (Renshaw, 1974). The parents' contributions include a family history and the child's medical, developmental, and behavioral histories. The teacher reports on the child's learning capacity and style and behavioral and perceptual difficulties. The school psychologist contributes the results of a psychological evaluation. The physician's evaluation includes information on the pregnancy, a family history, and a history of the child's birth, neonatal years, development, and behavior.

A full physical examination includes laboratory tests (blood and urine), a skull X-ray examination, and a neurological examination, including an electroencephalogram (EEG), if needed. The physician may prescribe medication on a trial basis as part of the diagnostic process.

A general physical examination is performed to *exclude* the possibility of diseases involving bodily systems that could account for the child's difficulties (Millichap, 1975). The neurological examination is performed to determine the probability of neurological malfunction and includes an evaluation of the individual's gait, coordination, deep tendon reflexes, muscular power and tone, handedness, sensory perception, speech, vision, and hearing.

Nutrition

Nutrition is defined as the relationship of nutrient intake to bodily needs (Kameya, 1972). In general, exact scientific relationships have not been demonstrated to exist between specific nutrients and specific behavior problems in children. However, a logical relationship between these factors in all probability does exist. Research has amply demonstrated the relationships between several nutrients and specific disorders of a physical nature.

Knapczyk (1979) noted three major diet-related conditions related to behavior disorders. These are (1) hypoglycemia, (2) vitamin/mineral deficiencies, and (3) allergies. Children with hypoglycemia may become either lethargic, unmotivated and withdrawn, or hyperactive and inattentive. Vitamin/mineral deficiencies are related to hyperactivity. Various specific food and food additives are related to allergic reactions in children.

It is hardly disputable that children suffering from malnutrition are neither happy nor productive. The malnourished child manifests signs of fatigue, sleepiness, and irritability and appears to lack motivation. Such a child is prone to infections, diseases, and injuries.

The importance of proper nutrition for children cannot be overemphasized. When parents are unable to provide for their children in the home, the school—using local, state and federal funds—must provide needy children with lunch and breakfast. Malnourishment is not confined to a specific socioeconomic group.

Diet

There is currently considerable activity and publicity on the effects of diet control on the hyperactive behaviors of children. Feingold (1973, 1975) hypothesized that naturally occurring salicylates and artificial food additives may cause the hyperkinetic syndrome in children who have a genetically determined predisposition.

Elimination of these substances from a child's diet would eliminate the symptoms of the hyperkinetic syndrome. Feingold claims that 48% of his patients were effectively treated by the diet and that symptoms can be reversed within a few hours if the diet is broken. Cook and Woodhill (1976) supported Feingold's claim in a clinical study of 15 hyperkinetic children. The parents of 10 children were "quite certain" and those of three others were "fairly certain" their child's behavior improved with the diet and relapsed when the diet was broken. Cook and Woodhill cautioned against the generalization of their finding because the sample was limited and the study did not meet rigorous research standards.

In a study of 59 children, Brenner (1977) reported that of 32 children able to tolerate the diet, 11 showed marked improvement as reported by teachers, parents, and physicians. Eight other children were judged "probably improved." No changes were reported in 13 children. In a control group of 27 children not on the diet, only two were improved without medication after 8 months. Brenner noted that the placebo effect could not be ruled out in the study.

Weiss, Williams, Margen, Abrams, Citron, Cox, McKibben, and Ogar (1980) conducted a challenge study of 22 children with regard to behavioral responses to artificial food colors. Twenty of the 22 children displayed no convincing evidence of sensitivity to the color challenge as reported by parents. Swanson and Kinsbourne (1980) studied the effects of food dyes on children's laboratory learning performance. Twenty children were classified as hyperactive, 20 were not. Both groups were challenged with food dyes. The performance of the hyperactive children was impaired on the days they received food dyes. Performance of the nonhyperactive children was not affected.

In a review of the pertinent empirical investigations with regard to the Feingold diet, Baker (1980) concluded that the differential results reported by Feingold, parents and others using the diet may be due to variables other than the eliminated substances. He found that in properly controlled studies, the positive effects of the diet evaporated. At this time, the debate remains unsettled as to whether a diet intervention is truly effective.

Megavitamin Therapy

The term *orthomolecular medicine,* or *megavitamin therapy,* was originally applied in the treatment of mental disorders, such as schizophrenia, to provide the optimum molecular environment for brain function, especially the optimum concentration of substances normally present in the human body. Megavitamin therapy refers specifically to the administration of large doses of vitamins, particularly nicotinic acid, pyridoxine, calcium pantothenate, ascorbic acid (Millichap, 1975), and other substances.

Some researchers have claimed positive results for megavitamin therapy (Pauling, 1968). However, according to Kameya (1972) and Millichap (1975), there is scant research evidence to support these claims. A task force of the American Psychiatric Association concluded that the claims of megavitamin therapists have not been confirmed in psychopharmacological research (Millichap, 1975).

Medication

Although behavior-modifying medications have been prescribed for children and youth with behavior disorders since the late 1930s (Wilson & Sherrets, 1979), the treatment-evaluation process remains complicated (Baldwin, 1973). The physician must not only be concerned with the individual child's personal status, but also must evaluate the child's environment, potentially biased evaluations of those associated with the child, and the actual and potential effects of other interventions being applied with the child such as special education.

Several reviews have been published (Gadow, 1979; Epstein & Olinger, 1987) describing the use of medication with children, particularly in the treatment of hyperactivity. These reviews are summarized in the following paragraphs.

Central Nervous System Stimulants. Stimulants are prescribed for their calming effect on prepubertal children of both sexes. This is called a paradoxical effect. Although at this time the specific reasons for this effect are unknown, stimulants have a calming and quieting effect on some children, whereas an adult is generally stimulated. Trade names of stimulants include Ritalin, Dexedrine, and Cylert.

The sought-for positive effects of the stimulants are (a) increased controlled physical activity, (b) increased goal-directedness, (c) decreased impulsivity and disruptiveness, (d) decreased distractibility, (e) increased attending, (f) improved performance, cognition, and perception, (g) improved motor coordination, (h) improved cooperation, and (i) decreased negative and increased positive behavior.

Stimulants have several possible side effects. Students may experience nausea, loss of appetite, and weight loss. There may be a disruption in sleep patterns, with insomnia or infrequent drowsiness both observed. Nervousness, depression, and crying are also noted. When the stimulant is first introduced, severe shaking and fear may be observed.

Antianxiety and Antipsychotic Drugs. These drugs are prescribed for calming effects. Trade names include Mellaril, Thorazine, Librium, Miltown, and Equanil among others. Mellaril and Thorazine are the most frequently prescribed tranquilizers for children.

Desired positive effects of tranquilizers are increased calmness and improved behavior and social functioning. Possible negative effects include nausea, drowsiness, dry mouth and nasal congestion, nervousness, rashes, increased appetite and weight gain.

Anticonvulsants and Antihistamines.   Anticonvulsants are used to treat children whose behavior and learning problems are complicated by seizures. Trade names for these medications include Dilantin, Mysoline, and Valproic Acid among others.

Antihistamines are used to counteract the effects of various allergies. Trade names include Benadryl, Vistaril, and Phenergan. According to Renshaw (1974), these medications are exceptionally safe. They are often prescribed for their sedative effects on children in pain and as a nighttime sedative.

In summary, teachers should remember that although properly prescribed and monitored medication can have a beneficial effect on the child, it cannot (1) compensate for "lost" years of learning, (2) provide the discipline needed to develop acceptable functioning, (3) improve the self-esteem needed for self-acceptance, (4) provide the love the child needs for normal development, or (5) reverse essential deficits, such as mental retardation and cerebral palsy (Renshaw, 1974).

Educator's Role in Biophysical Interventions

The educator plays an important supportive role to medical personnel in the application of biophysical interventions. This supportive role includes (1) referral, (2) collaboration with and reporting of observations to the physician, (3) modification of classroom structure and curriculum content to meet the needs of the child, (4) obtaining permission to administer medication, and (5) safeguarding and administering medication to the child in school.

Referral.   The educator is not in a position by experience, training, or function to refer a child directly to a physician. Neither is the educator in a position to suggest the prescribing of medication to a physician for a specific child. In addition, the educator should not attempt to coerce parents to accept any particular biophysical treatment.

It is proper for teachers to inform parents of a child's problems. The school initiates contact with medical personnel on behalf of a particular child only with parental consent. It is suggested that an educator not directly involved with the child in school serve as a contact person and intermediary between the teacher and parents during the referral process (Report of the Conference on the Use of Stimulant Drugs, 1971).

Collaboration with and Reporting of Observations to the Physician.   A primary role of the teacher in biophysical interventions is the provision of current and objective feedback to the physician on the observable effects of the treatment on the child's behavior and learning (Wilson and Sherrets, 1979). The majority of the present-day medications are experimental substances, the effects of which on a particular child cannot be predicted with exactitude. Thus meaningful feedback to the prescribing physician will assist in maximizing the positive effects of medication. The teacher, a trained observer who is with the child throughout the day, is in an excellent position to observe the effects of the medication and report, through proper channels, to the physician.

Modification of Classroom Structure and Curriculum Content. During the biophysical treatment process, especially during the beginning weeks, the child's behavior and learning styles may change radically. Consequently, it will be necessary for the teacher to modify, as necessary, both classroom structure and curriculum content to respond to the child's needs. Classroom structure may have to be increased or decreased to permit the child to adjust to his or her "new" behavior. The curriculum may have to be changed to allow the child to learn the knowledge and skills neglected during the "lost" years.

Obtaining Permission to Dispense Medication. The educator must obtain permission to dispense medication in the school when medical personnel (physician and/or nurse) are not available. A child should not be dismissed from school because medical personnel are not immediately available to administer medication. In some circumstances, teachers may dispense medication with proper permission. However, school personnel must investigate and adhere to their state's laws and regulations governing the dispensing of medication in the schools. In some cases, the school may need legal advice. A permission form suggested by Renshaw (1974) is shown in Figure 7.1.

Safeguarding and Administration of Medication. In a survey of 149 teachers who were members of the Illinois Council for Children with Behavioral Disorders, Epstein (1989) found that 49% of the schools represented by the teachers did not have a policy on medication practices in their schools. He urged all schools to develop a reasonable and comprehensive policy. When medication is dispensed in the school, the following guidelines should be used:

1. Proper permission forms, completed by parents and physicians, should be obtained and filed in the child's record folder (see Figure 7.1).
2. All medications should be stored in a central location. This facility should be clean, ventilated, and lighted and should contain a locked cabinet. A water tap is needed. A refrigerator is necessary for some medications.
3. All medication must be properly labeled with the child's name and the physician's name. The label should include directions for use.
4. All medication, including new prescriptions and refills, received from and returned home should be logged in and out of the school. Medication should be inventoried frequently. One individual from the school's faculty or staff should be appointed

School Medication Consent and Directions

Parent permission: Date _____

Child _____Birthdate _____

Address _____Phone _____

School _____Grade _____ Teacher _____

_____

I hereby consent for the above-named school to supervise the medication prescribed below by my physician for my child.

_____

Physician's direction: Date _____

Child _____

Medication and instruction _____

_____

Doctor requests teacher's comments:

Please observe the following _____

Phone _____ Best time to call _____

_____

Physician's signature
Physician/Clinic name

Address _____

FIGURE 7.1
School medication consent form and directions.

(From Renshaw, D. C. *The hyperactive child,* p. 127, Chicago: Nelson-Hall Publishers, 1974.)

to inventory the medication and function as a contact person in all communications with parents, physicians, and other medical personnel in relation to medication.

5. A responsible adult must be present when a child takes a medication.
6. A log, to be filled in each time a child takes a medication, should be affixed to the wall in the medication center. This form is presented in Figure 7.2. The completed forms should be retained in a file.

Medication Log

Child's name	Date	Time	Medication	Person dispensing medication	Notes

FIGURE 7.2
Medication log.

SUMMARY

In this chapter several biophysical and environmental interventions of relevance to the teacher interested in a broad understanding of behavior management are presented.

The careful reader will note that significant overlap exists between the behavior management interventions presented in this and the previous chapter. The educator should seek to synthesize the various conceptual frameworks (theories) and their intervention into a personal perspective of behavior management.

PROJECTS

1. Write a brief essay (300 words) on the following topics:
   a. The advantages and disadvantages of the environmental interventions.
   b. The advantages and disadvantages of the biophysical interventions from the educator's point of view.
2. Discuss the role of the educator in biophysical interventions.
3. Invite a physician or nurse to discuss biophysical interventions with your class.
4. Survey your community and school to ascertain which, if any, of the environmental interventions discussed in the chapter are applied to assist children with behavior problems.
5. Using the questions presented under the critical elements in the milieu, interview a teacher and principal to determine the character of the milieu in which they function.

REFERENCES

Anderson, N., & Marrone, R. T. (1979). Therapeutic discussion groups in public school classes for emotionally disturbed children. *Focus on Exceptional Children, 12*(1), 1-15.

Baker, R. W. (1980). The treatment of behavior disorders with medication. In S. G. Sapir & A. C. Nitzberg (Eds.), *Children with learning problems.* New York: Brunner/Mazel.

Baldwin, R. W. (1973). The treatment of behavior disorders with medication. In S. G. Sapir & A. C. Nitzberg (Eds.), *Children with learning problems.* New York: Brunner/Mazel.

Bartlett, L. (1988). Doe v. Honig and school discipline. *Behavior In Our Schools, 2*(3), 10-11.

Bartlett, L. (1988). To expel or not to expel: Discipline of special education students from a legal perspective. *Behavior In Our Schools, 2*(2), 14-16.

Bauer, A. M. (1980). *Head teacher's handbook.* St. Louis: Special District of St. Louis County, Missouri.

Bauer, A. M., Shea, T. M., & Keppler, R. (1986). Levels systems: A framework for the individualization of behavior management. *Behavioral Disorders, 12*(1), 28-35.

Bauer, A. M., & Shea, T. M. (1988). Structuring classroom through levels systems. *Focus on Exceptional Children, 21*(2), 1-12.

Blankenship, C. S. (1986). Managing pupil behavior during instruction. *Teaching Exceptional Children, 19*, 52-53.

Brenner, A. (1977). A study of the efficacy of the Feingold diet on hyperkinetic children. *Clinical Pediatrics, 16*, 652-656.

Carducci, D. J. (1980). Positive peer culture and assertiveness training. *Behavioral Disorders, 5*(3)156-162.

Center, D. B., & McKittrick, S. (1987). Disciplinary removal of special education students. *Focus on Exceptional Children, 20*(2), 1-10.

Cheney, C. O. (1989, August). First time in the classroom? Start off strong! *Exceptional Times, 4.*

Clark County Special Education Cooperative. (1984) *Day treatment program agreement.* Jeffersonville, IN: Clark County Special Education Cooperative.

Coleman, M., & Webber, J. (1988). Behavior problems? Try groups! *Academic Therapy, 23*(3), 265-275.

Cook, P. S., & Woodhill, J. M. (1976). The Feingold dietary treatment of the hyperkinetic syndrome. *Medical Journal of Australia, 2,* 85-89.

Costello, A. (1988). The psychosocial impact of genetic disease. *Focus on Exceptional Children, 20*(7), 1-8.

Coughlan, A. J., Gold, S. R., Dohrenwend, E.F., & Zimmerman, R. S. (1973). A psychobehavioral residential drug abuse program: A new adventure in adolescent psychiatry. *International Journal of Addiction, 8*(5), 767-777.

Englert, C. S. (1984). Measuring teacher effectiveness from the teacher's point of view. *Focus on Exceptional Children, 17,* 1-14.

Epstein, M. H. (1989). *Survey of teachers of children and adolescents with behavior disorders on the use of medication.* DeKalb, IL: Northern Illinois University.

Epstein, M. H., & Olinger, E. (1987). Use of medication in school programs for behaviorally disordered pupils. *Behavioral Disorders, 12*(2), 138-145.

Eskey, M., & Hauser, S. (1984). *Pals (Personal adjustment level system).* Hinsdale, IL: Hinsdale South High School.

Evertson, C. M., Emmer, E. T., Clements, B. S., Sanford, J. P., Worsham, M. E., & Williams, E. L. (1981). *Organizing and managing the elementary school classroom.* Austin: Research and Development Center for Teacher Education, University of Texas.

Feingold, B. F. (1973). Food additives and child development. *Hospital Practice, 8,* 11.

Feingold, B. F. (1975). *Why your child is hyperactive.* New York: Random House.

Gable, R. A., & Strain, P. S. (1981). Individualizing a token economy system for the treatment of children's behavior disorders. *Behavioral Disorders, 1,* 39-45.

Gadow, K. (1979). *Children on medication: A primer for school personnel.* Reston, VA: Council for Exceptional Children.

Gallagher, P. A. (1988). *Teaching students with behavior disorders* (2nd ed.). Denver: Love.

Genetic counseling. (1987). *The Exceptional Parent, 17*(5), 44-45, 47, 49.

Goss v. Lopez, 95 S. Ct. 729 (1975).

Grosenick, J. K., Huntze, S. L., Kochan, B., Peterson, R. L., Robertshaw, C. S., & Wood, F. (1982). *National needs analysis in behavior disorders working paper.* Columbia, MO: Department of Special Education, University of Missouri.

Harth, R., & Morris, S. M. (1976). Group processes for behavior change. *Teaching Exceptional Children, 8*(4), 136-139.

Hindman, S. E. (1986). The law, the courts, and the education of behaviorally disordered students. *Behavioral Disorders, 11*(4), 280-289.

Joyce, B. G., Joyce, J. H. & Chase, P. N. (1989). Considerations for the use of rules in academic settings. *Education and Treatment of Children, 12,* 82-92.

Kameya, L. I. (1972). Biophysical interventions in emotional disturbance. In W. C. Rhodes & M. L. Tracy (Eds.), *A study of child variance: Vol 2. Interventions.* Ann Arbor: University of Michigan Press.

Knapczyk, D. R. (1979). Diet control in the management of behavior disorders. *Behavioral Disorders, 5*(1), 2-9.

LaNunziata, L. J., Hunt, K. P., & Cooper, J. O. (1984). Suggestions for phasing out token economy systems in primary and intermediate grades. *Techniques, 1,* 151-156.

Legare, A. F. (1984). Using symbols to enhance classroom structure. *Teaching Exceptional Children, 17,* 69-70.

Long, N. J., Morse, W. C., & Newman, R. G. (1980). Milieu therapy. In N. J. Long, W. C. Morse, & R. G. Newman (Eds.), *Conflict in the classroom: The education of emotionally disturbed children* (4th ed.), Belmont, CA: Wadsworth Publishing Co.

Loughmiller, C. (1965). *Wilderness road.* Austin: University of Texas, Hogg Foundation for Mental Health.

Mastropieri, M. A., Jenne, T., & Scruggs, T. E. (1988). A levels system for managing problem behaviors in a high school resource program. *Behavioral Disorders, 13*(3), 202-208.

Millichap, J. G. (1975). *The hyperactive child with minimal brain dysfunction.* Chicago: Year Book Medical Publishers.

Mitchell, J. D., & Cockrum, D. L. (1980). Positive peer culture and a level system: A comparison in an adolescent treatment facility. *Criminal Justice and Behavior, 7*(4), 399-406.

Morris, P. (1987). The restricted use of traditional disciplinary procedures with handicapped youngsters. In A. Rotatori, M. Banbury, & R. Foxx (Eds.), *Issues in special education.* Mountain View, CA: Mayfield.

Morris, S. M. (1982). A classroom process for behavior change. *The Pointer, 26*(3), 25-28.

Morse, W. C., & Wineman, D. (1957). Group interviewing in a camp for disturbed boys. *Journal of Social Issues, 13*(1), 23-31.

Olson, J. (1989). Managing life in the classroom: Dealing with the nitty gritty. *Academic Therapy, 24,* 545-553.

Pauling, L. C. (1968). Orthomolecular psychiatry. *Science, 160,* 265-271.

Redl, F. (1959). The concept of the life-space interview. *American Journal of Orthopsychiatry, 29,* 1-18.

Reid, I. (1979). Developing a behavioral regime in a secure youth treatment centre. *Bulletin of the British Psychological Society, 32,* 207.

Renshaw, D. C. (1974). *The hyperactive child.* Chicago: Nelson-Hall Publishers.

Report of the Conference on the Use of Stimulant Drugs in the Treatment of Behaviorally Disturbed Young School Children. (1971). *Journal of Learning Disabilities, 4,* 523-530.

Rieth, H., & Evertson, C. (1988). Variables related to the effective instruction of difficult-to-teach children. *Focus on Exceptional Children, 20,* 1-8.

Rhodes, W. C., & Gibbins, S. (1972). Community programming for the behaviorally deviant child. In H. C. Quay & J. F. Werry (Eds.), *Psychopa-*thological disorders of childhood. New York: John Wiley & Sons.

Rosenberg, M.S. (1986). Maximizing the effectiveness of structured classroom management programs: Implementing rule-review procedures with disruptive and distractible students. *Behavioral Disorders, 11*(4), 239-248.

Rosenkoetter, S. E., & Fowler, S. A. (1986). Teaching mainstreamed children to manage daily transitions. *Teaching Exceptional Children, 19,* 20-23.

Rosenshine, B. (1977). Review of teaching variables and student achievement. In G. D. Borich & K. S. Fenton (Eds.), *The appraisal of teaching: Concepts and process.* Menlo Park, CA: Addison Wesley.

Rosenstock, H. A., & Levy, H. J. (1978). On the clinical superiority of the level system. *Journal of the National Association of Private Psychiatric Hospitals, 9*(3), 32-36.

Shea, T. M. (1977). *Camping for special children.* St. Louis: C. V. Mosby Co.

Shea, T. M., & Bauer, A. M. (1987). *Teaching children and youth with behavior disorders* (2nd ed.). Englewood Cliffs, NJ: Prentice-Hall.

Shea, T. M., Bauer, A. M., & Lynch, E. M. (1989, September). *Changing behavior: Ethical issues regarding behavior management and the control of students with behavioral disorders.* Paper presented at CEC/CCBD Conference, Charlotte, NC.

Slade, D., & Callaghan, T. (1988). Preventing management problems. *Academic Therapy, 23,* 229-235.

Stainback, W., Stainback, S., Etscheidt, S., & Doud, J. (1986). A nonintrusive intervention for acting-out behavior. *Teaching Exceptional Children, 19*(1), 38-41.

Swanson, J. M., & Kinsbourne, M. (1980) Food dyes impair performance of hyperactive children on a laboratory learning test. *Science, 207*(28), 1485-1486.

Swanson, H. L., & Reinert, H. R. (1984). *Teaching strategies for children in conflict.* St. Louis: C.V. Mosby Co.

Terez, T. (1986, January). Geel. *New Ways,* 24-29.

Tinker v. Des Moines Independent Community School District, 393 U.S. 503, 89 S. Ct. 733, 21

L. Ed. 2d 721 (1969).

Wagner, M. (1972). Environmental interventions in emotional disturbance. In W. C. Rhodes & M. L. Tracy (Eds.), *A study of child variance: Vol 2. Interventions.* Ann Arbor: University of Michigan Press.

Weinstein, L. (1968). Project Re-Ed: Schools for emotionally disturbed children—effectiveness as viewed by referring agencies, parents, and teachers. *Exceptional Children, 35,* 703-711.

Weiss, B., Williams, J. H., Margen, S., Abrams, B., Citron, L. J., Cox, C., McKibben, J., & Ogar, D. (1980). Behavioral responses to artificial food colors. *Science, 207*(28), 1487-1488.

Wilson, J. E., & Sherrets, S. D. (1979). A review of past and current pharmacological interventions in the treatment of emotionally disturbed children and adolescents. *Behavioral Disorders, 5*(1), 60-69.

CHAPTER EIGHT

Parent Training and Home-School Behavior Management

Mr. and Mrs. Wagnal arrived at the counseling center for their appointment with Dr. Murphy promptly at 3 PM. They were visiting the center to consult with Dr. Murphy, a psychologist, concerning the behavior problems of their 3-year-old son, Dennis. Dennis is their first child.

The Wagnals were disturbed about Dennis because of his poor eating habits, his lack of interest in other children, his frequent tantrums, and his toilet training problems. They reported that Dennis would eat only pickles, potato chips, chocolate candy, white bread, and frankfurters. He drank only water and cola. Needless to say, the Wagnals were concerned about Dennis's physical well-being.

Mrs. Wagnal stated that she had tried "everything" in an effort to bladder train Dennis. She had placed him on a rigid drinking schedule to control his liquid intake; she had awakened him every hour throughout the night and took him to the bathroom; she had set an egg timer to remind her to take him to the bathroom each hour throughout the day; and she had even purchased a musical potty chair. All of this had no influence on the boy's behavior.

The Wagnals' greatest concern was Dennis's behavior toward other children. Whenever another child of Dennis's age visited the home, Dennis would ignore the other child until he or she began playing with one of his toys. When the other child touched his possessions, Dennis immediately had a tantrum. He would kick and scream until the other child was removed from the home.

The Wagnals were desperate for help. Neither parent had relatives to whom they could turn for help with Dennis.

The Wagnals realized their need for some training and counseling if they were to help Dennis.

Mr. and Mrs. Mitchell arrived at room 210 of Collinsdale Junior High School promptly at 7:30 PM. They were to confer with Mr. Boyle, their 13-year-old daughter Eileen's homeroom teacher. This was the first time they had been summoned to a conference because of one of their children.

Neither parent was anxious to visit with Mr. Boyle. Eileen's last report card contained two Fs, three Cs, and a B. Her conduct grades were at the bottom of the school's 5-point scale. In addition to the report card, the Mitchells had received a dozen or more negative notes from Eileen's teachers.

They had yelled and hollered, scolded and punished, and even grounded Eileen during the preceding 3 months without effect. The Mitchells realized that without cooperation from their daughter's teachers they could not successfully help her.

There must be some techniques available for implementation to increase the consistency with which the home and school could manage Eileen's behavior and academic performance.

After studying the literature on parent education and training from a variety of theoretical and methodological perspectives, Clements and Alexander (1975) concluded: "Extensive research demonstrates unequivocally that children learn more, adjust better, and progress faster when parent training is effected" (p. 7).

Parent training is an integral part of a successful home-school management program. According to Beale and Beers (1982), there are three broad categories from which to work with parents. They are (1) parent education, (2) parent collaboration, and (3) parent-teacher communication. These may be rephrased as (1) "teach them what they need to know," (2) "work *with* them," and (3) "I talk, you talk, we talk."

The primary purposes of this chapter are to present a systematic methodology designed to facilitate (1) the effectiveness with which parents manage their children's behavior in home and community settings, (2) collaboration between the parents and teacher in the implementation of effective behavior management interventions on behalf of the child for whom they have a shared responsibility, and (3) the teacher's efforts to plan and conduct a parent behavior management training program.

The parent training perspective presented here is but one of many discussed in the literature. Extensive references to other approaches, such as those developed by Dinkmeyer and McKay (1973), Shea and Bauer (1985), Croft (1979), Kroth and Otteni (1985), Winton (1986), Ehly, Conoley, and Rosenthal (1985), Seligman (1979), and Dunst, Trivette, and Deal (1988), as well as references to several other methods of conducting parent education and training, are presented at the end of the chapter. The reader should find these references an excellent point of departure for a comprehensive study of parent education and training.

CHAPTER OBJECTIVES

After completing this chapter, you will be able to do the following:

1. Analyze the integrative framework or perspective of parent education and training.
2. Understand the need for and desirability of parent education and training.
3. Characterize the reactions, problems, and needs of parents of children with behavioral problems and other exceptionalities.
4. Explain the purpose and objectives of parent behavior management training.
5. Implement assessment strategies used to aid parents conducting a behavior change program.

6. List potentially effective reinforcers available in the home.
7. Execute the eight-session behavior management training course with parents.
8. Implement techniques to facilitate parent-teacher collaboration.

Need for and Desirability of Parent Education and Training

There remains among present-day regular and special education teachers, as well as educational administrators and other professionals, skepticism concerning the need for and desirability of school-sponsored programs for parents. Our experience, however, as parents and educators, indicates that parent education and training is a necessary component of a comprehensive school service program.

Clements and Alexander (1975) agree:

> It is unnecessary to revisit the already proven axiom that parents are effective change agents in the lives of exceptional children. It is, perhaps, equally as extravagant to indulge in outlining the boundaries of social and academic learning and perpetuate the pseudo-issue of who governs which set of constructs when, in reality, these are shared and interactive responsibilities. We must instead face an important issue in the third quarter of the twentieth century; parents are moving both physically and intellectually back into the mainstream of American education. (p. 1)

The question is not whether parent training is needed but how educators can effectively and efficiently conduct parent programs for the ultimate benefit of all children. Clements and Alexander suggest that the teacher is the school-based professional primarily responsible for parent services. All teachers of regular and special classes must acknowledge their responsibility and take steps to provide appropriate programs with parents.

Gardner (1974) maintains that cooperative home-school endeavors are more effective in responding to the needs of behavior-disordered children than are school endeavors alone. The Pathfinder School (Susser, 1974) perceives parents and educators as partners. According to Susser, success in the classroom is lasting only if there is 24-hour-a-day follow-through; the approach of school and home, teacher and parent, must be consistent. Karnes and Zehrbach (1972) have suggested that programs for handicapped children can be significantly improved if parents are meaningfully involved in them.

Opinions relative to the need for and desirability of programs for parents are not exclusively the domain of professionals. Many parents are aware of their need for education and training. Stigen (1976) writes repeatedly of her need for assistance through meaningful education and training. She discusses the inadequacy of the guidance and supportive services for parents offered by hospitals, schools, clinics, and other social service agencies.

Kratoville (1975a, 1975b) and Jogis (1975), both parents of handicapped children, have described their need for sensitive, practical assistance in their role as primary therapist for their children. These parents noted a lack of meaningful assistance and understanding of their problems by professionals in hospitals, schools, clinics, and community agencies. They discovered the obvious lack of training and sensitivity of professionals toward parents.

The opinions of the parents and professionals just cited and those of many others, including parents and teachers involved primarily with nonhandicapped children, lead us to the following conclusions (Shea & Bauer, 1985):

1. Both parents and professionals recognize the need for parent education and training.
2. Parent programs are desirable because they not only respond to the needs of the parents but also have a significant positive effect on the children.
3. The teacher, a specialist in instructional processes and behavior management techniques, is the logical professional to coordinate and conduct parent programs in cooperation with the school counselor, psychologist, or social worker.
4. Children benefit most when the behavior management approaches of the home and school are consistent.
5. Parent programs must be practical, concrete, specific, and meaningful to the parents.

Although the literature cited is primarily concerned with children administratively classified as handicapped, the conclusions drawn from the literature are relevant to all children and their parents. "Normal" children also have problems and are frequently a behavior management concern to their parents.

Parents' Reactions, Problems, and Needs

The parents of a child with a problem are first and foremost human beings, and like all human beings they react as individuals to the problems of loved ones. A particular parent's reaction is in large part determined by that individual's personal characteristics, life experiences, education and training, expectations, socioeconomic circumstances, and a variety of other variables. The parent's reaction is influenced by the characteristics of the child and the specific problem and, to some degree, by the educator's and other's reaction to the problem (Shea & Bauer, 1985).

Educators should keep in mind that parents with problem children are not necessarily "problem parents." They do not necessarily need personal counseling. The majority are normal persons who are responding in a normal manner to unanticipated trauma.

Ross (1964) discussed parental reactions to the birth or diagnosis of a child with exceptionality from a psychoanalytic perspective. The recognition of a handicap in a child causes an increase in the parents' level of anxiety. This anxiety appears to be caused by recognition of the unanticipated discrepancy between the parents' expectations for the child and the way the child is in reality. In their efforts to control anxiety, the parents employ one or more of a broad range of personal coping mechanisms. These mechanisms are used to regain emotional equilibrium, which has been threatened by the crisis. Although coping mechanisms are applied for positive reasons; that is, the regaining of emotional equilibrium, they may be destructive to the individual parent and child if they are overused or if they become habitual. According to Ross, counseling and similar supportive therapeutic services are required to aid parents in dealing with their initial anxiety and consequent reactions resulting from their child's problem.

A crisis reaction to a child's problems is not the exclusive province of parents of children classified as deviant, special, exceptional, or handicapped (Gordon, 1976). Emotional reactions to problems with a child are a natural human response for any parent confronted with a crisis or perceived crisis. Also, all parents do not employ the same coping mechanisms. Parental reactions are as varied as the individual parents confronted with a crisis situation (Gordon, 1976).

Among the coping mechanisms parents may apply in response to their recognition of a problem with their child are the following:

□ *Self doubt:* The parents may doubt their worth as human beings and as parents. Their self-worth may be in doubt because of a perceived inability to give birth to or raise a child according to their expectations and the expectations of society.

□ *Unhappiness and mourning:* The child's problem is perceived as so severe that the parents' joy of life is gone. It is impossible for them to smile, laugh, converse, or take an active part in any of life's common pleasures. This parental reaction has been compared to the mourning that occurs after the death of a loved one.

□ *Guilt:* Because of the uncertain cause of their child's problem, many parents feel guilty. They believe that the child's problem is their fault. At times parents will go to extreme lengths to find a reason for the child's difficulty and may discover some insignificant personal behavior or incident in the past on which to place blame.

□ *Denial:* The parents may react to the child's problem by denying its existence. They reason that if the existence of the problem is denied, they do not have to concern themselves with it.

□ *Projection:* Many parents who recognize the existence of a problem may blame it on another person. They may blame the child's difficulty on a physician, nurse, caseworker, counselor, baby-sitter, or teacher. Occasionally they will project blame onto their spouse or other children.

□ *Withdrawal:* The parents may react to the child's problem by withdrawal, believing that they can find a solution if they give the problem sufficient time and personal consideration. In some cases, withdrawal leads to depression requiring professional attention.

□ *Avoidance and rejection:* To some parents the birth or diagnosis of an exceptional child is so traumatic that they avoid contact with the child; they are unable to feed, clothe, or play with the child.

- □ *Embarrassment and social isolation:* Many parents of handicapped children are embarrassed by them. In some cases this embarrassment leads to social isolation. Neither parent nor child leaves the home for shopping, walks, visits, or entertainment.
- □ *Hostility:* Some parents report feelings of hostility and, on occasion, overt anger toward others who stare or ask questions about the child. The object of this hostility and anger may be anyone: a passenger on a bus, a person in the street, a friend, a neighbor, a relative, or a child.
- □ *Overdependency and helplessness:* The parents may react with overdependency on their spouse, a child, a relative, or a professional.
- □ *Confusion:* Most parents are confused by the child's problem. They are confused about the cause of the problem, its normal course, and its treatment. Such confusion is largely a result of a lack of factual information and guidance from professionals.
- □ *Frustration:* Many parents who have decided on a course of action that is appropriate for their child become frustrated in their efforts to obtain services. They are confronted with insensitive and inadequately trained professionals. They are frustrated by the lack of appropriate services in the community.

The educator must recognize that many of the foregoing emotional reactions are not under a parent's conscious control. Parents must be aided in dealing with their emotional reactions before they can fully participate in and benefit from a training program.

Teachers realize that they need a variety of communication and instructional skills. They must learn to listen to the meaning behind the parents' words, as well as the words themselves. They must be sensitive to the parents' feelings. They must be able to empathize with the problems confronting the parents and child. Although parent educators must approach their task with honesty and forthrightness, they must not be cruel, give the impression that the parents, child, and problem are hopeless, or indicate that they have all the answers. Parent educators must have sufficient confidence in their teaching ability to permit parents to develop confidence in them—and through them, in themselves. Teachers must recognize the limits of their knowledge and skills when working with parents. Teachers are neither counselors nor therapists. As a consequence, they must refer parents to the appropriate individuals and agencies for services that are beyond the scope of their professional expertise.

An Integrative Framework

The ecological contexts that affect children with a behavior problem are described in detail in Chapter 1. The reader is encouraged to review the Chapter 1 sections on traditional models of human behavior, the integrative framework, and Figure 1.6 before studying this section.

The integrative framework stresses that the understanding of human development and behavior requires examination of the contexts of interactions in several settings (Bronfenbrenner, 1977). The mesosystem—the interrelations among the major settings the child inhabits at a particular point in life—includes both home and school. To effectively respond to student needs, the teacher must involve those in the mesosystem (parents, guardians, siblings, and surrogate parents) in the child's behavior management program.

The integrative or ecological approach invites consideration of the joint impact of two or more settings on their elements. School and home jointly impact on children with behavior problems. The subsystems that are significant when working with children and their families include parent-child, parent-teacher-child, teacher-child, sibling-child, sibling-parent-child (Shea & Bauer, 1987). According to Bronfenbrenner, the design of an ecological intervention for an individual functioning in more than one setting should take into account the possible subsystems and effects that exist, or could exist, across settings. Consequently, programming with parents in behalf of children should take several subsystems into account. Those to be examined by teachers wishing to collaborate with parents in behalf of children with behavior problems include:

- Nature and requirements of the parents' work
- Neighborhood, health, and community services
- School and community relations
- Informal social networks
- Patterns of recreation and social life
- Family type (traditional or neolocal nuclear family, extended family, one-parent family, and so on)
- Delegation of child care to others outside the home
- Existence and character of explicit and implicit societal values with reference to parenting, children, handicapping conditions, and behavior.

By examining the child and the parents and family with reference to these ecological contexts, the teacher can develop, in collaboration with the parents, an individualized behavior management training program responsive to the needs of the child and parents.

Purposes and Objectives of Parent Training

McDowell (1976) has classified parent programs under three headings: (1) informational, (2) psychotherapeutic, and (3) training.

The informational program is designed primarily to present knowledge to parents about a variety of topics. Among the focuses of such informational programs are (1) child-raising techniques, (2) child development, (3) educational program designs, objectives, and procedures, (4) the causes, effects, and treatment of handicapping conditions, and (5) techniques of behavior management. The primary purpose of these parent programs is the transmission of information.

The psychotherapeutic strategy is employed to assist parents in their efforts to deal with personal feelings and conflicts related to the child's problem and its impact and contingencies. It is assumed that parents must adjust emotionally before they can plan and implement an action program.

Parent training programs are designed to assist parent's efforts to effectively interact with and manage the behavior of their children. These programs can be exemplified by several contemporary parent training programs. Parent Effectiveness Training (Gordon, 1970) focuses primarily on assisting parents in establishing effective and positive communications with children. The C-Group strategy (Dinkmeyer & McKay, 1973) focuses on training parents to solve practical child management problems. Both programs are action oriented. They necessitate parental involvement and commitment. In these programs it is assumed that once parents have learned appropriate and effective problem-solving skills and have made them a habit, they will continue to apply them in the management of child behavior.

The program for parent-teacher cooperation in child management presented in this chapter can be classified as a parent training program. It focuses primarily on training and implementation of behavior management techniques as an effective and efficient means of managing behavior. As a consequence of this focus, the program is limited in its effectiveness with those parents in need of psychotherapeutic or basic informational services.

Objectives of the Parent Training Program

The specific objectives of the parent training program presented in this chapter are the following:

☐ To increase the parents' knowledge of the techniques of behavior modification.
☐ To increase the parents' skills in the application of behavior modification techniques in the management of their children's behavior.
☐ To provide both the parents and the teacher with a common perspective of child behavior management and facilitate collaborative child behavior management efforts.

These objectives are attained by instructing the parents in behavior modification techniques and by assisting the parents' application of these techniques in home and home-school behavior management interventions.

The steps in the behavior change process applied in the parent training program are identical to those presented in Chapter 3. These steps are repeated here for reader convenience. Those wishing to review in depth the steps in the behavior change process are referred to Chapter 3. The steps are as follows:

Step 1: Selecting a target behavior.
Step 2: Collecting and recording baseline data.
Step 3: Identifying appropriate reinforcers.
Step 4: Implementing an intervention and collecting and recording intervention data.
Step 5: Evaluating the effects of intervention.

It must be remembered that in parent training, the teacher is generally once removed from direct observation of the child's behavior in the home setting; thus the teacher must rely on the parents' observations and reports. Consequently, assessment strategies must be implemented to facilitate the parents' selection and objectification of a target behavior.

In addition, reinforcers applied in the home setting differ somewhat from those available and applicable in the school; thus attention is given to the parents' recognition and application of home reinforcers.

Selecting the Target Behavior: Assessment Techniques

To be of practical assistance to parents wishing to improve their behavior management skills, the educator must obtain specific information about the child's behavior. The information needed includes (Blackham & Silberman, 1980):

- ☐ The history of the problem
- ☐ Specific areas of conflict
- ☐ A description of the behavior that makes it receptive to direct observation and measurement
- ☐ The identity of the person or persons present when the behavior occurs
- ☐ Reinforcers that appear to maintain the behavior
- ☐ The roles and responsibilities of the parents and other family members in the child's life
- ☐ Parental expectations and behavior requirements and the reasonableness of these expectations and requirements
- ☐ Methods presently used to change the behavior
- ☐ Rewards that are available or that can be made available in the home
- ☐ Observational data on the rate or frequency of the behavior

Blackham and Silberman have suggested four methods for obtaining data on parent-child interactions and problem areas:

1. Direct observation of the child and other family members in the home
2. Direct observation of the child and other family members in the clinic or school setting

3. Parental observation of the child's interaction within the family at home, and the reporting of the resultant data to the educator
4. A personal interview with the parents and child

As a result of the administrative organization of the public school system, the first two methods are not feasible; that is, the teacher is usually unable to spend the needed time observing parent-child interaction in either the home or the school. The third and fourth methods are most practical and can be implemented by means of the psychosituational assessment interview.

Psychosituational Assessment Interview

The psychosituational assessment interview is primarily an information-gathering technique. The interview focuses primarily on obtaining from the parent or parents descriptive data about the child's behavior and the circumstances surrounding it.

The psychosituational interview technique was designed by Bersoff and Grieger (1971) and applied by Shea and others (1974). The purpose of the interview is to analyze the unacceptable behavior and uncover the antecedents and consequences that elicit, reinforce, and sustain it. This information about the child is elicited from the parent or parents and contributes to decisions concerning interventions to modify the behavior.

By means of the interview, it is possible to determine to what extent the behavior is reinforced and maintained by the environment and to what extent it may be modified by the manipulation of the environment. Thus the primary aspects of the setting in which the behavior occurs are analyzed. These aspects are (1) the child's behavior, (2) the environmental variables surrounding the behavior, and (3) the attitudes and expectations of the parents.

Behavior refers to the actual behaviors for which the child was referred, including the antecedents and consequences of that behavior, that is, teacher, parental, and peer responses. *Environments* and *situations* refer to the specific places and circumstances in which the behavior occurs, including the presence of significant others. *Attitudes* refer to the beliefs and feelings of the referring agent, that is, the parent or parents.

A parent's concern about a child's behavior may be based on irrational ideas and attitudes that lead to unwarranted expectations, demands, and feelings—all of which may result in inappropriate actions toward the child following emission of the target behavior. *Expectation* has a dual meaning: It refers to the specific performance that the adult would like the child to achieve (short-term goals) and to the long-range aspirations that the adult has for the child.

The four major tasks to be accomplished during the interview are (1) defining the target behavior(s), (2) explicating specific situations in which the behavior occurs, (3) uncovering the contingencies (antecedents and consequences) that seemingly sustain the behavior, and (4) detecting any irrational ideas that make it difficult for the parent or parents to objectively understand, accept, and modify the behavior.

Defining the target behavior involves analyzing the following: (1) its *frequency rate,* the number of times the behavior occurs within a particular time period; (2) its *intensity,* the strength or force of the behavior; and (3) its *duration,* the length of time that the behavior is maintained. A careful analysis of the problem within a behavioral framework helps delineate and define it so that it becomes remediable. This process helps the parents check their perceptions and focus on the relevant problem.

Obtaining information about the specific situations in which the behavior occurs is important because behavior is considered a function of interaction between the learned response of the child and the situation in which the behavior occurs. This information helps the interviewer plan the intervention.

Exploring the antecedents and consequences of the behavior is the next interviewer task. The parents must be aware that *they are part of the problem* and may have a role in sustaining the behavior.

Finally, the interviewer must be aware of the parent or parents' irrational and unrealistic ideas about the child. The following irrational ideas of parents are frequently apparent:

1. The notion that the child is infallible and has wide-ranging competence. When the parents' expectation is that the child is competent in all respects, inefficiency in one or two areas of functioning is regarded as general failure.
2. The maintenance of absolutistic, supportable, and unreasonable expectations of the child. These ideas are usually expressed in "ought" and "should" terms. A parent may say, "He should be able to sit longer" or "He ought to know better."
3. The feeling that it is helpful to become angry over the child's misbehavior. This feeling may lead to guilt and anxiety on the part of the parents that may further interfere with parent-child interactions.
4. The belief that the child is blameworthy and needs to be punished for misdeeds. The failure to accept things as they exist inhibits rational problem solving.

It is recommended that both parents be present at the interview. A joint interview is desirable because differing perceptions and inconsistencies in parental behavior management strategies can be uncovered. It also allows the interviewer to gauge the amount and frequency of mutual support that the parents provide to each other.

The interview may be a single session or a series of sessions. If the interviewer is primarily concerned with obtaining data in an effort to design an intervention that includes parental participation, two or three sessions may be sufficient. However, frequently the strategy can be applied in an ongoing intervention program.

To assist the parent, the interviewer may suggest that the parents gather behavioral data. A form for this purpose is presented in Figure 8.1, along with instructions for completing the form.

The following are specific interviewer tasks:

1. Establish rapport with the parent or parents.
   Example Questions
   □ How are you doing today?

Behavior Log Form

Target behavior _____

Child _____

Observer _____

Date	Time		Antecedents	Consequences	Applied interventions	Comments
	Begins	Ends				

FIGURE 8.1
Parents' behavior log for home use.

Behavior Log Form

INSTRUCTIONS

1. Complete the top portion of the form, that is, the target behavior to be observed, the child's name, the observer's name, and date.
2. Write *day* and *date* of the first observation in first column, for example, M/8/3 or Th/11/3.
3. Upon each occurrence of the target behavior write the time it begins and ends in the second and third columns, respectively. If the target behavior is nearly instantaneous, write the time of the occurrence in the second column.
4. Upon each occurrence of the target behavior, write what happened immediately *before* the behavior in the fourth column.
5. In column six write what you or another person interacting with or supervising the child did to either *encourage* or *discourage* the behavior. If there was no reaction to the behavior, it should be noted in this column.
6. In column seven write any comments you have regarding the occurrence of the behavior that are out of the ordinary, for example, child was tired, grandmother was visiting, bad day in school, marital conflict occurring, and so on.

   It is recommended that a behavior log be maintained for a minimum of 1 week before an intervention is implemented.

FIGURE 8.1
Continued.

    ☐ Did work go well today?
    ☐ Would you care for something to drink? Coffee? Tea? Soda?
    ☐ Is that seat comfortable enough?

2. Have the parents specify the target behavior(s), that is, the specific behavior(s) that are disturbing to them. Explore the frequency, intensity, and duration of the behavior.
   Example Questions
   ☐ What exactly does the child do that you find unacceptable or annoying?
   ☐ What exactly does the child do that makes you say he or she is hyperactive, nonresponsive, or disobedient?
   ☐ What else does the child do that makes you say he or she is hyperactive, nonresponsive, or disobedient?
   ☐ In the course of an hour (day) how often is the child hyperactive, nonresponsive, or disobedient?

3. Have the parents delineate the specific situations and environments in which the behavior occurs. Establish where the behavior takes place and who is present when the behavior occurs.
   Example Questions
   ☐ Where does this behavior occur? In the house? In the yard? On the playground? In a store?

      □ Does it occur when the child is working on a particular project? With a particular group? While watching TV? When getting ready to go to bed? When getting up in the morning?

      □ Who is present when the behavior occurs? Mother? Father? Brothers? Sisters? Playmates? Visitors?

4. Explore the contingencies that may stimulate and sustain the behavior. Determine what happens immediately before and after the behavior occurs; that is, the antecedents and consequences of the behavior.

   Example Questions
   - □ What happens just before the behavior occurs?
   - □ What happens just after the behavior occurs?
   - □ What do you usually do when the child engages in this behavior?
   - □ How do other people indicate to the child that the behavior is unacceptable?

5. Attempt to determine the ratio of positive-to-negative interactions between the child and the parents.

   Example Questions
   - □ Is your relationship with the child usually pleasant or unpleasant?
   - □ Do you usually praise his or her accomplishments?
   - □ Do you reprimand the child's failures and ignore his or her success?

6. Explore the methods the parents use for behavior control. Explore the type of punishment and the conditions for application.

   Example Questions
   - □ Do you punish the behavior?
   - □ How do you punish inappropriate behavior?
   - □ Who is responsible for administering the punishment?
   - □ Do you always use this method of punishment?
   - □ Which other methods do you use?

7. Determine to what degree the parents are aware of how praise or punishment is communicated and its effect on the child's behavior.

   Example Questions
   - □ Can the child tell when you are angry? How?
   - □ Can the child tell when you want him or her to stop doing something? How?

8. Explore the manner in which expectations and consequences are communicated by the parents to their child.

   Example Questions
   - □ Are the rules you expect the child to follow clearly spelled out?
   - □ Does the child know what you expect him or her to do?

9. Detect irrational and unrealistic ideas that make it difficult for the parents to understand, accept, or modify the child's behavior. Be alert for and explore irrational ideas that may be expressed by the parents. Restate irrational ideas but avoid reinforcing them.

10. Conclude the session by restating the unacceptable behavior and presenting the desirable behavior. You may suggest that the parents keep a log of the child's behavior. (Refer to Figure 8.1.) Explain to the parents how the log should

be used. You may suggest one or two techniques for changing the behavior. (This is only done if additional sessions are prohibited.) Make arrangements for a future meeting.

A careful reading of the parent-teacher psychosituational assessment interview that follows will clarify the use of this technique.

Parent-Teacher Interview

T: Good afternoon, Mr. _____.

P: Hello, Mrs. _____, how are you?

T: Fine, thank you. Glad to meet you. Sit down, please. I'm Mark's special education teacher this year, and I'd like to ask you some questions about Mark. Let's see. He's 9 years old, and he's presently in Mrs. Lee's class—that's third grade.

P: Yes.

T: Mrs. Lee has told me that Mark does rather well in some of his subjects. He's particularly good in math. He enjoys that very much. He has a little bit of difficulty with reading and writing, however. And behaviorally, she finds some problems with him leaving his seat frequently. He's rather active in the classroom.

P: Yeah, she's not the only one who has problems with him.

T: I see.

P: He's a bad boy. We have trouble with him at home all the time.

T: Oh, you do?

P: Yeah, I'm, well, I know Mrs. Lee does, too, because my wife tells me that Mrs. Lee calls, and the principal calls about him and about sending him home from school all the time. My wife should be here today—she really spends most of the time with Mark, but she didn't want to come because she wasn't feeling very good. I drive a truck, and I'm on the road most of the time. I don't see much of him.

T: It was very nice of you to come today.

P: Well . . . thank you.

T: I'd like to ask you some more questions about Mark's behavior at home. You said that he seems to . . . you have some trouble with him, too. Would you explain that to me a little?

P: He fights all the time. He's just always getting in fights. Like I said, I'm gone a lot, but my wife tells me that she has trouble with him all the time. Fights with his brothers, and every once in a while he fights with the neighbors—he is just always getting into trouble. That seems to be about it.

T: Fighting seems to be the biggest problem.

P: Oh, yeah, he fights all the time. Always in trouble.

T: Could you give me an example of how one of these fights occurs?

P: Well, my wife was telling me last night that he and the older boy were playing Chinese checkers, and he lost. Mark lost, and Bill picked up a handful of—not Bill, but Mark—picked up a handful of marbles and threw them at Bill and went at him with his fists.

T: He became so agitated by losing that he started a fight.

P: He can't lose . . . he just goes . . . losing . . . he fights. That's just automatic—one, two. He just can't stand to lose. As long as he's winning, he gets along fine.

T: Are there any cases you can tell about when he wins—how he acts?

P: Well, I take the boys fishing in the spring and in the summer.

T: That's nice.

P: Oh, yeah. I like to fish. Actually, it's comforting and it's a lot of fun. We enjoy it—being out—and usually Mark, when he goes with us, he catches most of the fish.

T: Oh, really.

P: Oh, yeah. And, yeah, he has a good time then, bragging around and measuring, comparing the size of his fish and the other boys' fish and boasting about it. Yeah, he likes that.

T: He doesn't seem to fight much when you go fishing, does he?

P: Well, it all depends. Now, if one of the other boys catches a bigger fish or more fish, then he'll fight. He'll go at them, hit them, holler at them. Yeah, he can't stand to lose.

T: But if he's winning, and especially when he's fishing, he must enjoy that—going with you.

P: Yeah, he likes to go fishing. We have a good time.

T: Do you ever go with him by yourself?

P: We all go fishing. I tried to get my wife to go, but she doesn't care much for fishing. She doesn't like to bait the hook. You know how women are.

T: Oh, yes. So fishing is the one thing that Mark really enjoys, especially when he's winning. And he's pretty good at it, from what you say.

P: That's right.

T: He must have had some good training. Let's talk about the fighting that goes on at home. Could you tell me a little bit more about it? You said that if losing is involved, then he seems to fight.

P: Yeah, that's right.

T: One example was with the Chinese checkers and his older brother. Could you give me any other examples?

P: Yeah, if he thinks one of the other kids gets more ice cream—like his younger brother—he'll poke him and start a fight. You know. It's really bad. My wife says that he's on the younger boy all the time at home, and she has to spank him or send him out of the house or send him up to bed, and it keeps going on. He's really a bad boy at home.

T: And you say he fights all the time. It probably seems like it's all the time because it's rather upsetting.

P: She's always complaining about it.

T: Do you have any idea of how often exactly this happens? Once a night, twice a night, once a week?

P: Well, it may be two or three times a week.

T: Two or three times a week?

P: Yeah, about two or three times a week—mainly because he wins the other 2 or 3 days.

T: Oh, I see.

P: Yeah, he's pretty good.

T: On the winning days he's really not that much of a problem?

P: No problem. As long as he's winning, he gets along with everyone really well.

T: Let's talk about these fights a little. You mentioned that he gets into almost real fisticuffs. Do you mean that he actually punches?

P: Not *almost.* He really does. Punches. And he keeps punching until the other kid gives up.

T: That's how the fight is usually settled?

P: That's how it's settled, unless one of the adults steps in and stops it.

T: By one of the adults, I assume you mean yourself or your wife?

P: My wife is home most of the time—she does this. When I'm home, I'm watching television, and if he starts a ruckus, I stop it right away. I don't let anything go on. I stop it unless it's a tight inning, and then I may wait until the action's over and then I stop it. But it doesn't stop until I stop it.

T: You mentioned shaking him to stop it.

P: Yeah, I shake him.

T: Does that seem to work?

P: Well, you know, shake them till their teeth rattle—that straightens them out. That's what my daddy always said.

T: Do you use any other forms of punishment besides shaking?

P: Well, if that doesn't work, yeah, sure. I spank them when I feel that I should, and sometimes I just send them out of the house.

T: How long do these fights last? Just until . . . someone gives up? Maybe a minute? Two, 5 minutes?

P: If an adult's not there, sometimes they'll go on sometimes 5 or 10 minutes, 15 minutes. If an adult's there, of course, the adult stops it. Or an older kid can stop it, but they usually like to watch the fight.

T: Do you think what you're doing—this shaking and spanking—has changed his behavior any? Has it stopped the fighting?

P: It stops it then.

T: It stops it for that time?

P: Yeah.

T: When he loses, he fights, and when he fights, it's physical. It's dangerous to the other person.

P: Sometimes he yells and just hollers and screams at the other kids. One time he hit his older brother with a chair because he was losing the fight. And I mean, he really gets violent. He really wants to win.

T: These fights, even though they are violent, last sometimes less than 5 minutes? Sometimes up to 15 minutes?

P: Yeah, that's about right.

T: And they seem to happen two or three times a week?

P: Yeah, that's about right.

T: But it seems like, otherwise, the rest of the time he's really pretty agreeable and easy to get along with. Things seem to go all right as long as he's winning.

P: As long as things are going his way and nobody steps on him or steps on his toes, he's all right.

T: Fine. Most of the time when you're dealing with Mark, is it a pleasant interaction or are there problems? Let's say for the most part.

P: See, I'm not home very much, and when I'm home I like to do what I like to do. I like to watch television and sports and so forth. And you know, of course, we do go fishing in the spring and summer, and then we get along fine—unless, of course, someone catches more fish than he does. But when I'm home, I like to watch television. I really don't pay that much attention to the kids. But my wife says that, you know, some days he can be very nice. But most of the time he's a bad, rotten kid.

T: Well, I think maybe we should start to work on this fighting behavior. I could help you with some suggestions.

P: Well, I'll tell you, we'd appreciate anything you could suggest.

T: Well, one thing I think would be a good idea is if you and your wife could keep what we call a log. We train our teachers to keep this. All it is, is that you would write down every day whether or not there was a fight. Then, what time the fight occurred, what the behavior was just before the fight happened, and how it was resolved. So, an example of this, which was done by another parent, would show that, like, Monday there was a fight, Tuesday nothing, Wednesday nothing—but Thursday there were two fights. Then, if you and your wife together would keep this kind of log . . .

P: Well, I know what a log is. That's what I do because I'm a truck driver. We keep a log, and I can show my wife how to do it. I can't guarantee she'll do it, but I can show her how, and . . .

T: That would be very helpful.

P: Yeah, fine.

T: I think that you can probably explain it better than I could.

P: Probably so, right.

T: Then maybe in 3 weeks' time, we'll make another appointment for an interview, and you and your wife can come together.

P: Well, I'm not sure that I'll be able to make it because I'm on the road. But I think if my wife has something to talk about and hold onto, why, she'll probably be willing to come and chat with you.

T: Let's see if we can't arrange it for the three of us.

P: All right.

T: I'll do it at your convenience.

P: OK, right.

T: And if you will bring in the log for the next 3 weeks of behavior—how many times he fights—we won't worry about anything else, just the fighting behavior. Until that time, I'd also like you maybe to take some time with Mark alone and let me know how it works out with you just dealing with him individually, apart from his brothers. Just once in a while. I realize that you're very busy, but that may give us some insights.

P: Kind of father-son talks.

T: That kind of thing; that might work out well.

P: I'll try that.

Home Reinforcers

In this section, a list of potentially effective home reinforcers is presented. These have been found useful to parents needing suggestions on reinforcers they may apply at home. Additional suggestions are presented in the extensive list of reinforcers in Chapter 3, Supplement Two.

Consumable Food Reinforcers

Fruits	Cookies
Candies	Cake
Snack foods	Crackers
Gum	Milk
Ice cream	Soda
Yogurt	Juice

Reinforcing Activities in Relation to Food Reinforcers

Baking cookies or a cake with a parent
Preparing dinner with a parent
Operating a toaster, mixer, or another
    appliance
Washing dishes or operating the
    dishwasher
Setting the table for snack time
Serving snacks
Cleaning the table after snack time

Tangible Reinforcers

Pencils or pens
Colored, broad-tipped markers
Erasers
Money to purchase desired items
Records
Surprise gifts
Toys
Games
Coloring books
Pads of paper
Books
Jewelry
Clothing
Pets
Pet supplies

Token Reinforcers

Points
Stars
Chips
Play money
Check marks

Game Activity Reinforcers

Playing outdoors alone with friends or a
    parent
Participating in organized sports
Flying a kite
Participating in table games: checkers,
    backgammon, cards, and so on
Playing computer games

Social Reinforcers

Smiles
Hugs
Pats
Kisses
Attention from parents
Compliments about activities, efforts,
    appearance

Reinforcing Activities

Reading or looking at books,
    magazines, catalogs
Using the home computer
Watching television
Getting additional playtime
Going to the zoo
Fishing
Caring for a pet
Spending the night with a friend or
    relative
Shopping with a parent
Having a friend spend the night
Going to the movies
Using the stereo
Getting telephone privileges
Receiving help from a parent on a
    homework assignment or chore
Attending a recreational activity or
    sporting event
Attending or having a party
Staying out later than usual
Accompanying parents instead of
    remaining with a sitter
Driving the family car
Going for ice cream, hamburgers,
    french fries

Working on a project with a parent
Visiting a parent's place of work
Joining and participating in a club or
team

Taking lessons (music, dance,
swimming)
Using the family typewriter or computer
Listening to a story as a parent reads

Parent Training Program

The parent training program presented in this section has two objectives: (1) to train parents in the theory and application of behavior modification principles and practices and (2) to assist parents' efforts to systematically modify selected target behaviors exhibited by their children. Although not a primary objective of the program, a benefit derived by many parents is mutual support and understanding of their child management problems from other members of the group and educator.

The program includes these three phases: preparation, instructional, and follow-up.

Preparation Phase

Before beginning the instructional phase of the training program, the educator should conduct one or more psychosituational interviews with each parent or couple. The objective of these interviews is (1) to determine the parent or parents' needs, interests, and readiness to participate in a formal training program, and (2) to clarify at least one behavior they wish to modify.

The individual interview sessions are an excellent time for the educator to discuss the program objectives, organization, and requirements and to invite the parent or parents' participation.

Instructional Phase

The instructional phase of the parent training program includes 8 weekly sessions. The 1 1/2-hour sessions are divided into two 40-minute segments and a 10-minute break.

The first 40-minute segment is devoted to brief formal presentations by the educator on the principles and practices of behavior modification. The remainder of this segment is devoted to a question-and-answer session, group discussion, and practice exercises and activities.

The 10-minute break is devoted to informal discussion. Coffee, tea, milk, and soft drinks as well as snacks can be served. These items may be furnished by the educator or by the parents.

The second 40-minute segment of the weekly session is devoted to planning, implementing, and evaluating the parents' behavioral intervention programs. These programs are concerned with the behaviors selected during the preparation phase.

During this second segment, time is devoted to participants' reports of their interventions. All members of the group are expected and encouraged to question, discuss, and make suggestions for improving the interventions. A positive and helpful attitude must be maintained by all participants throughout this segment. Maintaining a positive tone in the group is a primary function of the educator.

Meetings are conducted in a mutually agreed-upon location. The educator's or participants' homes are *not* recommended, in large part to avoid potential competition or inconvenience to the participants. A school, YMCA, YWCA, or community center is an excellent location for meeting. The facility must be accessible to the participants. If necessary, car pools can be arranged among the participants. In some cases, child care services will be needed. In addition, the meeting room should ensure the group's privacy. Appropriate adult furnishings are necessary. A worktable should be available.

Group membership is limited to 12 or 14 persons, excluding the educator. Teachers of the parent-members' children can become group members. Groups are open to both mothers and fathers. Participation by both parents is desirable.

Attendance should be regular because of the cumulative nature of the material. If parents are unable to attend a particular session, the educator must update them in an individual session. However, absences should be discouraged for the sake of group cohesion.

The educator functions as an instructor and group facilitator during weekly sessions. Although the educator's function as an instructor remains relatively constant throughout the program, parents should be permitted and encouraged to make instructional presentations. The educator's function as group facilitator should diminish as the instructional phase progresses and the participants begin to assert leadership.

Occasionally a team of two educators may present the training program. This is an excellent idea, particularly if one assumes the functions of instructor and the other the functions of facilitator. Of course, success in team teaching assumes personal-professional compatibility as well as fundamental agreement on the subject matter and instructional methods.

Any person who is knowledgeable of the principles and practices of behavior modification, child behavior, and group processes can serve as an educator. This includes parents, regular and special education teachers, college instructors, counselors, psychologists, nurses, social workers, and others.

The instructional materials needed for the parent training program are in this text, especially the work sheets at the back. Each participant should have a copy of the text. Additional instructional aids are suggested in the lesson plans that follow.

Follow-Up Phase

Contacts with the parents should not be terminated at the end of the 8-week training program. It is suggested that the educator develop a follow-up plan, maintaining periodic contact with the group and with individual members to reinforce their efforts and assist in the planning and implementation of additional interventions. Contact can be maintained by individual interviews, telephone conversations, and monthly meetings.

The periodic reinforcement offered the participants during the follow-up phase will increase the probability that the skills learned during the training program will not fall into disuse.

Parent Training Lessons

Lesson 1: Introduction to Behavior Modification*

Goals
1. To familiarize participants with the models of causation of human behavior and with the behavior change process
2. To enable participants to exemplify each of the principles of behavior modification
3. To enable participants to complete two or more target behavior selection checklists correctly
4. To enable participants to accurately observe and record a target behavior

Content
1. Models of causation of human behavior
2. Principles of behavior modification
3. Overview of the behavior change process
4. Selecting a target behavior
5. Observing and recording a target behavior

Instructional methods
1. Lecture
2. Discussion
3. Demonstration
4. Completion of a target behavior selection checklist
5. Recording the target behavior rate or frequency

Activities
1. Segment A (40 minutes)
   a. Introduction of the educator and individual participants
   b. Overview of the course organization and content
   c. Brief lecture on contemporary theories of causation of human behavior
   d. Brief lecture or overview of the behavior change process

---

*Time constraints may necessitate dividing this lesson into two sessions.

    e. Lecture on the principles of behavior modification; each participant requested to cite a personal example of each principle (may be written)

    f. Examples of target behaviors presented and explanation of the target behavior selection process; demonstration of how to complete a target behavior selection checklist; each participant requested to select a target behavior and complete a target behavior selection checklist

    g. Procedures for observing and recording target behaviors presented, exemplified, and discussed

2. Break (10 minutes)
3. Segment B (40 minutes)

    a. Target Behavior 1 (home behavior)

      (1) Each participant (or mother and father) presents to the group the target behavior selected during the psychosituational assessment interview of the course preparation phase. Participants also present and discuss the data that they recorded on the behavior log form.

      (2) Each participant completes a target behavior selection checklist on Target Behavior 1.

      (3) Each participant transfers the data on the behavior log form to an appropriate tally form (see Table 3.2).

Resources*

1. Segment A

    a. Parent educator and individual participants

    b. Chapter 8: Preparation phase of program and lesson titles

    c. Chapter 1: Models of human behavior

    d. Chapter 3: Entire chapter

    e. Chapter 2: Principles of reinforcement

    f. Chapter 3: Selecting a target behavior; target behavior selection checklist (back of text)

    g. Chapter 3: Collecting and recording baseline data

2. Break
3. Segment B

    a. Target Behavior 1

      (1) Behavior log form (back of text)

      (2) Target behavior selection checklist (back of text)

      (3) Chapter 3: Collecting and recording baseline data

Evaluation

1. Quiz on or written examples of the principles of reinforcement
2. Completed behavior log form, target behavior selection checklist, and tally form

---

*Where appropriate, the numbers and letters in this section are in agreement with those in the activities section.

Home assignment
1. Observe and record baseline data on Target Behavior 1
2. Read:
   a. Chapter 2: Consequences of behavior; Schedules of reinforcement
   b. Chapter 3: Collecting and recording baseline data

Lesson 2: Consequences of Behavior

Goals
1. To familiarize participants with the consequences of human behavior and the common reinforcement schedules
2. To enable participants to accurately chart baseline data on Target Behavior 1

Content
1. Review of Lesson 1
2. Consequences of behavior
3. Schedules of reinforcement
4. Collecting and recording baseline data
5. Charting baseline data

Instructional methods
1. Lecture
2. Demonstration
3. Discussion
4. Completion of a behavior chart

Activities
1. Segment A (40 minutes)
   a. Review
   b. Lecture/demonstration on the consequences of human behavior, the common reinforcement schedules, and the procedure of charting baseline data
   c. Discussion of (b)
   d. Examples of baseline data presented; each participant requested to chart example baseline data on a behavior chart
2. Break (10 minutes)
3. Segment B (40 minutes)
   a. Target Behavior 1 (home behavior)
      (1) Each participant charts baseline data collected between Lessons 1 and 2 (Baseline 1 data).
      (2) Participants present their raw data to the group for discussion, clarification, and practice charting.

Resources
1. Segment A
   a. Lesson 1 resources
   b. Chapter 2: Consequences of behavior; Schedules of reinforcement; Chapter 3: Collecting and recording baseline data
   c. Parent educator and participants
   d. Chapter 3: Collecting and recording baseline data; behavior chart (back of text)
2. Break
3. Segment B
   a. Target Behavior 1
      (1) Behavior chart (back of text)
      (2) Behavior tally form used during Week 1

Evaluation
1. Quiz on or written examples of the consequences of behavior and the common schedules of reinforcement
2. Completed tally form and behavior chart

Home assignment
1. Continue observing and recording Baseline 1 data on target Behavior 1
2. Observe and note those things and activities the child likes to do during free time
3. Read:
   a. Chapter 3: Identifying appropriate reinforcers
   b. Chapter 8: Home reinforcers

Lesson 3: Selecting Effective Reinforcers

Goals
1. To familiarize participants with the behavior modification intervention strategies for increasing, maintaining, and decreasing behavior
2. To enable participants to compile a list of potentially effective home-based reinforcers
3. To enable participants to accurately chart Baseline 1 data on Target Behavior 1
4. To facilitate participants' selection of reinforcers, a reinforcement schedule, and an intervention strategy for Target Behavior 1

Content
1. Review of Lesson 2
2. Selecting potentially effective reinforcers
3. Overview of behavior modification intervention strategies
4. Charting or graphing baseline data
5. Selecting an appropriate reinforcement schedule and intervention strategy

Instructional methods
1. Lecture
2. Discussion
3. Completion of behavior chart
4. Individual/group project

Activities
1. Segment A (40 minutes)
   a. Review
   b. Lecture on selecting potentially effective reinforcers and on behavior modification intervention strategies
   c. Discussion of (b)
   d. Individual/group development of a list of children's rewards observed as home assignment
2. Break (10 minutes)
3. Segment B (40 minutes)
   a. Target Behavior 1 (home behavior)
      (1) Each participant charts Baseline 1 data collected between Lessons 2 and 3.
      (2) Each participant (with educator's assistance) selects reinforcers, a reinforcement schedule, and an intervention strategy to modify Target Behavior 1.

Resources
1. Segment A
   a. Lesson 2 resources
   b. Chapter 3: Identifying appropriate reinforcers; Chapter 4: Entire chapter; Chapter 5: Entire chapter; Chapter 8: Home reinforcers
   c. Parent educator and participants
   d. Chapter 3: Identifying appropriate reinforcers
2. Break
3. Segment B
   a. Target Behavior 1
      (1) Behavior chart (back of text)
      (2) Participant with assistance of parent educator and other participants

Evaluation
1. Quiz on methods of selecting appropriate reinforcers
2. Results of individual/group list of children's rewards
3. Behavior chart on Target Behavior 1

Home assignment
1. Implement intervention strategy for Target Behavior 1 and continue observing and recording data
2. Read Chapter 4: Shaping; Modeling; Contingency contracting

Lesson 4: Strategies To Increase Behavior

Goals
1. To familiarize participants with modeling, shaping, and contingency contracting intervention strategies
2. To enable participants to accurately chart intervention data on Target Behavior 1
3. To enable participants to accurately complete a target behavior selection checklist on Target Behavior 2 (home or home-school behavior)

Content
1. Review of Lesson 3
2. Intervention strategies: shaping , modeling, and contingency contracting
3. Charting intervention data
4. Selecting a target behavior

Instructional methods
1. Lecture
2. Discussion
3. Completion of contingency contract form
4. Completion of target behavior selection checklist
5. Completion of behavior chart

Activities
1. Segment A (40 minutes)
   a. Review
   b. Lecture/demonstration on shaping, modeling, and contingency contracting
   c. Discussion of (b)
   d. Participants requested to present examples of shaping and modeling from home setting (may be written)
   e. Completion of one or more contingency contracts
2. Break (10 minutes)
3. Segment B (40 minutes)
   a. Target Behavior 1 (home behavior)
      (1) Each participant charts or graphs intervention data collected between Lessons 3 and 4 (Intervention 1 data).
      (2) Participants discuss charts.
   b. Target Behavior 2 (home or home-school behavior)
      (1) Each participant completes a target behavior selection checklist.
      (2) Participants discuss checklists.

Resources
1. Segment A
   a. Lesson 3 resources
   b. Chapter 4: Shaping; Modeling; Contingency contracting
   c. Parent educator and participants

     d. Same as (c)

     e. Contingency contract form (back of text)

2. Break
3. Segment B

     a. Target Behavior 1

        (1) Behavior chart (back of text)

        (2) Parent educator and participants

     b. Target Behavior 2

        (1) Target behavior selection checklist (back of text)

        (2) Parent educator and participants

Evaluation
1. Quiz on or written examples of shaping and modeling
2. Completing contingency contract forms
3. Behavior chart on Target Behavior 1
4. Target Behavior selection checklist on Target Behavior 2

Home assignment
1. Observe and record Intervention 1 data on Target Behavior 1
2. Observe and record Baseline 1 data on Target Behavior 2
3. Read Chapter 4: Token economy

Lesson 5: Strategies To Increase Behavior—Continued

Goals
1. To familiarize participants with the token economy intervention strategy
2. To enable participants to accurately chart Intervention 1 data on Target Behavior 1
3. To enable participants to assess the effectiveness of the behavior change program for Target Behavior 1
4. To enable participants to plan an evaluation of Target Behavior 1 by means of observing and recording new baseline data following the intervention (Baseline 2 data)
5. To enable participants to chart Baseline 1 data on Target Behavior 2

Content
1. Review of Lesson 4
2. Token economy intervention strategy
3. Charting data
4. Assessing intervention effectiveness
5. Planning evaluation phase (charting Baseline 2 data)

Instructional methods
1. Lecture
2. Discussion
3. Completion of behavior charts

Activities
1. Segment A (40 minutes)
   a. Review
   b. Lecture/demonstration on token economy
   c. Discussion of (b)
   d. Participants requested to present an example of a home token economy including target behavior(s), reinforcement schedule, reward menu, and proposed point card or tally form (may be written)
2. Break (10 minutes)
3. Segment B (40 minutes)
   a. Target Behavior 1 (home behavior)
      (1) Each participant charts or graphs Intervention 1 data collected between Lessons 4 and 5.
      (2) Each participant assesses the effectiveness of the intervention by analyzing the behavior chart.
      (3) Each participant plans an evaluation phase based on Baseline 2 data.
   b. Target Behavior 2 (home or home-school behavior)
      (1) Each participant charts or graphs Baseline 1 data collected between Lessons 4 and 5.

Resources
1. Segment A
   a. Lesson 4 resources
   b. Chapter 4: Token economy
   c. Parent educator and participants
   d. Participants
2. Break
3. Segment B
   a. Target Behavior 1
      (1) Behavior chart (back of text)
      (2) Participant with assistance of parent educator and other participants
      (3) Same as (2)
   b. Target Behavior 2
      (1) Behavior chart (back of text)

Evaluation
1. Quiz on or written examples of token economy
2. Behavior chart on Target Behavior 1
3. Behavior chart on Target Behavior 2

Home assignment
1. Observe and record evaluation (Baseline 2) data on Target Behavior 1
2. Observe and record Baseline 1 data on Target Behavior 2

3. Read:
   a. Chapter 5: Extinction; Time-out; Reinforcement of incompatible behaviors
   b. Chapter 8: Aids to communication

Lesson 6: Strategies To Decrease Behavior

Goals
1. To familiarize participants with extinction, time-out, and reinforcement of incompatible behaviors intervention strategies
2. To familiarize participants with the aids to communication between home and school
3. To enable participants to chart evaluation (Baseline 2) data and plan the reimposition of the intervention (Intervention 2) for Target Behavior 1
4. To enable participants to chart Baseline 1 data and plan the specific reinforcers, reinforcement schedule, and intervention strategy to modify Target Behavior 2

Content
1. Review of Lesson 5
2. Extinction, time-out, and reinforcement of incompatible behaviors intervention strategies
3. Aids to communication
4. Charting or graphing data
5. Planning the reimposed intervention (Intervention 2) phase for Target Behavior 1
6. Planning the initial intervention (Intervention 1) phase for Target Behavior 2

Instructional methods
1. Lecture
2. Discussion
3. Completion of behavior charts

Activities
1. Segment A (40 minutes)
   a. Review
   b. Lecture/demonstration on extinction, time-out, and reinforcement of incompatible behaviors
   c. Lecture/demonstration on aids to communication
   d. Discussion of (b) and (c)
   e. Participants requested to present examples of extinction, time-out, and reinforcers (may be written)
2. Break
3. Segment B (40 minutes)
   a. Target Behavior 1 (home behavior)

    (1) Each participant charts Baseline 2 data collected between Lessons 5 and 6.

    (2) Each participant compares Baseline 2 data with Baseline 1 and Intervention 1 data.

    (3) Each participant plans the reimposition of the intervention strategy.

  b. Target Behavior 2 (home or home-school behavior)

    (1) Each participant charts Baseline 1 data collected between Lessons 5 and 6.

    (2) Each participant selects a reinforcement schedule, reinforcers, and an intervention strategy to modify Target Behavior 2.

Resources
1. Segment A
   a. Lesson 5 resources
   b. Chapter 5: Extinction; Time-out; Reinforcement of incompatible behaviors
   c. Chapter 8: Aids to communication
   d. Parent educator and participants
   e. Participants
2. Break
3. Segment B
   a. Target Behavior 1
      (1) Behavior chart (back of text)
      (2) Participants
      (3) Participant with assistance of parent educator and other participants
   b. Target Behavior 2
      (1) Behavior chart (back of text)
      (2) Participants

Evaluation
1. Quiz on or written examples of extinction, time-out, reinforcement of incompatible behaviors, and aids to communication
2. Behavior chart on Target Behavior 1
3. Behavior chart on Target Behavior 2

Home assignment
1. Observe and record behavior data on the reimposed intervention (Intervention 2) for Target Behavior 1
2. Observe and record behavior data on the initial intervention (Intervention 1) for Target Behavior 2
3. Read Chapter 5: Punishment; Desensitization.

Lesson 7: Strategies To Decrease Behavior—Continued

Goals
1. To familiarize participants with punishment and desensitization intervention strategies

2. To enable participants to chart Intervention 2 data on Target Behavior 1
3. To enable participants to chart Intervention 1 data on Target Behavior 2

Content
1. Review of Lesson 6
2. Punishment and desensitization intervention strategies
3. Charting data

Instructional methods
1. Lecture/demonstration
2. Discussion
3. Completion of behavior charts

Activities
1. Segment A (40 minutes)
   a. Review
   b. Lecture/demonstration on punishment and desensitization
   c. Discussion of (b)
   d. Participants requested to present examples of punishment and desensitization (may be written)
2. Break (10 minutes)
3. Segment B (40 minutes)
   a. Target Behavior 1 (home behavior)
      (1) Each participant charts Intervention 2 data collected between Lessons 6 and 7.
      (2) Each participant compares Intervention 2 data with previously collected data: Baseline 1, Intervention 1, and Baseline 2 data.
   b. Target Behavior 2 (home or home-school behavior)
      (1) Each participant charts Intervention 1 data collected between Lessons 6 and 7.

Resources
1. Segment A
   a. Lesson 6 resources
   b. Chapter 5: Punishment; Desensitization
   c. Parent educator and participants
   d. Participants
2. Break
3. Segment B
   a. Target Behavior 1
      (1) Behavior chart (back of text)
      (2) Participants
   b. Target Behavior 2
      (1) Behavior chart (back of text)

Evaluation
1. Quiz on or written examples of punishment and desensitization
2. Behavior chart on Target Behavior 1
3. Behavior chart on Target Behavior 2

Home assignment
1. Observe and record behavior data on Intervention 2 for Target Behavior 1
2. Observe and record behavior data on Intervention 1 for Target Behavior 2
3. Read Chapter 9: Some guidelines for application; Some principles concerning individual rights of children.

Lesson 8: Ethical and Effective Application

Goals
1. To familiarize participants with the principles concerning the individual rights of children
2. To enable participants to chart Intervention 2 data for Target Behavior 1
3. To enable participants to plan the phasing out of the intervention imposed on Target Behavior 1
4. To enable participants to chart Intervention 1 data for Target Behavior 2 and assess the effectiveness of the intervention
5. To enable participants to plan the remainder of the behavior change program for Target Behavior 2, which may include Baseline 2 data, Intervention 2, and phasing out
6. To establish procedures for follow-up of course participation

Content
1. Review of Lessons 1 through 7
2. Principles concerning the individual rights of children
3. Charting data
4. Planning intervention phases and phasing out

Instructional methods
1. Lecture/demonstration
2. Discussion
3. Completion of behavior charts

Activities
1. Segment A (40 minutes)
   a. Review
   b. Lecture/demonstration on the principles concerning the individual rights of children
   c. Discussion of (b)

    d. Participants requested to present examples of the principles (may be written)

    e. Plans agreed on for course follow-up activities

2. Break (10 minutes)
3. Segment B (40 minutes)
    a. Target Behavior 1 (home behavior)
        (1) Each participant charts Intervention 2 data.
        (2) Each participant plans the phasing out of the intervention.
    b. Target Behavior 2 (home or home-school behavior)
        (1) Each participant plans the remainder of the behavior change program, which may include Baseline 2 data, Intervention 2, and phasing out.
        (2) Discussion of (1).

Resources
1. Segment A
    a. Lessons 1 through 7 resources
    b. Chapter 9: Some principles concerning individual rights of children
    c. Parent educator and participants
    d. Participants
    e. Parent educator and participants
2. Break
3. Segment B
    a. Target Behavior 1
        (1) Behavior chart (back of text)
        (2) Participant with assistance of parent educator and other participants
    b. Target Behavior 2
        (1) Participant with assistance of parent educator and other participants
        (2) Parent educator and participants

Evaluation
1. Quiz on or written examples of application of principles
2. Behavior chart on Target Behavior 1 and phasing out plan
3. Behavior chart on Target Behavior 2 and plan or remainder of intervention

Home assignment
1. Continue application of course content and learned skills
2. Attend follow-up session

Aids to Home-School Communication

During the implementation phase of a home-school behavior change intervention, the parents and educator need to communicate precisely and frequently to ensure the integrity of the program. Although it is possible to use telephone conversations and handwritten notes to communicate, the parents and teacher may find these methods imprecise and inordinately demanding of time.

In this section, several aids to parent-teacher communication that appear to minimize inconvenience for both parties are presented.

The Passport

Schmalz (1987) recommended a home-school notebook for parents and teachers who wished to communicate on a daily basis on the behavior of the student in both home and school. The "passport" (Runge et al., 1975) is an effective technique for increasing and maintaining parent-teacher communication and cooperation.

The passport is an ordinary spiral notebook that the child carries daily to and from home and to and from the classrooms in which the child is instructed. The passport is a medium for communications among parents, special teachers, regular teachers, paraprofessionals, bus drivers, and others concerned with the child's behavior change or academic remediation program. All concerned adults are encouraged to make notations in the notebook.

Before the actual initiation of a behavior change program, the passport procedures are explained to the child, who is told that he or she will be rewarded for carrying the notebook and presenting it to the appropriate adults.

The child is rewarded with points for carrying the passport and for appropriate efforts, accomplishments, and behavior in the home, in the classroom, on the bus, in the gym, and so on. Points may be awarded at home for appropriate behavior and home-study activities. If the child forgets or refuses to carry the "passport," he or she cannot earn points. At the appropriate time, the accumulated points are exchanged for tangible as well as social rewards.

Most elementary school students respond enthusiastically to carrying the passport, receiving points and awards, and reading the comments written about their behavior and achievement by adults.

Parents are introduced to the passport concept and procedures at an evening meeting. At this meeting the method is explained and discussed. Parents' questions and concerns must be appropriately responded to by the teacher. At this session, instructions for making notations in the passport are given. Similar meetings or informal discussions should be held with other adults who will be using the passport, such as classroom teachers, special teachers, administrators, bus drivers, and so on.

The guidelines for writing comments in the passport are as follows:

1. Be brief. (Parents are busy, too.)
2. Be positive. (Parents know their child has problems. They don't need to be reinforced.)
3. Be honest. (Don't say a child is doing fine if he is not. However, rather than writing negative notes, write neutral ones or request a parent visit).
4. Be responsive. (If a parent asks for help, respond immediately.)

5. Be informal. (You are a professional, but parents are still your equal.)
6. Be consistent. (If you use the passport, do so consistently and expect the same from the parent.)
7. Avoid jargon. (Parents don't understand educators' jargon. For that matter, do we?)
8. Be careful. (If you are having a bad day, personally, do not project your feelings onto the child or his parents.) (p. 92*)

Points are awarded to the child on the basis of a mutually agreed-on reinforcement schedule and rate. The procedures applied in the passport are similar to those presented in the section on the token economy in Chapter 4. Points are recorded on a point card similar to those presented in that section. The card is usually affixed to the inside of the front or back cover of the notebook.

Examples of the types of notations to be made in the passport are presented in Figures 8.2 and 8.3. The first set of examples involves an exchange of information among an elementary school teacher, a bus driver, a physical education teacher, and the child's parents. The second set of examples involves an exchange between an elementary school teacher and parents.

Daily Report Cards

It is generally true that report cards or grades issued periodically by elementary and secondary schools (and universities) have positive effects on student performance. It is also true that this positive effect is of short duration. During our years as secondary school and university teachers, it became obvious that students study more and behave better in the few weeks immediately before and after report cards or grades are issued. Unfortunately this high level of student performance does not persist during those times when report card issuance is not imminent (Kroth & Otteni, 1985).

It would appear that acceptable levels of student performance, both academic and behavioral, can be maintained if feedback on performance is provided frequently to the student and parents. This proposition has led to several efforts to explore the use of daily report cards with normal and exceptional children at various grade levels (Dickerson et al., 1973; Fairchild, 1987; Powell, 1980).

In 1969, Edlund designed and implemented a daily reporting system that uses rewards available in the home to improve children's school performance. The system focuses on both academic performance and social-personal behavior.

Edlund's daily report card system is introduced to the parents during individual and small group sessions. In these sessions parents are introduced to the principles and procedures of behavior modification as applied in the reporting system. Specific attention is given to the daily checklist, principles of reinforcement, selecting rewards,

---

*From "A Passport to Positive Parent-Teacher Communications" by A. Runge, J. Walker, and T. M. Shea, 1975, *Teaching Exceptional Children,* 7(3), pp. 91-92. Copyright 1975 by The Council for Exceptional Children, 1920 Association Drive, Reston, VA 22091. Reprinted by permission.

10/25/90
9:00 AM

To: Ms. Dolores

Good day on the bus. Tom sat in his assigned seat and waited his turn to leave the bus. I praised his behavior and gave him two points.

Mr. Parker, Bus Driver

10/25/90
10:30 AM

To: Ms. Dolores

During PE today the group played kickball. Tom was well behaved but had difficulty participating effectively. I awarded him six points. He was praised for his behavior. Can we meet to discuss some means of increasing his participation?

Ms. Minton, PE

10/25/90
2:30 PM

To: Mr. and Mrs. Hogerty

As you can see from the notes above, Tom had a good day at school.

He received 89% on his reading test this morning. That's real progress. Please praise him for this accomplishment.

This evening, Tom is to read pp. 1–5 in his new reading book.

Even better news! Tom remembered to walk in the hallways today. He is very proud of himself.

I shall talk to Ms. Minton today about increasing Tom's participation at PE. I'll let you know what we decide at parent meeting tomorrow night.

Ms. Dolores

10/25/90
9:00 PM

To: Ms. Dolores

We praised and rewarded Tom for his hard work on the reading test, the bus, and the hallways. You're right, he feels good about himself today.

Tom read pp. 1–5 in the new book with his father. The words he had trouble with are underlined.

We will be at parent meeting tomorrow night.

Mary Hogerty

FIGURE 8.2
Sample passport notations between school staff and parents.

and the application of the Premack principle. This initial training is followed up throughout the program by means of weekly parent-professional conferences or telephone communication.

Before the daily reporting system is implemented, baseline data are gathered by the educator and/or parents on the child's academic performance and social-personal behaviors. Using the baseline data, the reporting system is individualized for the child as a response to his or her particular learning or behavior problems.

5/6/90

Dear Mr. and Mrs. Barea:

John received 98% on his reading test to-day. Isn't that terrific? He should be praised for his progress.

Please let him read pp. 1–5 in his new reading book to you this evening.

Even better news! John remembered to walk in the hallways. He was really pleased with himself.

Don't forget—parent-teacher group discussion tomorrow night. See you then.

Ms. Anita

5/6/90

Dear Ms. Anita:

We told John what a good job you said he did on his test.

John read pp. 1–5 in the new book with his father. He had trouble with a lot of the words.

He did his math paper.

Mrs. Barea

5/7/90

Dear Mr. and Mrs. Barea:

John and Mr. Miner, the student teacher, went over the difficult reading words today.

Thanks for marking them in the book.

Please review pp. 1–5 in the reading book again. John also has a math paper to complete.

It was a good day. See you at 7 PM.

Ms. Anita

5/8/90

Dear Ms. Anita

Certainly enjoyed the parent discussion last night. Mr. Barea and I appreciated the explanation of John's report card.

John had his math done when we got home. I checked it. He did a good job on his reading.

Mrs. Barea

FIGURE 8.3
Sample passport notations between parents and teachers.

Children earn points for completing academic assignments and for acceptable school behavior. Points are recorded on a checklist. Although not presented here, Edlund designed three checklists: (1) a report for academic performance only, (2) a report of personal-social behavior only, and (3) a composite report such as that presented in Figure 8.4.

The teacher awards points in the form of check marks at the end of predetermined periods of time or activities throughout the day. At the end of the day, the teacher reviews the child's checklist and initials it. The checklist is taken home by the child and reviewed by the parents, who initial it. The child returns the checklist to the teacher the following day.

Composite Academic Performance and Personal-Social Behavior Report

DAILY REPORT CHECKLIST

Child's Name _____

	Reading		Spelling		Arithmetic		Health		Social Studies		PE		Initials	
	Acad	Beh	Acad	Beh	Acad	Beh	Acad	Beh	Acad	Beh	Acad	Beh	Parent	Teacher
M														
T														
W														
Th														
F														
M														
T														
W														
Th														
F														
M														
T														
W														
Th														
F														

FIGURE 8.4
Composite behavior checklist for gathering baseline data.

If a child fails to take the checklist home, he is sent back to school for it or a duplicate. A child cannot be rewarded without the checklist.

Rewards for school performance are given to the child at home during the afternoon and evening hours. The rewards are individualized. Care is taken to ensure that the child receives only those rewards that are earned and that are meaningful to him or her. A child who fails to earn rewards is assigned undesirable tasks at home, such as housekeeping chores, yardwork, homework, and so on. Special rewards are given to a child for a "perfect day" or several perfect days.

After several weeks of acceptable academic performance and/or behavior, the reward system is phased out over a period of days or weeks.

Edlund concluded that his daily report card system did improve the children's academic performance and acceptable social-personal behavior. He noted that the desirable behavior continued after the rewards were discontinued. The children learned to respond to the verbal praise and social recognition provided by parents and teachers, which naturally occurred as a result of their high level of performance.

The Edlund daily report card system has been applied successfully with children from kindergarten to high school. It has been used successfully with exceptional children classified as emotionally disturbed, mentally retarded, disruptive, school phobic, truant, economically deprived, and culturally different.

The Teacher-Parent Communication Program (TPCP), a daily report card system, was developed by Dickerson and others (1973). This cooperative parent-teacher communication system is designed to help children improve their inschool academic performance and social behavior in exchange for rewards at home.

During a 4-year period, the TPCP was used with more than 1000 children, ages 5 to 15 years in regular and special education settings. Although Dickerson and others do not view the program as a "cure-all," it was reported by teachers who used it as effective in modifying social behavior and academic performance.

The TPCP centers around report cards issued by the teacher to the child periodically throughout the school day. The completed cards are taken home at the end of the school day. On the basis of the information on the cards, the parents either reward or do not reward the child's performance. Example report cards are presented in Figures 8.5 and 8.6.

The cards have a space for the teacher's evaluation of the child's academic performance and social behavior. The teacher may make notations on the back of the card if desired. Dickerson and his associates recommend that the teacher's notations be neutral and positive. The cards are dated and signed by the teacher.

Although not included on the TPCP card, it may be helpful if the card provided space for the parent's signature and notations. The card could be returned to the teacher on the following school day by the child. Such a procedure would ensure that the parents received the card, that the child was rewarded, and that both parents and teacher were attending to the appropriate objectives.

The cards are issued to the child approximately every 40 minutes throughout the school day. At the end of the day, the child usually has 10 completed cards to take home.

Daily Report Card for Grades K to 3

Consider card satisfactory *only* when boxes 1 and 3 are checked.

1. 🙂 ☐ Social behavior good

2. ☹️ ☐ Social behavior bad

3. 🙂 ☐ School work done

4. ☹️ ☐ School work not done

_____/_____/_____   _____
          Date   Teacher's signature

FIGURE 8.5
Daily report card.

(From Let the cards do the talking—a teacher-parent communication program by D. Dickerson, C. R. Spellman, S. Larsen, and L. Tyler, *Teaching Exceptional Children, 4*(4), 1973, pp. 170-178. Copyright 1973 by The Council for Exceptional Children. Reprinted with permission.)

Although not included in the Dickerson program, it may be desirable to provide space on the card for identification of the activity in which the child participated during the various time periods. This procedure would help the parents identify more precisely the child's problem subjects and situations. It may also be helpful to both parents and teacher if a master card were developed that presented "at a glance" the totals of the child's 10 daily cards.

With few exceptions, the TPCP cards are not acceptable for rewards unless both social behavior and academic performance are checked acceptable by the teacher. Thus a child who behaves appropriately but fails to do this work acceptably is not rewarded. The reverse of this is also true; that is, a child who completes his work but behaves inappropriately is not rewarded.

The presentation of rewards at home is based on the number of acceptable cards the child earns during the school day. The number of cards needed for a reward is initiated at the child's present level of functioning. This performance level is mutually agreed on by parent and teacher. As the child's overall level of performance improves, the number of acceptable cards needed for rewards is systematically increased.

If an acceptable number of cards is earned, the child is praised and encouraged by the parent. The child is permitted to engage in rewarding activities, for example, a later bedtime hour, television viewing, and the like. Special rewards are available for exceptional performance. If the child fails to earn the acceptable number of daily report cards, after-school and evening activities are restricted, or the child is

---

Daily Report Card for Grades 4 to 6

Consider card satisfactory *only* when boxes 1 and 3 are checked.

1. ☐ Social behavior satisfactory
2. ☐ Social behavior unsatisfactory
3. ☐ Academic work satisfactory
4. ☐ Academic work unsatisfactory

_____/_____/_____
     Date   Teacher's signature

FIGURE 8.6
Daily report card.

(From Let the cards do the talking—a teacher-parent communication program by D. Dickerson, C. R. Spellman, S. Larsen, and L. Tyler, *Teaching Exceptional Children, 4*(4), 1973 pp. 170-178. Copyright 1973 by The Council for Exceptional Children. Reprinted with permission.)

assigned undesirable tasks, such as yardwork, housekeeping tasks, homework, and the like.

The TPCP is initiated by the teacher, who solicits the parents' cooperation and participation. During an orientation conference, the teacher explains the program to the parents. The purpose and benefits of the TPCP for the child are discussed. The teacher outlines the duties and responsibilities of the child, parent, and teacher. Dickerson and associates prepared the checklist in Figure 8.7 to facilitate parent-orientation. The checklist ensures that all elements of the daily reporting system are reviewed.

After the parents and teacher agree to implement the TPCP, the teacher informs the child and makes him or her aware of the parents' participation. The child is given instructions concerning the purpose, objectives, and functioning of the system. The child is encouraged to participate in the process of determining his or her initial acceptable performance level and rewards.

The designers of the TPCP recommend that the daily report card system remain in force as long as the child needs it. However, after several weeks of acceptable performance by the child, the teacher, in cooperation with the parents, should begin to phase out the TPCP. Presumably the rewards for a high level of academic performance and social behavior that naturally occur in the child's school behavior and home environments will maintain the acceptable performance levels without the TPCP.

In *It's Positively Fun* (Kaplan et al., 1974) and *It's Absolutely Groovy* (Kaplan & Hoffman, 1981) a variety of certificates, award forms, and other unique forms are presented. Many of these forms can be used in daily report card programs.

TPCP Conference Checklist

CHECK LIST OF MAJOR POINTS COVERED IN PARENT ORIENTATION CONFERENCE

1. Ten cards will be sent home each day whether academic work is done or not.
2. One bad check makes a card unacceptable.
3. Cards must be signed by the teacher and free of erasures and extra marks.
4. The minimum number of good cards necessary to earn privileges should be explained.
5. The number of acceptable cards will be increased sometime in the future.
6. The program will at first emphasize the quantity of work and later the quality of work.
7. The backs of the cards should always be examined for notations.
8. Weekend bonuses may be earned for each week the specified number of good cards have been earned.
9. After-school and evening activities should be a direct result of performance in school.
10. Cards not received at home should be counted as unacceptable.
11. Cards should be reviewed with the child as soon as he or she arrives home.
12. The cards should be counted each day.
13. Praise and encourage the child for earning the acceptable number of good cards.
14. *Let the cards do the talking.*

FIGURE 8.7

Parent orientation for daily report cards.

(From Let the cards do the talking—a teacher-parent communication program by D. Dickerson, C. R. Spellman, S. Larsen, and L. Tyler, *Teaching Exceptional Children,* 4(4), 1973, pp. 170-178. Copyright 1973 by The Council for Exceptional Children. Reprinted with permission.)

The authors provide a brief outline for planning and implementing a daily home-school communication program. These texts are excellent references for professionals wishing to implement a daily report card system.

Kroth and others (1970) presented a parent-teacher communication system that included a daily reporting program as an integral part of a behavior modification intervention. This system provides several specific guidelines for professionals desiring a daily reporting system to focus primarily on student behavior.

The purpose of the daily report card system is to improve parent-professional communication for the benefit of the child. Attention is focused on both social-personal behavior and academic performance.

Teachers wishing to implement a daily report card program should consider several characteristics of the systems presented and individualize these in response to the needs of the children and parents with whom they work.

The mechanism used for reporting (communicating) should be specific and easy to complete. Complex mechanisms requiring extensive time and energy inhibit the conduct and effectiveness of the program.

The daily report card program should accentuate the child's positive social-personal behavior and/or academic performance. The child should be rewarded for attaining the mutually agreed-on objectives of the program and ignored if the objectives are not attained. Punishment should be avoided.

Both parents and teachers must remain cognizant of the fact that the conduct of a daily report card program is a shared responsibility. If either teacher or parents fail to meet their responsibilities, the program's effectiveness is inhibited.

Everton and Heshusius (1985) developed a weekly reporting system that they found to be effective in application with mainstreamed secondary school students. The system was recommended for communication among resource teachers, regular teachers, and parents. An additional benefit of this system was that it provided frequent feedback to the students on their performance.

SUMMARY

In this chapter, a method that may be applied by the educator interested in training parents in behavior modification procedures and principles is presented. The program is designed primarily to increase parental knowledge and skill in the application of behavior modification techniques. The training program also has the potential to increase parent-teacher collaboration. Although not a primary objective of the program, parents are provided a setting in which they may receive emotional support as they struggle with their child's problem.

PROJECTS

1. Write a 300-word essay on the topic "Parent Education and Training: A Significant Component of the School Service Program."
2. List 25 home reinforcers not presented in this chapter. Classify these as social or tangible.
3. Conduct a psychosituational assessment interview in which a classmate plays the role of a parent. Record and analyze the interview.
4. Obtain, study, and write a report for verbal presentation to your class on one of the checklists and inventories listed in the chapter. As part of the verbal presentation, demonstrate to the group the administration of the instrument.
5. Using one of the lesson plans in the chapter, prepare, present, and evaluate a parent training session. Your classmates can role play as parents.

REFERENCES

Beale, A., & Beers, C. S. (1982). What do you say to parents after you say hello? *Teaching Exceptional Children, 15*(1), 34-38.

Bersoff, D. N., & Grieger, R. M. II (1971). An interview model for the psychosituational assessment of children's behavior. *American Journal of Orthopsychiatry, 41*(3), 483-493.

Blackham, G. J., and Silberman, A. (1980). *Modification of child and adolescent behavior* (3rd ed.). Belmont, CA: Wadsworth.

Bronfenbrenner, U. (1977). Toward an experimental ecology of human development. *American Psychologist, 32*, 513-531.

Clements, J. E., & Alexander, R. N. (1975). Parent training: Bringing it all back home. *Focus on Exceptional Children, 7*(5), 1-12.

Croft, D. J. (1979). *Parents and teachers: A resource book for home, school, and community relations.* Belmont, CA: Wadsworth.

Dickerson, D., Spelllman, C. R., Larsen, S., & Tyler, L. (1973). Let the cards do the talking—a teacher-parent communication program. *Teaching Exceptional Children, 4*(4), 170-178.

Dinkmeyer, D., & McKay, G. D. (1973). *Raising a responsible child: Practical steps to successful family relationships.* New York: Simon & Schuster.

Dunst, C.J., Trivette, C. M., & Deal, A. G. (1988). *Enabling and empowering families: Principles and guidelines for practice.* Cambridge, MA: Brookline Books.

Edlund, C. V. (1969). Rewards at home to promote desirable school behavior. *Teaching Exceptional Children, 1*(4), 121-127.

Ehly, S. W., Conoley, J. C., & Ronsethal, D. (1985). *Working with parents of exceptional children.* St. Louis, MO: C. V. Mosby.

Everton, J., & Heshusius, L. (1985). Feedback on secondary mainstreaming. *Teaching Exceptional Children, 17*(3), 223-224.

Fairchild, T. N. (1987). "The daily report card." *Teaching Exceptional Children, 19*(2), 72-73.

Gardner, W. I. (1974). *Children with learning and behavior problems: A behavior management approach.* Boston: Allyn & Bacon.

Gordon, S. (1976). A parent's concerns. *The Exceptional Parent, 6*(3), 19-22.

Gordon, T. (1970). *Parent effectiveness training.* New York: Wyden Books.

Jogis, J. L. (1975). To be spoken sadly. In L. Buscaglia (Ed.), *The disabled and their parents: A counseling challenge.* Thorofare, NJ: Charles B. Stack.

Kaplan, P. G., & Hoffman, A. G. (1981). *It's absolutely groovy.* Denver: Love Publishing Co.

Kaplan, P., Kohfeldt, J., & Sturla, K. (1974). *It's positively fun: Techniques for managing learning environments.* Denver: Love Publishing Co.

Karnes, M.B., & Zehrbach, R. R. (1972). Flexibility in getting parents involved in the school. *Teaching Exceptional Children, 5*(1), 6-19.

Kratoville, B. L. (1975a). What parents feel. In L. Buscaglia (Ed.), *The disabled and their parents: A counseling challenge.* Thorofare, NJ: Charles B. Stack.

Kratoville, B. L. (1975b). What parents need to hear. In L. Buscaglia (Ed.), *The disabled and their parents: A counseling challenge.* Thorofare, NJ: Charles B. Stack.

Kroth, R. L., & Otteni, H. (1985). *Communicating with parents of exceptional children: Improving parent-teacher relationships* (2nd ed.). Denver: Love Publishing Co.

Kroth, R. L., Whelan, R. J., & Stables, J. M. (1970). Teacher application of behavior principles in home and classroom environments. *Focus on Exceptional Children, 1*(3), 1-10.

McDowell, R. L. (1976). Parent counseling: The state of the art. *Journal of Learning Disabilities, 9*(10), 614-619.

Powell, T. H. (1980). Improving home-school communication: Sharing daily reports. *The Exceptional Parent, 10*(5), 824-826.

Ross, A. O. (1964). *The exceptional child in the family: Helping parents of exceptional children.* New York: Grune & Stratton.

Runge, A., Walker, J., & Shea, T. M. (1975). A passport to positive parent-teacher communications. *Teaching Exceptional Children, 7*(3), 91-92.

Schmalz, N. (1987). Home-school notebook: How to find out what your child did all day. *Exceptional Parent, 17*(6), 18-19, 21-22.

Seligman, M. (1979). *Strategies for helping parents of exceptional children: A guide for teachers.* New York, NY: The Free Press.

Shea, T. M., & Bauer, A. M. (1985). *Parents and teachers of exceptional students: A handbook for involvement.* Boston: Allyn & Bacon.

Shea, T. M., Whiteside, W. R., Beetner, E. G., & Lindsey, D. L. (1974). *Microteaching module: Psychosituational interview.* Edwardsville: Southern Illinois University.

Shea, T. M., & Bauer, A. M. (1987). *Teaching children and youth with behavior disorders* (2nd ed.). Englewood Cliffs, NJ: Prentice-Hall.

Stigen, G. (1976). *Heartaches and handicaps: An irreverent survival manual for parents.* Palo Alto, CA: Science & Behavior Books.

Susser, P. (1974). Parents and partners. *The Exceptional Parent, 4*(3), 41-47.

Winton, P. (1986). Effective strategies for involving families in intervention efforts. *Focus on Exceptional Children, 19*(2), 1-12.

CHAPTER NINE

Critical Issues in
Behavior Management

Mr. Bauer is the teacher of 26 inner-city, street-wise tenth-grade adolescents. He is having little success teaching the subjects (consumer education and practical mathematics) outlined on the city curriculum guide for the tenth grade. In his opinion very little, if any, formal learning takes place in his classroom. Each school day is filled with verbal and physical aggression among the students. Mr. Bauer is in constant fear for his physical safety. He is anxious throughout the day and emotionally fatigued when he arrives home in the evening.

Although he dislikes his present work assignment, he enjoys teaching. However, he has contemplated leaving the profession for employment in business. Mr. Bauer is desperate for some way to control the behavior of his students.

As usual on Friday after school, Mr. Bauer joins a group of other teachers for a little relaxation and libation at Archie's Place before going home. The conversation turns to behavior problems and behavior management. Several of Mr. Bauer's colleagues, who are more effective behavior managers than he, offer a variety of interventions they apply with success.

Mr. Glove said: "I punch the little idiots. They cut the bull quick."

Mr. Pine offered: "I carry my paddle, and the first turkey that wiggles a finger gets it. I don't like it, but it works."

Ms. Weeping relates: "I scream at them. I can outshout them. If all else fails, I cry."

Ms. Fox stated: "I don't fool with them. It's in the door—shut up—get to work—and out the door. No discussion, no questions, no group work, and no jokes—no nothing."

Mr. Power brags: "I've got the best solution. This fall I bought an electric wand—you know, a cattle prod. It's cheap and effective. The first kid who opens his mouth when he's not supposed to gets it. One good, fast shock usually does it."

As Mr. Bauer sat in the subway on his way home, he reviewed his colleagues' suggestions. Which, if any, should he use with his students? How to decide?

Ms. Jan was employed as a teacher of elementary school-aged severely behavior-disordered children in a private facility. Although she enjoyed her work and believed she was an effective teacher, she was concerned about one of the interventions her supervisors ordered her to implement. Although they had discussed the intervention and Ms. Jan's professional reasons for viewing it as inappropriate and unethical, the supervisor remained adamant about its use.

The intervention was "extinction"—ignoring the head-slapping behavior of Tyrone. Tyrone slapped the sides of his head on an average of 61 times an hour during the school day. He slapped himself with such force that the hair on the side of his head had been pulled out and his temples were swollen and severely bruised.

Ms. Jan recognized that she must do something. But what? She needed her job, and she needed a positive recommendation from her supervisor if she were to be considered for her annual pay raise.

Before implementing the interventions suggested in this text, the reader is encouraged to study and contemplate several important issues concerning behavior management presented in this chapter. These issues are (1) the question of ethics, (2) continua of management interventions, and (3) the rights of children. This chapter concludes with a discussion of behavior management as a preventive technique.

CHAPTER OBJECTIVES

After completing this chapter, you will be able to do the following:

1. Explain ethical issues with regard to the use of behavior management interventions.
2. Describe various perspectives of the ethics of behavior management.
3. Discuss ethical and professional guidelines for the application of behavior management interventions.
4. Characterize a continuum of behavior management interventions and its purposes.
5. Understand the principles of normalization, fairness, and respect for the dignity and worth of the individual.

The Question of Ethics

Both empirical and nonexperimental inquiry have led to the development of the principles of learning and their resultant interventions for the management of human behavior. It is difficult to refute the findings of experimental studies: the principles of learning presented in Chapter 2 are in operation, and the results of controlled research studies are, in the main, positive.

However, practitioners cannot sweep aside the ethical issues created by the application of these principles to the processes of human learning. The principles of learning have caused confusion, concern, and, in some cases, anxiety among those individuals holding more traditional views of human behavior and human freedom. Many scholars have discussed these issues in a depth that is not possible in this text. The reader is referred to works by Bandura (1969), Bellack and Hersen (1977), and Skinner (1971) for an in-depth study of these important issues. Recently, there has been considerable controversy with regard to the use of aversive stimuli and punishment with children and youth. The reader is referred to the works of Evans and Meyer (1985), Guess, Helmstetter, Turnbull, and Knowlton (1987), Rose (1989), and Shea, Bauer, and Lynch (1989).

The following are some basic metaphysical questions that all practitioners must address when considering the ethical practice of behavior management:

- ☐ What is a human being?
- ☐ Are human beings free; that is, do we have freedom of choice?
- ☐ Do we behave in accordance with specific principles of behavior that are observable, measurable, and repetitive?
- ☐ Can our behavior be changed by external forces?
- ☐ Who can modify whose behavior?

The readers who admit—regardless of their theoretical perspective— that control of human behavior is possible, must consider the following ethical questions:

- ☐ Who shall decide who will be the manager of behavior?
- ☐ Who shall decide whose behavior is to be managed?
- ☐ How can behavior managers be controlled?
- ☐ What type of interventions shall be applied?
- ☐ Who will determine the type of interventions to be legitimized?
- ☐ To what ends will the interventions be applied?

These questions have vast implications for our future (as individuals and as members of the human species) and for the future of society. They must be considered and responded to by the behavior management practitioner.

When these questions are applied to the training of children, they have profound implications for educational practice. The queries are rephrased here to emphasize these implications, which are not only philosophical issues but also pragmatic issues of immediate importance to educators.

- ☐ What is a child?
- ☐ Is a child free to make choices?
- ☐ Should a child be free to make choices?
- ☐ Does a child act in accordance with specific principles of behavior that are observable, measurable, and repetitive?
- ☐ Can a child's behavior be changed by external forces?
- ☐ Can an educator modify a child's behavior?
- ☐ Can another child or a parent change behavior?
- ☐ Who shall determine whose and which behaviors are to be changed?
- ☐ Which interventions shall be applied in the classroom and school to change children's behavior?

□ Who will legitimize and monitor the interventions being used to change the behavior of children?

□ To what ends will the interventions be applied?

That people can and do exert some control over behavior would not be denied by the majority of researchers and practitioners, both behaviorists and traditionalists.

The central issue, then, appears to focus on the relative influences of our nature and environment on behavior. The behaviorist emphasizes the importance of the external environment in the determination of behavior. The behaviorist maintains that the influence of the environment is systematic, constant, and the prime determinant of behavior. This systematic, constant influence is observable and measurable. As a result, actions can be explained by means of the principles of behavior (or learning as discussed in Chapters 2 through 5). The principles are derived by applying the scientific methods of discovery to the modification of overt human behavior.

Few would deny that, in general, the majority of persons respond in a predictable manner under specified conditions. For example, if they go to a sports event, they cheer; to a funeral, they cry or sigh; to a college class, they sit passively, praying for the end; and so on.

In addition to the issues of whether and how human beings can be controlled, professionals in psychology, the social sciences, and education have focused attention on the issue of the *means* of control. Many professionals suggest that the overt controls applied to human behavior by means of behavior modification interventions are unacceptable and can lead to unethical practices. These individuals fail to recognize or acknowledge that other, more traditional forms of interventions, such as those reviewed in Chapters 6 and 7, may exert equally potent, although less obvious, control over human behavior. For example, traditional nondirective and directive psychotherapeutic interventions, such as client-centered counseling, individual and group psychotherapy, psychoanalysis, and life-space interviewing, have as their objective to change the child's behavior or to encourage the child to change his or her behavior with the therapist's assistance. The silent, nondirective therapist and the permissive teacher influence the child's behavior, and this influence limits the child's freedom of choice. Such limiting (or controlling), rather than being denied, should be recognized, evaluated, and monitored for the child's benefit.

The reader is urged to devote time to systematic exploration of his or her responses to the questions listed in this section.

Ethical Perspective

The ethics of behavior management can be approached from several points of view: political, legal, professional, and research. An extensive discussion of each is not feasible in this text; thus, the reader is urged to complete the study of the ethics of behavior management using the chapter references.

From a political perspective, the current quest for excellence in the schools (National Commission on Excellence in Education, 1983) has become localized, with each district and school crafting its own approach to excellence (Down, 1985). In this effort, children and youth whose behavior continues to challenge the system are rarely treasured. It is at this point in development of education that educators find themselves discussing the ethics of behavior management. Behavior problem students, unequally valued to their complying, achieving peers, bring teachers, who are accountable for student achievement, to the point of using behavior management methods and strategies that would not be applied with the more highly valued students.

From a legal perspective, it must be recognized that proactive decisions are seldom found. It appears to be the nature of the courts and the legislatures to react to the misuse, or potential misuse, of various interventions—rather than to actively set standards. It also appears that decisions and laws are concerned primarily with normal students and confined to corporal punishment, suspension, and expulsion. Few decisions and laws focus on the use of aversives in general. The legal aspects of expulsion, suspension and inschool suspension were discussed in Chapter 7. Corporal punishment was discussed in Chapter 5. The reader is referred to those chapters for review.

In *Milonas v. Williams* (1982), the court held that a school for students with behavioral disorders violated students' civil rights, under the Rehabilitation Act of 1973, by using intrusive methods (prolonged isolation, physical punishment, and polygraph tests) even with parental consent.

Summarizing and defining the implications of research in behavior management must be approached with great caution. In general, however, there is little definitive empirical research; and much of the published research is about severely handicapped populations. Evans and Meyer (1985) reported that theoretical and review articles questioning the use of aversives generally conclude that (1) aversive procedures are associated with short-term improvement; (2) little long-term improvement and generalization data are reported; and (3) in comparison to information on the effects of aversives, relatively little research is available regarding outcomes associated with alternative nonaversive procedures.

Guess, Helmstetter, Turnbull, and Knowlton (1987) concur that although there are reports of dramatic short-term effects with aversives, there is little or no data to support maintenance and generalization of these short-term effects. In an issue-by-issue analysis of articles from 1985 to 1989 in 14 journals that publish research on behavior management, Shea, Bauer, and Lynch (1989) found only 30 studies of behavior management procedures. More than half of the studies failed to consider the question of generalization of intervention effect. Only four studies used aversives. They concluded that the existing research base was insufficient to make decisions on the long-term effects and generalization of aversives.

There has been considerable activity among professional, parent, and citizen organizations with regard to the use of aversive and other behavior management interventions. Few position statements discuss the use of any and all behavior management procedures regardless of the theories from which they are derived. Most statements are concerned with the use of behavioral strategies.

Morris (1985) recast a position statement by the Association for the Advancement of Behavioral Therapy (1977) to make it applicable to all interventions, both behavioral and nonbehavioral. The Accreditation Council for Services for the Mentally Retarded and Other Developmental Disabled Persons (1980) wrote a comprehensive statement including 63 proscriptions and prescriptions on the use of behavior management and behavior modification. These statements offered guidelines on policy, program planning, treatment goals, methods, clients' participation, clients' interest subordination, treatment evaluation, confidentiality, referral, practitioner qualifications, and the use of corporal punishment, seclusion, food deprivation, and time-out. Position statements by the Association for Retarded Citizens (1986), American Association on Mental Deficiency (1986), Association for Persons with Severe Handicaps (1981) and others organizations have focused on a broad range of behavioral interventions. As discussed in Chapter 5, the National Association of School Psychologists issued a position statement opposing corporal punishment in the schools. This statement listed 23 national organizations that opposed the use of corporal punishment in the school.

From an ethical perspective, it is generally agreed that the principles underlying behavior management interventions can provide practitioners with the means to an end, but the principles cannot decide the end of intervention: That decision depends on the practitioner's values (Turnbull & Associates, 1986). Ethics are defined as the rules that guide moral (right, good, or correct) behavior (Tymchuk, 1976). According to Sexton (1987), there are two general schools of ethics: formalism and utilitarianism. Formalism suggests that all individuals are born with rights and needs that are superordinate to the interests of society. From this point of view, behavior management interventions that intrude upon an individual's rights are unethical. Utilitarianism suggests that the interests of society precede the interests of the individual. Individuals' rights are given by society and individuals are valued for their actual, or potential, contributions to (or the degree of burden they place on) the society. From this perspective, the use of aversive management is deemed acceptable if it facilitates the movement of the individual from the position of "burden on society" to "contributing member." In a review of the literature, considerable support for both of these positions can be found (Blackham & Silberman, 1975; Singer & Irvin, 1987; Morrow & Gochros, 1970; Wood, 1978).

The following is a summary of the ethical and professional guidelines found in literature:

1. Explore alternative interventions prior to implementation of aversives (Hewett, 1978; Schloss & Smith, 1987).
2. Explore potential side effects and the extent of potential injury as a consequence of intervention (Hewett, 1978; Sabatino, 1983).
3. Determine whether the student understands the contingency (Hewett, 1978).

4. The individual administering the intervention must be trained and comfortable with the intervention (Bellack & Hersen, 1977; Hewett, 1978; Morris & Brown, 1983; Rose, 1989).
5. Empirical evidence should exist that the intervention is effective (Morris & Brown, 1983).
6. The student's program plan (IEP) should be consistent with the intervention and input from the parents and guardian (Morris & Brown, 1983; Singer & Irvin, 1987).
7. The program should be closely monitored and documented (Bellack & Hersen, 1977; Morris & Brown, 1983).
8. Informed consent should be obtained (Axelrod, 1983; Bellack & Hersen, 1977; Blackham & Silberman, 1975; Morris & Brown, 1983; Rose, 1989; Singer & Irvin, 1987). Informed consent should include full information on (a) the nature of the program, (b) benefits, (c) risks, (d) expected outcomes, and (e) alternative strategies (Kazdin, 1980).
9. The principle of normalization should be supported (Allen, 1969; Nirje, 1967). (This principle is discussed in another section of this chapter.)
10. The procedure should be fair; that is, appropriate in regard to the gravity of the offense, and it should provide the individual with an opportunity for success (Allen, 1969; Morris, 1987; Nirje, 1967; Sabatino, 1983). (This principle is discussed in another section of this chapter.)
11. The dignity and worth of the individual should be respected (Allen, 1969; Blackham & Silberman, 1977; Morris, 1987; Nirje, 1967). (This principle is discussed in another section of this chapter.)
12. Committee review and due process procedures should be applied (Singer & Irvin, 1987; Rose, 1989). Axelrod (1983) suggests a human rights committee to monitor the necessity, quality, and social acceptability of the proposed management program, as well as a peer-review committee to monitor the appropriateness of the proposed management program (Bellack & Hersen, 1977).
13. The least restrictive alternative principle should be applied (Morris & Brown, 1983; Singer & Irvin, 1987).

The principle of the least restrictive alternative leads to a consideration of continua of behavior management interventions, which is presented in the next section.

Continua of Behavior Management Interventions

It is unethical for practitioners to impose behavior management interventions that are unnecessary or more restrictive than necessary to change the child's behavior. For example, it would be unacceptable to impose seclusion time-out on a child if observational or exclusion time-out would effectively change the target behavior.

Likewise, it would be unacceptable to use a verbal counseling or extinction technique with a child who is physically assaulting other persons or is self-injurious when a more restrictive intervention is needed.

In the first example, seclusion time-out is considered unacceptable because it restricts the child's freedom more than is necessary. In this situation seclusion would be imposed only after the less restrictive time-out procedures—observational and exclusion time-out—have been systematically applied over a period of time without success.

In the second example, extinction and counseling are inappropriate because they are too benign to change the target behavior and thus protect the child and others from harm. Of necessity, the practitioner must impose a more restrictive intervention, for example, time-out.

Each classroom, school, and local education agency should conduct a periodic inventory among school and cooperating community agency personnel to determine the behavior management interventions available and to ensure that professionals are competent to change the behavior of children. These interventions may include many of the interventions discussed in Chapters 4 through 7 and many others not reviewed in this text.

The behavior management interventions included on the inventory are then ordered on a continuum. The interventions are placed on the continuum to range from the *least* restrictive to the *most* restrictive with regard to the child's freedom to function in comparison with the average child.

An example continuum using selected behavior modification interventions is presented in Figure 9.1. It is obvious that no continuum of interventions is perfect. The exact location of an intervention on the continuum should be accomplished through discussion and consensus among those responsible for the behavior of children in the school and community, including parents and administrators. The continuum presented in Figure 9.1 is based on the work of Lewellen (1980). Morris (1985) and Morris and Brown (1983) developed the continuum of aversive interventions presented in Figure 9.2. This continuum varies on the dimensions of (a) restrictiveness and intrusiveness, and (b) aversiveness. Level I includes interventions judged to be the least restrictive/intrusive and aversive, with Level III interventions judged to be the most restrictive/intrusive and aversive.

Educational agencies should develop procedures to ensure the ethical and effective use of behavior management interventions. Among the items to be considered when planning the procedures to be used in behavior management are the following:

1. The behaviors to be targeted for change must be noted in the child's individualized education program.
2. The behavior management interventions to be implemented are to be described in the child's IEP. The purpose for which the intervention is imposed must be stated. The procedures to be applied to evaluate the consistency of application and effectiveness of the intervention are stated.

Example of Continuum of Interventions

1. *Reinforcement of behavior other than the target behavior:* A reinforcer is given at the end of a specified period of time provided that a prespecified misbehavior has not occurred during the specified time interval.
2. *Reinforcement of an appropriate target behavior:* A reinforcer is given following the performance of a prespecified appropriate target behavior.
3. *Reinforcement of incompatible behaviors:* A reinforcer is given following the performance of a prespecified behavior that is physically and functionally incompatible with the target behavior.
4. *Extinction:* The reinforcer that has been sustaining or increasing an undesirable behavior is withheld.
5. *Stimulus change:* The existing environmental conditions are drastically altered to ensure that the target behavior is temporarily suppressed.
6. *Nonexclusionary time-out:*
   a. Head down on desk or table in work area in which target behavior occurred
   b. Restriction to chair in a separate area of the classroom but able to observe classroom activities
   c. Removal of materials (work, play)
   d. Reduction or elimination of room illumination
7. *Physical restraint.*
8. *Negative practice or satiation:* The target behavior is eliminated by continued and increased reinforcement of that behavior.
9. *Overcorrection:* The repeated practice of an appropriate behavior in response to the exhibition of an inappropriate target behavior.
10. *Exclusionary time-out:*
    a. In-school suspension
    b. Quiet room

FIGURE 9.1
Sample continuum of behavior modification interventions.

3. Initially the least restrictive intervention feasible is to be applied unless, in the judgment of the IEP team, to do so would be ineffective. The intervention is to be selected or designed through the process of consensus among the team members including the student's parent(s) or parent surrogate(s). During the meeting the team may list subsequent and more restrictive interventions to be imposed if the initial intervention is demonstrated to be ineffective.
4. Data collection procedures are to be developed before the implementation of the intervention. These procedures are applied by the practitioner throughout the time during which the intervention is imposed. A written record of the data collected is to be enclosed in the student's file.
5. Initial and all subsequent techniques are to be imposed for a specified number of school days before being changed or discontinued.

Level I Procedures

Reinforcement (including differential reinforcement techniques)

Group reinforcement

Shaping

Behavioral chaining

Modeling

Token economy system

Contingency contracting

Self-control

Reinforcement of incompatible behaviors

Relaxation training

Extinction

Situation control

Level II Procedures

Contingent observation

Exclusion time-out

Response cost system

Contact desensitization

Level III Procedures

Overcorrection

Seclusion time-out

Physical punishment

FIGURE 9.2
Levels system of aversive interventions.

6. Documents on the student's behavior management plan and its application are to be available in the student's IEP file for periodic review by appropriate persons.

In addition, practitioners should be knowledgeable about national, state, provincial and local statutes and policies governing behavior management practices in schools. Practitioners should be trained in a broad range of behavior management interventions from various theoretical perspectives. Finally, a human rights committee should be established in each school or district to supervise the practice of behavior management with children and youth.

Procedures such as those just mentioned safeguard the child from potential mistreatment and the practitioner from potential charges of wrongdoing.

The Rights of Children

In 1969 Allen proposed three legal principles to guide individuals in the helping professions in their actions toward clients (children and adults). These principles serve as the foundation of all behavior management decisions made by teachers of both regular and special education students.

They are (1) the principle of normalization, (2) the principle of fairness, and (3) the principle of respect for the dignity and worth of the individual.

Principle of Normalization

> To let the handicapped person obtain an existence as close to the normal as is possible. (Nirje, 1967; cited by Allen, 1969)

When applying this principle, the practitioner must use as a point of reference the child's real environment (including the behavior of the children and adults within it) as well as the ideal democratic environment. This principle demands understanding of the similarities and differences among various groups in society. The practitioner must base decisions on knowledge of the individual child's growth and development, needs, desires, strengths, and disabilities.

Before implementing an intervention, the practitioner must respond to the following queries: Will the implementation of this specific behavioral intervention facilitate the child's movement toward the normally anticipated and observed behavior in this setting, or will it simply eliminate the child (and the behavior) as an inconvenience or annoyance to others in the environment, such as the child's teacher, peers, administrator, and parents?

Many children who attend classes for retarded, disturbed, and learning-disabled children are in those classes simply because they are different; that is, they are black, Hispanic, Asian-American, native American, or slow learners, nonreaders, poor, and so on. These children may be segregated primarily because they are an annoyance or inconvenience to others; they challenge the system. In this "special placement" their opportunity to obtain "an existence as normal as possible" is grossly inhibited, if not totally frustrated.

Principle of Fairness

> Fundamental fairness—due process of law—requires that in decision-making affecting one's life, liberty, or vital interests, the elements of due process will be observed, including the right to notice, to a fair hearing, to representation by counsel, to present evidence, and to appeal an adverse decision. (Allen, 1969)

Although this principle is phrased in legal terminology, it can be simply stated: "Is the intervention I have selected to change this child's behavior fair to the child as an individual?"

At times interventions are arbitrarily applied on the whim of a practitioner without concrete evidence that the child is, in fact, exhibiting the target behavior. Frequently interventions are applied that only serve to prohibit the child from finding *any* success in school. For example, a child who had difficulty learning French grammar is prohibited from going to recess, playing on the school athletic teams, and so on. This child may only be capable of meeting success in these prohibited activities. As do all humans, the child has a need for success. Interventions such as these are unfair.

Unfairness is evidenced when a practitioner refuses to apply an intervention that is obviously needed if the child is to function in school. For example, we are confronted with practitioners who will not use tangible rewards simply because they do not "believe in them." Yet the child whom they are attempting to help is found to respond only to tangible rewards.

Other examples of unfairness might include:

□ Refusal to try to modify a child's behavior systematically
□ Arbitrary placement of a child in a special therapy or instructional program without first attempting classroom interventions
□ Unwillingness of teachers to provide needed services or request consultation because they believe that seeking help is a sign of incompetency

If the principle of fairness is to be implemented, we must begin all decisions from the point of view of the child's welfare: "What does this child need?"

Principle of Respect for the Dignity and Worth of the Individual

One's right to be treated as a human being, and not as an animal or a statistic. (Allen, 1969)

In actions toward children, are practitioners demonstrating respect for them as human beings? All interventions must be judged against this question. When the intervention is evaluated from this point of view, many common "therapeutic" practices are found to violate the principle of respect. The following are examples:

□ Physical punishment (spankings, slaps, paddlings)
□ Psychological punishment (sarcasm, embarrassment, name calling)
□ Deprivation (prohibiting a child normal opportunities for success)
□ Segregation (arbitrary special-class placement)
□ Isolation (inconsistent, long-term use of time-out and restraint)
□ Medication (capricious use of symptom-control medications)
□ Extrahuman punishment (use of restraints, electric shockers)

All of these interventions have been used and remain in use in this society. Generally they are applied by individuals who justify the use of any means to attain their end. All of these interventions have been justified by some as the "only way" to accomplish an objective. These techniques are used (and justified) frequently simply because they are convenient, efficient, and seemingly effective.

It cannot be denied that a beaten child will obey, that an electric cattle prod will get a child to pay attention, and that segregation and isolation will reduce conflict. However, practitioners must establish limits on the interventions that can be applied with children. They must judge these interventions in the light of this third principle; that is, could or do the interventions inflict damage on the individual child or relegate the child to a less-than-human classification?

It is absolutely necessary that all behavior management practitioners develop an ethical system that incorporates the principles of normalization, fairness, and respect for the dignity and the worth of the child. This value system must avoid the pitfall of justifying "any means to attain a desired end."

Any intervention can be misused and abused if the person using it lacks an ethical system of personal and professional values. Practitioners must never be allowed to forget that knowledge is power and that with power comes the responsibility to apply that power for the benefit of all persons.

The Council for Exceptional Children's Delegate Assembly (1983) adopted standards for the ethical application of behavior management interventions. These standards are as follows:

1.2.1. Special education professionals participate with other professionals and with parents in an interdisciplinary effort in the management of behavior. Professionals:

1.2.1.1. Apply only those disciplinary methods and behavioral procedures which they have been instructed to use and which do not undermine the dignity of the individual or basic human rights of exceptional persons (such as corporal punishment).

1.2.1.2. Clearly specify the goals and objectives for behavior management practices in the exceptional person's individual education program.

1.2.1.3. Conform to policies, statutes, and rules established by state/provincial and local agencies relating to judicious application of disciplinary methods and behavioral procedures.

1.2.1.4. Take adequate measures to discourage, prevent, and intervene when a colleague's behavior is perceived as being detrimental to exceptional persons.

1.2.1.5. Refrain from aversive techniques unless repeated trials of other methods have failed and then only after consultation with parents and appropriate agency officials. (p. 9)

Behavior Management Prevention

Most of the behavior management literature is concerned with the remediation of academic and behavior problems in the home, school, institution, and clinic. Efforts have generally been directed toward the increase of acceptable and decrease of unacceptable behaviors. Very few research reports and position statements have focused on the maintenance of the acceptable behaviors of normally functioning children.

There are many opportunities in the classroom to prevent the development of inappropriate behavior by systematically maintaining the existing acceptable behavior. If teachers understand and apply the principles of behavior management (presented in Chapter 2) as part of their normal teaching methodology, many potential problems and conflicts can be avoided.

Concerned teachers monitor and evaluate their personal teaching behaviors and the learning behaviors of their classroom groups. They do this by systematically evaluating the teaching-learning process. They recognize that children need positive reinforcement (rewards) and that only the child being rewarded can indicate with certitude what is rewarding.

Experienced practitioners understand that they can and do reinforce inappropriate behavior on occasion. Consequently they attempt to reward only appropriate behaviors. They realize that the younger, less experienced child needs to be immediately reinforced for exhibiting appropriate behavior. They also recognize that delayed rewards are more desirable, from a societal point of view, than immediate rewards and that social rewards are more desirable than tangible rewards. They always give the child social reinforcement in conjunction with tangible rewards.

Prevention-minded practitioners recognize that new behaviors must be rewarded more frequently and more consistently than established behaviors and that although continuous reinforcement is necessary when a new behavior is being established, intermittent reinforcement is ultimately desired and will effectively maintain established behaviors.

Prevention-conscious practitioners systematically use high-frequency behaviors to facilitate the development of low-frequency behaviors.

By using the principles of behavior management as a standard part of the teaching-learning process, practitioners need not anxiously wait for problems to arise in the classroom but can prevent them and use the time saved to teach children those things they must know to live productively in society.

SUMMARY

In this chapter, several critical issues in the application of behavior management interventions are emphasized. An effort is made to reinforce the need to apply all management interventions with care and to individualize the process in response to the needs of the student.

Several important ethical issues are discussed, and the various perspectives of the ethics of behavior management are presented. Ethics are discussed from a political, legal, professional and research perspective. It is recommended that the practitioner carefully follow the professional guidelines suggested by the Council for Exceptional Children as well as the other guidelines suggested in the chapter.

It is essential that each classroom and school develop a continuum of behavior management interventions. Practitioners should not apply interventions that are judged to be more restrictive of student functioning than are necessary to effectively assist the student to learn self-control.

The practitioner is urged to apply the principles of normalization, fairness, and dignity and worth of the individual in all interaction with students.

PROJECTS

1. Research the professional literature and write a 500-word essay on "The Ethics of Behavior Management."
2. Research the professional literature and write a 500-word essay "for" or "against" the use of physical punishment in the school.
3. Invite an attorney or a specialist in civil rights to discuss with your class the rights of children as enumerated in this text.
4. As a group, conduct an inventory of behavior management interventions in a school.
5. As a group, organize the results of the inventory conducted in Project 4 into a continuum of behavior management interventions. Make an effort to obtain consensus on the location of each intervention on the continuum.
6. As a group, discuss the ordering of the interventions as listed in this chapter.

REFERENCES

Accreditation Council for Services for Mentally Retarded and Other Developmentally Disabled Persons (1980). *Standards for services for developmentally disabled individuals.* Washington, DC: Author.

Allen, R. C. (1969). *Legal rights of the disabled and disadvantaged* (GPO 1969-0-360-797). Washington, DC: U.S. Department of Health, Education, and Welfare, National Citizens Conference on Rehabilitation of the Disabled and Disadvantaged.

American Association on Mental Deficiency (1986). *Position statement on aversives.*

Association for the Advancement of Behavior Therapy (1977). Ethical issues for human services. *Behavior Therapy, 8,* v-vi.

Association for Persons with Severe Handicaps (1981). Resolution on aversive interventions. *TASH Newsletter, 7*(11), 1-2.

Association for Retarded Citizens of the United States (1986). *Position statement on behavior management.* Reno, NV: Author.

Axelrod, S. (1983). *Behavior modification for the classroom teacher.* NY: McGraw-Hill.

Bandura, A. (1969). *Principles of behavior modification.* New York: Holt, Rinehart & Winston.

Bellack, A. S., & Hersen, M. (1977). *Behavior modification: An introductory textbook.* Baltimore: Williams & Wilkins Co.

Blackham, G. J., & Silberman, A. (1975). *Modification of child and adolescent behavior* (2nd ed.). Belmont, CA: Wadsworth.

Council for Exceptional Children Delegate Assembly (1983). Code of ethics and standards for professional practice. *Exceptional Children, 50*(3), 8-12.

Down, A. G. (1985). Excellence and equity: The unfinished agenda of the 1980's. *Educational Horizons, 63,* 16-19.

Evans, I. M., & Meyer, L. H. (1985). *An educative approach to behavior problems: A practical decision model for intervention with severely handicapped learners.* Baltimore: Brookes.

Guess, D., Helmstetter, E., Turnbull, H. R., III, & Knowlton, S. (1987). Use of aversive procedures with persons who are disabled: An historical review and critical analysis. *TASH Monograph Series #2.* Seattle, WA: The Association for Persons with Severe Handicaps.

Hewett, F. M. (1978). Punishment and eductional programs for behaviorally disordered and emotionally disturbed children and youth: A personal perspective. In F. Wood & K. Lakin (Eds.), *Punishment and aversive stimulation in special education* (pp. 101-117). Minneapolis: University of Minnesota.

Kazdin, A. E. (1980). *Behavior modification in applied settings* (Revised). Homewood, IL: Dorsey.

Lewellen, A. (1980). *The use of quiet rooms and other time-out procedures in the public school.* Mattoon, IL: Eastern Illinois Area of Special Education.

Milonas v. Williams, 691 F. 2d 931 (1982).

Morris, R. J. (1985). *Behavior modification with exceptional children: Principles and practices.* Glenview, IL: Scott, Foresman.

Morris, R. J., & Brown, D. K. (1983). Legal and ethical issues in behavior modification with mentally retarded persons. In J. Matson & F. Andrasik (Eds.), *Treatment issues and innovations in mental retardation.* New York: Plenum.

Morris, P. (1987). The restricted use of traditional disciplinary procedures with handicapped youngsters. In A. Rotatori, M. Banbury, & R. Foxx (Eds.), *Issues in special education.* Mountain View, CA: Mayfield.

Morrow, W. R., & Gochros, H. L. (1970). Misconceptions regarding behavior modification. *Social Service Review, 44,* 293-307.

National Association of School Psychologists (1986). *NASP corporal punishment position statement.* Hollywood, FL: Author.

National Commission on Excellence in Education (1983). *A nation at risk.* Washington, DC: U.S. Government Printing Office.

Nirje, B. (1967). The normalization principle and its human management implications. In R. Kugel & W. Wolfensberger (Eds.), *Changing patterns in residential services for the mentally retarded.* Washington, DC: President's Committee on Mental Retardation.

Rose, T. L. (1989). Corporal punishment with mildly handicapped students: Five years later. *Remedial and Special Education, 10*(1), 43-52.

Sabatino, A. C. (1983). Discipline: A national issue. In A. C. Sabatino & L. Mann (Eds.), *Discipline and behavioral management.* Rockville, MD: Aspen, 1-27.

Schloss, P. J., & Smith, M. A. (1987). Guidelines for ethical use of manual restraint in public school settings for behaviorally disordered students. *Behavioral Disorders, 12,* 207-213.

Sexton, J. D. (1987). Involuntary euthanasia: Withholding treatment from infants with severe handicaps. In M. Rotatori, M. Banbury, & R. Foxx (Eds.), *Issues in special education.* Mountain View, CA: Mayfield.

Shea, T. M., Bauer, A. M., & Lynch, E. M. (1989, September). *Changing behavior: Ethical issues regarding behavior management and the control of students with behavioral disorders.* Paper presented at Find the Answer for the Decade Ahead, CEC/CCBD Conference, Charlotte, NC.

Singer, G. S., & Irvin, L. K. (1987). Human rights review of intrusive behavioral treatments for students with severe handicaps. *Exceptional Children, 54,* 46-52.

Skinner, B. F. (1971). *Beyond freedom and dignity.* New York: Alfred A. Knopf.

Turnbull, H. R., III, Guess, D., Backus, L. H., Barber, P. A., Feidler, C. R., Helmstetter, E., & Summers, J. A. (1986). A model for analyzing the moral aspects of special education and behavioral interventions: The moral aspects of aversive procedures. In P. Dokecki & R. Zaner (Eds.), *Ethics of dealing with persons with severe handicaps: Toward a research agenda* (pp. 167-210). Baltimore: Brookes.

Tymchuk, A. J. (1976). A perspective on ethics in mental retardation. *Mental Retardation, 14,* 44-47.

Wood, F. H. (1978). Punishment and special education: Some concluding comments. In F. Wood & K. Lakin (Eds.), *Punishment and aversive stimulation in special education.* (pp. 119-122). Minneapolis: University of Minnesota.

AUTHOR INDEX

SUBJECT INDEX

Work Sheets and Forms

Work sheets and forms used in this text may be copied from the following pages as needed.

Target Behavior Selection Checklist

1. What is the target behavior to be modified? _____

   _____

   _____

   _____

   _____

2. Each characteristic of the behavior that should be considered in the target behavior selective process is listed below. An X should be marked by each characteristic as it is considered. The pertinency of these characteristics varies with the specific target behavior under consideration.

(X)	Characteristic	Comment
( )	1. Frequency	
( )	2. Duration	
( )	3. Intensity	
( )	4. Type	
( )	5. Direction	
( )	6. Observability	
( )	7. Measurability	

3. Restate the target behavior in precise and specific terminology. _____

   _____

   _____

   _____

   _____

Behavior Chart

Child _____
Observer _____ Date _____
Target behavior _____

DIRECTIONS: Indicate rate, frequency, etc., for vertical axis; hours, days, etc., for horizontal axis. Enter ordinate and abscissa points.

Ordinate points (rate, frequency, duration, percent, etc.)

0

Abscissa points (hours, days, sessions, treatment, etc.)

323

Date _____

Contract

This is an agreement between _____
Child's name

and _____. The contract begins on
Teacher's name

_____ and ends on _____. It will be re-
Date   Date

viewed on _____
Date

The terms of the agreement are:

Child will _____

_____

_____

_____

_____

Teacher will _____

_____

_____

_____

If the child fulfills his or her part of the contract, the child will receive the agreed-on reward from the teacher. However, if the child fails to fulfill his or her part of the contract, the rewards will be withheld.

Child's signature _____

Teacher's signature _____

Contract Work Sheet

Child _____

Teacher _____ Date _____

(X)	Tasks	Comments
( )	1. Establish and maintain rapport.	
( )	2. Explain the purpose of the meeting.	
( )	3. Explain a contract.	
( )	4. Give an example of a contract.	
( )	5. Ask the child to give an example of a contract; if there is no response, give another example.	
( )	6. Discuss possible tasks.	
( )	7. Child-suggested tasks: _____ _____ _____ _____	
( )	8. Teacher-suggested tasks: _____ _____ _____ _____	
( )	9. Agree on the task.	
( )	10. Ask the child what activities he or she enjoys and what items he or she wishes to possess.	
( )	11. Record child-suggested reinforcers.	
( )	12. Negotiate the ratio of the task to the reinforcer.	

Continued.

Contract Work Sheet—cont'd

(X)	Tasks	Comments
( )	13. Identify the time allotted for the task.	
( )	14. Identify the criterion or achievement level.	
( )	15. Discuss methods of evaluation.	
( )	16. Agree on the method of evaluation.	
( )	17. Restate and clarify the method of evaluation.	
( )	18. Negotiate the delivery of the reinforcer.	
( )	19. Set the date for renegotiation.	
( )	20. Write two copies of the contract.	
( )	21. Read the contract to the child.	
( )	22. Elicit the child's verbal affirmation and give your own affirmation.	
( )	23. Sign the contract and have the child sign it.	
( )	24. Congratulate the child (and yourself).	

Point Card*

Child's name _____ Date _____

1	2	3	4	5	6	7	8	9	10
11	12	13	14	15	16	17	18	19	20
21	22	23	24	25	26	27	28	29	30
31	32	33	34	35	36	37	38	39	40
41	42	43	44	45	46	47	48	49	50
51	52	53	54	55	56	57	58	59	60
61	62	63	64	65	66	67	68	69	70
71	72	73	74	75	76	77	78	79	80
81	82	83	84	85	86	87	88	89	90
91	92	93	94	95	96	97	98	99	100

*Teacher circles the cumulative total.

Point Tally Form

Child _____ Date _____

Monday

Tuesday

Wednesday

Thursday

Friday

	TOTAL	
Monday		
Tuesday		
Wednesday		
Thursday		
Friday		
Week		

Point Card for Multipurpose Token Economy

Child _____ Day _____ Date _____

Work period	Readiness	Social behavior	Work effort	Work success	Teacher comments
9:00-9:15			★	★	
9:15-10:00					
10:00-10:30					
10:30-10:45			★	★	
10:45-11:30					
11:30-12:00					
12:00-1:00			★	★	
1:00-1:30					
1:30-2:45					
2:45-3:00			★	★	

*Points for work effort and work success are not available during these periods due to the nature of the activity: opening exercises, recess, lunch, and closing exercises.

Time-out Log

Child _____

Supervisor _____

Date _____

Time		Behavior before time-out	Behavior during time-out	Behavior after time-out
Enters	Leaves			

Behavior Log Form

Target behavior _____

Child _____

Observer _____

Date	Time		Antecedents	Consequences	Applied interventions	Comments
	Begins	Ends				